Cracking the

PSAT/ NMSQT®

with 2 Practice Tests, 2016 Edition

By the Staff of the Princeton Review

PrincetonReview.com

The Princeton Review, Inc.
24 Prime Parkway, Suite 201
Natick, MA 01760
E-mail: editorialsupport@review.com

ISBN: 978-1-101-91977-4
eBook ISBN: 978-1-101-91978-1
ISSN: 1549-6120

Editor: Sarah Litt
Production Editor: Kathy Carter
Production Artist: Deborah A. Silvestrini

Printed in the United States of America on partially recycled paper.

10 9 8 7 6 5 4 3 2 1

2016 Edition

Editorial

Rob Franek, Senior VP, Publisher
Casey Cornelius, VP Content Development
Mary Beth Garrick, Director of Production
Selena Coppock, Managing Editor
Meave Shelton, Senior Editor
Colleen Day, Editor
Sarah Litt, Editor
Aaron Riccio, Editor
Orion McBean, Editorial Assistant

Random House Publishing Team

Tom Russell, Publisher
Alison Stoltzfus, Publishing Manager
Melinda Ackell, Associate Managing Editor
Ellen Reed, Production Manager

Acknowledgments

Special thanks: Amy Minster, Aaron Lindh, Elizabeth Owens

Thanks: Jim Havens, Tony Krupp, Anne Goldberg

The Princeton Review would like to thank Johnathan Chiu, Debbie Silvestrini, and Kathy Carter for their work on this book.

Special thanks to Adam Robinson, who conceived of and perfected the Joe Bloggs approach to standardized tests, and many other techniques in this book.

Contents

Register Your

1 Go to **PrincetonReview.com/cracking**

2 You'll see a welcome page where you can register your book using the following ISBN: 9781101919774

3 After placing this free order, you'll either be asked to log in or to answer a few simple questions in order to set up a new Princeton Review account.

4 Finally, click on the "Student Tools" tab located at the top of the screen. It may take an hour or two for your registration to go through, but after that, you're good to go.

If you are experiencing book problems (potential content errors), please contact EditorialSupport@review.com with the full title of the book, its ISBN number (located above), and the page number of the error. Experiencing technical issues? Please e-mail TPRStudentTech@review.com with the following information:

- your full name
- e-mail address used to register the book
- full book title and ISBN
- your computer OS (Mac or PC) and Internet browser (Firefox, Safari, Chrome, etc.)
- description of technical issue

Book Online!

Once you've registered, you can...

- Find any late-breaking information released about the AP Computer Science Exam

- Take a full-length practice PSAT, SAT, and ACT

- Get valuable advice about the college application process, including tips for writing a great essay and where to apply for financial aid

- Sort colleges by whatever you're looking for (such as Best Theater or Dorm), learn more about your top choices, and see how they all rank according to *The Best 380 Colleges*

- Check to see if there have been any corrections or updates to this edition

Look For These Icons Throughout The Book

- Online Articles
- Proven Techniques
- Applied Strategies
- Study Break
- More Great Books

The **Princeton** Review®

Part I
Orientation

Chapter 1
What Is the PSAT/NMSQT?

The PSAT/NMSQT—from now on, we'll just call it the PSAT—is a standardized test given primarily to high school juniors to give them a "preliminary" idea of how well they could do on SAT question types. The test is also used to determine which students are eligible for National Merit Scholar recognition. This chapter will give you a general overview of the test and how it is used, along with the basics to start your preparation.

How Do You Pronounce PSAT/NMSQT, Anyway?

Ah, yes—first things first. Well, to be honest, we're not really sure. You can pronounce it *pee-sat-nim-squit* if you want. However, we think it's easier just to call it the PSAT.

When Is the PSAT Given?

The PSAT is officially administered twice each year, typically on a Wednesday and Saturday of the same week in October. Your school will announce the exact dates at the beginning of the school year, or you can find out at **PrincetonReview.com**, or the College Board at **CollegeBoard.com**.

Keep on Schedule
You'll officially take the PSAT in the fall of your junior year. Plan to take the SAT anytime between the winter of your junior year and the fall of your senior year.

How Do I Sign Up for the PSAT?

You don't have to do anything to sign up for the PSAT; your school will do all the work for you. Test registration fees can vary from school to school, so be sure to check with your guidance counselor if you have questions about how much the PSAT will cost you.

What About Students with Special Needs?

If you have a diagnosed learning difference, you will probably qualify for special accommodations on the PSAT. However, it's important that you get the process started early. The first step is to speak to your school counselor who handles learning differences. Only he or she can file the appropriate paperwork. You'll also need to gather some information (documentation of your condition) from a licensed practitioner and some other information from your school. Then your school counselor will file the application for you.

You will need to apply for accommodations only once; with that single application you'll qualify for accommodations on the PSAT, SAT, SAT Subject Tests, and AP tests. The one exception to this rule is that if you change schools, you'll need to have a counselor at the new school refile your paperwork.

Does the PSAT Play a Role in College Admissions?

No! The PSAT plays no role in college admissions. It's really just a practice test for the SAT.

The one exception is for that very small group of students, about 4 percent of all students nationwide, whose PSAT scores qualify them for National Merit recognition. (We'll tell you more than you ever wanted to know about that in the next section.) Recognition as a commended scholar, semifinalist, or finalist for National Merit is a fairly impressive addition to your college admissions portfolio, and is something that you should certainly pursue if you are seriously in contention for it.

What Happens to the Score Report from the PSAT?

Only you, your high school, and the National Merit Scholarship Corporation (which cosponsors the PSAT) will receive copies of your score reports. They won't be sent to colleges.

WHAT DOES THE PSAT TEST?

First off, while the PSAT may have recently changed, we at The Princeton Review understand that certain fundamentals of a test always stay the same. As you begin your prep, it's useful to remember that the PSAT is not a test of aptitude, how good of a person you are, or how successful you will be in life. The PSAT simply tests how well you take the PSAT. That's it. And performing well on the PSAT is a skill, one that can be learned like any other. The Princeton Review was founded more than 30 years ago on this very simple idea, and—as our students' test scores show—our approach is the one that works.

All of these changes to tests that you hear could heavily influence your college admission strategy can be extremely daunting. However, remember that any standardized test is a coachable test. A beatable test. Just remember:

The PSAT doesn't measure the stuff that matters. It measures neither intelligence nor the depth and breadth of what you're learning in high school. It doesn't predict college grades as well as your high school grades do, and many schools are still hesitant to use the score from your essay in their application decisions at all: That's why it's now optional. Colleges know there is more to you as a student—and as a person—than what you do on a single test administered on a Saturday morning.

Who Writes the PSAT, Anyway?

The PSAT is written and administered by Educational Testing Service (ETS) and by the College Board. You might think that the people at ETS and the College Board are educators, professors of education, or teachers. They're not. The people who work for ETS and the College Board are average folks who just happen to make a living writing tests. In fact, they write hundreds of tests, for all kinds of organizations. They're a group of "testers-for-hire" who will write a test for anyone who asks.

The folks at ETS and the College Board aren't really paid to educate; they're paid to write and administer tests. And even though you'll be paying them to take the PSAT, you're not their customer. The actual customers ETS and the College Board cater to are the colleges, who get the information they want at no cost. This means that you should take everything that ETS and the College Board says with a grain of salt and realize that its testing "advice" isn't always the best advice. (Getting testing advice from ETS and the College Board is a bit like getting baseball advice from the opposing team.)

Every test reflects the interests of the people who write it. If you know who writes the test, you will know a lot more about what kinds of answers will be considered "correct" answers on that test.

SO THEN WHAT IS THE PRINCETON REVIEW?

Shortcuts
The Princeton Review's techniques are the closest thing there is to a shortcut to the PSAT. However, there is no shortcut to learning these techniques.

The Princeton Review is the nation's leading test-preparation company. In just a few years, we became the nation's leader in SAT preparation, primarily because our techniques work. We offer courses and private tutoring for all of the major standardized tests, and we publish a series of books to help in your search for the right school. If you'd like more information about our programs or books, give us a call at 800-2-Review, or check out our website at **PrincetonReview.com**.

HOW TO USE THIS BOOK

This book is divided into two main parts. The first three parts of the book (Chapters 1–12 and the subsequent Drill Answers) contain both general testing strategies and question-specific problem-solving instruction. The back of the book contains two practice PSATs. The study guide on page 8 will give you a plan of attack for these things and the rest of the book. There is no single plan that will fit everyone, so be prepared to adapt to the plan that appears below and use it according to your own needs.

The first practice test will give you an idea of your strengths and weaknesses, both of which can be sources of improvement. If you're already good at something, additional practice can make you great at it; if you're not so good at something, what you should do about it depends on how important it is. If the concept is one that frequently appears on the test, you'll want to spend a lot of time on it; if it only comes up once in a while, you'll want to spend very little time working on it and remember that it's something you should put off until you've done easier things or skip entirely.

How do you know what's important? We'll tell you throughout the book when techniques like Plugging In come up, but you can also get an idea from the layout of the book. If you're not so great at Critical Reading, you're going to need to work on Reading questions because there will be a total of 47 questions. If you're not so hot at geometry, you can tell that these aren't as important as Plugging In or Math Basics, because geometry questions appear only in the Advanced section.

Time Management

To manage your PSAT preparation, make use of the study guide on the following pages. This guide will break down the seemingly daunting task of PSAT prep into bite-sized pieces we call sessions. We have mapped out tasks for each session to be sure you get the most out of this book. Sessions will generally take between an hour or two, unless you're taking a practice test. The tests will be the first and last sessions, so you should be sure to plan to have about two and a half hours for these sessions. Most other sessions will last between an hour and two hours, so plan to take a short break in the middle, and if it looks like the session is going to exceed two hours, feel free to stop and pick up where you left off on the next day.

When You Take a Practice Test

You'll see when to take practice tests in the session outlines. Here are some guidelines for taking these tests:

- Time yourself strictly. Use a timer, watch, or stopwatch that will ring, and do not allow yourself to go over time for any section. If you try to do so at the real test, your scores will probably be canceled.
- Take a practice test in one sitting, allowing yourself breaks of no more than two minutes between sections. You need to build up your endurance for the real test, and you also need an accurate picture of how you will do.
- Always take a practice test using an answer sheet with bubbles to fill in, just as you will for the real test. For the practice tests in the book, use the answer sheets provided at the back of this book. You need to be comfortable transferring answers to the separate sheet because you will be skipping around a bit.
- Each bubble you choose should be filled in thoroughly, and no other marks should be made in the answer area.
- As you fill in the bubble for a question, check to be sure you are on the correct number on the answer sheet. If you fill in the wrong bubble on the answer sheet, it won't matter if you've worked out the problem correctly in the test booklet. All that matters to the machine scoring the test is the No. 2 pencil mark.

Session-by-Session Study Guide

Session Zero   You're involved in this session right now. Finish reading the first chapter so you'll know what the test is about, why it is important for you to take, and what to expect from the rest of the book. This step probably won't take you long, so if you've got a couple of hours to devote to a session and you've finished these chapters, you can go on to Session One and take the first practice test.

Session One   Take Practice Test 1 (in the back of this book) and score it. You'll use this result to get an idea of how many questions you should attempt on each section and the parts of the math sections you should concentrate on.

Session Two   Work through Chapters 2 and 3 of the Orientation. Work through Chapter 4, Reading Comprehension.

Session Three   Work through the Math Basics in Chapter 5 and the corresponding drills.

Session Four   Read the Introduction to the Writing and Language Strategy section along with Chapter 10, Punctuation.

Session Five   Work through the Math Techniques section in Chapter 6 and associated drills. Take a look at Chapter 11, Words.

Session Six   Work through Advanced Math Principles, Chapter 7. Techniques like Plugging In are central to doing well on the math sections, so it's not like you can practice them too much. If there's time, start Chapter 8.

Session Seven   Work through the Additional Topics in Chapter 8. When you finish up, read through Chapter 12, Questions. This will give you a good idea of how the PSAT will put together all the things you've gone over for the Writing Skills section of the test.

Session Eight   Take Practice Test 2. Use the techniques you've been practicing throughout the book. Score your test and go through the explanations, focusing on where you may have missed the opportunity to use a technique and your decisions about whether you should have attempted a question or not, given your pacing goals and Personal Order of Difficulty.

Some of the terminology in the study guide may be unfamiliar to you now, but don't worry, you'll get to know it soon. Also, you'll want to refer back to this study guide at each session to keep yourself on track.

One important note: In this book, any sample question you see will have a question number that indicates where it would appear on the PSAT. That's why you may see a question 4 followed by a question 14—the question number indicates the PSAT question level instead of its order in the chapter. Chapter 3 has great advice on how to crack some of the most difficult questions.

HOW IS THE PSAT STRUCTURED AND SCORED?

Category	Redesigned PSAT/NMSQT (released fall 2015)
Time	2 hours and 45 minutes
Components	• Evidence-Based Reading and Writing: Reading; Writing and Language • Math
Number of Questions, Time by Section	Reading: 47 Questions, 60 minutes Writing and Language: 44 Questions, 35 minutes Math: 48 Questions, 70 minutes
Important Features	• Continued emphasis on reasoning alongside a clearer, stronger focus on the knowledge, skills, and understandings more important for college and career readiness and success • Greater emphasis on the meaning of words in extended contexts and on how word choice shapes meaning, tone, and impact • Rights-only scoring (a point for a correct answer but no deduction for an incorrect answer; blank responses have no impact on score)
Score Reporting	• Some scores will be reported on the same scale used for the SAT. This scale ranges from 400 to 1600 for total score, 200–800 for two section scores, and 10–40 for test scores
Subscore Reporting	Subscores for every test, providing added insight for students, parents, educators, and counselors
Answer Choices	4 answer choices

The More You Know...
These changes may be intimidating, but as long as you adopt a careful approach after mastering your fundamentals, you will do well on the new PSAT!

...The Less to Study
While higher-level math may sound scary at first, stay tuned for further information from us on the most effective techniques to use on the new PSAT that can, sometimes, drastically reduce the math complexity for many questions.

In addition to the obvious changes listed on the table above, such as the shift from five answer choices to four answer choices for multiple-choice questions, the PSAT suggests that it has increased the complexity of questions across the board. For the Reading and Writing and Language tests, this refers in part to the way in which all questions are now connected to full passages, which are themselves purportedly aligned with what introductory college courses and vocational training programs offer. This means that there will be an increase in history- and science-based reading material. More importantly, there are no longer any fill-in-the-blank Sentence Completion questions, nor stand-alone sentence-editing questions: Instead, you will be tested on your ability to demonstrate a full understanding of the source's ideas.

The math has also shifted, and not just in the number of questions (from 38 to 48). The actual scope of the content now focuses on a more specific set of problem-solving and analytical topics, and it includes higher-level content (like trigonometry). You are also likely to encounter more grid-in questions, and you will face topics that are both specifically geared to test your ability to use a calculator and for which calculators are not permitted.

The Math Test will be divided into two sections, one with the calculator, with 31 questions over the course of 45 minutes, and one without, with 17 questions administered in 25 minutes. Because of the tight time limit, particularly in the non-calculator section, it's important that you review the explanations for the problems in this book that you solved correctly, as you may discover techniques that help to shave seconds from your solutions. A large part of what's being tested is your ability to use the appropriate tools in a strategic fashion, and while there may be multiple ways to solve a given problem, you'll want to focus on the most efficient.

SCORING ON THE PSAT

Another major difference has to do with the way that the test is scored: The PSAT will now be scored on a scale of 320–1520 that will be the sum of the two section scores that range from 160–760. The two sections are the Evidence-Based Reading and Writing section and the Mathematics section. Wrong answers to multiple-choice questions will no longer be penalized, so you're advised never to leave a question blank—even if that means blindly picking a letter and bubbling it in for any uncompleted questions before time runs out.

In addition to the overall total score and the section scores, there will be other subscores reported on your PSAT score report:

An **Analysis in History/Social Studies** and **Analysis in Science** cross-test score is generated based on questions from all three of the subject tests (Math included!), and these assess the cross-curricular application of the tested skills to other contexts. Relax! This doesn't mean that you have to start cramming dates and anatomy—every question can be answered from the context of a given reading passage or the data included in a table or figure. The only changes have to do with the content of the passages and questions themselves.

Additionally, the Math test is broken into several categories, as we've done in this book. The **Heart of Algebra** subscore looks specifically at how well students understand how to handle algebraic expressions, work with a variety of algebraic equations, and relate real-world scenarios to algebraic principles. **Problem Solving and Data Analysis** focuses more on interpretation of mathematical expressions, graphical analysis, and data interpretation. Your ability to not only understand what a problem is asking, but also to represent it in your own words, will come in handy here. **Passport to Advanced Mathematics** questions showcase the higher-level math that's been added to the test, from quadratics and their graphs to the creation and translation of functions.

Finally, there is an **Additional Topics** domain that's filled with what you might consider wild-card material. Although these questions might not correlate directly to a subscore, six of these miscellaneous types will show up on the redesigned test. In the Verbal portions of the test, the **Command of Evidence** subscore measures how well you can translate and cite specific lines that back up your interpretation, while the **Relevant Words in Context** subscore ensures that you can select the best definition for how a word is used in a passage. The Writing and Language section additionally measures **Expression of Ideas**, which deals with revising language in order to make more logical and cohesive arguments, and **Standard English Conventions**, which assesses your ability to conform to the basic rules of English structure, punctuation, and usage.

HOW DOES THE SAT DIFFER FROM THE PSAT?

The SAT does not differ significantly from the PSAT in structure and timing! Indeed, the PSAT's Reading Test, which contains only 5 fewer questions, is only 5 minutes shorter than the SAT's Reading Test. The Writing and Language Test is the same in terms of length and timing for both tests. The PSAT's Math Test has only 10 fewer total questions as compared to those of the SAT's Math Test. The tables below summarize the differences—or actually, the similarities!—of the two tests.

Here's a breakdown of how the tests differ:

	SAT	PSAT
Structure	4 (+ optional Essay) sections	4 sections
Length	2 hours 55 minutes (+ 50 minutes for Essay)	2 hours 45 minutes
Purpose	College admissions	NMSQT (see Chapter 1)
Scoring	1600	1520

What Does the PSAT Score Mean for My SAT Score?

The SAT is scored on a 1600 scale whereas the PSAT is scored on a 1520 scale. However, because the PSAT and SAT are aligned by the College Board to be scored on the same scale, your PSAT score indicates the approximate SAT score you would earn were you to have taken the SAT on that same day.

How Much Should I Prepare for the PSAT?

If you're in that very small percentage of students who are in contention for National Merit recognition, it may be worth your while to put in a good deal of time to prepare for this test. After all, your extra hard work may well put you in a better position for National Merit recognition. Otherwise, you should prepare enough so that you feel more in control of the test and have a better testing experience. (Nothing feels quite as awful as being dragged through a testing experience feeling like you don't know what you're being tested on or what to expect—except perhaps dental surgery.) The other reason to prepare for the PSAT is that it will give you some testing skills that will help you begin to prepare for the tests that actually count, namely the SAT and SAT Subject Tests.

The bottom line is this: The best reason to prepare for the PSAT is that it will help you get an early start on your preparation for the SAT.

Study
If you were getting ready to take a biology test, you'd study biology. If you were preparing for a basketball game, you'd practice basketball. So, if you're preparing for the PSAT (and eventually the SAT), study the PSAT. The PSAT can't test everything, so concentrate on learning what it *does* test.

Chapter 2
All About National Merit Scholarships

The NMSQT part of the name PSAT/NMSQT stands for National Merit Scholarship Qualifying Test. That means that the PSAT serves as the test that will establish whether or not you are eligible for National Merit recognition. This chapter will help you figure out what that may mean for you.

How Do I Qualify for National Merit?

To participate in the National Merit Scholarship Program, a student must:

1. Take the PSAT/NMSQT in the specified year of the high school program and **no later than** the third year in grades 9 through 12, regardless of grade classification or educational pattern;
2. Be enrolled as a high school student (traditional or homeschooled), progressing normally toward graduation or completion of high school, and planning to enroll full time in college no later than the fall following completion of high school; and
3. Be a citizen of the United States; or be a U.S. lawful permanent resident (or have applied for permanent residence, the application for which has not been denied) and intend to become a U.S. citizen at the earliest opportunity allowed by law.

The Index

How does your PSAT score qualify you for National Merit? The National Merit Scholarship Corporation uses a selection index, which is the sum of your Critical Reading, Writing and Language, and Math Test scores that are each on a scale of 8–38. Those three test scores are added together and then multiplied by 2 to calculate your Selection Index score that has a range of 48–228. Qualifying scores for National Merit recognition will vary from state to state, so check with your guidance counselor as to what the cutoff score is that year for your particular state. For instance, if your PSAT scores were 24 Math, 22 Critical Reading, and 30 Writing and Language Skills, your index would be 152.

Math	+	Critical Reading	+	Writing and Language Skills	=	Test Scores Total
24	+	22	+	30	=	76

National Merit Selection Index

$$76 \times 2 = 152$$

The Awards and the Process

In the fall of their senior year, about 50,000 students will receive one of two letters from NMSC (National Merit Scholarship Corporation): either a Letter of Commendation or a letter stating that they have qualified as semifinalists for National Merit.

Commended Students   Roughly two-thirds of these students (about 34,000 total students each year) will receive a Letter of Commendation by virtue of their high scores on the test. This looks great on your college application, so if you have a reasonable chance of getting one, it's definitely worth your time to prepare for the PSAT. Make no mistake, though, these letters are not easy to get. They are awarded to students who score between the 95th and the mid-99th percentiles— that means to the top four to five percent in the country.

If you receive this honorable mention from NMSC, you should be extremely proud of yourself. Even though you won't continue in the process for National Merit scholarships, this commendation does make you eligible for special scholarships sponsored by certain companies and organizations, which vary in their amounts and eligibility requirements.

Semifinalists   The other third of these students—those 16,000 students who score in the upper 99th percentile in their states—will be notified that they are National Merit semifinalists. If you qualify, you'll get a letter announcing your status as a semifinalist, along with information about the requirements for qualification as a finalist. These include maintaining high grades, performing well on your SAT, and getting an endorsement from your principal.

Becoming a National Merit semifinalist is quite impressive, and if you manage it, you should certainly mention it on your college applications.

What does "scoring in the upper 99th percentile in the state" mean? It means that you're essentially competing against the other people in your state for those semifinalist positions. Since some states have higher average scores than others, this means that if you're in states like New York, New Jersey, Maryland, Connecticut, or Massachusetts, you need a higher score to qualify than if you live in other states.

Many students want to know exactly what score they need. Sadly, National Merit is notoriously tight-lipped about these numbers. It releases them only on rare occasions and generally doesn't like to announce them. However, it's not hard to get some pretty reliable unofficial data on what it takes to be a semifinalist. Below you'll find the most up-to-date qualifying scores for the class of 2015, and the estimated 2016 cutoff, for the National Merit semifinalists:

	2015	2016		2015	2016
Alabama	207	1,311	Montana	206	1,305
Alaska	210	1,330	Nebraska	209	1,324
Arizona	213	1,349	Nevada	208	1,317
Arkansas	206	1,305	New Hampshire	212	1,342
California	222	1,406	New Jersey	224	1,419
Colorado	213	1,349	New Mexico	210	1,330
Connecticut	220	1,393	New York	218	1,381
Washington, DC	224	1,419	North Carolina	212	1,342
Delaware	215	1,362	North Dakota	201	1,273
Florida	211	1,336	Ohio	213	1,349
Georgia	215	1,362	Oklahoma	206	1,305
Hawaii	214	1,355	Oregon	217	1,374
Idaho	211	1,336	Pennsylvania	216	1,368
Illinois	215	1,362	Rhode Island	212	1,342
Indiana	212	1,342	South Carolina	209	1,324
Iowa	207	1,311	South Dakota	203	1,286
Kansas	213	1,349	Tennessee	212	1,342
Kentucky	210	1,330	Texas	218	1,381
Louisiana	208	1,317	Utah	208	1,317
Maine	212	1,342	Vermont	213	1,349
Maryland	221	1,340	Virginia	219	1,387
Massachusetts	223	1,412	Washington	219	1,387
Michigan	210	1,330	West Virginia	201	1,273
Minnesota	215	1,362	Wisconsin	209	1,317
Mississippi	207	1,311	Wyoming	204	1,292
Missouri	209	1,324			

Note that scores can change from year to year, so these should be used only to give you a rough idea of the range of scores for National Merit recognition.

Finalists   The majority of semifinalists (more than 90 percent) go on to qualify as finalists. Students who meet all of the eligibility requirements will be notified in February of their senior year that they have qualified as finalists. This means that they are now eligible for scholarship money, though it doesn't necessarily mean that they'll get any. In fact, only about half of National Merit finalists actually win scholarships. What determines whether a student gets money or not? There is a final screening process, based on criteria that NMSC doesn't release to the public, to determine who actually gets these scholarships. There are typically 8,300 Merit Scholarship winners and 1,300 Special Scholarship recipients. Unlike the Merit Scholarships, which are given by the NMSC, the Special Scholarship recipients will receive awards from corporate sponsors and are selected from students who are outstanding, but not National Merit finalists.

Though the amounts of money may not be huge, every little bit helps, and the award itself looks great in your portfolio. So if you think you are in contention for National Merit recognition, practice diligently and smartly! If not, don't sweat it too much, but prepare for the PSAT anyway because it is good practice for the SAT.

But I'm Not a Junior in High School Yet...

If you are not yet a junior, and you're interested in National Merit, you will have to take the test again your junior year in order to qualify.

A certain number of schools give the PSAT to students in their sophomore year—and sometimes even earlier. These schools hope that earlier exposure to these tests will help their students perform better in later years. If you're not yet in your junior year, the PSAT won't count for National Merit scholarship purposes, so it's really just a trial run for you. It's still a good idea to go into the test prepared in order to feel and perform your best. After all, there's nothing more unpleasant than an unpleasant testing experience, except maybe having a tooth drilled or watching the sad downward spiral of certain pop stars.

What If I'm in a Three-Year or Other Nonstandard Course of Study?

If you're going to spend only three years in secondary school, you have two options for when to take the PSAT for National Merit purposes: You can take it either in your next-to-last year or in your last year of secondary school. However, our advice is this: If you're in any program other than a usual four-year high school, be sure to talk to your guidance counselor. He or she will consult with NMSC and help ensure that you take the PSAT at the right time. This is important, because not taking the PSAT at the right time can disqualify you from National Merit recognition.

What If I Miss the PSAT Administration My Junior Year?

If you aren't concerned about National Merit scholarships, there's no reason to do anything in particular—except, perhaps, to obtain a few PSAT booklets to practice on, just to see what fun you missed.

However, if you want to be eligible for National Merit recognition, then swift action on your part is required. If an emergency arises that prevents you from taking the PSAT, you should write to the National Merit Scholarship Corporation *immediately* to request alternate testing dates. If your request is received soon enough, it should be able to accommodate you. (NMSC says that this kind of request must absolutely be received by March 1 following the missed PSAT administration.) You'll also need a signature from a school official.

For More Information

If you have any questions or problems, the best person to consult is your school guidance counselor, who can help make sure you're on the right track. If you need further help, contact your local Princeton Review office at 800-2-REVIEW or **PrincetonReview.com**. Or, you can contact National Merit directly:

National Merit Scholarship Corporation
1560 Sherman Avenue, Suite 200
Evanston, IL 60201-4897
(847) 866-5100
NationalMerit.org

Chapter 3
Basic Principles

The first step to cracking the PSAT is to know how best to approach the test. The PSAT is not like the tests you've taken in school, so you need to learn to look at it in a different way. This chapter will show test-taking strategies that immediately improve your score. Make sure you fully understand these concepts before moving on to Part II. Good luck!

BASIC PRINCIPLES OF CRACKING THE TEST

What ETS Is Good At

The folks at ETS have been writing standardized tests for more than 80 years, and they write tests for all sorts of programs. They have administered the test so many times that they know exactly how you will approach it. They know how you'll attack certain questions, what sort of mistakes you'll probably make, and even what answer you'll be most likely to pick. Freaky, isn't it?

However, ETS's strength is also a weakness. Because the test is standardized, the PSAT has to ask the same type of questions over and over again. Sure, the numbers or the words might change, but the basics don't. With enough practice, you can learn to think like the test writers. But try to use your powers for good, okay?

The PSAT Isn't School

Our job isn't to teach you math or English—leave that to your supersmart school teachers. Instead, we're going to teach you what the PSAT is and how to crack the PSAT. You'll soon see that the PSAT involves a very different skill set.

> **No More Wrong-Answer Penalty!**
> Unlike the old PSAT, you will NOT be penalized on the new PSAT for any wrong answers. This means you should always guess, even if this means choosing an answer at random.

Be warned that some of the approaches we're going to show you may seem counterintuitive or unnatural. Some of these strategies may be very different from the way you learned to approach similar questions in school, but trust us! Try tackling the problems using our techniques, and keep practicing until they become easier. You'll see a real improvement in your score.

Let's take a look at the questions.

Cracking Multiple-Choice Questions

What's the capital of Azerbaijan?

Give up?

Unless you spend your spare time studying an atlas, you may not even know that Azerbaijan is a real country, much less what its capital is. If this question came up on a test, you'd have to skip it, wouldn't you? Well, maybe not. Let's turn this question into a multiple-choice question—just like all the questions on the PSAT Reading Test and Writing and Language Test, and the majority of questions you'll find on the PSAT Math Test—and see if you can figure out the answer anyway.

The capital of Azerbaijan is

A) Washington, DC.

B) Paris.

C) London.

D) Baku.

The question doesn't seem that hard anymore, does it? Of course, we made our example extremely easy. (By the way, there won't actually be any questions about geography on the PSAT.) But you'd be surprised by how many people give up on PSAT questions that aren't much more difficult than this one just because they don't know the correct answer right off the top of their heads. "Capital of Azerbaijan? Oh, no! I've never heard of Azerbaijan!"

These students don't stop to think that they might be able to find the correct answer simply by eliminating all of the answer choices they know are wrong.

You Already Know Almost All of the Answers

All but a handful of the questions on the PSAT are multiple-choice questions, and every multiple-choice question has four answer choices. One of those choices, and only one, will be the correct answer to the question. You don't have to come up with the answer from scratch. You just have to identify it.

How will you do that?

Look for the Wrong Answers Instead of the Right Ones

Why? Because wrong answers are usually easier to find than the right ones. After all, there are more of them! Remember the question about Azerbaijan? Even though you didn't know the answer off the top of your head, you easily figured it out by eliminating the three obviously incorrect choices. You looked for wrong answers first.

In other words, you used the Process of Elimination, which we'll call POE for short. This is an extremely important concept, one we'll come back to again and again. It's one of the keys to improving your PSAT score. When you finish reading this book, you will be able to use POE to answer many questions that you may not understand.

It's Not About Circling the Right Answer
Physically marking in your test booklet what you think of certain answers can help you narrow down choices, take the best possible guess, and save time! Try using the following notations:

- ✔   Put a check mark next to an answer you like.
- ∼   Put a squiggle next to an answer you kinda like.
- ?   Put a question mark next to an answer you don't understand.
- A̶   Cross out the letter of any answer choice you KNOW is wrong.

You can always come up with your own system. Just make sure you are consistent.

The great artist Michelangelo once said that when he looked at a block of marble, he could see a statue inside. All he had to do to make a sculpture was to chip away everything that wasn't part of it. You should approach difficult PSAT multiple-choice questions in the same way, by chipping away everything that's not correct. By first eliminating the most obviously incorrect choices on difficult questions, you will be able to focus your attention on the few choices that remain.

PROCESS OF ELIMINATION (POE)

There won't be many questions on the PSAT in which incorrect choices will be as easy to eliminate as they were on the Azerbaijan question. But if you read this book carefully, you'll learn how to eliminate at least one choice on almost any PSAT multiple-choice question, if not two or even three choices.

What good is it to eliminate just one or two choices on a four-choice PSAT question?

Plenty. In fact, for most students, it's an important key to earning higher scores. Here's another example:

2

The capital of Qatar is

A) Paris.

B) Dukhan.

C) Tokyo.

D) Doha.

On this question you'll almost certainly be able to eliminate two of the four choices by using POE. That means you're still not sure of the answer. You know that the capital of Qatar has to be either Doha or Dukhan, but you don't know which.

Should you skip the question and go on? Or should you guess?

Close Your Eyes and Point

There is no guessing penalty on the PSAT, so you should bubble something for every question. If you get down to two answers, just pick one of them. There's no harm in doing so.

You're going to hear a lot of mixed opinions about what you should bubble or whether you should bubble at all. Let's clear up a few misconceptions about guessing.

FALSE: Don't answer a question unless you're absolutely sure of the answer.

You will almost certainly have teachers and guidance counselors who tell you this. Don't listen to them! The pre-2016 PSAT penalized students for wrong answers, but the new PSAT does not. Put something down for every question: You might get a freebie.

FALSE: If you have to guess, guess (C).

This is a weird misconception, and obviously it's not true. As a general rule, if someone says something really weird-sounding about the PSAT, it's usually safest not to believe that person.

FALSE: Always pick the [fill in the blank].

Be careful with directives that tell you that this or that answer or type of answer is always right. It's much safer to learn the rules and to have a solid guessing strategy in place.

As far as guessing is concerned, we do have a small piece of advice. First and foremost, make sure of one thing:

> Answer every question on the PSAT. There's no penalty.

LETTER OF THE DAY (LOTD)

Sometimes you won't be able to eliminate any answers, and other times there are questions that you won't have time to look at. For those, we have a simple solution. Pick a "letter of the day," or LOTD (from A to D) and use that letter for all the questions from which you weren't able to eliminate any choices.

This is a quick and easy way to make sure that you've bubbled everything. It also has some potential statistical advantages. If all the answers show up about a fourth of the time and you guess the same answer every time you have to guess, you're likely to get a couple of freebies.

LOTD should absolutely be an afterthought; it's far more important and helpful to your score to eliminate answer choices. But for those questions you don't know at all, LOTD is better than full-on random guessing or no strategy at all.

Are You Ready?
Check out *Are You Ready for the SAT and ACT?* to brush up on essential skills for these exams and beyond.

PACE YOURSELF

LOTD should remind us about something very important: There's a very good chance that you won't answer every question on the test.

Think about it this way. There are 5 passages and 47 questions on the Reading Test. You've got 60 minutes to complete those questions. Now, everyone knows that the Reading Test is super long and boring, and 47 questions in 60 minutes probably sounds like a ton. The great news is that you don't have to work all 47 of these questions. After all, do you think you read most effectively when you're in a huge rush? You might do better if you worked only four of the passages and LOTD'd the rest. There's nothing in the test booklet that says that you can't work at your own pace.

Let's say you do all 47 Reading questions and get half of them right. What raw score do you get from that? That's right: 23 or 24.

Now, let's say you do only three of the 10-question Reading passages and get all of them right. It's conceivable that you could because you've now got all this extra time. What kind of score would you get from this method? You bet: 30—and maybe even a little higher because you'll get a few freebies from your Letter of the Day.

In this case, and on the PSAT as a whole, slowing down can get you more points. Unless you're currently scoring in the 650+ range on the two sections, you shouldn't be working all the questions. We'll go into this in more detail in the later chapters, but for now remember this:

> Slow down, score more. You're not scored on *how many questions you do.* You're scored on *how many questions you answer correctly.* Doing fewer questions can mean more correct answers overall!

EMBRACE YOUR POOD

Embrace your what now? POOD! It stands for "Personal Order of Difficulty." One of the things that PSAT has dispensed with altogether is a strict Order of Difficulty—in other words, an arrangement of problems that puts easy ones earlier in the test than hard ones. In the absence of this Order of Difficulty (OOD), you need to be particularly vigilant about applying your *Personal* Order of Difficulty (POOD).

Think about it this way. There's someone writing the words that you're reading right now. So what happens if you are asked, *Who is the author of Cracking the PSAT?* Do you know the answer to that question? Maybe not. Do we know the answer to that question? Absolutely.

So you can't exactly say that that question is "difficult," but you can say that certain people would have an easier time answering it.

As we've begun to suggest with our Pacing, POE, and Letter of the Day strategies, The Princeton Review's strategies are all about making the test your own, to whatever extent that is possible. We call this idea POOD because we believe it is essential that you identify the questions that you find easy or hard and that you work the test in a way most suitable to your goals and strengths.

As you familiarize yourself with the rest of our strategies, keep all of this in mind. You may be surprised to find out how you perform on particular question types and sections. This test may be standardized, but the biggest improvements are usually reserved for those who can treat the test in a personalized, nonstandardized way.

Summary

o   When you don't know the right answer to a multiple-choice question, look for wrong answers instead. They're usually easier to find.

o   When you find a wrong answer choice, eliminate it. In other words, use POE, the Process of Elimination.

o   There's no more guessing penalty on the PSAT, so there's no reason NOT to guess.

o   There's bound to be at least a few questions you simply don't get to or where you're finding it difficult to eliminate even one answer choice. When this happens, use the LOTD (letter of the day) strategy.

o   Pace yourself. Remember: You're not scored on how many questions you answer, but on how many questions you answer correctly. Take it slow and steady.

o   Make the test your own. When you can work the test to suit your strengths (and use our strategies to overcome any weaknesses), you'll be on your way to a higher score.

Part II
Cracking the
PSAT/NMSQT

Chapter 4
Reading
Comprehension

Half of your Evidence-Based Reading and Writing score comes from the Reading Test, a 60-minute test that requires you to answer 47 questions spread out over five passages. The questions will ask you to do everything from determining the meaning of words in context, to deciding an author's purpose for providing a detail, to finding the main idea of an entire passage, to pinpointing information on a graph. Each passage ranges from 500 to 750 words and has 9 or 10 questions. Time will be tight on this test. The purpose of this chapter is to introduce you to a basic approach that will streamline how you take the test and allow you to focus on only what you need to get your points.

PSAT READING: CRACKING THE PASSAGES

Answering passage-based reading questions is exactly like taking an open-book test: All of the information that you could be asked about is right in front of you, so you never have to worry about any history, literature, or chemistry that you may (or may not) have learned in school. Of course you will use the passage to answer the questions, but you will not need to read the passage from beginning to end, master all its details, and then carefully select the one choice that answers the question perfectly. Ain't nobody got time for that. What you need is a way to get in and get out of this section with as little stress and as many points as possible.

If someone asked you in what year Louis Pasteur invented pasteurization, would you read the Wikipedia entry on Pasteur from the beginning until you found the answer? Or would you quickly scan through it looking for words like "invented" and "pasteurization"? We're sure his childhood was fascinating, but your job is to answer a specific question, not read an entire text. This is exactly how to approach passage-based reading questions on the PSAT.

Your Mission:

Process five passages and answer 9 or 10 questions for each passage (or pair of passages). Get as many points as you can.

Okay…so how do you get those points? Let's start with ETS and the College Board's instructions for the Reading Test.

DIRECTIONS

Each passage or pair of passages below is followed by a number of questions. After reading each passage or pair, choose the best answer to each question based on what is stated or implied in the passage or passages and in any accompanying graphics (such as a table or graph).

Notice that the directions clearly state the correct answer is based on "what is stated or implied in the passage." This is great news! You do not have to rely on your outside knowledge here. All ETS and College Board care about is whether you can read a text and understand it well enough to answer some questions about it. Unlike in the Math or the Writing and Language Tests, there are no formulas to memorize, no comma rules to learn. You just need to know how to efficiently process the text, the questions, and the answer choices in order to maximize your score. A mantra you can use here: Don't think! Just read!

Another benefit of this open-book test format: You can (and should!) flip back and forth between the passage and the questions so that you are reading only what you need in order to answer a given question.

Your POOD and Your Reading Test

You will get all five of the Reading passages at the same time, so use that to your advantage. Take a quick look through the entire section and figure out the best order for you to do the passages. Depending on your target score, you may be able to temporarily skip (don't forget LOTD!) an entire passage or two, so figure out which passages are hardest, and save them for last (or for never).

How do you decide which ones to do and which ones to skip? Consider these concepts:

- **Type of passage:** You'll have one literature passage, two science passages, and two history/social studies passages. If you like to read fiction, the literature passage may be a good place for you to start. If you like to read nonfiction, the science or history/social studies might be a better starting place for you.
- **Topic of passage:** The blurb will give you some basic information about the passage that can help you decide whether to do the passage or skip it.
- **Types of questions:** Do the questions have a good number of Line References and Lead Words? Will you be able to find what you're looking for relatively quickly, or will you have to spend more time wading through the passage to find what you need?

Don't forget: On any questions or passages that you skip, always fill in your LOTD!

Basic Approach for the Reading Test

Follow these steps for every Reading passage. We'll go over these in greater detail in the next few pages.

Where the Money Is

A reporter once asked notorious thief Willie Sutton why he robbed banks. Legend has it that his answer was, "Because that's where the money is." While reading comprehension is safer and slightly more productive than larceny, the same principle applies: Concentrate on the questions and answer choices because that's where the points are. The passage is just a place for ETS to stash facts and details. You'll find them when you need to. What's the point of memorizing all 67 pesky details about plankton if ETS asks you about only 12?

1. **Read the Blurb**. The little blurb at the beginning of each passage may not contain a lot of information, but it can be helpful for identifying the type of passage.
2. **Select and Understand a Question**. For the most part, do the questions in order, saving the general questions for last and using your LOTD on any questions or passages you want to skip.
3. **Read What You Need.** Don't read the whole passage! Use Line References and Lead Words to find the reference for the question, and then carefully read a window of about 10–12 lines (usually about 5 or 6 lines above and below the Line Reference/Lead Word) to find the answer to the question.

4. **Predict the Correct Answer**. Your prediction should come straight from the text. Don't analyze or paraphrase. Often, you'll be able to find something in the text that you can actually underline to predict the answer.
5. **POE**. Eliminate anything that isn't consistent with your prediction. Don't necessarily try to find the right answer immediately, because there is a good chance you won't see anything that you like. If you can eliminate answers that you know are wrong, though, you'll be closer to the right answer. If you can't eliminate three answers with your prediction, use the POE criteria (which we'll talk about in a few pages.)

Let's see these steps in action!

A sample passage and questions appear on the next few pages. Don't start working the passage right away. In fact...you can't! The answer choices are missing. Just go ahead to page 36, where we will begin going through the steps of the Basic Approach, using the upcoming passage and questions.

SAMPLE PASSAGE AND QUESTIONS

Here is an example of what a reading comprehension passage and questions look like. We will use this passage to illustrate the reading Basic Approach throughout this chapter. You don't need to do the questions now, but you might want to paperclip this page so it's easy to flip back to later.

Questions 21-30 are based on the following passage.

The passage below is adapted from an article discussing minor Elizabethan dramatists. It focuses on the works of Thomas Heywood and Thomas Middleton, two influential playwrights of the early seventeenth century.

Thomas Heywood, of whom little is known, was one of the most prolific writers the world has ever seen. In 1598 he became an actor, or, as
Line Henslowe, who employed him, phrases it, "came
5 and hired himself to me as a covenanted servant for two years." The date of his first published drama is 1601; that of his last published work, a "General History of Women," is 1657. As early as 1633 he represents himself as having had
10 an "entire hand, or at least a main finger," in two hundred and twenty plays, of which only twenty-three were printed. "It is true," he says, "that my plays are not exposed to the world in volumes, as others are: one reason is that many of them,
15 by shifting and change of companies, have been negligently lost; others of them are still retained in the hands of some actors, who think it against their peculiar profit to have them come in print; it was also never any great ambition in me to be in
20 this kind voluminously read." It was said of him, by a contemporary, that he "not only acted every day, but also obliged himself to write a sheet every day for several years; but many of his plays being composed loosely in taverns, occasions them to
25 be so mean." Besides his labors as a playwright, he worked as translator, versifier, and general maker of books. Late in life he conceived the design of writing the lives of all the poets of the world, including his contemporaries. Had this
30 project been carried out, we should have known something about the external life of Shakespeare; for Heywood must have carried in his brain many of those facts which we of this age are most curious to know.
35 Heywood's best plays evince large observation, considerable dramatic skill, a sweet and humane

spirit, and an easy command of language. His style, indeed, is singularly simple, pure, clear, and straightforward; but it conveys the impression of
40 a mind so diffused as almost to be characterless, and incapable of flashing its thoughts through the images of imaginative passion. He is more prosaic, closer to ordinary life and character, than his contemporaries.
45 With less fluency of diction, less skill in fastening the reader's interest to his fable, harsher in versification, and generally clumsier in construction, the best plays of Thomas Middleton are still superior to Heywood's in force of
50 imagination, depth of passion, and fullness of matter. It must, however, be admitted that the sentiments which direct his powers are not so fine as Heywood's. He depresses the mind, rather than invigorates it. The eye he cast on human life
55 was not the eye of a sympathizing poet, but rather that of a sagacious cynic. His observation, though sharp, close, and vigilant, is somewhat ironic and unfeeling. His penetrating, incisive intellect cuts its way to the heart of a character as with a knife;
60 and if he lays bare its throbs of guilt and weakness, and lets you into the secrets of its organization, he conceives his whole work is performed. This criticism applies even to his tragedy of "Women Beware Women," a drama which shows a deep
65 study of the sources of human frailty, considerable skill in exhibiting the passions in their consecutive, if not in their conflicting action, and a firm hold upon character; but it lacks pathos, tenderness, and humanity; its power is out of all
70 proportion to its geniality; the characters, while they stand definitely out to the eye, are seen through no visionary medium of sentiment and fancy
There is, indeed, no atmosphere to Middleton's
75 mind; and the hard, bald caustic peculiarity of his genius, which is unpleasingly felt in reading any one of his plays, becomes a source of painful weariness as we plod doggedly through his works. This is most powerfully felt in his tragedy of "The

80 Changeling," at once the most oppressive and
impressive effort of his genius. The character
of De Flores in this play has in it a strangeness
such as is hardly paralleled in the whole range
of the Elizabethan drama. The passions of this
85 brute imp are not human. They are such as might
be conceived of as springing from the union of
animal with fiendish impulses, in a nature which
knew no law outside of its own lust, and was as
incapable of a scruple as of a sympathy.

These are the questions for the passage. We've removed the answer choices because, for now, we just want you to see the different question types the PSAT will ask. Don't worry about answering these here.

21

The primary purpose of the passage is to

22

According to the information in the passage, the author most likely would agree that Heywood

23

Which choice provides the best evidence for the answer to the previous question?

24

The author's reaction to Middleton is best described as a mix of

25

According to the information in the passage, one primary difference between Heywood and Middleton is that Heywood

26

Which choice provides the best evidence for the answer to the previous question?

27

Heywood claims that all of the following are reasons that many of his plays were not published EXCEPT

28

As used in line 28, "design" most nearly means

29

As used in line 53, "fine" most nearly means

30

The information in lines 58-62 serves primarily to

Step 1: Read the Blurb

You should always begin by reading the blurb (the introductory material above the passage). The blurb gives you the title of the piece, as well as the author and the publication date. Typically the blurb won't have much more information than that, but it'll be enough to let you know whether the passage is literature, history/social studies, or science. It will also give you a sense of what the passage will be about and can help you make a POOD decision about when to do the passage.

Read the blurb at the beginning of the passage on page 33. Based on the blurb, is the passage literature, history/social studies, or science? What will the passage be about?

_____

_____

Step 2: Select and Understand a Question

Select...

Notice that the steps of the Basic Approach have you jumping straight from the blurb to the questions. There is no "Read the Passage" step. You get points for answering questions, not for reading the passage, so we're going to go straight to the questions.

On a test you take in school, you probably do the questions in order. That seems logical and straightforward. However, doing the questions in order on a Reading passage can set you up for a serious time issue. ETS and College Board say the order of the questions "is also as natural as possible, with general questions about central ideas, themes, point of view, overall text structure, and the like coming early in the sequence, followed by more localized questions about details, words in context, evidence, and the like." So to sum it up: The general questions come first, followed by the specific questions.

That question structure works great in an English class, when you have plenty of time to read and digest the text on your own. When you're trying to get through five passages in only an hour, you don't have time for that. Instead of starting with the general questions and then answering the specific questions, we're going to flip that and do the specific questions first.

Look back at the questions on page 35.

What does the first question ask you about?

In order to answer that question, you'd have to read what part of the passage?

And what we don't want to do is read the whole passage! So skip that first question. You'll come back to it, but not until you've done the specific questions. Once you go through and answer all (or most) of the specific questions, you'll have a really good idea what the test writers think is important. You'll also have read most of the passage, so answering the general questions at the end will be easier than it would if you'd started with them.

Remember we mentioned earlier that the questions are in chronological order? Look at the Line References in the specific questions. What do you notice about them?

Yep! They're in order through the passage! So work through them as they're given, and you'll work through the passage from beginning to end. Do not get stuck on a hard question, though. If you find yourself stumped, use your LOTD and move on to the next question. You can always come back if you have time.

Based on that logic, let's skip the first question and move on to the second question.

...and Understand

Once you've selected a question, you need to make sure you understand what it's asking. Reading questions are often not in question format. Instead, they will make statements such as, "The author's primary reason for mentioning the gadfly is to," and then the answer choices will follow. Make sure that you understand the question by turning it into a question—that is, back into a sentence that ends with a question mark and begins with Who/What/Why.

According to the information in the passage, the author most likely would agree that Heywood

What is this question asking?

Notice the phrase *most likely would agree that*. This phrase lets you know that the question can be rephrased as a "what" question. So for this particular question, you want to figure out "What does the author most likely think about Heywood?" Notice also the phrase *according to the information in the passage* at the start of the question. This phrase lets you know that you don't have to be psychic! You just need to find something the author actually said about Heywood, and use that information to answer the question.

Step 3: Read What You Need

Line Reference and Lead Words

Many questions will refer you to a specific set of lines or to a particular paragraph, so you won't need to read the entire passage to answer those questions. Those are Line References. Other questions may not give you a Line Reference, but may ask about specific names, quotes, or phrases that are easy to spot in the text. We'll call those Lead Words. It's important to remember that the Line Reference or Lead Word shows you where the *question* is in the passage, but you'll have to read more than that single line in order to find the *answer* in the passage.

If you read a window of about five lines above and five lines below each Line Reference or Lead Word, you should find the information you need. It's important to note that while you do not need to read more than these 10–12 lines of text, you usually cannot get away with reading less. If you read only the lines from the Line Reference, you will very likely not find the information you need to answer the question. Read carefully! You should be able to put your finger on the particular phrase, sentence, or set of lines that answers your question. If you save the general questions that relate to the passage as a whole for last, then by the time you begin those questions, you'll have a greater understanding of the passage even if you haven't read every word of it.

> Read a window of about 5 lines above and 5 lines below your Line Reference to get the context for the question.

The Strategy
1. Read the Blurb
2. Select and Understand a Question
3. Read What You Need

5 Above, 5 Below
5 is the magic number when it comes to Line Reference questions. Read 5 lines above the Line Reference and then 5 lines below it to get all of the information you need in order to answer the question correctly.

24

> The author's reaction to Middleton is best described
> as a mix of

What are the Lead Words in this question?

What lines will you need to read to find the answer?

Once you use the Lead Words to find your window, draw a bracket around the window so that you can find it easily. The more you can get out of your brain and onto the page, the better off you'll be. Because the Lead Word is *Middleton*, you'll want to skip to line 48 and start reading there. In this case, the first half of the third paragraph would be a good window.

Now it's time to read. Even though you're reading only a chunk of the text, make sure you read it carefully.

Step 4: Predict Your Answer

ETS and College Board do their best to distract you by creating tempting—but nevertheless wrong—answers. However, if you know what you're looking for in advance, you will be less likely to fall for a trap answer. Before you even glance at the answer choices, take the time to think about what specific, stated information in your window supplies the answer to the question. Be careful not to paraphrase too far from the text or try to analyze what you're reading. Remember: What might be a good "English class" answer may lead you in the wrong direction on the PSAT! Stick with the text.

As you read the window, look for specific lines or phrases that answer the question. Often what you're looking for will be in a sentence before or after the Line Reference or Lead Word, so it's crucial that you read the full window.

Once you've found text to answer the question, underline it if you can! Otherwise, jot down a prediction for the answer, sticking as close to the text as possible.

Let's keep looking at question 24, this time with the window.

24

The author's reaction to Middleton is best described as a mix of

Here's your window from the passage. Read it and see if you can find something that answers the question. Underline your prediction if you can.

> With less fluency of diction, less skill in fastening the reader's interest to his fable, harsher in versification, and generally clumsier in construction, the best plays of Thomas Middleton are still superior to Heywood's in force of imagination, depth of passion, and fullness of matter. It must, however, be admitted that the sentiments which direct his powers are not so fine as Heywood's. He depresses the mind, rather than invigorates it. The eye he casts on human life was not the eye of a sympathizing poet, but rather that of a sagacious cynic. His observation, though sharp, close, and vigilant, is somewhat ironic and unfeeling.

Did you underline some negative terms as well as some positive ones? The passage gives you clear evidence that the author's reaction to Middleton involves both a positive and a negative judgement. The sentence *His observation, though sharp, close, and vigilant, is somewhat ironic and unfeeling* shows this ambivalence.

The Strategy
1. Read the Blurb
2. Select and Understand a Question
3. Read What You Need
4. Predict Your Answer
5. Use Process of Elimination

Step 5: Use Process of Elimination

A multiple-choice test is a cool thing because you have all the right answers on the page in front of you. All you have to do is eliminate anything that isn't correct. Sometimes, especially on Reading, it's easier to find wrong answers that aren't supported by the passage rather than trying to find the right answer that might not look the way you think it should.

Process of Elimination, or POE, involves two steps. The first step will be the question, "What can I eliminate that doesn't match—or is inconsistent with—my prediction?" For many of the easy and medium questions, this step will be enough to get down to the right answer.

24

The author's reaction to Middleton is best described as a mix of

Remember, on the previous page, you used the text to predict that the author reacted to Middleton with a mix of positive and negative judgement. Start by eliminating anything that does not fit that prediction.

	Keep?	Eliminate?
A) admiration for his ingenuity but criticism for his absence of warmth.		
B) disgust for his style but appreciation for his displays of tenderness.		
C) confusion about his use of diction but curiosity about his sentiments.		
D) apathy toward his ability to dishearten readers but dislike of his coldness.		

Did you eliminate (C) and (D) right away? Neither choice involves a mix of positive and negative. That was fast! Now that you're down to two answer choices that fit your prediction, use the text to get the right one. On the negative side, what's the author's criticism? Middleton *depresses* us because he is *unfeeling*. Does that better match (A) criticism or (B) disgust? Disgust seems too extreme. If you're not sure yet, look at the positive side: What does the author like about Middleton? The *force of imagination, depth of passion, and fullness of matter*. Does that match (A) admiration for his ingenuity? Maybe. Does that match (B) appreciation for his displays of tenderness. Not at all. Either way you slice it, (A) is better than (B). Pick (A).

POE Criteria

On most of the Easy and Medium questions, you'll be able to eliminate three of the four answers simply by using your prediction. On other questions, usually the Hard questions, your prediction will help you get rid of one or two answers, and then you'll need to consider the remaining answers a little more carefully. If you're down to two answers, and they both seem to make sense, you're probably down to the right answer and the trap answer. Luckily, there are some common traps that ETS and College Board will set for you, and knowing them can help you figure out which is the trap answer and which is the right answer. Here are a few of those traps:

Predictions and POE
Use these criteria after you have eliminated anything that doesn't match your prediction.

- **Mostly Right/Slightly Wrong**: These answers look just about perfect except for a word or two that doesn't match what's in the text.
- **Could Be True**: These answers might initially look good because they make sense or seem logical. You might be able to support these answers in an English class, but they lack the concrete support from the text to make them correct PSAT answers.
- **Deceptive Language**: These answer choices have individual words that look exactly like what you saw in the passage, but the words are put together in such a way that they don't actually say what you need them to say. Make sure you're reading carefully and not just matching words.

QUESTION TYPES AND FORMATS

Now that you know the steps of the Basic Approach, let's consider the different types of questions you'll be answering. It's not important that you can identify the question types by the names we give them. But it is extremely important that you can read a question and know how to respond. Is the question asking you WHAT the author says, WHAT the author means, WHAT a particular word means, WHAT evidence supports a point, etc.? The next section of this chapter will help you decode those question types and formats. The final section will help you make sense of questions that ask HOW or WHY an author does something. Your score will depend on your ability to figure out if a question is asking you WHAT, WHY, or HOW.

Question Types and Formats

- Detail
- Vocabulary in Context
- Infer/Imply/Suggest
- Except/Not/Least
- Paired Questions

DETAIL (*What?*)

When you see a question that contains the phrase *according to the passage* or *according to the author*, your job is fairly simple. Get to that part of the text, find the detail that tells you WHAT the passage or the author is saying, and then use POE to get rid of wrong answers. Carefully read the window and do not simply rely on your memory. The question writers are really good at tricking people who use their memories rather than their eyes.

———————————○———————————

25

According to the information in the passage, one primary difference between Heywood and Middleton is that Heywood

A) displayed a more cynical attitude toward humanity.

B) had fewer of his works published.

C) was a more disciplined writer.

D) showed less powerful creativity in his writing.

Here's How To Crack It

First you need to go back to the text and find a *primary difference* between the two writers. Since paragraphs 1 and 2 are about Heywood only, and paragraph 4 is about Middleton only, focus on paragraph 3. Since the second half of paragraph 3 is only about Middleton, focus on the first half, which contrasts both writers. As you read that window, underline whatever is true about Heywood but not Middleton. You should notice that, compared to Middleton, Heywood has more *fluency of diction* and *skill in fastening the reader's interest to his fable*, better *versification* and *construction*, but has less *force of imagination, depth of passion, and fullness of matter*. Once you have this prediction—based completely on the text, not on your opinion and not on your memory—use POE to work through the answer choices. Choice (A) doesn't match the prediction (and actually fits Middleton, rather than Heywood), so eliminate it. Choice (B) might seem logical, but it's not in the text and it doesn't match the prediction. Eliminate it. Choice (C) Could Be True because the text says he had more fluency and skill and better construction. If he's better at the technical parts of writing, it might make sense that he's a more disciplined writer. However, nothing in the text actually supports that. Watch out for answers that you might be able to justify in an essay. There has to be support in the text! Choice (C) does not have that support and it does not match the prediction. Eliminate it. Choice (D) totally matches the prediction. Remember: Don't think—read! Put another way: Don't remember—underline!

———————————○———————————

VOCABULARY IN CONTEXT (*What?*)

Another way that ETS and College Board will test your reading comprehension is with Vocabulary-in-Context (VIC) questions. The most important thing to remember is that these are ***IN CONTEXT!*** Gone are the days of "SAT Vocabulary" when you had to memorize lists of obscure words like *impecunious* and *perspicacious*. Now, ETS and College Board want to see that you can understand what a word means based on context. You'll see words that look familiar but may be used in ways that are a little less familiar. Do not try to answer these questions simply by defining the word in your head and looking for that definition. You have to go back to the text and look at the context for the word.

28

As used in line 28, "design" most nearly means

A) draft.

B) pattern.

C) biography.

D) intention.

Here's How To Crack It

With VIC questions, you don't need to read a full 10–12-line window. Typically a few lines before and a few lines after will give you what you need. Go to line 28 and find the word *design*. Underline it. When you read a bit before and after the word, say lines 25 through 29, the text says: *Besides his labors as a playwright, he worked as translator, versifier, and general maker of books. Late in life he conceived the <u>design</u> of writing the lives of all the poets of the world, including his contemporaries.* Now read the sentence and put in a different word than "design" that means the same thing. Did you use a word like "plan"? Did you use that exact word? Compare your prediction to the four answer choices, and you can quickly eliminate (A), (B), and (C).

Do not give in to the temptation to simply answer the question without looking at the text. Did you notice that at least two of the wrong answer choices do legitimately mean *design*? If you don't go back to the text, you can easily fall for such a wrong answer. But if you look at what the text actually says, VIC questions are among the easiest to answer. Don't think—just read!

Now try this one:

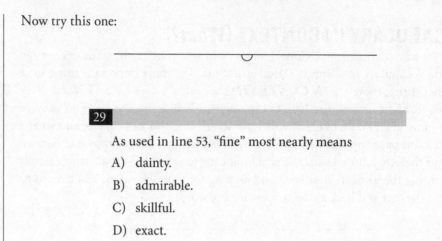

29

As used in line 53, "fine" most nearly means

A) dainty.

B) admirable.

C) skillful.

D) exact.

Here's How To Crack It

Here are lines 48–54: *[T]he best plays of Thomas Middleton are still superior to Heywood's in force of imagination, depth of passion, and fullness of matter. It must, however, be admitted that the sentiments which direct his powers are not so fine as Heywood's. He depresses the mind, rather than invigorates it.*

So it seems Middleton is *not so fine*, and Heywood is therefore *fine*. Great. But you don't have to guess! The sentence gives us some clues as to the meaning here: Since depressing the mind is Middleton's thing, depressing the mind is apparently *not so fine*. Well, then, invigorating the mind is apparently a *fine* thing. Thinking along these lines, what's a word you could now use where you've been using *fine*? How about "good/happy/invigorating/something like that"? Does "dainty" have the same meaning? No. Does "admirable"? Maybe. Does "skillful"? That fits "good," but doesn't fit the rest. Does "exact"? That also fits good, but not the rest. So using these predictions, (A) is out, (B) seems okay, and (C) and (D) both seem weakly possible. In a situation like this, choose (B)!

INFER/IMPLY/SUGGEST (*What*?)

When you see a question that contains the word *infer*, *imply*, or *suggest*, be extra careful. In real life, those words often signify a question asking your opinion. You may think that ETS and College Board want you to do some English-class-level reading between the lines. In actuality, though, they don't. It's still just a straight reading comprehension question. There may be a tiny bit of reading between the lines, so far as the answer will not be directly stated in the text as it will with a detail question, but there will still be plenty of evidence in the text to support the correct answer.

A few pages ago, we discussed this question:

> **24**
>
> The author's reaction to Middleton is best described as a mix of
>
> A) admiration for his ingenuity but criticism for his absence of warmth.
>
> B) disgust for his style but appreciation for his displays of tenderness.
>
> C) confusion about his use of diction but curiosity about his sentiments.
>
> D) apathy toward his ability to dishearten readers but dislike of his coldness.

Recall how we solved it by going back to the text, finding relevant evidence, predicting an answer, and then using POE to eliminate answer choices that didn't fit the prediction. If you rely on this procedure, you will improve your performance with these sorts of questions.

Inference questions can seem confusing, but remember that these are still WHAT questions. Whereas Detail questions ask WHAT the author says, Inference questions ask WHAT the author *really* says? The correct answer will have the same *meaning* as the text, even though the *words* may be different.

EXCEPT/NOT/LEAST (*What*???)

Now that you know how to answer a basic WHAT question, let's consider what changes when you get one of these three pesky words in the question stem. Consider this question stem:

> **27**
>
> Heywood claims that all of the following are reasons that many of his plays were not published EXCEPT

So apparently, three of the answer choices are true, and one is false. Except for that, this is a "detail" question. But now you have to be willing to find three parts of the passage that correspond to an answer choice, which you will eliminate. And you will select the lonely remaining answer choice with no support from the passage. These can be time-consuming (after all, you have to find three pieces of information in the text instead of just one), but carefully reading your window can help eliminate efficiently. Let's see how this works using the full question:

Heywood claims that all of the following are reasons that many of his plays were not published EXCEPT

A) many of his plays accidentally went missing.

B) Heywood lacked a strong desire for popularity.

C) a number of his plays feature mean characters.

D) some individuals kept the plays to prevent their publication.

Since lines 12–20 give a direct quote from Heywood explaining why his plays are not published, use that window and underline the reasons he gives.

"It is true," he says, "that my plays are not exposed to the world in volumes, as others are: one reason is that many of them, by shifting and change of companies, have been negligently lost; others of them are still retained in the hands of some actors, who think it against their peculiar profit to have them come in print; it was also never any great ambition in me to be in this kind voluminously read."

Notice that there are phrases that support (A) (*have been negligently lost*), (B) (*it was also never any great ambition in me to be in this kind voluminously read*), and (D) (*some actors…think it against their peculiar profit to have them come in print*). With support from the text, those three choices can all be eliminated, leaving (C) as the correct answer.

PAIRED QUESTIONS (BEST EVIDENCE)

Remember the full name of this section of the test? It's the PSAT Evidence-Based Reading Test. Throughout this chapter, you've been using evidence to answer all of these questions, so this next step won't come as a complete surprise. In fact, once you get a hold of how to manage best evidence questions, you'll be glad. You can do the work for one question and get points for two.

Best Evidence: Specific Paired Questions

We talked about, indeed we answered, question 25 earlier. This was the question:

25

According to the information in the passage, one primary difference between Heywood and Middleton is that Heywood

The correct answer was (D): *showed less powerful creativity in his writing*. Recall that we based this answer on the part of the text that said Heywood had less *force of imagination, depth of passion, and fullness of matter*.

So now you encounter the following question:

---○---

> **26**
>
> Which choice provides the best evidence for the answer to the previous question?
>
> A)   Lines 8-12 ("As early as . . . printed")
>
> B)   Lines 20-25 ("It was said . . . mean")
>
> C)   Lines 45-51 ("With less . . . matter")
>
> D)   Lines 54-56 ("The eye . . . cynic")

Here's How To Crack It

What to do? Since the text you already used to answer Question 25 (*force of imagination, depth of passion, and fullness of matter*) was in lines 49–51, simply pick (C) and move on! Buy one, get one free.

---○---

We're not kidding: Specific best evidence questions are like free points. Get them all!

Best Evidence: General Paired Questions

Sometimes, though, the best evidence question follows a general question, rather than a specific one. And that general question may have no Lead Words or Line References. You might think that you have to solve the general question first by rereading the entire passage, and then answering the evidence question based on that exhaustive research. But luckily, we have a time-saving and accuracy-improving strategy for you: Parallel POE.

Using Parallel POE, you'll be able to work through the questions at the same time! When you find yourself faced with a set of paired questions, you can start with the second question (the "best evidence" question) if (1) you aren't sure where to look for the answer or (2) the first question is a general question about the passage. Because the second question in the pair asks which lines provide the *best evidence* for the previous question, you can use those lines to help work through the answers for the previous question. Let's take a look.

Best Evidence
Not sure where to find the answer? Let the "best evidence" lines help!

22

According to the information in the passage, the author most likely would agree that Heywood

A) could have contributed more to our knowledge of influential seventeenth-century writers than he actually did.

B) was more involved in professions other than playwriting than many authorities today believe.

C) was an actor in more than two hundred plays, although only slightly more than twenty became popular productions.

D) would have been the most talented playwright of his day had he possessed more imagination and passion.

23

Which choice provides the best evidence for the answer to the previous question?

A) Lines 3-12 ("In 1598 . . . printed")

B) Lines 20-27 ("It was said . . . books")

C) Lines 27-34 ("Late . . . know")

D) Lines 37-44 ("His style . . . contemporaries")

Here's How to Crack It

Heywood is the subject of the first two paragraphs. At 44 lines, that's a pretty big window! What to do? That's where Parallel POE comes in. Notice that Question 23 gives you the only possible lines for your evidence. Choice (23A) references 10 lines, (23B) references 8 lines, (23C) references 8 lines, and (23D) references 8 lines. So what would you rather do: read the entire passage hoping you might find an answer somewhere or read these tiny chunks one at a time to see if they answer the question? We hope you answered the latter!

What's great about Parallel POE is that, in the first instance, the original question does not even matter. Think for a moment about how paired questions operate. The correct answer to the first question *must* be supported by an answer to the best evidence question, and the correct answer to the best evidence question *must* support an answer to the first question. In other words, if there is a best evidence answer that doesn't support an answer to the first question, it is wrong. Period. Likewise, if there is an answer to the first question that isn't supported by a best evidence answer, it too is wrong. Period.

Let's use this to our advantage! Rather than worry about what the first question is asking and what the answer might be, just start making connections between the two answer sets. If a best evidence answer supports a first question answer, physically draw a line connecting them. You should not expect to have four connections. If you are lucky, you will have only one connection, and you will have your answer pair. Otherwise, you might have two or three connections and will then (and only then) worry about the first question. The important thing to remember is that any answer choice in the first question that isn't physically connected to a best evidence answer—and any best evidence answer that isn't connected to an answer in the first question—must be eliminated.

———————○———————

Let's take a look at how this first Parallel POE pass would look. (The paired questions have been arranged in two columns to help understand this, and the lines have been written out for your convenience. This does not represent what you will see on the official test.)

22. According to the information in the passage, the author most likely would agree that Heywood	23. Which choice provides the best evidence for the answer to the previous question?
A) could have contributed more to our knowledge of influential seventeenth-century writers than he actually did.	A) Lines 3-12 ("In 1598 . . . printed")
B) was more involved in professions other than playwriting than many authorities today believe.	B) Lines 20-27 ("It was said . . . books")
C) was an actor in more than two hundred plays, although only slightly more than twenty became popular productions.	C) Lines 27-34 ("Late . . . know")
D) would have been the most talented playwright of his day had he possessed more imagination and passion.	D) Lines 37-44 ("His style . . . contemporaries")

Don't worry about the question itself yet. Go straight to the best evidence lines.

- Choice (23A) says *In 1598 he became an actor, or, as Henslowe, who employed him, phrases it, "came and hired himself to me as a covenanted servant for two years." The date of his first published drama is 1601; that of his last published work, a "General History of Women," is 1657. As early as 1633 he represents himself as having had an "entire hand, or at least a main finger," in two hundred and twenty plays, of which only twenty-three were printed.* Does this evidence support any of the answer choices for Question 22? Nope. So eliminate (23A) and move on.

- Choice (23B) says *It was said of him, by a contemporary, that he "not only acted every day, but also obliged himself to write a sheet every day for several years; but many of his plays being composed loosely in taverns, occasions them to be so mean." Besides his labors as a playwright, he worked as translator, versifier, and general maker of books.* So he wrote a lot. Does this evidence support any of the answer choices for Question 22? Choice (22B) looks possible, so draw a line physically connecting (23B) with (22B).

- Choice (23C) says *Late in life he conceived the design of writing the lives of all the poets of the world, including his contemporaries. Had this project been carried out, we should have known something about the external life of Shakespeare; for Heywood must have carried in his brain many of those facts which we of this age are most curious to know.* Does this evidence support any of the answer choices for Question 22? Yes, it very strongly supports (22A), so draw a line physically connecting (23C) with (22A).

- Choice (23D) says *His style, indeed, is singularly simple, pure, clear, and straightforward; but it conveys the impression of a mind so diffused as almost to be characterless, and incapable of flashing its thoughts through the images of imaginative passion. He is more prosaic, closer to ordinary life and character, than his contemporaries.* Does this evidence support any of the answer choices for Question 22? Nope. So eliminate (23D) and move on.

Look at your progress so far: (22C) and (22D) have no support from Question 23, so go ahead and eliminate (22C) and (22D). No matter how good they may sound, they CANNOT be right if there is no evidence supporting them from the best evidence question.

Your work should look something like this at this point:

22. According to the information in the passage, the author most likely would agree that Heywood	23. Which choice provides the best evidence for the answer to the previous question?
A) could have contributed more to our knowledge of influential seventeenth-century writers than he actually did.	A) ~~Lines 3-12 ("In 1598 . . . printed")~~
B) ~~was more involved in professions other than playwriting than many authorities today believe.~~	B) Lines 20-27 ("It was said . . . books")
C) ~~was an actor in more than two hundred plays, although only slightly more than twenty became popular productions.~~	C) Lines 27-34 ("Late . . . know")
D) ~~would have been the most talented playwright of his day had he possessed more imagination and passion.~~	D) ~~Lines 37-44 ("His style . . . contemporaries")~~

Now you're down to a very nice 50/50 split. Go back to the question. Of the two pairs, which one best describes Heywood in a way that *the author would most likely agree with*? Your strong reaction that (23C) strongly matched (22A) is a clue that this is what the author would most likely agree with, since it's something the author actually did say. The other pair was a weaker match, with a feeling of Could Be True. Eliminate (23B), eliminate (22B), choose the remaining answer (22A) and (23C), and get two points.

On the actual test, it would be too complicated for you to draw a full table like the one above, but all you need to do is create a column to the left of the best evidence answer choices for the answers to the previous question. Basically, it should look something like this:

Q23   23. Which choice provides the best evidence for the answer to
         the previous question?

A   A) Lines 3-12 ("In 1598 . . . printed")
B   B) Lines 20-27 ("It was said . . . books")
C   C) Lines 27-34 ("Late . . . know")
D   D) Lines 37-44 ("His style . . . contemporaries")

Parallel POE
Since you can't draw a full table on the actual exam, try making notations as shown in question 22; that is, create a column to the left of the best evidence answer choices listing out the choices to the previous question.

SAMPLE PASSAGE AND QUESTIONS

Here is another example of a Reading passage and questions. We will use this passage to further illustrate the Basic Approach to let you independently practice the questions you already know how to do (Detail, Infer) and to model for you how to manage some other question types you will encounter.

Questions 31-40 are based on the following passage.

This passage is excerpted from an article on the long-term effects of acid rain.

Remember acid rain? Resulting largely from the smokestack emissions of coal-fired power plants, acid rain was a serious environmental
Line concern in the 1980s. Studies showed that
5 because of the increasing acidity of rainfall, nearly a quarter of the lakes and streams in the Adirondack Mountains had become uninhabitable by fish. The urgency of the problem prompted amendments to the Clean
10 Air Act in 1990 and the creation of the world's first "pollution market," a cap-and-trade program in which power companies were required to buy permits to emit sulfur dioxide and nitrogen oxides, which cause acid rain. The result:
15 Today, acid rain has all but disappeared from news headlines.

Acid rain was rare among environmental problems in that it had a viable solution, and these days it's often hailed as an environmental
20 success story. The market worked as intended, sulfur and nitrogen emissions declined, and rain became less acidic.

But what about the lakes and streams that were already so acidic? Nearly 25 years since
25 those changes to the Clean Air Act, water bodies in the Northeast have recovered, while those further south have not.

There has been an impressive rebound in the Northeast. Declines in sulfate concentrations in
30 the water bodies of New York and Pennsylvania, for example, are a promising sign. But the effect has not been universal. The monitoring sites in the central Appalachian region show a different pattern. Streams here aren't recovering
35 from acidification like the water bodies in the Northeast are, and scientists have been working to figure out why.

The answer may lie in differences in local geology. The central Appalachians were not
40 glaciated during the last ice age, unlike the regions further north. One consequence is that Virginia's soils are older and therefore highly weathered. Weathered soil has a much higher capacity for sulfate to stick to it. When sulfate
45 was deposited on the landscape in its highest concentrations in the late 1980s, a large portion of that sulfate was retained in the soil, and not immediately deposited into water bodies. In the Adirondacks, sulfate from acid rain went straight
50 into the water bodies rather than stuck to the soil.

The problem today is that the sulfate stored in the soils of the central Appalachians is coming back out. With sulfate concentrations in rainfall on the decline, the soils are leaching
55 their stored sulfate back into the water. Evidence of this comes from Rick Webb of the University of Virginia, who coordinated the monitoring program in the central Appalachians for 25 years until his recent retirement. The program found
60 that in Adirondack lakes the consequences of acid rain occurred directly after the rain fell, and the recovery process began almost immediately after sulfate emissions declined. In the central Appalachians, however, the negative effects of
65 acidification occurred at a slower pace, but the recovery has also been slow. Geology cuts both ways. The coal veins that run rich in this region— as well as its highly weathered soils—are both a consequence of geologic history.

70 What can be done about the predicament of central Appalachian streams? The most obvious action, however unlikely, would be further reductions in emissions of sulfur and nitrogen oxides. A recent Supreme Court decision upheld
75 the federal government's authority to regulate these pollutants, but it merely set the stage for a larger battle with the power industry. The EPA intends to use the Clean Air Act, and the court's decision, to justify the first-ever limits on carbon

80 dioxide emissions from coal-fired power plants.
The agency is expected to announce the new
regulations next month.

   The soils of the central Appalachians will
continue to release sulfate into the water for years
85 to come, but lower additions from man-made
sources in the present would decrease the burden
on ecosystems haunted by the ghost of emissions
past.

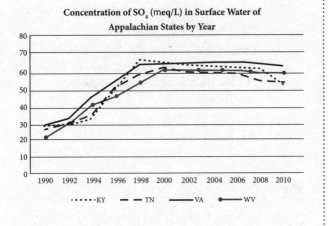

Concentration of SO$_4$ (meq/L) in Surface Water of
Appalachian States by Year

········ KY   — — TN   —— VA   ●— WV

31

What is the purpose of the opening line of the
passage?

A) To introduce a topic that was previously well
   known but is now widely forgotten

B) To test the reader on her knowledge of public
   health concerns

C) To reminisce over a previous victory on an
   environmental issue

D) To let the reader know the author also has
   trouble recalling what acid rain is

32

Which of the following models the structure of
the author's argument throughout the passage?

A) She acquaints the reader with an unknown
   phenomenon, describes solutions that were
   applied, and discusses the negative results
   that followed from those solutions.

B) She introduces a topic, compares the
   differing geographic effects that resulted, and
   makes predictions for future effects.

C) She provides a detailed description of the
   ways in which government regulation solves
   all environmental problems.

D) She offers a critical review of the ways
   in which markets both help and hinder
   environmental protection goals.

33

Which of the following best describes the role of
soil sulfate retention in local geologies in regards
to acid rain?

A) Soil sulfate retention is the primary cause of
   acidification of lakes.

B) It is soil sulfate retention that prevents the
   entry of acid into lakes.

C) Although soil sulfate retention initially acts
   as a protection for bodies of water, it can
   increase their long-term acidity.

D) Areas with lower levels of soil sulfate
   retention tend to be more adversely affected
   by acid rain for longer periods of time.

34

According to the passage, what was the effect of government regulation on the issue of acid rain?

A) The EPA's limitation of carbon dioxide emissions helped to decrease the effects of acid rain.

B) An amendment was introduced but was most effective after it was upheld by the Supreme Court.

C) The creation of the pollution market, which allowed the free trade of environmental pollutants without government interference or oversight.

D) The amendments to the Clean Air Act in 1990 resulted in a significant decrease in the occurrence of acid rain.

35

What is the main idea of the passage?

A) Despite positive steps to limit its occurrence, the long-term effects of acid rain are still evident and can be further addressed.

B) Now that acid rain has been eradicated, it is time to turn our focus to the environmental effects of carbon dioxide emissions.

C) The government did not go far enough to restrict pollutants from the power industries.

D) There is still a great deal of work to do for the recovery of Appalachian lakes.

36

Which statement best describes the function of the sentence in lines 66-67, "Geology cuts both ways"?

A) One learns the most from geology from cutting across soil to expose the layers of soil.

B) Environmental factors can result in both beneficial and deleterious effects for a region depending on specific circumstances.

C) Geology either helps or hurts the organisms within a region.

D) The geology of Virginia has been more hurtful than helpful in the long term.

37

Which of the following best illustrates the effect of the geology of the Adirondacks?

A) Because the soil near lakes had low levels of sulfate retention, the lakes recovered more quickly than those in other regions in North America.

B) Because the lakes were not sheltered by sulfate soil retention, they are showing slower signs of recovery than lakes in other regions in North America.

C) Despite having coal, the geology of the Adirondacks may in the end create more burden than benefit for the regional population.

D) The geology of the Adirondacks is the best outcome of acid rain.

38

In the seventh paragraph (lines 70-82), the author doubts that emissions of acid-rain-inducing pollutants will decrease further due to

A) the reluctance of commercial entities to reduce individual pollution outputs.

B) the lack of interest on the part of the EPA to regulate anything but carbon dioxide emissions.

C) the unwillingness of the Supreme Court to fight for the Clean Air Act.

D) the continued leaching of sulfate into lakes and rivers from sulfate retaining soils.

39

All of the following are true according to the passage EXCEPT

A) the creation of a "pollution market" helped decrease rates of acid-rain-causing emissions.

B) the more weathered soil is, the greater its rate of sulfate retention.

C) the decrease in acid rain has led to a decrease in acidification of the lakes of the Appalachians.

D) more can be done to improve the environmental quality of lakes in North America.

Which of the following is supported by the provided graph?

A) Although Kentucky experienced the highest concentration of SO_4, that state has demonstrated the lowest level of concentration for the last year recorded.

B) Virginia experienced the greatest protection from sulfate soil retention in the early 1990s.

C) Tennessee has had consistently higher rates of SO_4 concentration than West Virginia.

D) All four states of Appalachia have an observable decline in SO_4 concentration from 2008 to 2010.

Do you recognize questions 34, 38, and 39 as Detail questions? Do you recognize questions 33 and 37 as Infer questions? Try answering them on your own, using the procedures we've been discussing. So that leaves us with five questions and a few other mysterious question types. In the following pages, we will demystify them for you.

What? (Main Idea/General Questions)

For many of the Reading passages, the very first question will ask a general question about the passage. It might ask about the main idea or purpose of the passage, the narrative point of view, or a shift that occurs through the passage. Remember the Select a Question step? Those general questions are not good to do first because you haven't read the passage yet, but once you've answered most of the other questions, you have a good idea of the overall themes of the text.

Let's take a look at question 35:

What is the main idea of the passage?

Because this question asks about the *central claim* of the passage, there's no one place you can look. General questions don't have line references or lead words, so there's no way to use the text to predict an answer. It's okay, though: You've answered almost all of the questions about the passage, so you know what the main idea of the passage is. Not only that, but you also have a good sense of what the test writers found most interesting about the passage. While having this knowledge does not always help, it sure can sometimes. If there are answer choices that have nothing to do with either the questions or the answers you've seen repeatedly, you can eliminate them and instead choose the one that is consistent with those questions and answers.

Let's take a look at the answers:

A) Despite positive steps to limit its occurrence, the long-term effects of acid rain are still evident and can be further addressed.

B) Now that acid rain has been eradicated, it is time to turn our focus to the environmental effects of carbon dioxide emissions.

C) The government did not go far enough to restrict pollutants from the power industries.

D) There is still a great deal of work to do for the recovery of Appalachian lakes.

Remember, if it's a *main idea*, it's a central point of the text. What can you eliminate?

The first half of (A) fits paragraphs 1 and 2, and the second half of (A) fits the rest of the passage starting with paragraph 3, so keep this for now.

The first half of (B) says that acid rain has been eradicated, but the point of the article was to describe bad effects of acid rain that are still with us, so this claim seems extreme. The second half of (B) talks about carbon dioxide, which is not an issue in the passage at all. Eliminate (B).

Choice (C) expresses an opinion that one could certainly have. Can you find any words in the passage that show that the author expressed this opinion? No. Eliminate (C).

Choice (D) fits the second half of the passage. This is definitely an idea of the passage. But the question asked about the main idea, not just a true idea.

Since (A) fits more paragraphs than does (D), select (A).

Why? (Purpose Questions)

Take a look at this question, and think about how it's different from what we've been talking about.

> 31
>
> What is the purpose of the opening line of the passage?

Notice that it's not asking you WHAT the opening line says. It is asking about the purpose. The purpose for something is the reason it is there. How would you talk about that? You would explain WHY it is there, right? Yes! So when you see questions with phrases like "what is the purpose" or "the author says/does X/Y/Z in order to," just translate this into your own words as a question starting with WHY.

So question 31 is really asking WHY the author used the opening line of the passage. Doesn't that feel easier to deal with than the way it was originally worded? We think so too.

Well, the opening line of the passage is *Remember acid rain?* Having worked through the passage a bit, why do you think the author would start this way? Is the author doing a memory test? Giving a history lesson? Starting a chemistry experiment? No, no, and no. The passage was all about how the long-term effects of acid rain are still with us, so this opening line must be there to get us thinking about the issue. Let's compare that prediction to the answer choices.

A) To introduce a topic that was previously well-known but is now widely forgotten

B) To test the reader's knowledge of public health concerns

C) To reminisce about a previous victory on an environmental issue

D) To let the reader know the author also has trouble recalling what acid rain is

Choice (A) fits our prediction well enough. Choices (B), (C), and (D) do not. So choose (A)!

How? (Structure questions)

The last time someone asked you about a film you just saw, did you answer "A character was introduced, a problem emerged, possible solutions were explored and rejected, and a resolution emerged from an unexpected alliance with a former antagonist"? Doubtful. But if so, ETS and College Board might have a job for you!

Take a look at this question, and think about how it's different from what we've been talking about.

32

Which of the following models the structure of the author's argument throughout the passage?

Notice that it's not asking you WHAT the author says. The content doesn't matter here. It's also not asking you WHY the author says things. It's asking you HOW the author built an argument. The answer choices might be off-putting to you, since they are pretty abstract, but they will still be supported by the text. Just eliminate what is clearly wrong, and then look for specifics to justify keeping or eliminating the remaining answers.

A) She acquaints the reader with an unknown phenomenon, describes solutions that were applied, and discusses the negative results that followed from those solutions.

B) She introduces a topic, compares the differing geographic effects that resulted, and makes predictions for future effects.

C) She provides a detailed description of the ways in which government regulation solves all environmental problems.

D) She offers a critical review of the ways in which markets both help and hinder environmental protection goals.

What are the worst answer choices here, the ones that have nothing to do with what you saw in the passage? Choices (A) and (B) are both three-part sentences, which might represent three parts of the text, so keep them for now. Choice (C) says that the text describes in detail how *government regulation solves all of the problems*, and you know that the passage didn't do that. Choice (D) says the passage was all about how the markets affect environmental protection goals, and you know the passage didn't do that. So eliminate (C) and (D) right away.

Now you can compare (A) and (B). Choice (A) starts by saying that the author *acquaints the reader with an unknown phenomenon*; (B) starts by saying that the author *introduces a topic*. Which one seems right to you so far? Since the topic is not unknown, (A) is already flawed. Choice (B) is fine and true so far, and the rest of (B) also works just fine.

Try question 36 on your own using the same approach!

Charts and Graphs

Charts, graphs, and diagrams are no longer limited to the Math Test! You will now see a variety of graphics in the Reading Test and even in the Writing and Language Test! (More on the Writing and Language test later.) The good news is that the graphics you'll be dealing with in the Reading Test are very straightforward and do not require any computations. All you need to do is make sure you can put your pencil on the place on the graphic that proves a reason to keep or eliminate an answer choice. Let's take a look at an example.

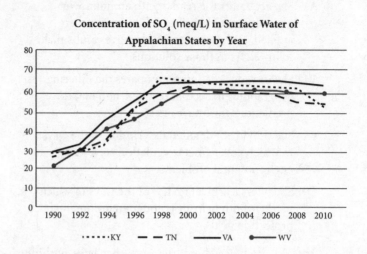

Concentration of SO$_4$ (meq/L) in Surface Water of Appalachian States by Year

········ KY   — — TN   —— VA   ——●—— WV

Step 1: Read the graphic.

Carefully look at the title, axis labels, and legend. Notice that on this graph we're looking at the concentration of SO$_4$ (measured in μeq/L, whatever that is) in the surface water of Appalachian states from 1990 to 2010. The years are on the horizontal axis, so the vertical axis must be measuring that concentration. According to the legend (the part below the chart), we are comparing these concentrations in four different states: KY, TN, VA, and WV.

Step 2: Read your question.

40

Which of the following is supported by the provided graph?

Since the question asks you what is supported by the graph, your job will be to compare all four answer choices with the graph. Make sure you can put your pencil on the data point you're using to keep or eliminate certain answers.

Step 3: Read your answers.

A) Although Kentucky experienced the highest concentration of SO$_4$, that state has demonstrated the lowest level of concentration for the last year recorded.

B) Virginia experienced the greatest protection from sulfate soil retention in the early 1990s.

C) Tennessee has had consistently higher rates of SO$_4$ concentration than West Virginia.

D) All four states of Appalachia have an observable decline in SO$_4$ concentration from 2008 to 2010.

Let's take another look at the graph, this time looking for specific reasons to keep or eliminate answers.

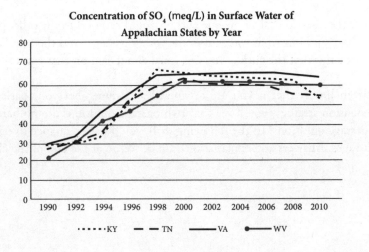

Concentration of SO$_4$ (meq/L) in Surface Water of Appalachian States by Year

Based on the data shown, (A) is the correct answer.

KY had the highest recorded amount of SO$_4$ concentration in 1998, but by 2010 it had the lowest concentration. Keep (A).

VA had a higher SO$_4$ concentration in surface water than did any of the other three states, so it was less protected by the soil retention of sulfate. Eliminate (B).

TN and WV's concentration levels fluctuated with no clear relationship between the two. Eliminate (C).

Between 2008 and 2010, WV showed no decline in SO$_4$ concentration. Eliminate (D).

Dual Passages

One of your Science or History/Social Studies passages will be a set of dual passages. There will be two shorter passages about one topic. Although the two passages will be about the same topic, there will also be differences that you'll need to pay attention to. Rather than attempting to read and understand both passages at the same time, just follow the Basic Approach and focus on one at a time.

The questions for Passage 1 will come before the questions for Passage 2, and the questions for each passage follow the order of the passage, just like single-passage questions. The questions about both passages will follow the questions for Passage 2.

Two-Passage Questions

For questions asking to compare or contrast both passages, it's helpful to consider one passage at a time rather than trying to juggle both passages at the same time. First, find the answer for the first passage (or the second passage if that one is easier) and use POE to narrow down the answer choices. Then find the answer in the other passage and use POE to arrive at the correct answer. This will save time and keep you from confusing the two passages when you're evaluating the answer choices. Always keep in mind that the same POE criteria apply, no matter how two-passage questions are presented.

- If a question is about what is supported by both passages, make sure that you find specific support in both passages, and be wary of all the usual trap answers.

- If a question is about an issue on which the authors of the two passages disagree or on how the passages relate to one another, make sure you find support in each passage for the author's particular opinion.

- If the question asks how one author would respond to the other passage, find out what was said in that other passage, and then find out exactly what the author you are asked about said on that exact topic.

The bottom line is that if you are organized and remember your basic reading comprehension strategy, you'll see that two-passage questions are no harder than single-passage questions! In the following drill, you'll have a chance to try a set of dual passages. Answers and explanations can be found at the end of the chapter.

Dual Passage Drill

The following are modified passages that explore the design and construction of drug delivery vehicles for biomedical applications.

Passage 1

The technology of drug delivery is one of the most important in the field of medicine and biomedical engineering. The more site-specific a delivery system is, the more effective the drug it is delivering will be; the more conservative a delivered drug dosage is, the less severe the side effects will be. This is especially true of different drugs used to predominantly treat infections and cancers. A new technology called electrostatic processing, or electrospinning, accomplishes both of these goals.

Electrospinning creates biodegradable scaffolds composed of fibers ranging from nanometers to micrometers in diameter, an attribute that is intrinsically difficult to obtain from other fiber-fabrication processes. The electrospinning process begins with a polymer solution at a prescribed charge and viscosity that is pumped through a spinneret. An electric field, powered by a high voltage power supply, is applied to this spinneret so that a droplet is formed at the tip of the spinneret. This droplet morphs into the shape of a cone, in which the surface tension of the droplet is counterbalanced by the applied external electrostatic forces. Once the applied voltage is strong enough to overcome the droplet's surface tension, a fibrous jet is emitted from the cone and captured on a grounded collecting plate. The distance between the spinneret and the collecting plate is where any residual solvent in the ejected jet stream evaporates, resulting in a collection of non-woven submicron-sized fibers that, ultimately, form a highly porous scaffold. Drug delivery via these electrospun scaffolds affords ample flexibility in creating an optimal delivery vehicle for therapeutic treatment.

The chemical properties of the materials utilized as base polymers determine how stable the electrospun scaffolds are and how well they function. Both synthetic and natural materials can be used as base polymers. Between the two, natural polymers typically possess lower levels of toxicity, immunogenicity, and improved biocompatibility. In other words natural polymers have a greater ability to perform more effectively than synthetic polymers do in the treatment of human disease. Examples of a natural base commonly used as a base for electrospun fibers include collagen and elastin. Collagen is the most prevalent protein in the extracellular matrix (ECM) of soft and hard tissues, and collagen types I, II, and III have all been utilized as the main component of electrospun scaffolds. Elastin has also been substantially utilized as a polymer in electrospinning, especially for vascular tissue engineering. Beyond the inherent advantages that natural polymers possess, the combination of natural polymers can sometimes provide a greater benefit toward constructing an ideal electrospun scaffold. For example, the combination of collagen and elastin in certain ratios has been demonstrated to produce ideally-sized fiber diameters. Thus, the potential to combine—or include—other natural polymers is tremendous in attempting to engineer a drug delivery vehicle with optimal biodegradable properties.

Passage 2

Although it has historically been the case that natural polymers were favored in the construction of electrospun fibers for drug delivery systems, there is a growing trend towards employing synthetic polymers. Synthetic polymers are used to enhance various characteristics of the drug delivery system goals. These characteristics include degradation time, mechanical properties, and cell attachment affinities. Synthetic polymers are able to improve these characteristics as they are more easily tailored to a wider range of properties such as hydrophilicity and hydrophobicity—in other words, the desired solubility of an electrospun scaffold. Because synthetic polymers can be created in laboratories, a nearly innumerable

number of possible products that are made from synthetic polymers can be engineered to address any particular clinical need. The most popular of
85 these are the most hydrophobic and biodegradable polymers such as poly(glycolide) (PGA) and poly(lactide).

Despite the clear benefits of synthetic polymers when compared to natural polymers, it
90 is of the utmost importance to not limit scientific or medical pursuit by a purist approach. The ability to blend the variety of synthetic polymers with the strong biocompatible properties of natural polymers may allow biomedical engineers
95 to more precisely fine-tune the properties of electrospun scaffolds. It is this wide-ranging flexibility of polymer compositions that gives electrospun scaffolds such huge promise in medical applications, causing the huge spike of
100 research done in this space in the last several decades. With even more to discover, it is both likely and lucky that this interest will continue for some time.

42

The author mentions infections and cancers (lines 8-9) in order to

A) provide an example of the types of diseases that electrospun scaffolds have cured.

B) point out illnesses that still do not have effective treatments.

C) illustrate types of medical conditions that are more effectively treated by precisely controlled internal drug delivery.

D) demonstrate the kind of vaccines electrospinning technology will help to develop.

43

In Passage 1, the reference to "nanometers to micrometers" (lines 13-14) serves to

A) give a precise measurement of fibers used in electrospinning.

B) further elaborate on the minuteness of electrospun fibers.

C) relate the size of the fibers in electrospun scaffolds to that of the cells of the human body.

D) inform the reader of one of the qualities of electrospun fibers absent in other similar technological approaches.

44

As used in line 30, "residual" most nearly means

A) durable.

B) remaining.

C) steadfast.

D) inhabiting.

45

In discussing the nature of natural polymers, the author of Passage 1 suggests that

A) they are more effective as an electrospun scaffold base as they may be less harmful to people than synthetic polymers.

B) they are not as effective as when blended with synthetic polymers such as poly(glyocide) and poly(lactide).

C) because they are natural materials that exist in the human body, the body is unable to reject them.

D) collagen and elastin are effective polymer bases only when blended together.

In Passage 2, the connection between natural and synthetic polymers is best described in which of the following ways?

A) Researchers are increasingly using synthetic polymers more than the historically preferred natural polymers, while more attention is being paid to electrospun fiber research that combines the two types of polymers.

B) Because synthetic polymers can be created in laboratories, they are easier to work with than natural polymers.

C) Because of the importance of a purist approach, it is important to separate research conducted on differing types of base polymers.

D) Synthetic polymers are more hydrophobic when compared to natural polymers.

The second paragraph of Passage 2 primarily serves to

A) confirm the author's assertion that synthetic polymers are the most effective polymers for electrospinning.

B) support the purist approach to polymer research in order to preserve the impeccable methods of scientific and medical study.

C) assert that it is because there has been a huge spike in research on polymers that scientists have learned how flexible polymers are.

D) acknowledge that both types of polymers have positive attributes that, when combined, may lead to even more effective electrospun scaffolds.

From the information presented in Passage 2, it can be inferred that

A) history favors things from nature.

B) it is the man-made nature of synthetic polymers that accounts for their flexibility.

C) the solubility of an electrospun scaffold depends more on its hydrophilicity than its hydrophobicity.

D) synthetic polymers degrade more quickly over time than natural polymers.

The authors of both passages would most likely agree with which of the following?

A) Hydrophilicity and Hydrophobicity are important factors to consider when selecting a base polymer material.

B) Differing electric charges and viscosity will result in differing constructions of electrospun scaffolding.

C) The more exact the system of drug delivery is, the more beneficial it is likely to be.

D) A blended polymer base will be more effective than a non-blended one.

The passages differ in that Passage 1

A) does not discuss the possibility of using multiple materials for base polymers while Passage 2 does.

B) provides information on electrospun scaffolding construction while Passage 2 looks to the future of electrospun scaffolding research.

C) is concerned only with drug delivery systems to address cancers, while Passage 2 aims to treat all diseases.

D) advocates that the type of polymer base used for electrospun scaffolds is unimportant while Passage 2 advocates that the type of polymer base is important.

What is the primary difference in the tones of Passages 1 and 2?

A) Passage 1 is belligerent while Passage 2 is enthusiastic.

B) Passage 1 biased while Passage 2 is subjective.

C) Passage 1 is unequivocal while Passage 2 is conciliatory.

D) Passage 1 is pessimistic while Passage 2 is optimistic.

DUAL-PASSAGE DRILL ANSWERS AND EXPLANATIONS

42. **C** The author mentions *infections and cancers* as examples of the types of ailments that site-specific and conservative drug doses can more effectively help than other drug delivery systems that are not characterized by these attributes. The answer that best matches this description is (C). Choice (A) is not supported because the passage discusses treating these types of illnesses, not curing them. Choice (D) is also incorrect as it references vaccines, rather than treatments. Choice (B) is disproven by the passage; the paragraph clearly refers to drugs *used to predominately treat infections and cancers*. This implies that there are currently effective treatments for cancers, but there may be even better ones out there. The best answer is (C).

43. **D** The author states that the fibers range in size from nanometers to micrometers, which is an attribute that is intrinsically difficult to obtain from other fiber-fabrication processes. The only answer choice that matches this is (D). Choices (A) and (C) are not correct because precise fiber measurements and cellular measurements are not mentioned in the passage. Choice (B) is deceptively worded; the passage is describing the sizes of the fibers for the first time. Because there is no additional information being given about the size, (B) cannot be correct.

44. **B** In context, "residual" refers to the solvent that evaporates, as opposed to that which forms the collection of non-woven fibers, so it is the extra material that results from the electrospinning process. Therefore, the correct answer should match the meaning "extra." Because *durable, steadfast*, and *inhabiting* do not match this meaning, eliminate (A), (C), and (D). The remaining answer does match this meaning, making (B) the best answer.

45. **A** The author of Passage 1 prefers natural polymers to synthetic polymers because they possess lower levels of toxicity, immunogenicity, and improved biocompatibility as compared to synthetic polymers. This is best supported by (A). The author of Passage 1 does not discuss blending natural polymers with synthetic polymers—that's the author of Passage 2, so eliminate (B). Choice (D) is too extreme—while the author states that when combined, these polymers can have greater benefit; it does not go so far to say that when used individually, collagen and elastin are not effective. Choice (C) is not discussed in either passage, so it cannot be the correct answer.

46. **A** Passage 2 begins by discussing why there has been an increase in research and use of synthetic polymers as opposed to natural ones and reviews the positive attributes of synthetic. It then goes on to say in the second and final paragraph that researchers should not limit themselves to a purist approach, and a blend of polymer types may result in the most beneficial base yet of electrospun scaffolds. This best matches (A). Choice (C) is the opposite of this—the author does not think a purist approach is important to have. Choice (D) is too specific and does not address the connection between natural and synthetic polymers. Choice (B) goes too far; although the passage does state that synthetic polymers can be created in laboratories, it does not say that they are easier to work with than natural fibers, only that many possible products can be made from them. The correct answer is (A).

47. **D** Although the author does state that synthetic polymers have clear benefits over natural ones, he goes on to urge that a blend of the two may create an even better option because they both have positive properties. Choice (D) is the only answer that matches the general point of the paragraph. Choice (A) is too specific because it addresses only the first line of the paragraph. Choice (B) is the opposite of what is stated in the paragraph; the author does not support the purist approach. Choice (C) is not addressed in the passage, so it is not correct. The best answer is (D).

48. **B** Don't forget to use POE! Passage 2 focuses on the positive aspects of synthetic polymers and the importance of keeping an open approach to building these drug delivery systems. Choice (B) is supported by the author's assertion that *because synthetic polymers can be created in laboratories… [they] can be engineered to address any particular clinical need.* Choice (A) is too vague and does not match the information presented in Passage 2 regarding synthetic polymers having many benefits over natural polymers. Eliminate (A). The passage states that the hydrophilicity and hydrophobicity of a polymer are related to its solubility, but it never states that one has more affect on solubility than the other. This makes (C) incorrect. Because there is no evidence from Passage 2 to support (D), the only possible answer is (B).

49. **C** Hydrophilicity and hydrophobicity are mentioned only in Passage 2, not in both passages. Therefore, eliminate (A). Differing electrical charges and viscosity are mentioned only in Passage 1, so (B) can be eliminated as well. The topics in (C) and (D) are addressed in both passages, but (D) goes too far. Passage 1 states that natural polymers *typically* possess positive aspects, not that they necessarily do, while Passage 2 argues for trying blended polymer bases. So eliminate (D). Passage 1 does state that site-specificity, stability, and dosage measurement all impact how well electrospun scaffolds work, while Passage 2 states that it is the aim of researchers to precisely fine-tune the properties of electrospun scaffolds. Choice (C) is the best-supported answer.

50. **B** Both passages discuss blended polymer bases: Passage 1 discusses the combination of collagen and elastin, while Passage 2 encourages research on synthetic and natural base blends, so eliminate (A). Choice (C) is incorrect because Passage 1 refers to both the efficacy of different drug delivery systems for cancers and infections, while Passage 2 does not refer to disease at all, just merely *medical applications.* Eliminate (C). Choice (D) is inaccurate for Passage 1 because the author of that passage clearly favors natural polymer bases. Only (B) matches both passages, as Passage 1 explains how electrospinning works, and Passage 2 discusses the need to look at combining polymer bases and continued interest in this field in the last paragraph.

51. **C** The tones differ in that Passage 1 strongly believes natural polymers are the best, while Passage 2 believes that, although synthetic polymers have more positive characteristics, both have benefits that should be utilized. This makes (C) the best answer. Choice (B) can be eliminated because *biased* and *subjective* mean the same thing. Choices (A) and (D) can be eliminated as the author of Passage 1 is neither belligerent nor pessimistic.

Summary

o The Reading Test on the PSAT makes up 50 percent of your score on the Evidence-Based Reading and Writing section.

o Reading questions are *not* presented in order of difficulty, but they are in chronological order. Don't be afraid to skip a hard question, and don't worry if you can't answer every question.

o Use your POOD to pick up the points you can get, and don't forget LOTD on the rest!

o Reading is an open-book test! Use that to your advantage by focusing only on the text you need to get each point.

o Translate each question back into a *what* or *why* question before you start reading your window.

o Use Line References, Lead Words, and chronology to help you find ETS's answer in the passage. Always start reading a few lines above the Line Reference or the Lead Words and read until you have the answer.

o Use the text to predict your answer to the question before you look at the answer choices.

o Use POE to eliminate answers that don't match your prediction.

o If you have more than one answer left after you eliminate anything that doesn't match your prediction, compare your remaining answers to see if any of them

• Are Mostly Right/Slightly Wrong
• Could Be True
• Contain Deceptive Language

o   For Paired Sets, make sure you're following the right strategy.
- Specific Paired Questions simply require you to follow the Basic Approach, making sure you've underlined the evidence for your prediction in the text.
- General Paired Questions will be much more straightforward if you use Parallel POE to consider the "best evidence" in tandem with the previous question.

o   For Dual Passages, do questions about the first passage first, questions about the second passage second, and dual questions last. Remember that even with dual questions, you must find support in the passages.

o   Save Main Idea or General Questions until the end of the passage. POE will be much more efficient once you've done all the other questions.

o   Don't get bogged down by hard or time-consuming questions! If you find yourself stuck or running short on time, use LOTD and move on!

Chapter 5
Math Basics

Although we'll show you which mathematical concepts are most important to know for the PSAT, this book relies on your knowledge of basic math concepts. If you're a little rusty, this chapter is for you. Read on for a review of the math basics you'll need to know before you continue.

HOW TO CONQUER PSAT MATH

So what do you need to do? There are three important steps:

1. **Know the basic content.** Obviously you do need to know the basics of arithmetic, algebra, and geometry. We'll cover what you need to know in this chapter.

2. **Learn some PSAT-specific problem-solving skills.** Since these basic concepts appear in ways you're probably not used to from math class, you need to prepare yourself with a set of test-specific problem-solving skills designed to help you solve PSAT Math problems. We'll cover the most important ones in the next chapter.

3. **Have a sound overall testing strategy.** This means knowing what to do with difficult questions or when calculator use is not allowed, and having a plan to pace yourself to get the maximum number of points in the time allotted. Be sure to read carefully the material in Chapter 3, to make sure you're using the strategy that will get you the greatest number of points in the time you have.

(PERSONAL) ORDER OF DIFFICULTY

The Math sections on the PSAT are Sections 3 and 4. Section 3 contains 13 multiple-choice questions and 4 grid-in questions. Section 4 contains 27 multiple-choice questions and 4 grid-in questions. Within each question type, there is a loose order of difficulty, with most of the questions being of medium difficulty. More important than any order of difficulty is your own Personal Order of Difficulty. Though the last questions of each type in a section are likely to be the hardest, use your own personal strengths and weaknesses to decide which questions to do and which to skip.

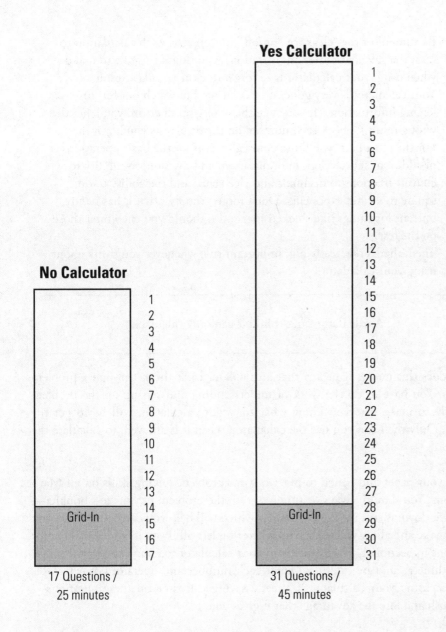

No Calculator

1
2
3
4
5
6
7
8
9
10
11
12
13
14
15
16
17

Grid-In

17 Questions /
25 minutes

Yes Calculator

1
2
3
4
5
6
7
8
9
10
11
12
13
14
15
16
17
18
19
20
21
22
23
24
25
26
27
28
29
30
31

Grid-In

31 Questions /
45 minutes

USING YOUR CALCULATOR

You are allowed to use a calculator on Section 4 of the PSAT, and you should definitely do so. You can use any graphing, scientific, or plain old four-function calculator, **provided that it doesn't have a keyboard**.

There are a few simple rules to remember when dealing with your calculator:

1. Use the calculator you're most comfortable with. You definitely don't want to be trying to find the right button on test day. Ideally, you should be practicing with the same calculator you'll use on test day.
2. Change your batteries the week before the test. If they run out during the test, there's nothing you can do about it.

3. Be sure to hit the "clear" or "on/off" button after each calculation to reset the calculator after an operation. A common mistake to make when using your calculator is to forget to clear your last result.

4. Your calculator is very good at calculating, but watch out for mis-keying information. (If you type the wrong numbers in, you'll get the wrong result.) Check each number on the display as you key it in.

5. For the most part, you'll use your calculator for the basic operations of addition, subtraction, multiplication, and division; the ability to convert fractions to decimals and vice versa; and the ability to do square roots and exponents. Don't forget, though, that it has handy buttons for things like sine, cosine, and i, should you encounter those on the test.

6. Then, there's one really big, important rule whenever you think about using your calculator:

A calculator can't think; it can only calculate.

What does this mean? It means that a calculator can't think through a problem for you. You have to do the work of understanding and setting up the problem correctly to make sure you know what the right calculation will be to get the answer. Only then can you use the calculator, when it is allowed, to calculate the answer.

So use your paper and pencil to practice your problem-solving skills on all Math questions. You should always be sure to set up the problem in your test booklet—writing it down is still the best method—which will help you catch any errors you might make and allow you to pick up where you left off if you lose focus. Then, for questions in Section 4, move quickly to your calculator to chug your way through the arithmetic, and be careful to enter each number and operator correctly. Remember, using your calculator is already saving you time on these questions—don't rush and lose the advantage that it gives you.

As you work through this book, look for calculator symbols next to questions on which calculator use would be allowed. If you don't see the symbol, don't use your calculator!

Drill 1

DEFINITIONS

One of the reasons that good math students often don't get the credit they deserve on the PSAT is that they've forgotten one or more of these definitions—or they read too fast and skip over these "little" words. Be sure you know them cold and watch out for them!

Match the words with their definitions, and then come up with some examples. Answers can be found in Part III.

1. integers

2. positive numbers

3. negative numbers

4. even numbers

5. odd numbers

6. factors

7. multiples

8. prime numbers

9. distinct

10. digit

a. numbers that a certain number can be divided by, leaving no remainder
   Examples: _____

b. integers that cannot be divided evenly by 2
   Examples: _____

c. numbers that have no fractional or decimal parts
   Examples: _____

d. numbers that are greater than zero
   Examples: _____

e. having a different value
   Examples: _____

f. integers that can be divided by 2 evenly (with no remainder)
   Examples: _____

g. numbers that are less than zero
   Examples: _____

h. numbers that have exactly two distinct factors: themselves and 1
   Examples: _____

i. numbers that can be divided by a certain number with no remainder
   Examples: _____

j. a figure from 0 through 9 that is used as a placeholder
   Examples: _____

11. consecutive numbers

12. divisible

13. remainder

14. sum

15. product

16. difference

17. quotient

18. absolute value

k. the result of addition
   Examples: _____

l. a whole number left over after division
   Examples: _____

m. the result of subtraction
   Examples:_____

n. can be divided with no remainder
   Examples: _____

o. a number's distance from zero; always a
   positive value
   Examples: _____

p. numbers in a row
   Examples: _____

q. the result of division
   Examples: _____

r. the result of multiplication
   Examples: _____

EXPONENTS AND SQUARE ROOTS

Exponents are just a shorthand for multiplication. Instead of writing $3 \times 3 \times 3 \times 3$, you can write 3^4. Thus, you can handle exponents by expanding them out if necessary.

$$y^2 \times y^3 = y \times y \times y \times y \times y = y^5$$

$$\frac{y^4}{y^2} = \frac{y \times y \times y \times y}{y \times y} = y \times y = y^2$$

However, you can also multiply and divide exponents that have the same base using a shortcut called MADSPM. MADSPM also helps you remember how to deal with raising exponents to another power. Let's see the breakdown:

- **MA** means when you see a MULTIPLICATION sign, ADD the exponents. So $y^2 \times y^3 = y^{2+3} = y^5$.
- **DS** means when you see a DIVISION sign (or fraction), SUBTRACT the exponents. So $\frac{y^5}{y^2} = y^{5-2} = y^3$.

- **PM** means when you see an exponent raised to a POWER, MULTIPLY the exponents. So $(y^2)^3 = y^{2 \times 3} = y^6$. (This is really easy to confuse with multiplication, so watch out!)

Be careful, because the rules of MADSPM don't work for addition and subtraction. For example, $3^2 + 3^5$ does NOT equal 3^7. (Crunch it on your calculator if you want to prove it.)

Here are some additional rules to remember about exponents:

- Anything to the zero power equals 1: $3^0 = 1$. Mathematicians argue about whether 0^0 is 1 or is undefined, but that won't come up on the PSAT.
- Anything to the first power equals itself: $3^1 = 3$.
- 1 to any power equals 1: $1^{3876} = 1$.
- A **negative exponent** means to take the reciprocal of what would be the result as if the negative weren't there: $2^{-2} = \frac{1}{2^2} = \frac{1}{4}$.

- A **fractional exponent** has two parts (like any other fraction), the numerator, which is the power the base is raised to, and the denominator, which is the root of the base. For example, $8^{2/3} = \sqrt[3]{8^2} = \sqrt[3]{64} = 4$.

Warning
The rules for multiplying and dividing exponents do not apply to addition or subtraction:
$2^2 + 2^3 = 12$
$(2 \times 2) + (2 \times 2 \times 2) = 12$
It does not equal 2^5 or 32.

Remember that in calculating the value of a root, you're looking for what number multiplied by itself results in the number under the radical. In the above example, $\sqrt[3]{64} = 4$ because $4 \times 4 \times 4 = 64$.

When you see the square root sign, that means to take the positive root only. So, $\sqrt{9} = 3$, but not -3.

Square roots work just like exponents: You can *always* multiply and divide roots, but you can add and subtract only with the *same* root.

Multiplication and Division:

$$\sqrt{8} \times \sqrt{2} = \sqrt{8 \times 2} = \sqrt{16} = 4$$

$$\sqrt{\frac{1}{4}} = \frac{\sqrt{1}}{\sqrt{4}} = \frac{1}{2}$$

$$\sqrt{300} = \sqrt{100 \times 3} = \sqrt{100} \times \sqrt{3} = 10\sqrt{3}$$

Addition and Subtraction:

$$2\sqrt{2} + 3\sqrt{2} = 5\sqrt{2}$$

$$4\sqrt{3} - \sqrt{3} = 3\sqrt{3}$$

$2\sqrt{3} + 3\sqrt{2}$ *Cannot be added without a calculator since the terms do not have the same root.*

Drill 2

Answers can be found in Part III.

a. $3^3 \times 3^2 =$ _____

b. $\dfrac{3^3}{3^2} =$ _____

c. $\left(3^3\right)^2 =$ _____

d. $x^6 \times x^2 =$ _____

e. $\dfrac{x^6}{x^2} =$ _____

f. $\left(x^6\right)^2 =$ _____

g. $\sqrt{8} =$ _____

h. $\sqrt[3]{-64} =$ _____

i. $\sqrt{12} + 5\sqrt{3} =$ _____

j. $\sqrt{y^3} =$ _____

k. $\sqrt[3]{-y^3} =$ _____

l. $\sqrt{x^2 y} + 5x\sqrt{y} =$ _____

3

If $3^4 = 9^x$, then $x =$

A) 2

B) 3

C) 4

D) 5

5

If $\left(3^x\right)^3 = 3^{15}$, what is the value of x ?

A) 3

B) 5

C) 7

D) 9

11

If $x^y x^6 = x^{54}$ and $\left(x^3\right)^z = x^9$, then $y + z =$

A) 11

B) 12

C) 48

D) 51

4

If $\sqrt{s} - 3 = 9$, which of the following is a possible value of s ?

A) 12

B) 36

C) 81

D) 144

9

Which of the following expressions is equivalent to

$\sqrt[4]{81b^3 c}$?

A) $3b^{\frac{3}{4}} c^{\frac{1}{4}}$

B) $3b^3 c$

C) $20.25 b^{\frac{3}{4}} c^{\frac{1}{4}}$

D) $20.25 b^3 c$

10

If $x^{\frac{5}{2}} = 8x$, then x could equal

A) 2

B) 4

C) 6

D) 8

EQUATIONS AND INEQUALITIES

An **equation** is a statement that contains an equal sign, such as $3x + 5 = 17$.

To solve an equation, you want to get the variable x alone on one side of the equal sign and everything else on the other side.

The first step is to put all of the variables on one side of the equation and all of the numbers on the other side, using addition and subtraction. As long as you perform the same operation on both sides of the equal sign, you aren't changing the value of the variable.

Then you can divide both sides of the equation by the *coefficient,* which is the number in front of the variable. If that number is a fraction, you can multiply everything by its reciprocal.

For example:

$$
\begin{array}{rl}
3x + 5 = 17 & \\
\underline{-5 \quad -5} & \text{Subtract 5 from each side.} \\
3x \quad = 12 & \\
\underline{\div 3 \qquad \div 3} & \text{Divide each side by 3.} \\
x \quad = 4 &
\end{array}
$$

Always remember the rule of equations:

> *Whatever you do to one side of the equation, you must also do to the other side.*

These are fairly simple examples. The PSAT may test this idea with more complex equations and formulas, though. Just keep trying to isolate the variable in question by undoing the operations that have been done to it. Here's an example.

14

Logging companies can use Doyle's Log Rule to estimate the amount of usable lumber, in board feet B, that can be milled from logs. The rule is defined as $B = L\left(\dfrac{d-4}{4}\right)^2$, where d is the diameter inside the bark measured in inches at the small end of the log and L is the log length measured in feet. Which of the following gives the value of d, in terms of B and L?

A) $d = \dfrac{1}{4}\left(\sqrt{\dfrac{B}{L}} + 16\right)$

B) $d = 4\left(\sqrt{BL} + 1\right)$

C) $d = 4\left(\sqrt{\dfrac{B}{L}} - 1\right)$

D) $d = 4\left(\sqrt{\dfrac{B}{L}} + 1\right)$

Here's How to Crack It
Start with the L on the outside of the parentheses on the right. Divide both sides by L to get $\dfrac{B}{L} = \left(\dfrac{d-4}{4}\right)^2$. Now undo the power of 2 outside the parentheses.

Take the square root of both sides of the equation to get $\sqrt{\dfrac{B}{L}} = \dfrac{d-4}{4}$. Multiply both sides by 4 to get $4\sqrt{\dfrac{B}{L}} = d - 4$. Add 4 to both sides to get $4\sqrt{\dfrac{B}{L}} + 4 = d$.

Factor out the 4 to get $4\left(\sqrt{\dfrac{B}{L}} + 1\right) = d$. The correct answer is (D).

An **inequality** is any statement with one of these signs:

<   (less than)
>   (greater than)
≤   (less than or equal to)
≥   (greater than or equal to)

You can solve inequalities in the same way you solve equations, with one exception: Whenever you multiply or divide an inequality by a negative value, you must change the direction of the sign: < becomes >, and ≤ becomes ≥.

For example:

$$3x + 5 > 17$$
$$\underline{\quad -5 \quad -5 \quad}\quad \text{Subtract 5 from each side.}$$
$$3x \quad > \quad 12$$
$$\underline{\div 3 \qquad \div 3}\quad \text{Divide each side by 3.}$$
$$x \quad > \quad 4$$

In this case, we didn't multiply or divide by a negative value, so the direction of the sign didn't change. However, if we were to divide by a negative value, we would need to change the direction of the sign.

$$-4x + 3 > 15$$
$$\underline{\quad -3 \quad -3 \quad}\quad \text{Subtract 3 from each side.}$$
$$-4x \quad > \quad 12$$
$$\underline{\div -4 \qquad \div -4}\quad \text{Divide each side by } -4.$$
$$x \quad < \quad -3$$

Now let's look at how the PSAT may make things more complicated with a question about a range of values.

6

Which of the following is equivalent to
$-12 \le 3b + 3 \le 18$?

A) $-5 \le b \le 5$

B) $-5 \le b \le 6$

C) $-4 \le b \le 6$

D) $\;\;3 \le b \le 5$

Here's How to Crack It

Like many problems on the PSAT, this question will be difficult if you try to do it all at once. Instead, let's break it down into bite-sized pieces. Let's start with just part of the inequality, $-12 \leq 3b + 3$. Remember that you can solve inequalities just like equations—provided that if you multiply or divide by a negative value, you swap the direction of the inequality sign. To solve this part of the inequality, though, you just need to subtract 3 from each side (giving us $-15 \leq 3b$) and then divide each side by 3, which leaves you with $-5 \leq b$. Now you can eliminate any choices that you know won't work: (C) and (D) don't have -5 in them. Now let's take the other part of the inequality: $3b + 3 \leq 18$. If you subtract 3 from each side and then divide by 3, you get $b \leq 5$. Now you can cross off (B), and you're left with (A).

SOLVING RATIONAL EQUATIONS

Since you are not always allowed to use your calculator on the PSAT, there will be some instances in which you will need to solve an equation algebraically. Even on the sections in which calculator use is permitted, you may find it faster and more effective to use your mathematical skills to efficiently answer a question. Another way ETS and the College Board may make your calculator less effective is by asking you to solve for an expression. A lot of the time, algebraic manipulation will be the means by which you can solve that problem.

Here is an example:

5

Which of the following is equivalent to

$$\frac{f}{f-2} - \frac{5}{f+3}?$$

A) $\dfrac{f-5}{2f+1}$

B) $\dfrac{-5f}{f^2-6}$

C) $\dfrac{f^2-2f+10}{f^2+f-6}$

D) $\dfrac{f^2+8f-10}{f^2+f-6}$

Here's How to Crack It

In order to be able to add these fractions, you need a common denominator.

Multiply both the top and the bottom of the left fraction by $(f + 3)$ and multiply both the top and bottom of the right fraction by $(f - 2)$. The expression becomes $\dfrac{f(f+3)}{(f-2)(f+3)} - \dfrac{5(f-2)}{(f+3)(f-2)}$ or $\dfrac{f^2+3f}{f^2+f-6} - \dfrac{5f-10}{f^2+f-6}$.

Now the numerators can be combined over the common denominator and you get $\dfrac{f^2+3f-5f+10}{f^2+f-6} = \dfrac{f^2-2f+10}{f^2+f-6}$, which is (C).

EXTRANEOUS SOLUTIONS

Sometimes solving a rational or radical expression makes funny things happen. Let's look at an example.

$$\frac{1}{z+2} + \frac{1}{z-2} = \frac{4}{(z+2)(z-2)}$$

Given the equation above, what is the value of z?

To add the fractions on the left side, you need a common denominator. Multiply the numerator and the denominator of the first fraction by $(z - 2)$ and the numerator and denominator of the second fraction by $(z + 2)$. Now the fractions can be added together."

The equation becomes

$$\frac{(z-2)+(z+2)}{(z+2)(z-2)} = \frac{4}{(z+2)(z-2)}$$

Since the denominators are equal, the numerators are equal. This gives you

$$(z-2) + (z+2) = 4$$

When you simplify the left side, you get $2z = 4$, so $z = 2$. Sounds great, right? However, you need to plug this solution back into the original equation to make sure that it works. You get

$$\frac{1}{2+2} + \frac{1}{2-2} = \frac{4}{(2+2)(2-2)}$$

Once simplified, two of the three denominators become zero. That is not allowed, so the solution you found isn't really a solution at all. It is referred to as an "extraneous solution." That term refers to any answer you get to an algebraic equation that results in a false statement when plugged back in to the original equation.

Here's how it might look on the PSAT.

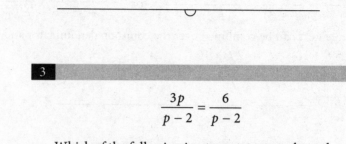

3

$$\frac{3p}{p-2} = \frac{6}{p-2}$$

Which of the following is a true statement about the equation above?

A) There are no solutions to the equation.

B) The solution is $p = 2$.

C) The solution is $p = 3$.

D) There are infinitely many solutions to the equation.

Here's How to Crack It

When given two fraction sets equal to one another, you often have to cross-multiply to solve. In this case, though, the fractions have the same denominator. This tells you that their numerators are equal. Therefore, $3p = 6$, so $p = 2$, right? But what if you put that value back into the denominators? They become 0, which can't happen. Therefore, 2 is an extraneous solution and the answer is (A).

An answer like (D) would occur if literally any value for a variable would make the equation true, such as would be the case in $x + 3 = x + 3$.

ABSOLUTE VALUES

Absolute value is just a measure of the distance between a number and 0. Since distances are always positive, the absolute value of a number is also always positive. The absolute value of a number is written as $|x|$.

When solving for the value of a variable inside the absolute value bars, it is important to remember that variable could be either positive or negative. For example, if $|x| = 2$, then $x = 2$ or $x = -2$ since both 2 and –2 are a distance of 2 from 0.

Here's an example:

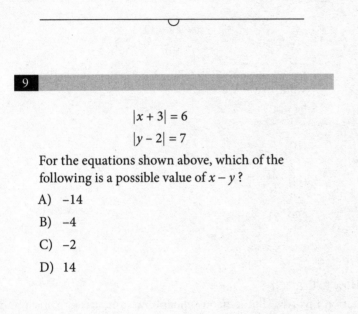

9

$$|x + 3| = 6$$
$$|y - 2| = 7$$

For the equations shown above, which of the following is a possible value of $x - y$?

A) –14

B) –4

C) –2

D) 14

PSAT Smoke and Mirrors
When you're asked to solve an equation involving an absolute value, it is very likely that the correct answer will be the negative result. Why? Because the test writers know that you are less likely to think about the negative result! Another way to avoid mistakes is to do all the math inside the absolute value symbols first, and then make the result positive.

Here's How to Crack It

To solve the first equation, set $x + 3 = 6$ and set $x + 3 = -6$. If $x + 3 = -6$, then the absolute value would still be 6. So, x can be either 3 or –9. Now, do the same thing to solve for y. Either $y = 9$ or $y = -5$.

To get the credited answer, you need to try the different combinations. One combination is $x = -9$ and $y = -5$. So, $x - y = -9 - (-5) = -4$, which is (B).

SIMULTANEOUS EQUATIONS

Simultaneous equations occur when you have two equations at the same time. Occasionally, all you have to do is stack the equations, and then add or subtract them, so try that first. Sometimes, it won't get you exactly what you want, but it will get you close to it.

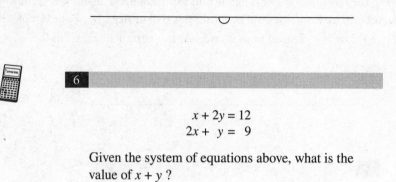

$$x + 2y = 12$$
$$2x + y = 9$$

Given the system of equations above, what is the value of $x + y$?

(A) 3

(B) 7

(C) $\dfrac{21}{2}$

(D) 21

Here's How to Crack It

This question involves simultaneous equations, so first try to stack and combine them. You're being asked for $x + y$, so even getting the same number of x variables as y variables would be useful.

Let's see what happens when you add the equations:

$$\begin{array}{r} x + 2y = 12 \\ + \underline{2x + y = 9} \\ 3x + 3y = 21 \end{array}$$

Now all you need to do is divide both sides of the equation by 3 to get the expression you're being asked for, $x + y$, and you end up with the answer, 7. The correct answer is (B).

That was pretty simple, but simultaneous equations on the PSAT are rarely that straightforward. Let's look at a really challenging one.

27

Two competing fast food restaurants sell both hamburgers and orders of French fries at the same prices. Burger Planet's lunchtime sales can be modeled as $40h + 70f = \$260.00$, where h is the cost of a hamburger and f is the cost of an order of French fries. If Slider Heaven sells 80 hamburgers and 60 orders of French fries over the same period and outsells Burger Planet by \$100, what is the total cost of three hamburgers and three orders of French fries at either establishment?

A) $5.00

B) $9.00

C) $11.00

D) $15.00

Here's How to Crack It

The sales equation at Burger Planet is given in the question. Create an equation for Slider Heaven's lunchtime sales so you can solve them. Slider Heaven's sales can be modeled as $80h + 60f = 260 + 100 = 360$. Adding these equations together or subtracting one from the other won't give you the 3 burgers and 3 fries that you want. Instead, you need to create a common coefficient for one of the variables and then add or subtract the two equations from each other to get rid of that variable. In this case, multiply the Burger Planet equation by -2 to get $-80h - 140f = -520$. Place the two equations on top of each other and add:

$$
\begin{array}{r}
-80h - 140f = -520 \\
+80h + 60f = 360 \\
\hline
-80f = -160
\end{array}
$$

Divide both sides by -2 to get $f = 2$. Plug 2 into the Burger Planet equation to get $40h + 70(2) = 260$. Solve for h to get $40h + 140 = 260$, or $40h = 120$, so $h = 3$. Therefore, the total cost of 3 hamburgers and 3 orders of French fries is $3(3) + 3(2) = 9 + 6 = 15$. The correct answer is (D).

WRITING YOUR OWN EQUATIONS

For the most part, we've been looking at solving equations given to you in questions. That last question, though, required you to create one of your own. The PSAT Math sections are testing not only your math skills, but also, and possibly even more importantly to your score improvement, your reading skills. It is imperative that you read the questions carefully and translate the words in the problem into mathematical symbols.

ENGLISH	MATH EQUIVALENTS
is, are, were, did, does, costs	=
what (or any unknown value)	*any variable (x, y, k, b)*
more, sum	+
less, difference	−
of, times, product	× *(multiply)*
ratio, quotient, out of, per	÷ *(divide)*

Sometimes you'll be asked to take a word problem and create equations or inequalities from that information. Usually they will not ask you to solve these equations/inequalities, so if you are able to locate and translate the information in the problem, you have a good shot at getting the correct answer. Always start with the most straightforward piece of information. What is the most straightforward piece of information? Well, that's up to you to decide. Consider the following problem.

3

Elom joined a gym that charges a monthly fee of \$35. A one-time enrollment fee of \$40 is charged when he joins. Which of the following represents the total amount of fees that Elom has paid to his gym after m months, in dollars?

A) $35m + 40$

B) $35 + 40m$

C) $35m - 40$

D) $(35 + 40)m$

Here's How to Crack It

The question states that there is a monthly fee of $35 and that the variable m represents the number of months. Therefore, the correct answer should include $35m$, so you can eliminate (B). The one-time enrollment fee of $40 has nothing to do with the number of months, so the 40 should be by itself. Eliminate (D), which multiplies the 40 by m. The fee should be added on, so the correct answer is (A).

Now let's look at harder one. The following question has a lot more words and more than one inequality in each answer choice. This makes it even more important to translate one piece at a time and eliminate after each step.

5

Kai has two different after-school jobs, one at a bookstore and one at a grocery store. He can only work a total of 10 hours each week due to his heavy homework load. When he works at the bookstore, he earns $10 per hour, and when he works at the grocery store, he earns $13 per hour. He never earns less than $100 in a week, and he always works more hours at the bookstore because he can get free coffee from the café. Solving which of the following systems of inequalities yields the number of hours at the bookstore, b, and the number of hours at the grocery store, g, that Kai can work in one week?

A) $\begin{cases} b - g \leq 10 \\ b < g \\ 10b + 13g \geq 100 \end{cases}$

B) $\begin{cases} b + g \leq 10 \\ b > g \\ 10b + 13g \geq 100 \end{cases}$

C) $\begin{cases} b + g \leq 10 \\ b > g \\ 13b + 10g \geq 100 \end{cases}$

D) $\begin{cases} bg \leq 100 \\ b > g \\ 10b + 13g \leq 100 \end{cases}$

Here's How to Crack It

Start with a straightforward piece of information to translate. If you start with the fact that Kai works more hours at the bookstore than at the grocery store, you can translate that into $b > g$. This would eliminate (A). If you start with the fact that Kai works no more than 10 hours each week, you can translate that into $b + g \leq 10$. This would eliminate (A) and (D). Now, to decide between (B) and (C), compare the answers and see what the differences are. Choice (B) has a coefficient of 10 in front of the variable b. Check the question to see if 10 should be associated with b. Since b is the number of hours Kai works at the bookstore, and he earns $10 per hour there, the correct answer should have $10b$, not $13b$. Eliminate (C) and choose (B).

Drill 3

Answers can be found in Part III.

3

If a certain number is 3 more than 7 times itself, what is the number?

A) −3

B) $-\dfrac{3}{2}$

C) $-\dfrac{1}{2}$

D) $-\dfrac{3}{8}$

5

Ann is writing a book that will include up to 98 recipes. She currently has 32 main dish recipes and 18 dessert recipes. If r represents the number of additional recipes that Ann could include in her book, which of the following inequalities represents all possible values of r?

A) $r - 50 \geq 98$

B) $r - 50 \leq 98$

C) $98 - (32 + 18) - r \leq 0$

D) $98 - (32 + 18) - r \geq 0$

4

If $\dfrac{3a}{4b} = \dfrac{5c}{6d}$, then which of the following is equal to bc ?

A) $\dfrac{a}{2b}$

B) $\dfrac{5a}{8d}$

C) $\dfrac{9ad}{10}$

D) $18ad$

8

A ski resort is renting skis for $30 and snowboards for $20 over a weekend. On Friday, a total of 40 skis and snowboards were rented, and the resort collected $1,100 in rental fees. On Saturday, 55 skis and snowboards were rented and the resort collected $1,400 in rental fees. On Sunday, the resort rented 85 skis and snowboards and collected $2,100 rental fees. Solving which of the following system of equations yields the number of skis, s, and the number of snowboards, b, that were rented over the three-day weekend?

A) $s + b = 50$
   $30s + 20b = 180$

B) $s + b = 180$
   $30s + 20b = 460$

C) $s + b = 180$
   $30s + 20b = 4,600$

D) $s + b = 4,600$
   $30s + 20b = 180$

12

$$\frac{m + 9}{3} + 2 = \frac{m - 2}{7} + 3$$

In the equation above, what is the value of m?

A) -17

B) -12

C) 5

D) 10

23

A group of students sells different types of cookies at a bake sale to raise funds for a school trip. When the students sell two snickerdoodle cookies, s, and seven cinnamon cookies, c, they raise $14.00. When the students sell eight snickerdoodle cookies and three cinnamon cookies, they raise $17.50. Assuming the price per cookie does not change, which of the following equations represents a sale the students could make during the fundraiser?

A) $2s + 3c = \$8.00$

B) $4s + 6c = \$16.25$

C) $6s + 5c = \$17.36$

D) $8s + 7c = \$24.50$

THE COORDINATE PLANE

You will definitely see some questions in the coordinate or *xy*-plane on the PSAT. Let's start by covering the basics here. You'll see more advanced concepts in the Advanced Math Principles chapter. So let's just review:

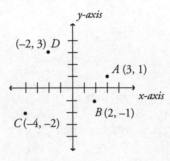

The *x*-axis is the horizontal axis, and the *y*-axis is the vertical axis. Points are given on the coordinate plane with the *x*-coordinate first. Positive *x*-values go to the right, and negative ones go to the left; positive *y*-values go up, and negative ones go down. So point *A* (3, 1) is 3 points to the right on the *x*-axis and 1 point up from there. Point *B* (2, –1) is two points to the right on the *x*-axis and 1 point down from there.

Slope is a measure of the steepness of a line on the coordinate plane. On most slope problems you need to recognize only whether the slope is positive, negative, or zero. A line that goes up and to the right has positive slope; a line that goes down and to the right has negative slope, and a flat line has zero slope. In the figure below, ℓ_1 has positive slope, ℓ_2 has zero slope, and ℓ_3 has negative slope.

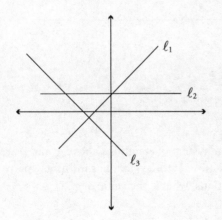

If you do need to calculate the slope, and the graph is drawn for you, here's how: slope = $\dfrac{y_2 - y_1}{x_2 - x_1}$. The *slope* of a line is equal to $\dfrac{rise}{run}$. To find the slope, take any two points on the line and count off the distance you need to get from one of these points to the other.

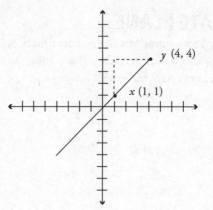

In the graph above, to get from point *x* to point *y*, we count up (rise) 3 units, and count over (run) 3 units. Therefore, the slope is $\frac{rise}{run} = \frac{3}{3} = 1$. Always remember to check whether the slope is positive or negative when you use $= \frac{rise}{run}$.

If you're not given a figure and you can't draw one easily using the points given, you can find the slope by plugging the coordinates you know into the slope formula. Just remember to plug the numbers into the formula carefully!

Knowing how to find the slope is useful for solving questions about perpendicular and parallel lines. **Perpendicular lines** have slopes that are negative reciprocals of one another. **Parallel lines** have the same slope and no solutions. You may also be given two equations that have infinitely many solutions.

Let's look at an example.

○

To Infinity…and Beyond!
When given two equations with infinitely many solutions, find a way to make them equal. The equations represent the same line.

20

$$gx - hy = 78$$
$$4x + 3y = 13$$

In the system of equations above, *g* and *h* are constants. If the system has infinitely many solutions, what is the value of *gh* ?

A) −432

B) −6

C) 6

D) 432

Here's How to Crack It

This question may have you scratching your head and moving on to the next question, but let's explore what you can do to solve this before you decide it's not worth your time. You may be surprised by how easy it is to solve a problem like this.

When they say that these equations have infinitely many solutions, what they are really saying is that these are the same equation, or that one equation is a multiple of the other equation. In other words, these two equations represent the same line. With that in mind, try to determine what needs to be done to make these equations equal. Since the right side of the equation is dealing with only a constant, first determine what you would need to do to make 13 equal to 78.

In this case, you need to multiply 13 by 6. Since we are working with equations, we need to do the same thing to both sides of the equation in order for the equation to remain equal.

$$6(4x + 3y) = 6 \times 13$$
$$24x + 18y = 78$$

Since both equations are now equal to 78, you can set them equal to one another, giving you this equation:

$$24x + 18y = gx - hy$$

You may know that when you have equations with the same variables on each side the coefficients on those variables must be equal, so you can deduce that $g = 24$ and $h = -18$. (Be cautious when you evaluate this equation. The test writers are being sneaky by using addition in one equation and subtraction in another.) Therefore, gh equals $24 \times -18 = -432$. Choice (A) is correct.

The equation of a line can take multiple forms. The most common of these is known as the **slope-intercept form**. If you know the slope and the y-intercept, you can create the equation of a given line. A slope-intercept equation takes the form $y = mx + b$, where m is the slope and b is the y-intercept.

Here's an example.

5

If c is a constant less than 0, which of the following could be the graph of $y = c(x + y)$ in the xy-plane?

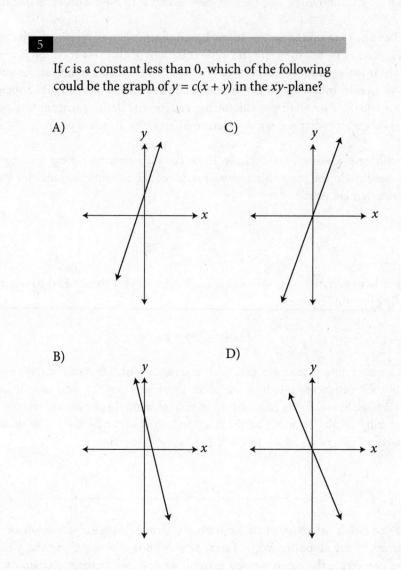

A)

C)

B)

D)

Here's How to Crack It

No points are labeled on the graphs in the answers, and the equation of the line has a mysterious c in it. If you knew the slope or y-intercept of the equation, you could use Process of Elimination. To see what is going on with this problem, make up a value for c that is less than 0. Let's say that $c = -2$, in which case $y = -2(x + y)$. Distribute the -2 to get $y = -2x - 2y$. Rewrite the equation so that it is in the slope-intercept form $y = mx + b$, to get $3y = -2x$ or $y = -\dfrac{2}{3}x$. Therefore, the slope is $-\dfrac{2}{3}$ and the y-intercept is 0. In fact, no matter what value you picked for c, if c is a constant less than 0, the slope will be negative, and the y–intercept will be 0. Eliminate (A) and (C) since both of these lines have positive slopes. Eliminate answer (B) because the y-intercept is not 0. The correct answer is (D).

The **distance formula** looks quite complicated. The easiest way to solve the distance between two points is to connect them and form a triangle. Then use the Pythagorean theorem. Many times, the triangle formed is one of the common Pythagorean triplets (3-4-5 or 5-12-13). We'll talk more about the Pythagorean theorem in the Additional Topics chapter.

The **midpoint formula** gives the midpoint of ST, with points $S\,(x_1,\,y_1)$ and $T\,(x_2,\,y_2)$. It's simply the average of the x-coordinates and the y-coordinates. In our example, the midpoint would be $\left(\dfrac{x_1 + x_2}{2},\, \dfrac{y_1 + y_2}{2}\right)$.

To find the **point of intersection** of two lines, find a way to set them equal and solve for the variable. If the equations are already in $y = mx + b$ form, set the $mx + b$ part of the two equations equal and solve for x. If the question asks for the value of y, plug the value of x back into either equation to solve for y. It may also be possible to plug in the answers or graph the equations on your calculator. These skills will also help find the points of intersection between a line and a non-linear graph such as a parabola.

Sometimes, it's a little trickier. Let's look at a difficult question that combines several of the previous concepts.

24

Line 1 contains the points (2, 1) and (1, –2) and line 2 contains the points (–2, 9) and (10, –3). What is the y-coordinate of the point of intersection of lines 1 and 2 ?

A) –1

B) 3

C) 4

D) 7

Here's How to Crack It

To solve this problem, first you need to find the equations of the two lines in order to set the equations equal to each other and find the value of x. Given two points on a line, you can find the slope using $\dfrac{y_2 - y_1}{x_2 - x_1}$. Therefore, the slope of line 1 can be calculated as $\dfrac{-2 - 1}{1 - 2} = \dfrac{-3}{-1} = 3$. Plug this and the coordinates of the easier point, (2, 1), into $y = mx + b$ to find the value of b. The equation for line 1 becomes $1 = 3(2) + b$. Solve for b to find that the value is -5, so line 1 is $y = 3x - 5$. The slope of line 2 can be calculated as $\dfrac{-3 - 9}{10 - (-2)} = \dfrac{-12}{12} = -1$. Find the value of b: $9 = -1(-2) + b$, so $b = 7$. The equation for line 2 is $y = -x + 7$. Set the two equations equal to each other to get $3x - 5 = -x + 7$. Solve for x to get $4x - 5 = 7$ or $4x = 12$, so $x = 3$. Finally, plug x into one of the equations to solve for y. Plug x into the equation $y = -x + 7$, to get $y = -3 + 7 = 4$. Therefore, the correct answer is 4, which is (C).

Drill 4

Answer can be found in Part III.

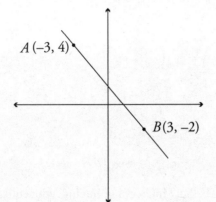

a.   How many units do you count up (rise) to get from point *B* to point *A* ? _____

b.   How many units must you count over (run) to get from point *A* to point *B* ? _____

c.   What is the slope of the line above? _____

(Remember, the line is going down to the right so it must have a negative slope.)

d.   What would be the slope of a line parallel to *AB*? _____

e.   What would be the slope of a line perpendicular to *AB*? _____

f.   What is the distance from point *A* to point *B*? _____

g.   What is the midpoint of line segment *AB*? _____

2

If $y = 6x + 3$ and $y = cx + 3$ are the equations of perpendicular lines, then what is the value of c ?

A)   –6

B) $-\dfrac{1}{6}$

C) $\dfrac{1}{6}$

D)   6

3

What is the y-intercept of the line with equation $2x + 3y = 12$?

A)   4

B)   3

C)   2

D) $\dfrac{1}{4}$

12

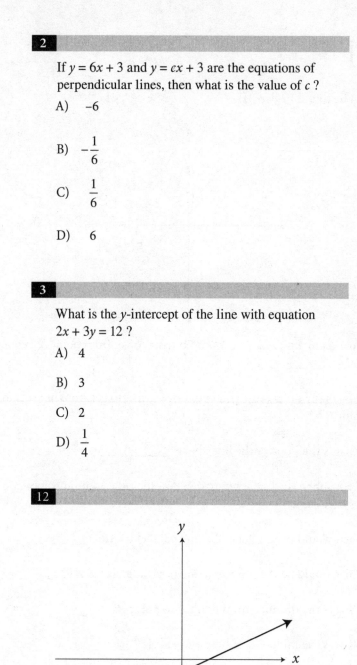

What is the x-intercept of the line in the graph above?

A)   –1

B)   0

C)   1

D)   2

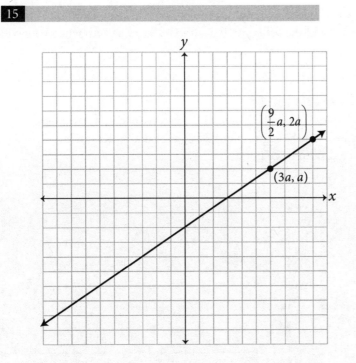

The graph of a line is shown in the *xy*-plane above. It contains the points $(3a, a)$ and $\left(\frac{9}{2}a, 2a \right)$, where *a* is a positive constant. Which of the following could be the equation of this line?

A) $y = \frac{2}{3}x - 2$

B) $y = \frac{2}{3}x + 2$

C) $y = \frac{4}{3}x - 2$

D) $y = \frac{3}{2}x - 2$

CHARTS AND GRAPHS

Another basic math skill you will need for the PSAT is the ability to read charts and graphs. The PSAT now includes charts, graphs, and tables throughout the test (not just in the Math sections) to present data for students to analyze. The test writers believe this will better reflect what students learn in school and need to understand in the real world. The situations will typically include real-life applications, such as finance and business situations, social science issues, and scientific matter.

Since you'll be seeing graphics throughout the test, let's look at the types you may encounter and the skills you'll need to be familiar with when you work with charts and graphs.

The Scatterplot

A scatterplot is a graph with distinct data points, each representing one piece of information. On the scatterplot below, each dot represents the number of televisions sold at a certain price point.

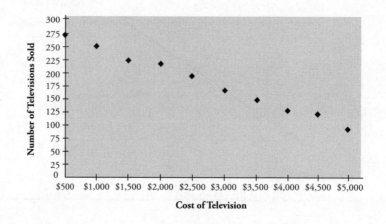

Here's How to Read It

To find the cost of a television when 225 televisions are sold, start at 225 on the vertical axis and draw a horizontal line to the right until you hit a data point. Use the edge of your answer sheet as a straightedge if you have trouble drawing your own straight lines. Once you hit a point, draw a straight line down from it to the horizontal axis and read the number the line hits, which should be $1,500. To determine the number of televisions sold when they cost a certain amount, reverse the steps—start at the bottom, draw up until you hit a point, then move left until you intersect the vertical axis.

A question may ask you to draw a "line of best fit" on a scatterplot diagram. This is the line that best represents the data. You can use the edge of your answer sheet as a ruler to help you draw a line that goes through most of the data.

The Line Graph

A line graph is similar to a scatterplot in that it shows different data points that relate the two variables. The difference with a line graph, though, is that the points have been connected to create a continuous line.

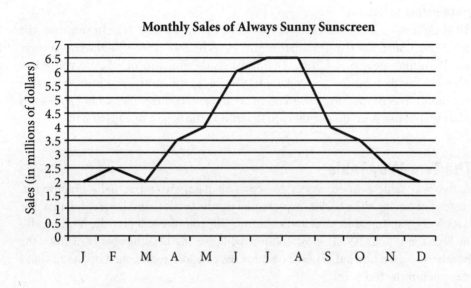

Monthly Sales of Always Sunny Sunscreen

Here's How to Read It

Reading a line graph is very similar to reading a scatterplot. Start at the axis that represents the data given, and draw a straight line up or to the right until you intersect the graph line. Then move left or down until you hit the other axis. For example, in February, indicated by an F on the horizontal axis, Always Sunny sunscreen had 2.5 million in sales. Make sure to notice the units on each axis. If February sales were only $2.50, rather than $2.5 million, then this company wouldn't be doing very well!

The Bar Graph (or Histogram)

Instead of showing a variety of different data points, a bar graph will show how many items belong to a particular category. If the variable at the bottom is given in ranges, instead of distinct items, the graph is called a histogram, but you read it the same way.

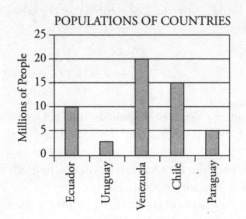

POPULATIONS OF COUNTRIES

Here's How to Read It

The height of each bar corresponds to a value on the vertical axis. In this case, the bar above Chile hits the line that intersects with 15 on the vertical axis, so there are 15 million people in Chile. Again, watch the units to make sure you know what the numbers on the axes represent. On this graph, horizontal lines are drawn at 5-unit intervals, making the graph easier to read. If these lines do not appear on a bar graph, use your answer sheet to determine the height of a given bar.

The Two-Way Table

A two-way table is another way to represent data without actually graphing it. Instead of having the variables represented on the vertical and horizontal axes, the data will be arranged in rows and columns. The top row will give the headings for each column, and the left-most column will give the headings for each row. The numbers in each box indicate the data for the category represented by the row and the column the box is in.

	Computer Production	
	Morning Shift	**Afternoon Shift**
Monday	200	375
Tuesday	245	330
Wednesday	255	340
Thursday	250	315
Friday	225	360

Here's How to Read It

If you wanted to see the number of computers produced on Tuesday morning, you could start in the Morning Shift column and look down until you found the number in the row that says, "Tuesday," or you could start in the row for Tuesday and look to the right until you found the Morning Shift column. Either way, the result is 245. Some tables will give you totals in the bottom row and/or the right-most column, but sometimes you will need to find the totals yourself by adding up all the numbers in each row or in each column. More complicated tables will have more categories listed in rows and/or columns, or the tables may even contain extraneous information.

Figure Facts

Every time you encounter a figure or graphic on the PSAT, you should make sure you understand how to read it by checking the following things:

- What are the variables for each axis or the headings for the table?
- What units are used for each variable?
- Are there any key pieces of information (numbers, for example) in the legend of the chart that you should note?

- What type of relationship is shown by the data in the chart? For instance, if the chart includes curves that show an upward slope, then the graph shows a *positive association*, while curves that show a downward slope show a *negative association*.
- You can use the edge of your answer sheet as a ruler to help you make sure you are locating the correct data in the graph or to draw a line of best fit if necessary.

Probability

One topic that is often tested with two-way tables is probability. Probability refers to the chance that an event will happen, and is given as a percent or a fractional value between 0 and 1, inclusive. A probability of 0 means that the event will never happen; a probability of 1 means that it is certain to happen.

$$\text{Probability} = \frac{\text{number of outcomes you want}}{\text{number of possible outcomes}}$$

For instance, if you have a die with faces numbered 1 to 6, what is the chance of rolling a 2? There is one face with the number 2 on it, out of 6 total faces. Therefore, the probability of rolling a 2 is $\frac{1}{6}$.

What is the chance of rolling an even number on one roll of this die? There are 3 faces of the die with an even number (the sides numbered 2, 4, and 6) out of a total of 6 faces. Therefore, the probability of rolling an even number is $\frac{3}{6}$, or $\frac{1}{2}$.

Let's look at how this concept will be tested on the PSAT.

A survey was conducted among a randomly chosen sample of full-time salaried workers about satisfaction in their current jobs. The table below shows a summary of the survey results.

Reported Job Satisfaction by Education Level (in thousands)

Highest Level of Education	Satisfied	Not Satisfied	No Response	Total
High School Diploma	17,880	12,053	2,575	32,508
Bachelor's Degree	24,236	8,496	3,442	36,174
Master's Degree	17,605	5,324	1,861	24,790
Doctoral Degree	12,210	2,081	972	15,263
Total	71,931	27,954	8,850	108,735

All persons who have earned a Master's or Doctoral degree must have previously earned a Bachelor's degree. What is the probability that a full-time salaried worker does NOT have a Bachelor's degree?

A) 29.9%

B) 33.3%

C) 36.8%

D) 66.7%

Here's How to Crack It

If everyone with a Master's or Doctoral degree has a Bachelor's degree, then the only people who do NOT have a Bachelor's degree are those whose highest level of education is a High School Diploma. Find the probability of choosing someone with a High School Diploma out of the total: $\frac{32,508}{108,735} = 0.299 = 29.9\%$, which is (A).

GRIDS-INS: THE BASICS

You will see 8 questions on the PSAT that ask you to bubble in a numerical answer on a grid, rather than answer a multiple-choice question. These questions are arranged in loose order of difficulty and can be solved according to the methods outlined for the multiple-choice problems on the test. The last two grid-ins in Section 4 will be a paired set, but each question can be answered separately. Don't worry that there are no answer choices—your approach is the same.

Keep Left
No matter how many digits in your answer, always start gridding in the leftmost column. That way, you'll avoid omitting digits and losing points.

The only difficulty with grid-ins is getting used to the way in which you are asked to answer the question. For each question, you'll have a grid like the following:

We recommend that you write the answer on top of the grid to help you bubble, but it's important to know that the scoring machine reads only the bubbles. *If you bubble incorrectly, the computer will consider the answer to be incorrect.*

Here are the basic rules of gridding:

1. If your answer uses fewer than four boxes, you can grid it anywhere you like.
   To avoid confusion, we suggest that you start at the leftmost box. For example:

2. You can grid your answer as either a fraction or a decimal, *if* the fraction will fit.

You can grid an answer of .5 as either .5 or $\frac{1}{2}$.

or

3. You do not need to reduce your fractions, *if* the fraction will fit.

If your answer is $\frac{2}{4}$, you can grid it as $\frac{2}{4}$, $\frac{1}{2}$, or .5.

or   or

4. If you have a decimal that will not fit in the spaces provided, you *must grid as many places as will fit.*

   If your answer is $\frac{2}{3}$, you can grid it as $\frac{2}{3}$, .666, or .667 but .66 is *not* acceptable.

   You do *not* need to round your numbers, so we suggest that you don't. There's no reason to give yourself a chance to make a mistake if you don't have to.

   or   or

5. You cannot grid mixed numbers. Convert all mixed numbers to ordinary fractions.

   If your answer is $2\frac{1}{2}$, you must convert it to $\frac{5}{2}$ or 2.5; otherwise the computer will read your 2 1/2 as 21/2.

   or

Don't Mix
Never grid in a mixed number. Change it into an improper fraction or decimal. To convert mixed fractions into improper fractions, all you have to do is multiply the denominator with the whole number in front of the fraction, then add that product to the numerator, and finally put that number over the denominator you started with.

6. You can't grid π, square roots, variables, or negative numbers, so if you get an answer with one of those terms, you've made a mistake. Check your work.

Drill 5

Answer can be found in Part III.

28

Estimated Numbers of Cell Phone Users by Type (in millions)

	Prepaid users	Contracted users	Totals
2008	45	225	270
2012	75	250	325
Totals	120	475	595

If a cell phone user is selected at random in 2008, what is the probability that user is a contracted user?

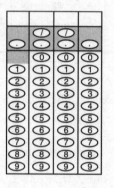

14

If $5x^2 = 125$, what could be the value of $5x^3$?

29

If $5 - \sqrt{z} = \sqrt{z - 5}$, what is the value of z ?

16

If $3a + 2b = 37$ and $7a + 4b = 85$, what is the value of $b^2 + 6b - 10$?

Summary

o   The Math sections are arranged in loose Order of Difficulty, which can make it easier to spot the less difficult problems. However, remember that the test writers' idea of "easier" problems is not necessarily the same as your idea. Let your Personal Order of Difficulty be your guide.

o   Write in your test booklet to set up problems, and then use your calculator (when allowed) to figure out solutions. And remember to type carefully—your calculator won't check for mistakes.

o   Review basic definitions again before the test to make sure you don't get stuck on the "little words."

o   When you have to manipulate exponents, remember your MADSPM rules.

o   To solve equations for a variable, isolate the variable. Make sure you perform the same operations on both sides of the equation.

o   Inequalities can be worked just like equations, until you have to multiply or divide by a negative. Then you need to flip the inequality sign.

o   When solving radical and rational equations, be on the lookout for extraneous solutions. They are answers you get that don't work when plugged back into the equation.

o   The absolute value of a number is the positive distance from zero, or practically, making the thing inside the || sign positive. Everything inside the || is equal to the positive and the negative value of the expression to which it is equal. Also remember that || work like ( ); you need to complete all the operations inside the || before you can make the value positive.

o   To solve simultaneous equations, simply add or subtract the equations. If you don't have the answer, look for multiples of your solutions. When the simultaneous equation question asks for a single variable and addition and subtraction don't work, try to make something disappear. Multiply the equations to make the coefficient(s) of the variable(s) you want go to zero when the equations are added or subtracted.

o   When writing a system of equations, start with the most straightforward piece of information.

o   You can also use the equations in the answer choices to help you narrow down the possibilities for your equations. Eliminate any answers in which an equation doesn't match your equation.

o   Parallel lines have the same slope and no solutions. If two lines have the same slope and infinitely many solutions, they are actually the same line. Perpendicular lines have slopes that are negative reciprocals of one another.

o   Rather than worrying about the distance formula, connect the two points and make it the hypotenuse of a right triangle. Then you can use the Pythagorean theorem to find the distance.

o   The coordinates of the midpoint of a line segment with endpoints (x_1, y_1) and (x_2, y_2) will be $\left(\dfrac{x_1 + x_2}{2}, \dfrac{y_1 + y_2}{2} \right)$.

o   When you encounter charts, carefully check the chart for information you should note, and remember that you can use your answer sheet as a ruler to help you locate information or to draw a line of best fit.

○ Probability is a fractional value between 0 and 1 (inclusive), and it is equal to the number of outcomes the question is asking for divided by the total number of possible outcomes. It can also be expressed as a percent.

○ When doing Grid-Ins, be sure to keep to the left, and don't bother reducing fractions if they fit in the allotted spaces.

Chapter 6
Math Techniques

In the previous chapter, we mentioned that one of the keys to doing well on the PSAT is to have a set of test-specific problem-solving skills. This chapter discusses some powerful strategies, which—though you may not use them in school—are specifically designed to get you points on the PSAT. Learn them well!

PLUGGING IN

One of the most powerful problem-solving skills on the PSAT is a technique we call Plugging In. Plugging In will turn nasty algebra problems into simple arithmetic and help you through the particularly twisted problems that you'll often see on the PSAT. There are several varieties of Plugging In, each suited to a different kind of question.

Plugging In Your Own Numbers

The problem with doing algebra is that it's just too easy to make a mistake.

> Whenever you see a problem with variables in the answer choices, PLUG IN.

Start by picking a number for the variable in the problem (or for more than one variable, if necessary), solve the problem using your number, and then see which answer choice gives you the correct answer.

Take a look at the following problem:

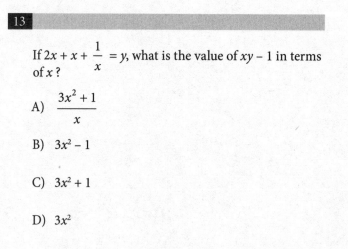

13

If $2x + x + \dfrac{1}{x} = y$, what is the value of $xy - 1$ in terms of x ?

A) $\dfrac{3x^2 + 1}{x}$

B) $3x^2 - 1$

C) $3x^2 + 1$

D) $3x^2$

Here's How to Crack It

First, start by choosing a value for one of the variables. Here, all the action is happening to the x, so choose a value for x. Make $x = 2$. Next, work the problem in Bite-Sized Pieces until you've come up with a numerical answer for the question.

When to Plug In
- Phrases like "in terms of" or "equivalent form" in the question
- Variables in the question and/or answers choices

If $x = 2$, then the equation becomes $2(2) + 2 + \dfrac{1}{2} = y$. Multiply; then add on the left side: $4 + 2 + \dfrac{1}{2} = y$; $\dfrac{13}{2} = y$. Note the question doesn't want the value of y, but rather $xy - 1$. Because $x = 2$ and $y = \dfrac{13}{2}$, $xy - 1 = (2)\left(\dfrac{13}{2}\right) - 1 = 13 - 1 = 12$. This is the Target Value; circle it.

Now that you have a Target Value, work your answer choices using Process of Elimination. Make $x = 2$ in each answer choice and eliminate any choice that doesn't equal your Target Value of 12:

A) $\dfrac{3(2)^2 + 1}{2} = \dfrac{13}{2}$ Not 12; eliminate!

B) $3(2)^2 - 1 = 11$ Not 12; eliminate!

C) $3(2)^2 + 1 = 13$ Not 12; eliminate!

D) $3(2)^2 = 12$ Is 12; keep!

Only (D) remains, so it must be the answer!

As you can see, Plugging In can turn messy algebra questions into more straightforward arithmetic questions. This technique is especially powerful when the PSAT asks for you to find the equivalent form of an expression:

16

The expression $x^2 + 4x - 4$ is written in the equivalent form $N^2 - 8$. What is the value of N?

A) $x^2 + 4x - 4$

B) $x^2 + 4x + 4$

C) $x - 2$

D) $x + 2$

Plugging In Quick Reference
- When you see *in terms of* or *equivalent form* and there are variables in the answer choices, you can Plug In.
- Pick your own number for an unknown in the problem.
- Do the necessary math to find the answer you're shooting for, which is the Target Value. Circle the Target Value.
- Use POE to eliminate every answer which doesn't match the Target Value.

Here's How to Crack It

The variable x is all over the place, so assign a value for x. Try $x = 2$. Next, work the problem in Bite-Sized Pieces. The first expression becomes $2^2 + 4(2) - 4 = 4 + 8 - 4 = 8$. The question then states that this is "written in the equivalent form" of $N^2 - 8$. If these expressions are equivalent, then $N^2 - 8$ must also equal 8. So set it equal to 8 and solve for N: $N^2 - 8 = 8$; $N^2 = 16$; $N = \pm 4$. The question is asking for N, so you're looking for any answer that equals either -4 or 4 (because there are two possible values). These are your Target Values; circle them. Make $x = 2$ in each answer choice and eliminate any option which doesn't match the Target Value:

A) $2^2 + 4(2) - 4 = 4 + 8 - 4 = 8$ Not -4 or 4; eliminate!

B) $2^2 + 4(2) + 4 = 4 + 8 + 4 = 16$ Not -4 or 4; eliminate!

C) $2 - 2 = 0$ Not -4 or 4; eliminate!

D) $2 + 2 = 4$ Yes!

The answer is (D).

———————————◯———————————

Plugging In is such a great technique because it turns hard algebra problems into medium and sometimes even easy arithmetic questions. Remember this when you're thinking of your POOD and looking for questions to do among the hard ones; if you see variables in the answers, there's a good chance it's one to try.

Don't worry too much about what numbers you choose to plug in; just plug in easy numbers (small numbers like 2, 5, or 10 or numbers that make the arithmetic easy, like 100 if you're looking for a percent). Also, be sure your numbers fit the conditions of the questions (if they say $x \leq 11$, don't plug in 12).

What If There's No Variable?

Sometimes you'll see a problem that doesn't contain an x, y, or z, but which contains a hidden variable. If your answers are percents or fractional parts of some unknown quantity (total number of marbles in a jar, total miles to travel in a trip), try using Plugging In.

Take a look at this problem:

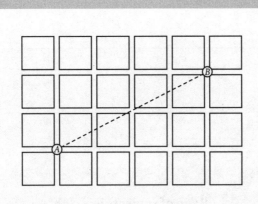

27

A neighborhood is comprised of square blocks, as shown above. Genna launches a drone from point *A*. The drone flies directly to point *B*, as shown by the dotted line. Genna then walks from point *A* to point *B* by following the streets by the shortest route possible. By approximately what percent was the distance Genna walked greater than the distance the drone flew?

A) 25%

B) 34%

C) 75%

D) 134%

Here's How to Crack It

Plug In for the size of the blocks. Assume each block is 1 unit by 1 unit. Genna must travel 4 blocks east and 2 blocks north, so she must travel 6 units total. (Note that it doesn't matter whether she goes north then east, east then north, or a zig-zag pattern from *A* to *B*; the shortest path will always be 6 units).

To find the distance the drone travels, make a right triangle with legs 4 units (the distance east) and 2 units (the distance north). Find the hypotenuse (which is the direct distance from *A* to *B*) using the Pythagorean theorem. The Pythagorean theorem is $a^2 + b^2 = c^2$, where c is the hypotenuse. Therefore $4^2 + 2^2 = c^2$; $16 + 4 = c^2$; $20 = c^2$; $\sqrt{20} = c$.

To find the percent difference, use the formula $\dfrac{\text{difference}}{\text{original}} \times 100$. Because you want percent greater, the original is the smaller value (in this case $\sqrt{20}$):

$\dfrac{6 - \sqrt{20}}{\sqrt{20}} \times 100 \approx 34.16$, which is closest to (B).

Try another one.

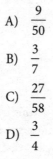

16

Ratio of students in a club

	Male	Female	Total
Junior	0.18	0.27	0.45
Senior	0.24	0.31	0.55
Total	0.42	0.58	100

The two-way table above shows the ratio of males and females and juniors and seniors in a particular club. If a male is chosen at random, what is the probability that he will be a junior?

A) $\dfrac{9}{50}$

B) $\dfrac{3}{7}$

C) $\dfrac{27}{58}$

D) $\dfrac{3}{4}$

Here's How to Crack It

The total ratio of students is 1.00, so Plug In for the total number of students. Make the number of students 100. To find the number of students in each category, you only need to multiply each number in the table by 100. This gives you the following:

	Male	Female	Total
Junior	18	27	45
Senior	24	31	55
Total	42	58	100

You're asked to find the probability of choosing a junior if you choose from the males. Probability is $\dfrac{what\ you\ want}{total\ possible\ outcomes}$. There are 18 male juniors and 42 total males, making the probability of choosing a junior from the males $\dfrac{18}{42}$, which reduces to $\dfrac{3}{7}$. This matches (B).

Drill 1

12

If $a = \dfrac{b}{c^2}$ and $c \neq 0$, then $\dfrac{1}{b^2} =$

A) ac^2

B) a^2c^4

C) $\dfrac{1}{ac^2}$

D) $\dfrac{1}{a^2c^4}$

13

If $p \neq 0$, then $\dfrac{\frac{1}{8}}{2p} =$

A) $\dfrac{1}{16p}$

B) $\dfrac{p}{4}$

C) $\dfrac{4}{p}$

D) $4p$

18

Jodi has x dollars in her bank account. She withdraws $\frac{1}{6}$ of the money in her account to pay her rent and another $\frac{1}{6}$ of the money in her account to make her car payment. Jodi then deposits her paycheck of y dollars into her account. A week later, she withdraws $\frac{1}{2}$ of the money in her account to spend on a new set of knives. In terms of x, how many dollars are left in Jodi's account?

A) $\dfrac{(4x-3y)}{6}$

B) $\dfrac{(3x-5y)}{6}$

C) $\dfrac{(3x-y)}{6}$

D) $\dfrac{(2x+3y)}{6}$

29

15% of the members of the incoming freshmen class at a certain university are left-handed, and the remaining members are right-handed. 65% of the same incoming freshmen class are female, and the rest are male. If $\frac{2}{3}$ of the left-handed students are male, then what percent of the female class is right-handed, to the nearest tenth of a percent? (Disregard the percent sign when gridding your answers. For example, if the answer is 43.2%, grid in 43.2.)

PLUGGING IN THE ANSWERS

You can also plug in when the answers to a problem are actual values, such as 2, 4, 10, or 20. Why would you want to do a lot of complicated algebra to solve a problem, when the answer is right there on the page? All you have to do is figure out *which* choice it is.

How can you tell which is the correct answer? Try every choice *until you find the one that works*. Even if this means you have to try all four choices, PITA is still a fast and reliable means of getting the right answer.

If you work strategically, however, you almost never need to try all four answers. If the question asks for either the greatest or the least answer, start there. Otherwise, start with one of the middle answer choices. If that answer works, you're done. If the answer you started with was too big, try a smaller answer. If the answer you started with was too small, try a bigger answer. You can almost always find the answer in two or three tries this way. Let's try PITA on the following problem.

PITA = Plugging In The Answers
Don't try to solve problems like this by writing equations and solving for *x* or *y*. Plugging In The Answers lets you use arithmetic instead of algebra, so you're less likely to make errors.

4

If the average (arithmetic mean) of 8 and *x* is equal to the average of 5, 9, and *x*, what is the value of *x* ?

A) 1

B) 2

C) 4

D) 8

Here's How to Crack It

Let's start with (C) and plug in 4 for *x*. The problem now reads:

4. If the average (arithmetic mean) of 8 and 4 is equal to the average of 5, 9, and 4 . . .

Does this work? The average of 8 and 4 is 6, and the average of 5, 9, and 4 is also 6. Therefore, (C) is the answer.

Neat, huh? Of course, the first answer you choose won't always be the correct one. Let's try one more.

If $(x - 2)^2 = 2x - 1$, which of the following is a possible value of x ?

A) 1

B) 2

C) 3

D) 6

Here's How to Crack It

If we try plugging in (C), 3, for x, the equation becomes 1 = 5, which is false. So (C) can't be right. If you're not sure which way to go next, just pick a direction. It won't take very long to figure out the correct answer. If we try plugging in (B), 2, for x, the equation becomes 0 = 3, which is false. If we try plugging in (A), 1, for x, the equation becomes 1 = 1, which is true. There's no need to try other answers, because there are no variables; only one answer choice can work. So the answer is (A).

Drill 2

3

$$2(n + 5) = 3(n - 2) + 8$$

In the equation above, what is the value of n ?

A) 1

B) 3

C) 4

D) 8

8

If $3^{x+2} = 243$, what is the value of x ?

A) 1

B) 2

C) 3

D) 4

10

If $\dfrac{24x}{4} + \dfrac{1}{x} = 5$, then $x =$

A) $-\dfrac{1}{6}$

B) $\dfrac{1}{6}$

C) $\dfrac{1}{4}$

D) $\dfrac{1}{2}$

DATA ANALYSIS

In the Calculator Permitted Math section, there will be questions that will ask you to work with concepts such as averages, percentages, and unit conversions. Luckily, The Princeton Review has you covered! The rest of this chapter will give you techniques and strategies to help you tackle these questions.

The Average Pie

You probably remember the average formula from math class, which says

Average (arithmetic mean) = $\dfrac{\text{total}}{\text{\# of things}}$. However, the PSAT rarely will ask you

to take a simple average. Of the three parts of an average problem—the average, the total, and the number of things—you're usually given two of these parts, but often in tricky combinations.

Therefore, the most reliable way to solve average problems is always to use the average pie:

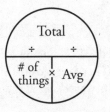

What the pie shows you is that if you know any two of these parts, you can always solve for the third. Once you fill in two of the elements, the pie shows you how to solve for the third part. If you know the total and the number of things, you can solve the average (total divided by number); if you know the total and the average, you can solve for the number of things (total divided by average); if you know the number of things and average, you can solve for the total (number times average).

Let's try this example.

9

The average (arithmetic mean) of 3 numbers is 22 and the smallest of these numbers is 2. If the remaining two numbers are equal, what are their values?

A) 22

B) 32

C) 40

D) 64

Total
When calculating averages, always find the total. It's the one piece of information that ETS loves to withhold.

Here's How to Crack It

Let's start by filling in our average pie. We know that 3 numbers have an average of 22. So we can fill in our pie, and the pie shows us that the sum total of these numbers must be 22×3, or 66.

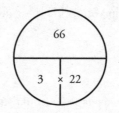

We know that one of the numbers is 2, so we can subtract it from the total we've just found, which leaves 64. What else do we know from the question? That the remaining two numbers are equal, so $64/2 = 32$. So the answer is (B).

Try one more.

8

Caroline scored 85, 88, and 89 on three of her four history tests. If her average (arithmetic mean) score for all four tests was 90, what did she score on her fourth test?

A) 90

B) 93

C) 96

D) 98

Here's How to Crack It

Let's start with what we know: We know that the average of all four of her tests was 90. So we can fill in an average pie with this information:

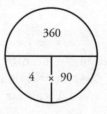

Now the pie tells us that the sum total of the scores on these four tests will be 4×90, or 360. Since three of these tests have a sum of $85 + 88 + 89$, or 262, we know that the score on the fourth test must be equal to 360 − 262, or 98. This makes the answer (D).

Median and Mode

Another two terms that are often tested along with average are median and mode. These are two more ways to describe the center of data.

The **median** of a group of numbers is the number in the middle, just as the "median" is the large divider in the middle of a road. To find the median, here's what you do:

- First, put the elements in the group in numerical order from lowest to highest.
- If the number of elements in your group is *odd*, find the number in the middle. That's the median.
- If you have an *even* number of elements in the group, find the two numbers in the middle and calculate their average (arithmetic mean).

Try this on the following problem:

3

If the 5 students in Ms. Jaffray's math class scored 91, 83, 84, 90, and 85 on their final exams, what is the median score for her class on the final exam?

A) 84

B) 85

C) 86

D) 88

Here's How to Crack It

First, let's place these numbers in order from lowest to highest: 83, 84, 85, 90, 91. The number in the middle is 85, so the median of this group is 85 and the answer is (B).

Finding a Median
To find the median of a set containing an even number of items, take the average of the two middle numbers after putting the numbers in order.

The **mode** of a group of numbers is the number that appears the most. (Remember: *Mode* sounds like *most*.) To find the mode of a group of numbers, simply see which element appears the greatest number of times.

28

If the 7 students in Ms. Holoway's math class scored 91, 83, 92, 83, 91, 85, and 91 on their final exams, what is the mode of her students' scores?

	⑦	⑦	
⊙	⊙	⊙	⊙
	⓪	⓪	⓪
①	①	①	①
②	②	②	②
③	③	③	③
④	④	④	④
⑤	⑤	⑤	⑤
⑥	⑥	⑥	⑥
⑦	⑦	⑦	⑦
⑧	⑧	⑧	⑧
⑨	⑨	⑨	⑨

Here's How to Crack It

Since the number 91 is the one that appears most often in the list, the mode of these numbers is 91. Pretty simple!

Range

Another measure of the spread of data is range. The range of a list of numbers is the difference between the greatest number on the list and the least number on the list. For the list 4, 5, 5, 6, 7, 8, 9, 10, 20, the greatest number is 20 and the least is 4, so the range is 20 − 4 = 16.

Let's look at a problem:

─────────────────○─────────────────

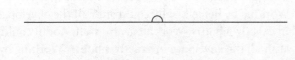

25

184	176	181	157	168
154	148	165	190	162

A group of patients is recruited for a clinical trial. Their heights, recorded in centimeters, are listed in the table above. Two more patients are recruited to the study. After these patients join, the range of the heights is 42 cm. Which of the following could NOT be the heights of the two new patients?

A)   154 cm and 186 cm

B)   146 cm and 179 cm

C)   150 cm and 188 cm

D)   148 cm and 185 cm

Here's How to Crack It

To determine the current range, take the difference of the greatest and least values: 190 − 148 = 42 cm. If the range is to remain 42 cm, then the new patients cannot be greater than 190 cm or less than 148 cm tall. Choice (B) violates this restriction. Because the question wants what could NOT be the heights of the new patients, the answer is (B).

─────────────────○─────────────────

Rates

Rate is a concept related to averages. Cars travel at an average speed. Work gets done at an average rate. Because the ideas are similar, you can also use a pie to organize your information on rate questions.

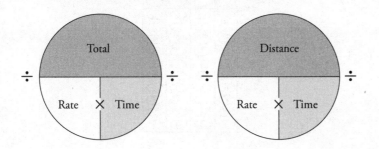

Here's a simple example:

Problem: If a fisherman can tie 9 flies for fly fishing in an hour and a half, how long does it take him to tie one fly, in minutes?

Solution: First, convert the hour and a half to 90 minutes, so your units are consistent. Then fill in the top of the pie with the amount (9 flies) and the lower right part with the time (90 minutes). Divide 9 by 90 to get the rate, $\frac{1}{10}$, or one fly every 10 minutes.

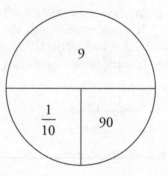

Let's look at an example:

28

Sally, Abdul, and Juanita have volunteered to stuff a certain number of envelopes for a local charity. Working by herself, Sally could stuff all the envelopes in exactly 3 hours. Working by himself, Abdul could stuff all the envelopes in exactly 4 hours. Working by herself, Juanita could stuff all the envelopes in exactly 6 hours. If Sally, Abdul, and Juanita work together at these rates to stuff all the envelopes, what fraction of the envelopes will be stuffed by Juanita?

Here's How to Crack It

Since the question doesn't tell you how many envelopes to stuff, this is a great problem to Plug In on in addition to using the Rate Pie. Because Sally takes 3 hours, Abdul takes 4 hours, and Juanita takes 6 hours, you want to choose a multiple of all those numbers. Make the total number of envelopes to stuff 120. Next, use the Rate Pie to determine each person's rate:

Sally

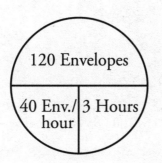

Abdul

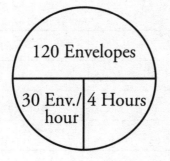

Juanita

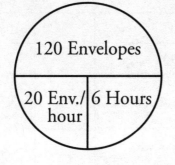

If all three people work together, their total rate will be $40 + 30 + 20 = 90$ envelopes/hour. During that hour Juanita will stuff 20 envelopes, meaning she does $\frac{20}{90}$ or $\frac{2}{9}$ of the job.

PERCENTS

Percent just means "divided by 100." So 20 percent = $\frac{20}{100} = \frac{1}{5}$ or .2.

Likewise, 400 percent = $\frac{400}{100} = \frac{4}{1} = 4$.

Any percent question can be translated into algebra—just use the following rules:

Percent	÷ 100
Of	×
What	x (or any variable)
Is, Are, Equals	=

Take a look at some examples of phrases you might have to translate on the PSAT:

8 percent of 10		$.08 \times 10 = .8$
10 percent of 80		$.1 \times 80 = 8$
5 is what percent of 80?	becomes	$5 = \frac{x}{100} \times 80$
5 is 80 percent of what number?		$5 = \frac{80}{100} x$
What percent of 5 is 80?		$\frac{x}{100} \times 5 = 80$

Percent Increase/Decrease

$$\textit{Percent Increase} \text{ or } \textit{Percent Decrease} = \frac{\textit{change}}{\textit{original amount}} \times 100$$

For example, if an $80 item is reduced to $60 during a sale, the percent decrease is the change in price ($80 – $60 = $20) divided by the original amount ($80), which gives us .25. Multiply by 100 to get 25 percent.

Try a question:

26

Estimated Numbers of Cell Phone Users by Type
(in millions)

	Prepaid users	Contracted users	Totals
2008	45	225	270
2012	75	250	325
Totals	120	475	595

By how much greater was the percent increase in prepaid users from 2008 to 2012 than the percent increase in contracted users over the same period, to the nearest percent?

A) 6%

B) 10%

C) 30%

D) 56%

Here's How to Crack It

First, find the percent increase in each group. Remember that percent increase is $\frac{\text{difference}}{\text{original}} \times 100$. For prepaid users, the equation would be $\frac{75-45}{45} \times 100 = 66\frac{2}{3}\%$. Contracted users: $\frac{250-225}{225} \times 100 = 11\frac{1}{9}\%$. Finally, subtract: $66\frac{2}{3} - 11\frac{1}{9} = 55\frac{5}{9}\%$, which is closest to (D).

GROWTH AND DECAY

Another aspect of percent questions may relate to things that increase or decrease by a certain percent over time. This is known as "growth and decay." Real-world examples include population growth, radioactive decay, and credit payments, to name a few. While Plugging In can help on these, it is also useful to know the growth and decay formula.

> When the growth or decay rate is a percent of the total population:
>
> *final amount = original amount* $(1 \pm rate)^{number\ of\ changes}$

Let's see how this formula can make quick work of an otherwise tedious question.

14

The population of Bethesda, Maryland is currently 61,000 and is growing at a rate of 2.5% every three months. If Bethesda's population, *P*, is a function of time in years, *t*, then which of the following functions represents the town's population growth?

A) $P(t) = 61,000(1.025)^t$

B) $P(t) = 61,000(1.1)^t$

C) $P(t) = 61,000(1.025)^{4t}$

D) $P(t) = 61,000(1.1)^{3t}$

Here's How to Crack It

Because the rate of growth is 2.5%, you need to add 0.025 (2.5% in decimal form) to 1 within the parenthesis. This would be 1 + 0.025 = 1.025. Eliminate (B) and (D) because they do not have this piece. The only difference between (A) and (C) is the exponent, which represents the number of changes. Here, *t* is in years, but the population increases every 3 months, which is 4 times a year. This means you want 4 changes when *t* = 1; this gives you (C) as your answer.

RATIOS AND PROPORTIONS

Some questions in the Calculator Permitted Math section will ask about ratios and proportions. With the strategies that you'll learn on the next few pages you'll be well prepared to tackle these concepts on the PSAT.

Ratios

Ratios are about relationships between numbers. Whereas a fraction is a relationship between a part and whole, a ratio is about the relationship between parts. So, for example, if there were 3 boys and 7 girls in a room, the fraction of boys in the room would be $\frac{3}{10}$. But the ratio of boys to girls would be 3 : 7. Notice that if you add up the parts, you get the whole. 7 + 3 = 10. That's important for PSAT ratio problems, and you'll see why in a moment.

Ratio problems usually aren't difficult to identify: The problem will tell you that there is a "ratio" of one thing to another, such as a 2 : 3 ratio of boys to girls in a club. When you see a ratio problem, drawing a ratio box will help you organize the information in the problem and figure out the correct answer.

For instance, suppose a problem tells you that there is a ratio of 2 boys to 3 girls in the physics club, which has 40 members total. Here's how you would put that information in a ratio box so that you can answer the question being asked:

The first line of a ratio box is where you put the *ratio* from the problem. These are parts of the whole; they're not actual numbers of people, animals, books, or anything else. By themselves, they don't tell you *how many* of anything you have.

The second line of a ratio box is for the **multiplier**. The multiplier tells you how much you have to multiply the ratio by to get an actual number of something. The multiplier is the same all the way across; it doesn't change from column to column. And usually, the multiplier isn't in the problem; you have to figure it out yourself.

The third line is for *actual numbers*, so when the problem gives you a number of people (or animals, books, or whatever), that information goes in the third line.

$$\text{Fraction} = \frac{\text{part}}{\text{whole}}$$

$$\text{Ratio} = \frac{\text{part}}{\text{part}}$$

One more thing to notice: See how there's a column for "whole"? This is where you add up the numbers in the ratio row and actual numbers row. Don't forget to add a column for the whole—it's usually key in figuring out the problem.

Now that you know some information from the problem and you know how the ratio box works, you can fill in the rest of the box.

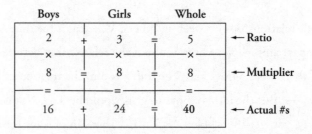

The first step is adding the ratio columns to find the whole, which is 5. Then you can find the multiplier by figuring out what you need to multiply 5 by to get 40. Once you fill in 8 for the multiplier all the way across the middle row, finding the actual number of boys and girls in the club is a snap.

Gridding In

A ratio is usually expressed as 2 : 3 or 2 to 3, but if you need to grid a ratio, grid it as $\frac{2}{3}$.

Now you can answer all kinds of questions about the membership of the physics club. There are 16 boys and 24 girls. Take the $\frac{part}{whole}$ from the ratio row to figure out that $\frac{3}{5}$ of the members are girls. That means $\frac{2}{5}$, or 40 percent, of the members are boys.

Sometimes you won't need to use the Ratio Box to solve a ratio problem. Instead, remember that you can treat ratios as fractions and, like fractions, you can use your calculator to turn the ratio into a decimal to simplify your calculations.

Try this one.

5

The ice cream flavor preferences of a randomly selected group of young Americans aged 3-18 are represented in the table below. Survey participants were asked to choose their favorite flavor among the following five: Vanilla, Chocolate, Mint Chocolate Chip, Cookies and Cream, and Coffee.

Reported favorite ice cream flavor by age group

Age	Vanilla	Chocolate	Mint Chocolate Chip	Cookies and Cream	Coffee
3–6	8,534	7,835	6,135	4,526	254
7–10	9,250	10,936	4,019	7,530	497
11–15	5,093	7,591	9,495	1,076	760
16–18	11,024	7,345	2,026	4,620	1,062

According to the data in the table above, the ratio of the most- to least-favorite flavors among the 7-10 age group is approximately how many times greater than the ratio of the most- to least-favorite flavors among the 11-15 age group?

A) 1.8

B) 3.4

C) 4.2

D) 6.7

Here's How to Crack It

First, you need to find the ratio of the most- to least-favorite flavor for each of the two age groups in question. For the 7–10 age group, the most favorite flavor is chocolate, with 10,936 votes, and the least favorite is coffee, with 497 votes. The ratio is thus $\frac{10,936}{497} = 22.0$. For the 11–15 age group, the most favorite flavor is mint chocolate chip, with 9,495 votes, and the least favorite flavor is coffee, with 760 votes. The ratio is thus $\frac{9,495}{760} = 12.5$. To find out how many times greater the first ratio is, divide these numbers: $\frac{22.0}{12.5} = 1.8$, which is (A).

Direct Proportion/Variation

Direct Proportion problems generally ask you to make a conversion (such as from ounces to pounds) or to compare two sets of information and find a missing piece. For example, a proportion problem may ask you to figure out the amount of time it will take to travel 300 miles at a rate of 50 miles per hour.

> To solve proportion problems, just set up two equal fractions. One will have all the information you know, and the other will have a missing piece that you're trying to figure out.

$$\frac{50 \text{ miles}}{1 \text{ hour}} = \frac{300 \text{ miles}}{x \text{ hours}}$$

Be sure to label the parts of your proportion so you'll know you have the right information in the right place; the same units should be in the numerator on both sides of the equal sign and the same units should be in the denominator on both sides of the equal sign. Notice how using a setup like this helps us keep track of the information we have and to find the information we're looking for, so we can use bite-sized pieces to work through the question.

Now we can cross-multiply and then solve for x: $50x = 300$, so $x = 6$ hours.

Let's try the following problem.

2

John receives $2.50 for every 4 pounds of berries he picks. How much money will he receive if he picks 90 pounds of berries?

A) $36.00

B) $42.25

C) $48.50

D) $56.25

Here's How to Crack It

To solve this, set up a proportion.

$$\frac{\$2.50}{4\,\text{pounds}} = \frac{x}{90\,\text{pounds}}$$

Now we can cross-multiply. $4x = 2.50 \times 90$, so $4x = 225$, and $x = 56.25$. The answer is (D).

Occasionally, you may see a problem that tells you there are two equal ratios. For example, if a problem says that the ratio of 24 to 0.6 is equal to the ratio of 12 to y, you can solve for y by setting up a proportion. A proportion, after all, is really just two ratios set equal to each other.

$$\frac{24}{0.6} = \frac{12}{y}$$

Then you can cross-multiply and solve to get 0.3 for your answer.

Inverse Proportion/Variation

Inverse Proportion is simply the opposite of a direct, or ordinary, proportion. In a direct proportion when one variable increases, so does the other; however, in an inverse variation or proportion, when one variable *increases*, the other variable *decreases*, or vice versa. These types of problems are generally clearly labeled and all you have to do is apply the inverse variation formula:

$$x_1 y_1 = x_2 y_2$$

Once you memorize the formula, applying it will become second nature to you.

Now try this one.

18

On a particular survey, the percentage of people answering a question with the same response is inversely proportional to the number of the question. If 80% of the people surveyed answered the same response to the 8th question, then, approximately, what percentage of the people surveyed answered the same answer to the 30th question?

A) 3%

B) 13%

C) 18%

D) 21%

Here's How to Crack It

The problem tells us that the numbers are inversely proportional, so we need to figure out what to put into the formula. The first piece of information is that 80 percent of the people answered the 8th question correctly; we need to know the percent of people who answered the 30th question correctly. Let's make x the percent and y the question number. Your equation should look like this:

$$(80)(8) = (x_2)(30)$$

When you solve the equation, you should end up with $\frac{640}{30}$ or $21\frac{1}{3}$, which is (D) (remember, when the problem says "approximately," you'll probably have to round up or down).

Drill 3

a.   If a student scores 70, 90, 95, and 105, what is the average (arithmetic mean) for these tests? _____

b.   If a student has an average (arithmetic mean) score of 80 on 4 tests, what is the total of the scores received on those tests? _____

c.   If a student has an average of 60 on tests, with a total of 360, how many tests has the student taken? _____

d.   If the average of 2, 8, and x is 6, what is the value of x? _____

2, 3, 3, 4, 6, 8, 10, 12

e.   What is the median of the group of numbers above? _____

f.   What is the mode of the group of numbers above? _____

g.   What is the range of the group of numbers above? _____

h.   What percent of 5 is 6? _____

i.   60 percent of 90 is the same as 50 percent of what number? _____

j.   Jenny's salary increased from $30,000 to $33,000. By what percent did her salary increase? _____

k.   In 1980, factory X produced 18,600 pieces. In 1981, factory X produced only 16,000 pieces. By approximately what percent did production decrease from 1980 to 1981? _____

The amount of money in a savings account after m months is modeled by the function $f(m) = 1{,}000(1.01)^m$.

l.   What was the original amount in the bank account? _____

m.   By what percent does the amount in the account increase each month? _____

n.   In a certain bag of marbles, the ratio of red marbles to green marbles is 7 : 5. If the bag contains 96 marbles, how many green marbles are in the bag? _____

o.   One hogshead is equal to 64 gallons. How many hogsheads are equal to 96 gallons? _____

p.   The pressure and volume of a gas are inversely related. If the gas is at 10 kPa at 2 liters, then what is the pressure when the gas is at 4 liters? _____

2

If 10 pecks are equivalent to 2.5 bushels, then 4 bushels are equivalent to how many pecks?

A) 4

B) 10

C) 12.5

D) 16

24

A student took five tests. He scored an average (arithmetic mean) of 80 on the first three tests and an average of 90 on the other two. Which of the following must be true?

    I. The student scored more than 85 on at least one test.

    II. The average (arithmetic mean) score for all five tests is less than 85.

    III. The student scored less than 80 on at least two tests.

A) I only

B) II only

C) I and II

D) II and III

28

Marcia can type 18 pages per hour, and David can type 14 pages per hour. If they work together, how many minutes will it take them to type 24 pages?

Summary

o   The test is full of opportunities to use arithmetic instead of algebra—just look for your chances to use Plugging In and Plugging In The Answers (PITA).

o   If a question has *in terms of* or variables in the answer choices, it's a Plugging In problem. Plug in your own number, do the math, find the target value, and use POE to get down to one correct answer.

o   If a question doesn't have variables but asks for a fraction or a percent of an unknown number, you can also plug in there. Just substitute your own number for the unknown and take the rest of the problem step by step.

o   If a question has an unknown and asks for a specific amount, making you feel like you have to write an equation, try PITA instead.

o   The Average Pie can help you tackle any question about the average (arithmetic mean)—just fill what you know from the problem into the correct spots for *Total*, *Number of Things*, and *Average*.

o   The median is the middle value in a list of consecutive numbers. If there are an odd number of elements, the median is the average of the two middle values.

o   The mode is the most commonly occurring value in a list of numbers.

o   The range is the difference between the greatest and least values in a list of numbers.

o   Rates are closely related to averages. Use the Rate Pie just like you use the Average Pie. Remember that the PSAT likes to make you find the totals (distance or work in the Rate Pie).

o   Percent simply means "per 100." Many percent questions can be tackled by translating English to math.

o Percent increase or decrease is $\dfrac{\text{difference}}{\text{original}} \times 100$.

o Growth and decay are given by the formula *final amount = original amount*$(1 \pm$ *rate*$)^{\textit{number of changes}}$.

o Use the ratio box on questions that ask about a ratio. Fill in the ratio box with information from the problem, calculate the missing piece, and then solve for whatever the problem is asking for.

o Sometimes you'll need to treat ratios like fractions or decimals. Use your calculator to turn the numbers into the easiest form to work the problem.

o Direct proportion means as one value goes up, the other goes up. The formula is $\dfrac{x_1}{y_1} = \dfrac{x_2}{y_2}$.

o Inverse proportion means as one value goes up, the other goes down. The formula is $x_1 y_1 = x_2 y_2$.

Chapter 7
Advanced Math Principles

So far we've covered basic knowledge and some PSAT-specific problem-solving skills. Now we'll look at some of the more advanced skills tested on the PSAT.

FUNCTIONS

In the Math Basics chapter, we looked at some concepts related to the *xy*-plane. Here, we will look at some more complicated topics involving functions and graphs. The functions on the PSAT mostly look like this:

$$f(x) = x^2 + 6x + 24$$

Most questions of this type will give you a specific value to plug in for *x* and then ask you to find the value of the function for that *x*. Each function is just a set of instructions that tells you what to do to *x*—or the number you plug in for *x*—in order to find the corresponding value for *f(x)* (a fancy name for *y*). Just plug your information into that equation and follow the instructions.

Let's try an easy one.

Just Follow the Instructions
Functions are like recipes. Each one is just a set of directions for you to follow. ETS and the College Board provide the ingredients and you work your magic.

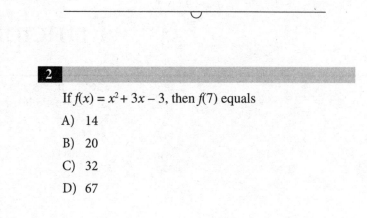

2

If $f(x) = x^2 + 3x - 3$, then $f(7)$ equals

A) 14

B) 20

C) 32

D) 67

Here's How to Crack It

Function questions are just trying to see if you can follow the directions, so follow them! The instructions, in this case, are in the equation. So plug 7 into the equation and it should look like this: $f(7) = 7^2 + 3(7) - 3$. Do the math and $f(7) = 67$. Therefore, the answer is (D).

Sometimes you'll get more complicated questions. As long as you know that when you put in x, your function will spit out another number, you'll be fine. Try this next one:

20

Let the function g be defined by $g(x) = 5x + 2$. If $\sqrt{g\left(\dfrac{a}{2}\right)} = 6$, what is the value of a ?

A) $\dfrac{1}{\sqrt{6}}$

B) $\dfrac{1}{\sqrt{2}}$

C) $\dfrac{34}{5}$

D) $\dfrac{68}{5}$

Here's How to Crack It

This may look complicated, but just follow the directions. You know that $g(x) = 5x + 2$. You also know that $\sqrt{g\left(\dfrac{a}{2}\right)} = 6$. First, get rid of the square root by squaring both sides. Now you have $g\left(\dfrac{a}{2}\right) = 36$. Usually there's an x inside the parentheses. Treat this the same. This statement says that g of some number equals 36. We also know that g of some number is the same as $5x + 2$. So $5x + 2 = 36$. Simplify and you get $\dfrac{34}{5}$. Careful, you're not done. You now know that $\dfrac{a}{2} = \dfrac{34}{5}$, so $a = \dfrac{68}{5}$, or (D).

PITA!
Don't forget that you can often plug in the answer choices on function questions!

Another way the PSAT can make functions more complicated is to give you two functions to deal with together. If you approach these problems one piece at a time, they will be easier to handle.

Here's an example:

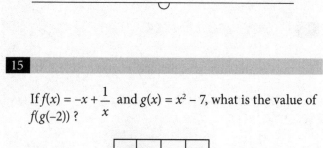

15

If $f(x) = -x + \dfrac{1}{x}$ and $g(x) = x^2 - 7$, what is the value of $f(g(-2))$?

Here's How to Crack It

With compound functions like this one, start from the inside and work your way out. Plug -2 into the g function to get $g(-2) = (-2)^2 - 7 = 4 - 7 = -3$. Plug this value into the f function to get $f(-3) = -(-3) + \dfrac{1}{-3} = 3 - \dfrac{1}{3} = 2\dfrac{2}{3}$. You can't grid in mixed fractions, so convert it to an improper fraction $\dfrac{8}{3}$ or the decimal 2.66 or 2.67. Any of these would be acceptable answers.

Sometimes the PSAT will use a word problem to describe a function, and then ask you to "build a function" that describes that real-world situation.

Try one of those:

6

A scientist noted that the rate of growth of a tree which he had been observing is directly proportional to time. The scientist first measured the height of the tree to be 20 feet; two years later, the tree was 21 feet tall. If the tree continues to grow at a constant rate, which of the following represents the height of the tree in feet, y, as a function of time, x, in years since the scientist's first measurement?

A) $y(x) = 0.5x + 20$

B) $y(x) = 21x + 20$

C) $y(x) = x + 20$

D) $y(x) = 20x + 21$

Here's How to Crack It

Instead of trying to write your own equation, use the ones in the answer choices. According to the question, 2 years after the first measurement, the tree was 21 feet tall. Therefore, when $x = 2$, $y(x) = 21$. Plug these points into the answers to see which answer works. Choice (A) becomes $21 = 0.5(2) + 20$. Solve the right side of the equation to get $21 = 1 + 20$, or $21 = 21$. The correct answer is (A).

Roots of a Function

You may also be asked about the roots of a function. These are the solutions for x that you get when you solve the function or the places where the graph of the function crosses the x-axis. Here's how this concept may be tested on the PSAT.

11

The graph of the function f in the xy-plane contains the points $(-3, 0)$, $(0, -2)$, and $(4, 0)$. Which of the following is a factor of function f?

A) $x - 2$

B) $x + 2$

C) $x + 3$

D) $x + 4$

Here's How to Crack It

The roots of an equation, found by setting the factors equal to 0, are the same as the x-intercepts of the equation. At the x-intercept, $y = 0$. Therefore, the point $(0, -2)$ is not a root, so you can eliminate (A) and (B) because they include 2. According to the question, one of the x-intercepts is at $(-3, 0)$. This means that one solution to the function can be found by $x + 3 = 0$, and one of the factors of the function is $x + 3$. The other factor would be $(x - 4)$, but that's not a choice. The correct answer is (C).

Drill 1

15

If $f(x) = x^2 - x + 4$, a is non-negative, and $f(a) = 10$, then what is the value of a ?

21

If $f(x) = x^{-\frac{2}{3}}$, what is the value of $\dfrac{f(8)}{f(3)}$?

A) $\dfrac{4}{\sqrt[3]{9}}$

B) $\dfrac{8}{3}$

C) $\sqrt{\dfrac{512}{27}}$

D) $\dfrac{\sqrt[3]{9}}{4}$

Questions 30 and 31 refer to the following information.

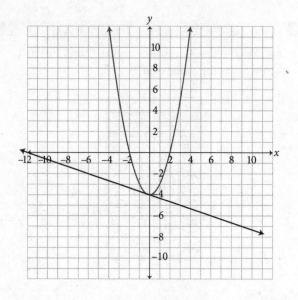

In the above graph, parabola $f(x)$ is represented by

the equation $f(x) = x^2 - 4$ and line $g(x)$ is represented

by the equation $g(x) = -\dfrac{1}{3}x - 4$. Line $g(x)$ intersects

parabola $f(x)$ at point $(0, -4)$, as shown on the graph.

30

For $x = 12$, how much greater is the value of $f(x)$ than $g(x)$?

31

A new line, $h(x)$, is added to the graph. The line $h(x)$ is perpendicular to line $g(x)$, intersecting with line $g(x)$ at the point $(-12, 0)$. What is the x-coordinate of the point where line $h(x)$ will intersect parabola $f(x)$ in Quadrant I?

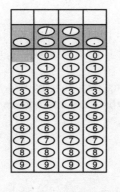

▲

QUADRATIC EQUATIONS

Ah, quadratics. You're likely to see several questions on the PSAT that require you to expand, factor, or solve quadratics. You may even need to find the vertex of a parabola or the points of intersection of a quadratic and a line. So let's review, starting with the basics.

Expanding

Most often you'll be asked to expand an expression simply by multiplying it out. When working with an expression of the form $(x + 3)(x + 4)$, multiply it out using the following rule:

> FOIL = First Outer Inner Last

Start with the *first* figure in each set of parentheses: $x \times x = x^2$

Now do the two *outer* figures: $x \times 4 = 4x$

Next, the two *inner* figures: $3 \times x = 3x$

Finally, the *last* figure in each set of parentheses: $3 \times 4 = 12$.

Add them all together, and we get $x^2 + 4x + 3x + 12$, or $x^2 + 7x + 12$.

Factoring

If you ever see an expression of the form $x^2 + 7x + 12$ on the PSAT, there is a good chance that factoring it will be the key to cracking it.

The key to factoring is figuring out what pair of numbers will multiply to give you the constant term (12, in this case) and add up to the coefficient of the x term (7, in this question).

Let's try an example:

Step 1: Draw two sets of parentheses next to each other and fill an x into the left side of each. That's what gives us our x^2 term.
Step 2: 12 can be factored a number of ways: 1×12, 2×6, or 3×4. Which of these adds up to 7? 3 and 4, so place a 3 on the right side of one parenthesis and a 4 in the other.
Step 3: Now we need to figure out what the correct signs should be. They should both be positive in this case, because that will sum to 7 and multiply to 12, so fill plus signs into each parenthesis.

$$x^2 + 7x + 12$$

$$(x \quad)(x \quad)$$

$$(x \quad 3)(x \quad 4)$$

$$(x + 3)(x + 4)$$

If you want to double-check your work, try expanding out $(x + 3)(x + 4)$ using FOIL and you'll get the original expression.

Now try the following problem.

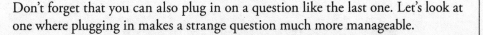

8

Travis determines that the average speed of his kayak traveling down the river when he is not paddling can be calculated using the formula $4r^2 - 40r + 100$, where r represents the strength of the river's current in feet per second. Which of the following expressions would be an equivalent formula that Travis could use to determine his kayak's speed?

A) $(2r + 10)^2$

B) $(2r + 10)(2r - 10)$

C) $4(r + 5)^2$

D) $4(r - 5)^2$

Here's How to Crack It

To compare the equation in the question to the answer choices, you need to either factor the equation in the question or expand out the answer choices. The first option is probably faster. Start by factoring a 4 out of the entire equation to get $4(r^2 - 10r + 25)$. Now, determine what two numbers can be added to get −10 and multiplied to get 25. In this case, it's −5 and −5. The equation becomes $4(r - 5)$ $(r - 5)$ or $4(r - 5)^2$, which is (D).

Don't forget that you can also plug in on a question like the last one. Let's look at one where plugging in makes a strange question much more manageable.

8

If the expression $x + 2(x - 4)$ is multiplied by R to form the expression $3x^2 - 5x - 8$, then which of the following is equivalent to R ?

A) $x + 1$

B) $x + 2$

C) $x + 3$

D) $x + 4$

Here's How to Crack It

Whenever the question and the answers include variables, see if you can plug in. If $x = 2$, the first expression becomes $2 + 2(2 - 4) = 2 + 2(-2) = 2 + (-4) = -2$, and the second expression becomes $3(2^2) - 5(2) - 8 = 3(4) - 10 - 8 = 12 - 10 - 8 = -6$. To find R, set up the following equation: $-2R = -6$. Solve for R to get $R = 3$. Plug 2 in for x in the equations to see which answer equals the target number of 3. Choice (A) becomes $2 + 1 = 3$. Keep (A), but check the remaining answers just in case. Choice (B) becomes $2 + 2 = 4$, (C) becomes $2 + 3 = 5$, and (D) becomes $2 + 4 = 6$. Eliminate (B), (C), and (D). The correct answer is (A).

Solving Quadratic Equations

Sometimes you'll want to factor to solve an equation. In this case, there will be two possible values for x, called the roots of the equation. To solve for x, use the following steps:

Step 1: Make sure that the equation is set equal to zero.
Step 2: Factor the equation.
Step 3: Set each parenthetical expression equal to zero. So if you have $(x + 2)(x - 7) = 0$, you get $(x + 2) = 0$ and $(x - 7) = 0$. When you solve for each, you get $x = -2$ and $x = 7$. Therefore, -2 and 7 are the solutions or roots of the equation.

Try the following problem.

4

If $b^2 + 2b - 8 = 0$, and $b < 0$, what is the value of b ?

A) -6

B) -4

C) -2

D) 0

Here's How to Crack It

Begin by using Process of Elimination. Since the question states that $b < 0$, eliminate (D). Now follow the steps:

1. The equation is already set equal to zero.
2. You can now factor the left side of the equation to get $(b + 4)(b - 2) = 0$.
3. When you set each parenthetical expression equal to zero, you get $b = -4$ and $b = 2$. Since $b < 0$, the answer is (B).

An alternative approach to this question is to plug in the answers. For (A), plug $b =$ −6 into the equation to get $(-6)^2 + 2(-6) - 8 = 0$. Solve the left side of the equation to get $36 - 12 - 8 = 0$, or $16 = 0$. Since this statement is not true, eliminate (A). For (B), plug $b = -4$ into the equation to get $(-4)^2 + 2(-4) - 8 = 0$. Solve the left side of the equation to get $16 - 8 - 8 = 0$, or $0 = 0$. Since, this statement is true, the correct answer is (B).

Sometimes, solving will get a little trickier. When quadratics do not factor easily and there are no answer choices to plug in, you can use the quadratic formula to solve.

> The values of x for a quadratic equation in the form $y = ax^2 + bx + c$ are
>
> $$x = \frac{-b \pm \sqrt{b^2 - 4ac}}{2a}$$

Let's try one.

Triangle Tip
An easy way to figure out the height of an equilateral triangle is to take half of its side and multiply it by the square root of 3.

29

If $y = x^2 - 4x + 3.75$, what is one possible value of x ?

Here's How to Crack It

This one is not easy to factor, so try the quadratic formula. In the given equation, $a = 1$, $b = -4$, and $c = 3.75$. Therefore,

$$x = \frac{-(-4) \pm \sqrt{(-4)^2 - 4(1)(3.75)}}{2(1)} = \frac{4 \pm \sqrt{16 - 15}}{2} = \frac{4 \pm 1}{2}.$$

So x equals $\frac{5}{2}$ (or 2.5) and $\frac{3}{2}$ (or 1.5). Any of these 4 options could be entered into the grid.

You may have noticed that this is a calculator question. Another option for this one would be to graph the equation on your calculator to determine the x-intercepts, which are the roots or solutions to the equation.

Other Quadratic Questions

Sometimes, quadratic equations will be tested with word problems or charts. Let's look at these types of questions.

29

An Olympic shot-putter throws a heavy spherical object that follows a parabolic trajectory. The equation describing the trajectory of the shot-putter's throw is $y = -0.04x^2 + 2.02x + 5.5$ where y represents the height of the object in feet and x represents the horizontal distance in feet traveled by the object. What is the original height of the object (in feet) immediately before it leaves the shot-putter's hand?

Here's How to Crack It

According to the question, x represents the horizontal distance in feet traveled by the object, and y represents the height. Before the shot-putter throws the object, $x = 0$. Plug 0 into the equation and solve for y. The equation becomes $y = -0.04(0^2) + 2.02(0) + 5.5 = 0 + 0 + 5.5 = 5.5$. The correct answer is 5.5.

Now look at an example of a chart-based quadratic question.

---○---

14

Trajectory of a Dolphin's Jump

Horizontal Distance (feet)	Vertical Height (feet)
0	0
1	2.7
2	4.8
3	6.3
4	7.2
5	7.5
6	7.2
7	6.3
8	4.8
9	2.7
10	0

The table above shows the horizontal distance and vertical height, both in feet, of a typical dolphin jumping out of the water (a height of 0 represents the surface of the water). If d represents the horizontal distance and h represents the vertical height, which of the following equations would best represent the trajectory of the dolphin's jump?

A) $h = -0.3d^2 + 3d$

B) $h = -0.4d^2 + 4d$

C) $h = -0.5d^2 + 5d$

D) $h = -0.6d^2 + 6d$

Here's How to Crack It

This is a similar task to "building a function" that we discussed earlier in this chapter. You should plug values from the table into the equations in the answer choices to see which equation works. According to the table, when $d = 1$, $h = 2.7$. Plug these values into (A) to get $2.7 = -0.3(1^2) + 3(1)$. Solve the right side of the equation to get $2.7 = -0.3 + 3$ or $2.7 = 2.7$. Keep (A), but check the remaining answers just in case. Choice (B) becomes $2.7 = -0.4(1^2) + 4(1)$. Solve the right side of the equation to get $2.7 = -0.4 + 4$ or $2.7 = 3.6$. This is not true, so eliminate (B). Choice (C) becomes $2.7 = -0.5(1^2) + 5(1)$. Solve the right side of the equation to get $2.7 = -0.5 + 5$ or $2.7 = 4.5$. Eliminate (C). Choice (D) becomes $2.7 = -0.6(1^2)$

+ 6(1). Solve the right side of the equation to get 2.7 = –0.6 + 6 or 2.7 = 5.4. Eliminate (D). The correct answer is (A).

———————○———————

Forms of Quadratics

When graphed in the *xy*-plane, quadratics form a parabola. The PSAT will ask questions using two different forms of the equation for a parabola.

> The standard form of a parabola equation is as follows:
>
> $$y = ax^2 + bx + c$$

In the standard form of a parabola, the value of *a* tells whether a parabola opens upwards or downwards (if *a* is positive, the parabola opens upwards, and if *a* is negative, the parabola opens downwards).

> The vertex form of a parabola equation is as follows:
>
> $$y = a(x - h)^2 + k$$
>
> In the vertex form, the point (*h*, *k*) is the vertex of the parabola.

Simply knowing what the vertex form looks like may help you answer a question, like the following example.

———————○———————

6

Which of the following equations has its vertex at (–4, 3) ?

A) $y = (x - 4)^2 + 3$

B) $y = (x + 4)^2 + 3$

C) $y = (x - 3)^2 + 4$

D) $y = (x + 3)^2 - 4$

Here's How to Crack It

If you know the vertex form, you can create the correct equation for the parabola. Be careful with the signs, though, as the signs are all changing in the answer choices. In the vertex $(-4, 3)$, -4 is h and 3 is k. The correct answer should end in $+ 3$, so eliminate (C) and (D). For the $(x - h)^2$ part of the equation, it becomes $(x - (-4))^2$, or $(x + 4)^2$, so the correct answer is (B).

Knowing the form makes Process of Elimination a quick way to answer these, but if you forget the form, you can always plug in the given point to see which equation is true.

The vertex form is great for answering questions about the minimum or maximum value a parabolic function will reach or the x-value that results in that minimum or maximum y-value. So another good thing to know is the method for turning a quadratic in the standard form into the vertex form. Here are the steps to do that.

> To convert a parabola equation in the standard form to the vertex form, complete the square.
>
> 1. Make $y = 0$, and move any constants over to the left side of the equation.
> 2. Take half of the coefficient on the x-term, square it, and add it to both sides of the equation.
> 3. Convert the x terms and the number on the right to square form: $(x - h)^2$.
> 4. Move the constant on the left back over to the right and set it equal to y again.

Say you were given the equation $y = x^2 - 4x - 12$. You would make it $0 = x^2 - 4x - 12$, and then $12 = x^2 - 4x$. You'd add 4 to both sides to get $16 = x^2 - 4x + 4$, and then convert the right side to the square form to get $16 = (x - 2)^2$. Finally, you'd move the 16 back over and set it equal to y to get $y = (x - 2)^2 - 16$.

Drill 2

Answers can be found in Part III.

Answers can be found in Part III.

4

If $12 - (t + 2)^2 = 3$, which of the following could be the value of t ?

A) −9

B) −5

C) 5

D) 7

6

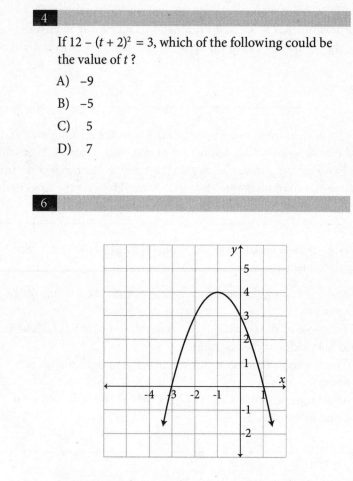

Which of the following equations is shown in the graph above?

A) $y = -(x - 3)(x + 1)$

B) $y = -(x + 3)(x - 1)$

C) $y = -(x + 3)(x + 4)$

D) $y = -(x - 1)(x + 4)$

14

The profit that a donut shop makes can be expressed by the equation $P = -4(x - 3)^2 + 2,000$, where x is the price per donut sold (in dollars). What price, in dollars, should the donut shop charge its customers in order to maximize its profit?

23

In the equation $x^2 + 24x + c = (x + 9)(x + p)$, c and p are constants. If the equation is true for all values of x, what is the value of c ?

A)   33

B)   135

C)   144

D)   216

ANALYSIS IN SCIENCE

If some of the questions you've seen so far are reminding you of science class, you're not crazy. One of the "Cross-Test scores" the PSAT aims to measure is called Analysis in Science. This means that questions on science-based ideas will show up in Reading and Writing passages and also in Math questions.

One way this concept will be tested is through word problems. Many of the strategies we've already discussed, such as translating or Plugging In, will help you to answer these questions, regardless of the scientific context.

Here's an example.

17

The electric potential of a point charge Q is given by the equation $V = \dfrac{kQ}{r}$, where V is the charge in volts or Joules per Coulomb, Q is the charge in Coulombs, r is the distance from the charge in meters, and k is a constant equal to $9.0 \times 10^9 \ \text{Nm}^2/\text{C}^2$. If a point charge has an electric potential of 225 volts at a distance of 1 meter from the charge, what is the charge in nanocoulombs? (Note: 1 Coulomb = 10^9 nanocoulombs.)

Here's How to Crack It

Start by identifying the values of all of the variables given. According to the question, $r = 1$, $k = 9.0 \times 10^9$, and $V = 225$ coulombs. The question asks for the charge in nanocoulombs, so multiply 225 by 10^9 and you find that $V = 225 \times 10^9$. Plug these values into the equation to get $225 \times 10^9 = \dfrac{(9.0 \times 10^9)Q}{1}$. Solve for Q by dividing both sides by 9.0×10^9 to get $\dfrac{225 \times 10^9}{9.0 \times 10^9} = Q$, or $\dfrac{225}{9.0} = Q$. So $25 = Q$, and that's your answer.

Sometimes, you will be asked science questions based on a chart or graph. In those cases, carefully look up the numbers in question, do the required calculations, and eliminate answers that aren't true.

Let's look at one.

───────────────○───────────────

4

Marble Ramp Rolling Times

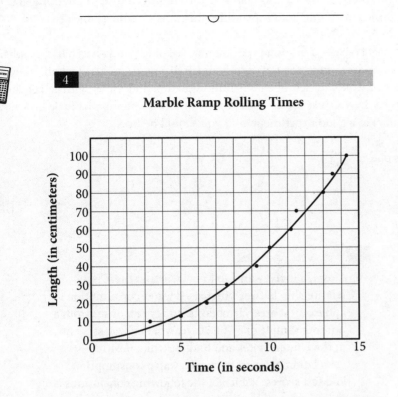

A student is rolling a marble down ramps of varying lengths. The scatterplot above shows the time, in seconds, it takes the marble to roll down each ramp. Based on the curve of best fit to the data represented, which of the following is the closest to the expected length of a ramp if a marble takes 12 seconds to roll down?

A) 61

B) 72

C) 79

D) 84

Here's How to Crack It

Roll time is shown on the horizontal axis of the graph, given in seconds. Look for the mark indicating 12 seconds on this axis; then draw a vertical line from that mark to the curve of best fit. Once you hit it, draw a horizontal line over to the vertical axis. It should hit between 60 and 80 centimeters, right around 70. This makes (B) the credited response, since it is slightly closer to the mark for 80. Draw your lines carefully, using your scantron as a straightedge if necessary, since three of these answer choices are between 60 and 80.

───────────────○───────────────

You may also be asked to graph the data presented in a table. Your knowledge of graphing in the *xy*-plane should help you with most of those. If anything gets too tricky, consider skipping it and spending your time on something else.

The last science-based question type you may see doesn't involve charts, graphs, or equations. In fact, these don't even look much like math problems at all. They will have a lot of words to describe a scientific situation and ask about the conclusion that can be drawn. Just use a lot of Process of Elimination and a little knowledge of what makes a good experiment, and you should be fine.

Try this one.

15

A psychologist wants to know whether there is a relationship between increased water consumption and exam scores. He obtains survey responses from a random sample of 3,500 20-year-old college students in the United States and finds a strong positive correlation between increased water consumption and test scores. Which of the following conclusions is well-supported by the data?

A) There is a positive association between increased water consumption and test scores for 20-year-olds in the United States.

B) There is a positive association between increased water consumption and test scores for adults in the United States.

C) High test scores are caused by increased water consumption for 20-year-olds in the United States.

D) High test scores are caused by increased water consumption for adults in the United States.

Here's How to Crack It

Consider each answer choice one at a time and use Process of Elimination. Choice (A) merely restates what the evidence says, which makes it a safe conclusion, so keep it. Choice (B) is similar but shifts from "20-year-old college students" to "adults." This is a less safe conclusion than (A), because it generalizes from a more particular group, so eliminate (B). Choices (C) and (D) both introduce the idea of causation. This is a problem—no information was given about cause. Maybe people who tend to score higher on tests are also smart enough to drink more water, or maybe there is another factor causing both high test scores and increased water consumption. Eliminate (C) and (D) and choose (A).

MEANING IN CONTEXT

Some questions, instead of asking you to come up with an equation, just want you to recognize what a part of the equation stands for. It sounds like a simple enough task, but when you look at the equation, they have made it really hard to see what is going on. For this reason, Meaning in Context questions are a great opportunity to plug in real numbers and start to see how the equation really works!

First things first, though, you want to think about your POOD: Does this question fit into your pacing goals? It might take a bit of legwork to get an answer, and you may need that time to go collect points on easier, quicker questions.

If this question does fit into your pacing plan, you should read carefully, label everything you can in the equation, and POE to get rid of any answer choices that are clearly on the wrong track. Then, it's time to plug some of your own numbers in to see what is going on in there.

Here's an example:

7

$$n = 1,273 - 4p$$

The equation above was used by the cafeteria in a large public high school to model the relationship between the number of slices of pizza, n, sold daily and the price of a slice of pizza, p, in dollars. What does the number 4 represent in this equation?

A) For every $4 the price of pizza decreases, the cafeteria sells 1 more slice of pizza.

B) For every dollar the price of pizza decreases, the cafeteria sells 4 more slices of pizza.

C) For every $4 the price of pizza increases, the cafeteria sells 1 more slice of pizza.

D) For every dollar the price of pizza increases, the cafeteria sells 4 more slices of pizza.

Here's How to Crack It

First, read the question very carefully, and use your pencil to label the variables. You know that p is the price of pizza, and n is the number of slices, so you can add that information to the equation. If you can, eliminate answer choices that don't make sense. But what if you can't eliminate anything, or you can eliminate only an answer choice or two?

Even with everything labeled, this equation is difficult to decode, so it's time to plug in! Try a few of your own numbers in the equation, and you will get a much better understanding of what is happening.

Let's try it out with $p = 2$. When you put 2 in for p, $n = 1,273 - 4(2)$ or $1,265$.

So, when $p = 2$, $n = 1,265$. In other words, at \$2 a slice, the cafeteria sells 1,265 slices.

When $p = 3$, $n = 1,261$, so at \$3 a slice, the cafeteria sells 1,261 slices.

When $p = 4$, $n = 1,257$, so at \$4 a slice, the cafeteria sells 1,257 slices.

So now, let's use POE. First of all, is the cafeteria selling more pizza as the price goes up? No, as the price of pizza goes up, the cafeteria sells fewer slices of pizza. That means you can eliminate (C) and (D).

Choice (A) says that for every \$4 the price goes down, the cafeteria sells 1 more slice of pizza. Does your plugging in back that up? No. The cafeteria sells 8 more slices of pizza when the price drops from \$4 to \$2, so (A) is no good.

Now, let's take a look at (B). Does the cafeteria sell 4 more slices of pizza for every dollar the price drops? Yes! Choice (B) is the correct answer.

───────○───────

Here are the steps for using Plugging In to solve Meaning in Context questions:

Meaning In Context

1. Read the question carefully. Make sure you know which part of the equation you are being asked to identify.
2. Use your pencil to label the parts of the equation you can identify.
3. Eliminate any answer choices that clearly describe the wrong part of the equation, or go against what you have labelled.
4. Plug in! Use your own numbers to start seeing what is happening in the equation.
5. Use POE again, using the information you learned from plugging in real numbers, until you can get it down to one answer choice. Or, get it down to as few choices as you can, and guess.

Let's look at a slightly different one now.

10

$$7x + y = 133$$

Jeffrey has set a monthly budget for purchasing frozen blended mocha drinks from his local SpendBucks coffee shop. The equation above can be used to model the amount of his budget, y, in dollars that remains after buying coffee for x days in a month. What does it mean that (19, 0) is a solution to this equation?

A) Jeffrey starts the month with a budget of $19.

B) Jeffrey spends $19 on coffee every day.

C) It takes 19 days for Jeffrey to drink 133 cups of coffee.

D) It takes 19 days for Jeffrey to run out of money in his budget for purchasing coffee.

Here's How to Crack It

Start by labeling the x and the y in the equation to keep track of what they stand for. Use your pencil to write "days" above the x and "budget" above the y. So $7 \times$ days + budget = 133. Hmm, still not very clear, is it? One way to approach this is to plug in the point (19, 0). If x = days = 19 when y = budget = 0, then Jeffrey will have no budget left after 19 days. This matches (D).

If you have trouble seeing this, you can use the answer choices to help you plug in. If (A) is true, the budget at the start of the month, when days = 0, is $19. Plug these values into the equation to see if it is true. Is $7 \times 0 + 19 = 133$? Not at all, so eliminate (A). If (B) is true, Jeffrey drinks a lot of coffee! Let's try some numbers and see if it works. For $x = 1$, the equation becomes $7(1) + y = 133$ or $y = 126$, and for $x = 2$, it is $7(2) + y = 133$ or $y = 119$. The difference in y, the budget remaining, is $126 - 119 = 7$, so that's not $7 per day. Eliminate (B) so only (C) and (D) remain. These both have 19 for the number of days, and the point (19, 0) would indicate that 19 is the x value, or days. If you saw that right away—great! That would allow you to skip right to testing (C) and (D).

For (C), you can plug in 19 for days in the equation to get $7 \times 19 + $ budget = 133, or budget = 0. Does that tell you how many cups of coffee Jeffrey drank? You have no information about the cost of a single cup of coffee, so the answer can't be (C). It does tell you, however, that after 19 days, Jeffrey has no budget left, so (D) is not only the one remaining answer, but it is also the correct one!

Drill 3

Answers can be found in Part III.

6

A shipping company pays a driver a fixed fee for each delivery, and deducts a separate fee daily for the use of the company's delivery truck. The driver's net pay in dollars, P, for one day is given by the equation $P = 8d - 40$, where d is the number of deliveries made in one day. What does the number 40 most likely represent?

A) The amount, in dollars, that the company deducts for use of the delivery truck

B) The amount, in dollars, that the driver is paid for each delivery

C) The average number of deliveries per hour made by the driver

D) The total number of deliveries made per day by the driver

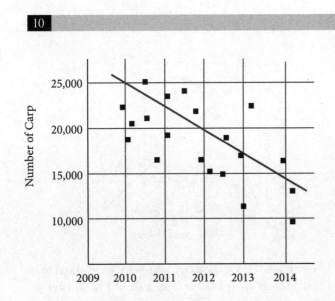

Between 2009 and 2014, researchers tracked populations of Crucian carp in the Ohio River. The graph above displays population sizes as counted by the researchers. According to the best-fit line, what is the approximate average yearly decrease in the number of Crucian carp?

A)   1

B)   2.5

C)   1,200

D)   2,500

A group of students decided to have a car wash to raise funds for the school. The students charged the same rate to wash each car, and they paid for cleaning supplies out of the proceeds. If the net amount, $N(c)$, in dollars, raised from washing c cars is given by the function $N(c) = 8c - 0.40c$, which of the following can be deduced from the function?

A)   The students paid a total of $8 for cleaning supplies.

B)   The students paid a total of $40 for cleaning supplies.

C)   The students paid $0.40 per car for cleaning supplies.

D)   The students paid $8 per car for cleaning supplies.

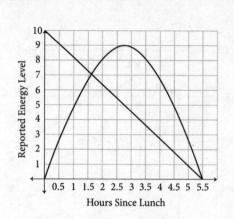

Hours Since Lunch

Two employees at a certain company were asked to gauge their energy levels on a scale of 1 to 10 after eating lunch at noon. The results were averaged and plotted as illustrated in the above figure. Which of the following statements is most consistent with the given data?

A) Both employees experienced the same fluctuation in energy during the afternoon hours.

B) Both employees were drowsy after eating big lunches.

C) One of the employees consumed energy-boosting foods and drinks and became less energetic throughout the afternoon.

D) One of the employees consumed foods that resulted in her feeling more energetic throughout the day.

11

Delphine is studying the growth of bacteria in a petri dish. She grows 100 colonies of bacteria in dishes at varying temperatures to find the optimal temperature for bacteria growth. The temperature of the 10 colonies with the most rapid growth is used to determine the optimal temperature range, which Delphine finds to be from 30° to 37° C, inclusive. Which of the following inequalities represents the optimal temperature range, t, for bacteria growth?

A) $|t + 7| \leq 37$

B) $|t - 3.5| \leq 33.5$

C) $|t - 30| \leq 7$

D) $|t - 33.5| \leq 3.5$

Summary

o   Given a function, you put an x value in and get an $f(x)$ or y value out.

o   Look for ways to use Plugging In and PITA on functions questions.

o   For questions about the graphs of functions, remember that $f(x) = y$.

o   If the graph contains a labeled point or the question gives you a point, plug it into the equations in the answers and eliminate any that aren't true.

o   To find a point of intersection, set the equations equal, plug a given point into both equations to see if it works, or graph the equations on your calculator when it is allowed.

o   When solving quadratic equations, you may need to FOIL or factor to get the equation into the easiest form for the question task.

o   To solve for the roots of a quadratic equation, set it equal to zero by moving all the terms to the left side of the equation, or use the quadratic formula:

$$x = \frac{-b \pm \sqrt{b^2 - 4ac}}{2a}$$

o   The vertex form of a parabola equation is $y = a(x - h)^2 + k$, where (h, k) is the vertex. To get a parabola in the standard form into vertex form, complete the square.

o   Plugging In can also be used on Meaning In Context questions. If a question asks you to identify a part of an equation, plug your own amounts into the equation so you can start to see what is going on.

o   Analysis in Science questions may seem weird, but they can usually be handled with the same strategies as those used for other math questions. Plug in or translate, read the chart or text carefully, and always use Process of Elimination to get rid of answers that don't match the data or don't make sense.

o   If you come across a hard Meaning in Context question or Science question, see if you can eliminate anything and make a guess. If not, find another question to do!

Chapter 8
Additional Topics

The PSAT has a clever name for the rest of the concepts tested—Additional Topics. Well, maybe it's not that clever. It consists of some geometry concepts and possibly a question about imaginary numbers. While there are a wide variety of geometry ideas that could be tested, these Additional Topics will really make up only a small fraction of the PSAT. Spend time on this chapter only after you have mastered the topics and techniques in the previous three chapters.

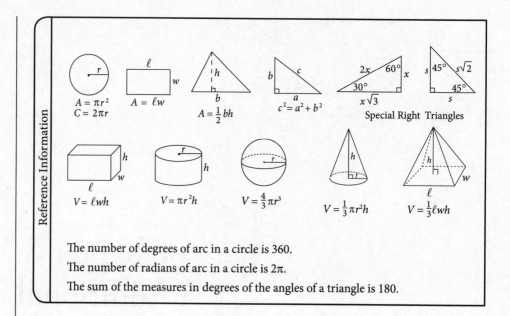

The number of degrees of arc in a circle is 360.

The number of radians of arc in a circle is 2π.

The sum of the measures in degrees of the angles of a triangle is 180.

GEOMETRY

LINES AND ANGLES

Common sense might tell you what a line is, but for this test you are going to have to learn the particulars of a line, a ray, and a line segment.

A **line** continues on in each direction forever. You need only two points to form a line, but that line does not end at those points. A straight line has 180 degrees on each side.

A **ray** is a line with one distinct endpoint. Again, you need only two points to designate a ray, but one of those points is where it stops—it continues on forever in the other direction. A ray has 180 degrees as well.

A **line segment** is a line with two distinct endpoints. It requires two points, and it is the length from one point to the other. A line segment has 180 degrees.

Whenever you have angles on a line, remember *the rule of 180*: The angles on any line must add up to 180. These angles are called *supplementary angles*. In the figure below, what is the value of x? We know that $2x + x$ must add up to 180, so we know that $3x = 180$. This makes $x = 60$.

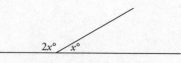

If two lines cross each other, they make *vertical angles*—that is, angles opposite each other when two lines intersect. These angles will always have the same measure. In the figure below, z and x are vertical angles, and y and the 130° angle are vertical angles. Also, we know that z must equal 50, since $130 + z$ must equal 180. We know that y is 130, since it is across from the angle 130. We also know that x is 50, since it is across from z.

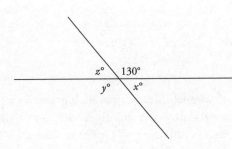

Any time you have two parallel lines and a line that crosses them, you have two kinds of angles: big angles and small angles. All of the big angles have the same measure, and all of the small angles have the same measure. In the following figure, angles a, d, e, and h all have the same measure; angles b, c, f, and g also all have the same measure. The sum of the measure of any big angle plus any small angle equals 180 degrees.

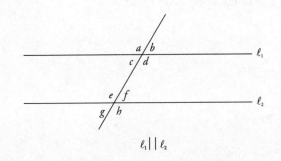

FOUR-SIDED FIGURES

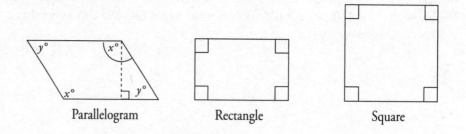

Parallelogram   Rectangle   Square

Thinking Inside the Box
Here's a progression of quadrilaterals from least specific to most specific:
quadrilateral = 4-sided figure
↓
parallelogram = a quadrilateral in which opposite sides are parallel
↓
rectangle = a parallelogram in which all angles equal 90°
↓
square = a rectangle in which all angles and all sides are equal

A figure with two sets of parallel sides is a **parallelogram**. In a parallelogram, the opposite angles are equal, and any adjacent angles add up to 180 degrees. (In the left-hand figure above, $x + y = 180$ degrees.) Opposite sides are also equal. The sum of all angles of a parallelogram is 360 degrees.

If all of the angles are also right angles, then the figure is a **rectangle**. And if all of the sides are the same length, then the figure is a **square**.

The *area* of a square, rectangle, or parallelogram is *length × width*. (In the parallelogram above, the length is shown by the dotted line.)

The *perimeter* of any figure is the sum of the lengths of its sides. A trapezoid with sides of 6, 8, 10, and 8 has a perimeter of 32.

Drill 1

Answers can be found in Part III.

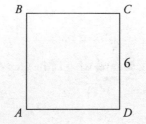

a. What is the area of square *ABCD* above? _____

b. What is the perimeter of square *ABCD* above? _____

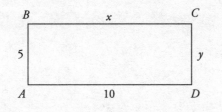

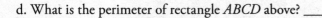

c. If *ABCD* is a rectangle, $x =$ _____ $y =$ _____

d. What is the perimeter of rectangle *ABCD* above? _____

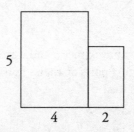

e. If the above figure is composed of two rectangles, what is the perimeter of the figure?_____

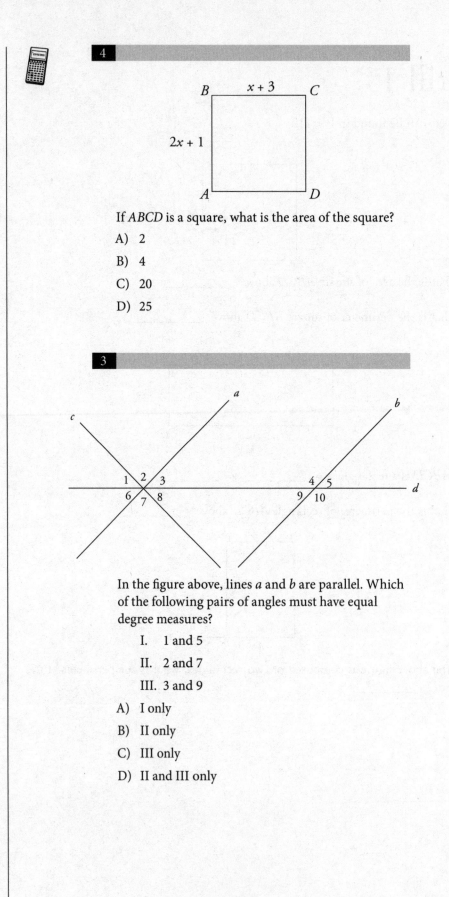

4

If *ABCD* is a square, what is the area of the square?

A) 2

B) 4

C) 20

D) 25

3

In the figure above, lines *a* and *b* are parallel. Which of the following pairs of angles must have equal degree measures?

    I.   1 and 5

    II. 2 and 7

    III. 3 and 9

A) I only

B) II only

C) III only

D) II and III only

TRIANGLES

The sum of the angles inside a triangle must equal 180 degrees. This means that if you know two of the angles in a triangle, you can always solve for the third. Since we know that two of the angles in the following figure are 90 and 60 degrees, we can solve for the third angle, which must be 30 degrees. (Note: The little square in the bottom corner of the triangle indicates a right angle, which is 90°.)

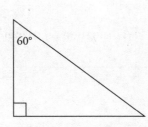

An **isosceles triangle** is a triangle that has two sides that are equal. Angles that are opposite equal sides must be equal. In the figure below, we have an isosceles triangle. Since $AB = BC$, we know that angles x and y are equal. And since their sum must be 150 degrees (to make a total of 180 degrees when we add the last angle), they each must be 75 degrees.

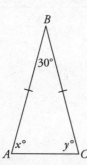

The **area** of a triangle is $\frac{1}{2}$ *base* × *height*. Note that the height is always perpendicular to the base.

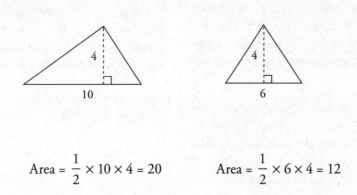

$$\text{Area} = \frac{1}{2} \times 10 \times 4 = 20 \qquad \text{Area} = \frac{1}{2} \times 6 \times 4 = 12$$

An **equilateral triangle** has all three sides equal and all of its angles equal to 60 degrees.

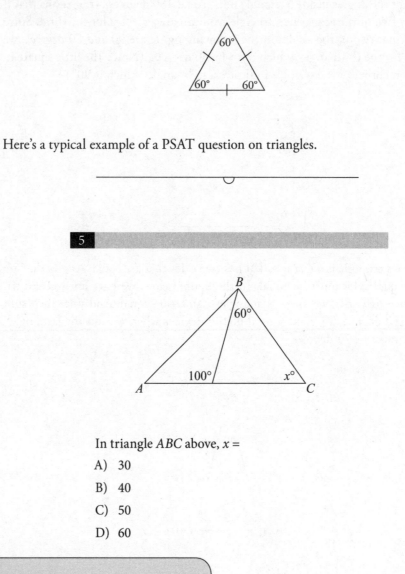

Here's a typical example of a PSAT question on triangles.

5

In triangle *ABC* above, *x* =

A) 30

B) 40

C) 50

D) 60

Being Aggressive on Geometry Problems

The most important problem-solving technique for tackling PSAT geometry is to learn to be aggressive. This means, whenever you have a diagram, ask yourself: *What else do I know?* Write everything you can think of on your booklet. You may not see right away why it's important, but write it down anyway. Chances are good that you will be making progress toward the answer, without even knowing it.

ETS is also fond of disguising familiar figures within more complex shapes by extending lines, overlapping figures, or combining several basic shapes. So be on the lookout for the basic figures hidden in complicated shapes.

Here's How to Crack It

We know that the angle adjacent to the 100-degree angle must equal 80 degrees since we know that a straight line is 180 degrees. Fill it in on your diagram. Now, since we know that the sum of the angles contained in a triangle must equal 180 degrees, we know that $80 + 60 + x = 180$, so $x = 40$. That's (B).

The Pythagorean Theorem

Whenever you have a right triangle, you can use the Pythagorean theorem. The theorem says that the sum of the squares of the legs of the triangle (the sides that form the right angle) will equal the square of the hypotenuse (the side opposite the right angle).

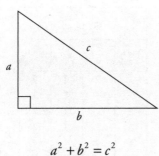

$$a^2 + b^2 = c^2$$

Two of the most common ratios of sides that fit the Pythagorean theorem are $3 : 4 : 5$ and $5 : 12 : 13$. Since these are ratios, any multiples of these numbers will also work, such as $6 : 8 : 10$, and $30 : 40 : 50$.

Try the following example.

_____

14

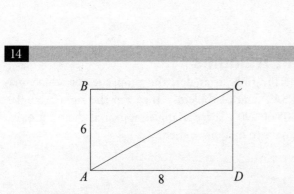

If *ABCD* is a rectangle, what is the perimeter of triangle *ABC* ?

	⑦	⑦	
⊙	⊙	⊙	⊙
	⓪	⓪	⓪
①	①	①	①
②	②	②	②
③	③	③	③
④	④	④	④
⑤	⑤	⑤	⑤
⑥	⑥	⑥	⑥
⑦	⑦	⑦	⑦
⑧	⑧	⑧	⑧
⑨	⑨	⑨	⑨

Here's How to Crack It

We can use the Pythagorean theorem to figure out the length of the diagonal of the rectangle—since it has sides 6 and 8, its diagonal must be 10. (If you remembered that this is one of those well-known Pythagorean ratios, you didn't actually have to do the calculations.) Therefore, the perimeter of the triangle is 6 + 8 + 10, or 24.

2	4		
	⊘	⊘	
⊙	⊙	⊙	⊙
	⓪	⓪	⓪
①	①	①	①
●	②	②	②
③	③	③	③
④	●	④	④
⑤	⑤	⑤	⑤
⑥	⑥	⑥	⑥
⑦	⑦	⑦	⑦
⑧	⑧	⑧	⑧
⑨	⑨	⑨	⑨

Special Right Triangles

There are two specific right triangles, the properties of which may play a role in some harder PSAT math problems. They are the right triangles with angles 45°-45°-90° and 30°-60°-90°. These triangles appear at the front of each Math section, so you don't have to memorize them.

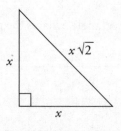

An isosceles right triangle has angles that measure 45, 45, and 90 degrees. Whenever you have a 45°-45°-90° triangle with sides of x, the hypotenuse will always be $x\sqrt{2}$. This means that if one of the legs of the triangle measures 3, then the hypotenuse will be $3\sqrt{2}$.

This right triangle is important because it is half of a square. Understanding the 45°-45°-90° triangle will allow you to easily find the diagonal of a square from its side, or find the side of a square from its diagonal.

Here's an example.

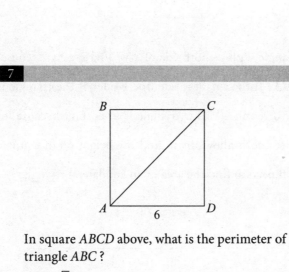

In square *ABCD* above, what is the perimeter of triangle *ABC* ?

A) $6\sqrt{2}$

B) 8

C) $12 + \sqrt{2}$

D) $12 + 6\sqrt{2}$

Here's How to Crack It

This question looks like a question about a square, and it certainly is in part, but it's really more about the two triangles formed by the diagonal.

In this square, we know that each of the triangles formed by the diagonal *AC* is a 45°-45°-90° right triangle. Since the square has a side of 6, using the 45°-45°-90° right triangle rule, each of the sides is 6 and the diagonal is $6\sqrt{2}$. Therefore, the perimeter of the triangle is $6 + 6 + 6\sqrt{2}$, or $12 + 6\sqrt{2}$ and the answer is (D).

The other important right triangle to understand is the 30°-60°-90° right triangle.

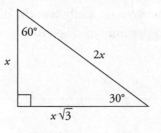

A 30°-60°-90° triangle with a short side of x will have a hypotenuse of $2x$ and a middle side of $x\sqrt{3}$. If the smallest side (the x side) of the triangle is 5, then the sides measure 5, $5\sqrt{3}$, and 10. This triangle is important because it is half of an equilateral triangle, and it allows us to find the height of an equilateral triangle, which is what we'll need to find the area of an equilateral triangle.

Try the following.

Triangle Tip
An easy way to figure out the height of an equilateral triangle is to take half of its side and multiply it by the square root of 3.

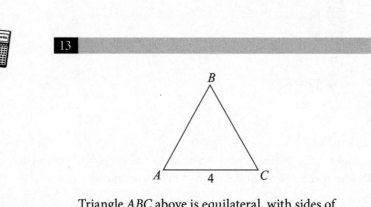

13

Triangle ABC above is equilateral, with sides of length 4. What is its area?

A) 3

B) $4\sqrt{2}$

C) $4\sqrt{3}$

D) 8

Here's How to Crack It

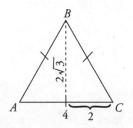

To find the area of the triangle, we need to know the base and the height. The question tells you that the base (line segment *AC*) is 4; now we need to find the height, which is *perpendicular* to the base. You can create the height by drawing a line from angle *B* straight down to the base, as you can see in the drawing above. Now you have two 30°-60°-90° triangles, and you can use the rules of 30-60-90 triangles to figure out the height. Half of the base would be 2, and that's the side across from the 30 degree angle, so you would multiply it by $\sqrt{3}$ to get the height.

Now we know that the base is 4 and the height is $2\sqrt{3}$, so plugging those numbers into the formula for area of a triangle, we get $A = \dfrac{1}{2} \times 4 \times 2\sqrt{3}$, which equals $4\sqrt{3}$. Thus, (C) is the correct answer.

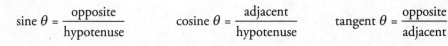

SOHCAHTOA

Trigonometry will likely appear on your PSAT. But fear not! Many trigonometry questions you will see mostly require you to know the basic definitions of the three main trigonometric functions. SOHCAHTOA is a way to remember the three functions:

SOHCAHTOA stands for:

$$\text{sine} = \frac{opposite}{hypotenuse}$$

$$\text{cosine} = \frac{adjacent}{hypotenuse}$$

$$\text{tangent} = \frac{opposite}{adjacent}$$

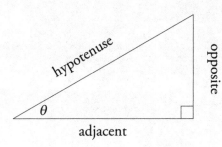

$$\text{sine } \theta = \frac{opposite}{hypotenuse} \qquad \text{cosine } \theta = \frac{adjacent}{hypotenuse} \qquad \text{tangent } \theta = \frac{opposite}{adjacent}$$

Let's see an example:

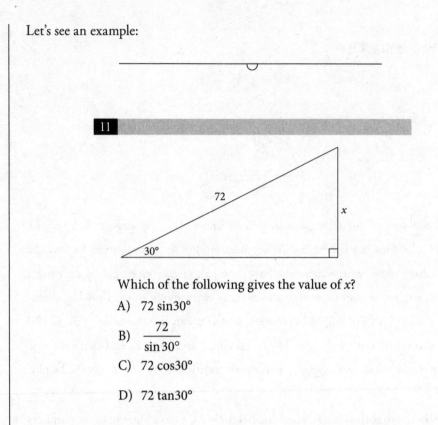

11

Which of the following gives the value of x?

A) 72 sin30°

B) $\dfrac{72}{\sin 30°}$

C) 72 cos30°

D) 72 tan30°

Here's How to Crack It

You know the hypotenuse of the triangle, and you want to find the side opposite the angle. SOHCAHTOA tells you that sine is $\dfrac{\text{opposite}}{\text{hypotenuse}}$, so you want sine. You can eliminate (C) and (D), which do not contain sine. Next, set up the equation using the definition of sine: $\sin 30° = \dfrac{x}{72}$. To solve for x, multiply both sides by 72 and you get 72 sin30° = x. This matches (A).

Similar Triangles

Similar triangles have the same shape, but they are not necessarily the same size. Having the same shape means that the angles of the triangles are identical and that the corresponding sides have the same ratio. Look at the following two similar triangles:

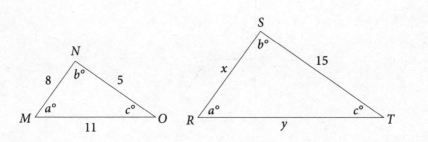

These two triangles both have the same set of angles, but they aren't the same size. Whenever this is true, the sides of one triangle are proportional to those of the other. Notice that sides NO and ST are both opposite the angle that is $a°$. These are called corresponding sides, because they correspond to the same angle. So the lengths of $\overline{NO}$ and $\overline{ST}$ are proportional to each other. In order to figure out the lengths of the other sides we set up a proportion: $\dfrac{MN}{RS} = \dfrac{NO}{ST}$. Now fill in the information that you know: $\dfrac{8}{x} = \dfrac{5}{15}$. Cross-multiply and you find that $x = 24$. You could also figure out the length of y: $\dfrac{NO}{ST} = \dfrac{MO}{RT}$. So, $\dfrac{5}{15} = \dfrac{11}{y}$, and $y = 33$. Whenever you have to deal with sides of similar triangles, just set up a proportion.

Give it a try.

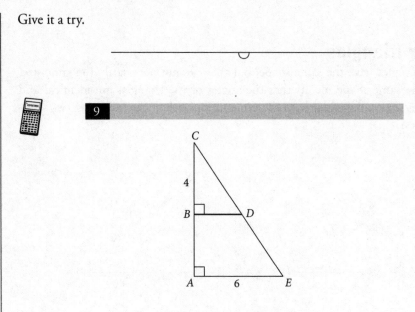

9

Note: Figure not drawn to scale.

If the area of triangle *ACE* is 18, what is the area of triangle *BCD*?

Here's How to Crack It

The formula to find the area of a triangle is $A = \dfrac{1}{2} bh$. Plugging in the area and base of triangle *ACE* as given in the formula gives you the equation $18 = \dfrac{1}{2}(6)h$. Simplify the fraction and you will get $18 = 3h$. Divide both sides by 3 and you can see that the height of triangle *ACE* is 6. Because triangle *ACE* and triangle *BCD* have the same angle measures, they are similar. Therefore, you should create a proportion to find the length of $\overline{BD}$. The proportion should look like this: $\dfrac{4}{x} = \dfrac{6}{6}$, if *x* represents the length of $\overline{BD}$. Simplify your fractions and cross-multiply to see that $x = 4$. Plug the base and height of triangle *BCD* into the area formula: $A = \dfrac{1}{2}(4)(4)$. Simplify the equation and you will see that the area of triangle *BCD* is 8.

Drill 2

Answers can be found in Part III.

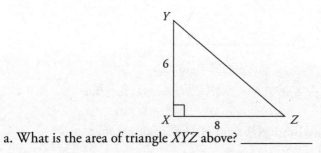

a. What is the area of triangle *XYZ* above? _____

b. What is the length of *YZ*? _____

c. What is the sine of ∠*Z*? _____

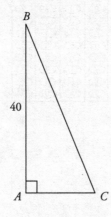

d. If the area of the triangle above is 400, what is the length of *AC*? _____

e. What is the length of *BC*? _____

f. What is the cosine of ∠*C*? _____

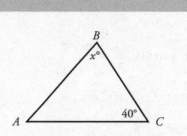

Note: Figure not drawn to scale.

In triangle *ABC* above, if *AB = BC*, what is the value of *x* ?

(Disregard the degree symbol when gridding your answer.)

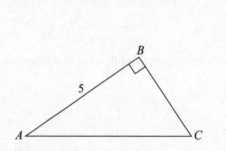

Note: Figure not drawn to scale.

In the figure above, if triangle *ABC* is isosceles, what is the perimeter of the triangle?

A) 12.5

B) $10\sqrt{2}$

C) $10+5\sqrt{2}$

D) $15\sqrt{2}$

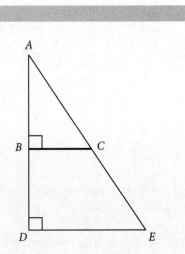

Note: Figure not drawn to scale.

In the figure above, if $AB = 5$, $AC = 13$, and $DE = 24$, what is the value of BD?

A) 12

B) 10

C) 8

D) 5

CIRCLES

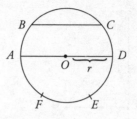

The **radius** of a circle is the distance from the center to the edge of the circle. In the figure above, *OD* is a radius. So is *OA*.

The **diameter** is the distance from one edge, through the center, to the other edge of the circle. The diameter will always be twice the measure of the radius and will always be the longest line you can draw through a circle. In the figure above, *AD* is the diameter.

A **chord** is any line drawn from one point on the edge of the circle to the other. In the figure above, *BC* is a chord. A diameter is also a chord and also the longest chord in a circle.

An **arc** is any section of the circumference (the edge) of the circle. *EF* is an arc in the figure above.

The **circumference** is the distance around the outside edge of the circle. The circumference of a circle with radius *r* is $2\pi r$. A circle with radius of 5 has a circumference of 10π.

The **area** of a circle with radius *r* is πr^2. A circle with a radius of 5 has an area of 25π.

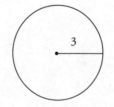

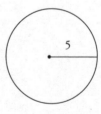

Area = 9π

Circumference = 6π

Area = 25π

Circumference = 10π

Proportionality in a Circle

Here's another rule that plays a role in more advanced circle problems.

> Arc measure is proportional to interior angle measure,
> which is proportional to sector area.

Quick Review
- An interior angle is an angle formed by two radii.
- A sector is the portion of the circle between the two radii.

This means that whatever fraction of the total degree measure is made up by the interior angle, the arc described by that angle is the same fraction of the circumference, and the pie piece created has the same fraction of the area.

Take a look at the figure below:

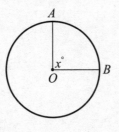

If angle x is equal to 90 degrees, which is one-quarter of 360 degrees, then the arc AB is equal to one-quarter of the circumference of the circle and the area of the sector of the circle enclosed by radii OA and OB is equal to one-quarter of the area of the circle.

To see how this works, try the following question.

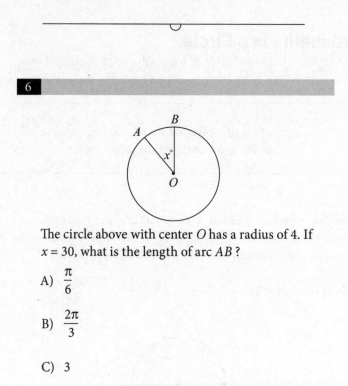

6

The circle above with center O has a radius of 4. If $x = 30$, what is the length of arc AB ?

A) $\dfrac{\pi}{6}$

B) $\dfrac{2\pi}{3}$

C) 3

D) $\dfrac{3\pi}{2}$

Here's How to Crack It

Since the interior angle x is equal to 30 degrees, which is $\dfrac{1}{12}$ of 360 degrees, we know that the arc AB will be equal to $\dfrac{1}{12}$ of the circumference of the circle. Since the circle has radius 4, its circumference will be 8π. Therefore, arc AB will measure $\dfrac{1}{12} \times 8\pi$, or $\dfrac{2\pi}{3}$, (B).

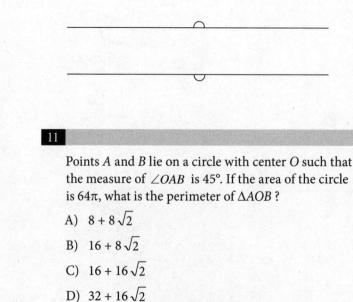

11

Points A and B lie on a circle with center O such that the measure of $\angle OAB$ is 45°. If the area of the circle is 64π, what is the perimeter of $\triangle AOB$?

A) $8 + 8\sqrt{2}$

B) $16 + 8\sqrt{2}$

C) $16 + 16\sqrt{2}$

D) $32 + 16\sqrt{2}$

Here's How to Crack It

This time a diagram isn't given, so drawing the circle should be your first step. Since points A and B lie on the circle, $\overline{OA}$ and $\overline{OB}$ are both radii, and equal in length, making $\triangle AOB$ isosceles. The problem indicates that $\angle OAB$ is 45 degrees, which means that $\angle OBA$ is also 45 degrees, which makes $\triangle AOB$ a 45-45-90 triangle (remember those special right triangles?).

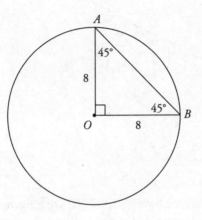

Given the circle's area of 64π, the radii of the circle (which are the legs of the isosceles right triangle) are 8, and the hypotenuse is $8\sqrt{2}$, making the perimeter $8 + 8 + 8\sqrt{2}$, or $16 + 8\sqrt{2}$, which is answer (B).

Tangents to a Circle

A tangent is a line that intersects the edge of a circle at exactly one point. A radius drawn to the point of tangency forms a 90 degree angle with the tangent line. This comes up occasionally on hard problems, so take a look at the example below. As you work through this question, if you're thinking that you'd never know how to do it yourself, there's still a valuable lesson here, and it's that this question is not in your POOD, so you should look instead for a plug in or something you're more familiar with.

27

In the figure above, $\overline{NP}$ and $\overline{NQ}$ are tangent to the circle with center O at points P and Q, respectively. If the area of the shaded region is 24π, what is the circumference of the circle?

A) 8π

B) 12π

C) 16π

D) 40π

Here's How to Crack It

The key is remembering that any line or line segment drawn tangent to a circle is perpendicular to a radius drawn from the center of the circle to that tangent point; this means both $\angle OQN$ and $\angle OPN$ equal 90 degrees. With $\angle QNP$ given as 45 degrees, that leaves the central $\angle QOP$ of quadrilateral $QNPO$. Since all quadrilaterals contain 360 degrees and since 45 of the remaining 180 degrees are accounted for, that remaining angle must be 135 degrees. As all circles contain 360 degrees of arc, this means the shaded area represents $\frac{135}{360}$ or $\frac{3}{8}$ of the area of the entire circle.

Remember, we want to write down the formulas for quantities the question talks about, so that's $A = \pi r^2$ and $C = 2\pi r$. So far we don't have anything we can put directly into a formula, so what do we know? We're told that the area of the shaded sector is 24π, so we can use that to figure out the area of the whole circle, because we know it's proportional to the central angle. In fact, we've figured out that this part of the circle is $\frac{3}{8}$ of the whole, so the whole area must be $\frac{8}{3}$ times the sector, so $\left(\frac{8}{3}\right) \times 24\pi = 64\pi$ (this is a shortcut to using a proportion, which looks like this: $\frac{3}{8} = \frac{24\pi}{x}$, which if we cross-multiply and solve for x gives us 64π). Now we can use the first formula and solve for $r = 8$. We can put this right into the second formula and get $C = 16\pi$, so the answer is (C).

The Equation of a Circle

One last thing you may need to know about a circle is what the equation of a circle in the *xy*-plane looks like.

The equation of a circle is as follows:

$$(x - h)^2 + (y - k)^2 = r^2$$

In the circle equation, the center of the circle is the point (h, k), and the radius of the circle is r.

Let's look at one.

13

What is the equation of a circle with center $(2, 4)$ that passes through the point $(-6, -2)$?

A) $(x + 2)^2 + (y + 4)^2 = 100$

B) $(x + 2)^2 + (y + 4)^2 = \sqrt{20}$

C) $(x - 2)^2 + (y - 4)^2 = 100$

D) $(x - 2)^2 + (y - 4)^2 = \sqrt{20}$

Here's How to Crack It

Take the given center and put it into the circle equation above. Plugging in $h = 2$ and $k = 4$, you get $(x - 2)^2 + (y - 4)^2 = r^2$. In the circle equation, x and y are the coordinates of a point on the circle. Plugging in the point $(-6, -2)$, you get $(-6 - 2)^2 + (-2 - 4)^2 = r^2$, which simplifies to $(-8)^2 + (-6)^2 = r^2$, or $64 + 36 = r^2$. This means $r^2 = 100$, so the equation is $(x - 2)^2 + (y - 4)^2 = 100$. The correct answer is (C).

There is a chance that you might see a circle equation that is not in the form shown above. If this happens, you will need to complete the square to get the given equation into the proper form. Just follow the steps listed for completing the square in the Quadratics section of the previous chapter. The only difference is that you'll have to do it twice—for the x terms and for the y terms. You may decide, however, that such a question is not worth your time. In that case, move on to something else!

Drill 3

Answers can be found in Part III.

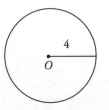

a. What is the area of the circle above with center O? _____

b. What is its circumference? _____

16

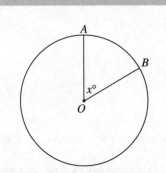

The circle shown above has its center at O. If $x = 60$ and the length of arc AB is 2π, what is the area of circle O?

A) 36π

B) 12π

C) 6π

D) 6

18

A circle with center O has diameter $\overline{AB}$. Segment $\overline{AC}$ is tangent to the circle at point A and has a length of 5. If the area of the circle is 36π, what is the perimeter of triangle ABC?

A) 15

B) 25

C) 30

D) 60

VOLUME

Volume questions on the PSAT can seem intimidating at times. The PSAT sometimes gives you questions featuring unusual shapes such as pyramids and spheres. Luckily, at the beginning of the Math sections (and the beginning of this chapter), you're given a box with all the formulas you will ever need for volume questions on the PSAT.

Let's look at an example:

15

A sphere has a volume of 36π. What is the surface area of the sphere? (The surface area of a sphere is given by the formula $A = 4\pi r^2$.)

A) 3π

B) 9π

C) 27π

D) 36π

Here's How to Crack It

Start by writing down the formula for volume of a sphere from the beginning of the chapter: $V = \frac{4}{3}\pi r^3$. Put what you know into the equation: $36\pi = \frac{4}{3}\pi r^3$. From this you can solve for r. Divide both sides by π to get $36 = \frac{4}{3}r^3$. Multiply both sides by 3 to clear the fraction: $36(3) = 4r^3$. Note we left 36 as 36, because the next step is to divide both sides by 4, and 36 divided by 4 is 9, so $9(3) = r^3$ or $27 = r^3$. Take the cube root of both sides to get $r = 3$. Now that you have the radius, use the formula provided to find the surface area: $A = 4\pi(3)^2$, which comes out to 36π, which is (D).

PLUGGING IN ON GEOMETRY

You can also plug in on geometry questions, just as you can for algebra. Any time that you have variables in the answer choices, or hidden variables, plug in! As long as you follow all the rules of geometry while you solve, you'll get the answer.

Take a look at this problem.

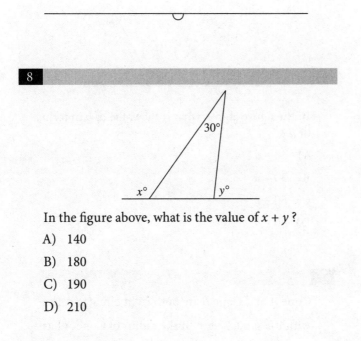

In the figure above, what is the value of $x + y$?

A) 140

B) 180

C) 190

D) 210

Here's How to Crack It

We could solve this problem using algebra, but why? We can plug in whatever numbers we want for the other angles inside the triangle—as long as we make sure that all the angles in the triangle add up to 180 degrees. So let's plug in 60 and 90 for the other angles inside that triangle. Now we can solve for x and y: If the angle next to x is 60 degrees, then x will be equal to 120. If the angle next to y is equal to 90 degrees, then y will be equal to 90. This makes the sum $x + y$ equal to 120 + 90, or 210. No matter what numbers we pick for the angles inside the triangle, we'll always get the same answer, (D).

Drill 4

Try to plug in on the following questions. Answers can be found in Part III.

3

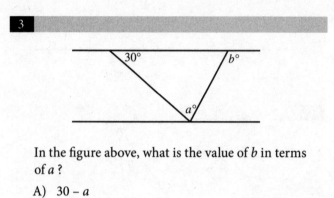

In the figure above, what is the value of b in terms of a ?

A) $30 - a$

B) $30 + a$

C) $60 + a$

D) $80 - a$

7

Cone A and Cone B are both right circular cones with the same height. If the radius of Cone A has $\dfrac{3}{4}$ of the radius of Cone B, which of the following is the ratio of the volume of Cone A to the volume of Cone B?

A) $27 : 64$

B) $9 : 16$

C) $3 : 4$

D) $4 : 3$

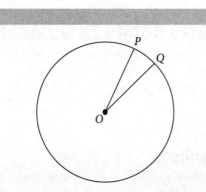

In the figure above, O is the center of the circle, the radius of the circle is x and the length of minor arc PQ is $\dfrac{\pi x}{18}$. What is the area of sector POQ?

A) $\dfrac{\pi x^2}{36}$

B) $\dfrac{\pi x^2}{18}$

C) $\dfrac{\pi x^2}{9}$

D) $\dfrac{\pi x^2}{3}$

IMAGINARY AND COMPLEX NUMBERS

So far you have been working with real numbers, which are any numbers that you can place on a number line. The PSAT may ask you to do mathematical operations with imaginary or complex numbers.

Imaginary Numbers

An imaginary number, very simply, is the square root of a negative number. Since there is no way to have a real number that is the square root of a negative number, mathematicians needed to come up with a way to represent this concept when writing equations. They use an italicized lowercase "I" to do that: $i = \sqrt{-1}$, and the PSAT will likely tell you that in any problem involving imaginary numbers.

Another common piece of information you will need to know about i is how it behaves when it is raised to a power. Here is i raised to the powers 1 through 8. Can you complete the next four values of i in the series?

$$i = \sqrt{-1} \qquad\qquad i^5 = \sqrt{-1} \qquad\qquad i^9 = ?$$

$$i^2 = -1 \qquad\qquad i^6 = -1 \qquad\qquad i^{10} = ?$$

$$i^3 = -\sqrt{-1} = -i \qquad\qquad i^7 = -\sqrt{-1} = -i \qquad\qquad i^{11} = ?$$

$$i^4 = 1 \qquad\qquad i^8 = 1 \qquad\qquad i^{12} = ?$$

Did you notice anything about the answer? If you said that there is a repeating pattern, then you are correct. This pattern will be helpful in answering questions containing imaginary and complex numbers.

Complex Numbers

Complex numbers are another way in which the PSAT may test the concept of imaginary numbers. A complex number is one that has a real component and an imaginary component connected by addition or subtraction. $8 + 7i$ and $3 - 4i$ are two examples of complex numbers.

You may be tested on complex numbers in a variety of ways. ETS may ask you to add or subtract the complex numbers. When you are completing these operations, you can treat i as a variable. Just combine the like terms in these expressions and then simplify (don't forget to distribute the subtraction sign).

Here is an example:

7

If $i = \sqrt{-1}$, which of the following is equivalent to $(4 + 3i) - (2 - 2i)$?

A) 3

B) $2 + i$

C) $6 + i$

D) $2 + 5i$

Here's How to Crack It

Start by distributing the negative sign: $(4 + 3i) - (2 - 2i) = 4 + 3i - 2 + 2i$. Be careful with the negative signs, which are often the trickiest part of imaginary number questions. The real parts are 4 and -2, which can be added together to get 2. The imaginary parts are $3i$ and $2i$. These can also be added together to get $5i$. Note you cannot combine real parts and imaginary parts in a complex number, so the answer is simply (D).

The PSAT may also ask you to multiply complex numbers. Again you can treat i as a variable as you work through the multiplication as if you were multiplying binominals. In other words, use FOIL to work through the problem. The only difference is that you substitute -1 for i^2.

Let's look at one.

10

If $i^2 = -1$ and $a = (i + 6)$, which of the following is the result of squaring a ?

A) $36i$

B) $i + 36$

C) $12i + 35$

D) $12i + 36$

Here's How to Crack It

The question states that $a = (i + 6)$, so the square of a must be $(i + 6)^2$. Expand the squared term using FOIL and you get $i^2 + 6i + 6i + 36$. Combine like terms to get $i^2 + 12i + 36$. Since $i^2 = -1$, you can simplify further to $(-1) + 12i + 36$, or $12i + 35$, which is (C).

Note that this question would appear in the calculator section. Your calculator has a handy i button, so feel free to use it when allowed if things get tricky.

Summary

o Be sure to review your basic geometry rules before the test; often, problems hinge on knowing that vertical angles are equal or that a quadrilateral is 360°.

o On all geometry problems, draw figures out and aggressively fill in everything you know.

o When two parallel lines are cut by a third line, the small angles are equal, the big angles are equal, and the sum of a big angle and a small angle is 180°.

o The perimeter of a rectangle is the sum of the lengths of its sides. The area of a rectangle is *length × width*.

o The perimeter of a triangle is the sum of the lengths of its sides. The area of a triangle is 1/2 *base × height*.

o Knowing the Pythagorean theorem, common right triangles (such as 3-4-5 and 5-12-13), and special right triangles (45°-45°-90° and 30°-60°-90°) will help you figure out angles and lengths in a right triangle.

o For trigonometry questions, remember SOHCAHTOA:

- sine $= \dfrac{opposite}{hypotenuse}$

- cosine $= \dfrac{adjacent}{hypotenuse}$

- tangent $= \dfrac{opposite}{adjacent}$

o Similar triangles have the same angles and their lengths are proportional.

o   The circumference of a circle is $2\pi r$. The area of a circle is πr^2.

o   Circles that show an interior angle (an angle that extends from the center of the circle) have proportionality. The interior angle over the whole degree measure (360°) equals the same fraction as the arc enclosed by that angle over the circumference. Likewise, both of these fractions are equal to the area of the segment over the entire area of the circle.

o   When you see a line that is "tangent to" a circle, remember two things:
    • The line intersects the circle at exactly one point.
    • The radius of the circle that intersects the tangent line is perpendicular (90°) to that tangent line.

o   The formulas to compute the volumes of many three-dimensional figures are supplied in the instructions at the front of both Math sections.

o   When plugging in with geometry problems, remember to use your knowledge of basic geometry rules; e.g., there are still 180° in a triangle when you're using Plugging In.

o   The imaginary number $i = \sqrt{-1}$, and there is a repeating pattern when you raise i to a power: i, -1, $-i$, 1. When doing algebra with i, treat it as a variable, unless you are able to substitute -1 for i^2 when appropriate.

Chapter 9
Introduction
to Writing and
Language Strategy

CAN YOU REALLY TEST WRITING ON A MULTIPLE-CHOICE TEST?

We'd say no, but the PSAT (and a heck of a lot of other tests) seems to think the answer is yes. To that end, the PSAT is giving you 35 minutes to answer 44 multiple-choice questions that ask about a variety of grammatical and stylistic topics. If you like to read and/or write, this test may frustrate you a bit because it may seem to boil writing down to a couple of dull rules. But as you will see, we will use the next few chapters to suggest a method that keeps things simple for pro- and anti-grammarians alike.

It is worth noting also that the breakdown of the test is exactly that of the SAT. While other sections of this test may provide slightly easier or shorter versions of what is to come on the real SAT, the Writing and Language Test is a carbon copy. Even the topics tested and the difficulty levels are likely to be the same.

WHERE DID ALL THE QUESTIONS GO?

One thing that can seem a little strange about the Writing and Language section of the PSAT is that many of the questions don't have, well, questions. Instead, many of the questions look something like this:

The history of **1** standardized testing although it may seem pretty dull, is in many ways a story about beliefs about how people learn and succeed.

1

A) NO CHANGE

B) standardized testing, although it may seem pretty dull

C) standardized testing, although it may seem, pretty dull,

D) standardized testing, although it may seem pretty dull,

How are you supposed to pick an answer when there's no question?

Well, actually, what you'll find throughout this chapter and the next two is that the PSAT gives you a *lot* of information in this list of answer choices. (The answer is (D), by the way, but stick with us for a second here.)

Look at these pairs, and you'll see just what we mean. As you read through these pairs of answer choices, think about what each question is probably testing.

i.   A)   could of
     B)   could have
ii. A)   tall, dark, and handsome
     B)   tall, dark and handsome
iii. A)   let them in
     B)   let Sister Susie and Brother John in
iv. A)   We arrived in Paris on a Sunday. Then we took the train to Nantes. Then we took the train to Bordeaux.
     B)   We arrived in Paris on a Sunday. Then we took the train to Bordeaux. Then we took the train to Nantes.

If you were able to see the differences in these answer choices, you're already more than halfway there. Now, notice how the differences in these answers can reveal the question that is lurking in the heart of each list of answer choices.

i.   The difference between the word "of" and "have" means that this question is asking *Is the correct form "could of" or "could have"?*
ii. The difference between having a comma after the word "dark" and not having one there means that this question is asking *How many commas does this sentence need, and where do they belong?*
iii. The difference between "them" and "Sister and Susie and Brother John" means that this question is asking *Is "them" adequately specific, or do you need to refer to people by name?*
iv. The difference in the order of these sentences asks *What order should the sentences be in?*

Therefore, what we have noticed in these pairs of answer choices is something that may seem fairly simple but which is essential to success on the PSAT.

THE ANSWER CHOICES ASK THE QUESTIONS

At some point, you've almost certainly had to do the English-class exercise called "peer editing." In this exercise, you are tasked with "editing" the work of one of your fellow students. But this can be really tough, because what exactly does it mean to "edit" an entire essay or paper when you aren't given any directions? It's *especially* tough when you start getting into the subtleties between whether things are *wrong* or whether they could merely be improved.

Look, for example, at these two sentences:

It was a beautiful day outside birds were singing cheerful songs.

It was a beautiful day outside; birds were singing cheerful songs.

You'd have to pick the second one in this case because the first has a grammatical error: It's a run-on sentence. Or for the non-grammarians out there, you have to break that thing up.

Now, look at these next two sentences:

> *The weather was just right, so I decided to play soccer.*
>
> *Just right was how I would describe the weather, so a decision of soccer-playing was made by me.*

In this case, the first sentence is obviously better than the second, but the second technically doesn't have any grammatical errors in it. The first may be *better*, but the second isn't exactly *wrong*.

What made each of these pairs of sentences relatively easy to deal with, though, was the fact that you could compare the sentences to one another. In doing so, you noted the differences between those sentences, and so you picked the *better* answer accordingly.

Let's see how this looks in a real PSAT situation.

In particular, the early history of standardized **2** tests reveals some of the basic assumptions about what education was supposed to do.

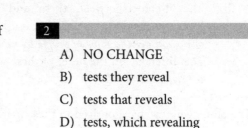

2

A) NO CHANGE
B) tests they reveal
C) tests that reveals
D) tests, which revealing

Here's How to Crack It

First, look at what's changing in the answer choices. The word *tests* remains the same in each, but what comes after it changes each time. This question, then, seems to be asking *Which words will best link the two ideas in the sentence?*

Choices (A) and (D) make the sentence incomplete, so those should be eliminated. Choice (B) creates a run-on sentence, so that should also be eliminated. It looks like only (C) appropriately links the ideas without adding new errors.

Notice how that entire process starting with asking *What's changing in the answer choices?* With that question, we figured out what was being tested, and we used POE to do the rest.

Let's try another.

In many ways, a civilization's self-image can be assessed through what that civilization expects **3** their citizens to know.

3

A) NO CHANGE
B) they're citizens
C) their citizen
D) its citizens

How to Crack It

As always, start with what is changing in the answer choices. It looks like the main change is between the words *their*, *they're*, and *its* with a minor change between the words *citizen* and *citizens*. As such, this question seems to be asking *What is the appropriate pronoun to use in this context, and just how many citizens are we talking about?*

Start wherever is easiest. In this case, we're talking about many *citizens*, not just one, so (C) can be eliminated. Now, let's work with the pronoun. What does it refer back to? In this sentence, it seems that the pronoun refers back to *civilization*, which is a singular noun (even though it describes a lot of people). Therefore, the only possible answer that could work is (D), which contains the singular pronoun "its."

LEARN FROM THE ANSWER CHOICES

Let's think about the previous question a bit more. If someone said to you *a civilization's self-image can be assessed through what that civilization expects their citizens to know*, you might not necessarily hear that as wrong. That's because the way we speak is often very different from the way we write. The PSAT is more concerned on this test with how we write and with the stricter set of rules that go along with writing.

As such, not only can the answer choices tell us what a particular question is testing, they can also reveal mistakes that we might not have otherwise seen (in the original sentence) or heard (in our heads). In the previous question, we might not have noted the mistake at all if we hadn't looked at what was changing in the answer choices.

Let's see another.

A good standardized test can be an effective way **4** to try a different tact at assessing student learning.

4
A) NO CHANGE
B) to try a different tack
C) for those trying a different tact
D) for those trying a different tack

Here's How to Crack It

First, as always, check what's changing in the answer choices. In this case, that step is especially important because you can't really hear the error. People misuse this idiom all the time because they so rarely see it written; each pair of answer choices sounds basically the same. The fact that they are not the same, that they *change*, tells us precisely what to pay attention to when we use POE.

Start the Process of Elimination. There's no good reason to add a bunch of extra words that don't make things any more precise, so eliminate (C) and (D). Then, if you're not sure, take a guess. The correct form of the saying here is (B).

Notice, though, that looking at the answer choices revealed the problem that you might not have otherwise been able to see or hear. Then, POE got you the rest of the way.

POE DOES THE BIG WORK

Once you have a sense of what the question is testing, POE can get you closer and closer to the answer. POE is especially helpful when you're dealing with sentences that have lots of issues, like this one:

It may seem that what you learn in school is too different from what you **5** are doing on the test. However, they would say that the underlying skills are the same.

5
A) NO CHANGE
B) do on the test, however, they'd
C) are doing on the test; however, the creators of the test would
D) do on the test; however, the creators of the test would

Here's How to Crack It

First, as always, check what's changing in the answer choices. In this case, there are three things changing: the difference between *do* and *are doing*, the difference between *they* and *the creators of the test*, and some differences in punctuation. While this may seem like a lot, this is actually a huge POE opportunity! Start with the one you find easiest, and work backwards from there.

Because the semicolon is not commonly used, let's save the punctuation part for last. Hopefully we can get the right answer without having to deal with the punctuation at all. Let's start with the difference between *they* and *the creators of the test*. If we use the pronoun *they*, it's not entirely clear whom the sentence is talking about, so eliminate (A) and (B). Then, to choose between the last two, *do* is more concise and more consistent with the rest of the sentence than is *are doing*, which makes (D) better than (C). In this instance, we got to the correct answer without having to deal with all of the messiness in the question!

ALL OF THE QUESTIONS CAN'T BE WRONG ALL OF THE TIME

Now that our strategy is basically set, let's look at one more tough one.

---

[6] Your attitude toward these test creators may not be entirely sympathetic, but it might make you feel better to know that the tests were designed with you in mind.

6

A) NO CHANGE

B) You're attitude toward these test creators may not be entirely sympathetic,

C) Your attitude toward these test creators may not be sympathetically entire,

D) You're attitude toward these test creators may not be sympathetic or entire,

Here's How to Crack It

As always, check the answers first. In this case, here's what's changing: the answers are switching between *your* and *you're* and some weirdness with *entire* and *sympathetic*. Let's do the easy parts first!

First of all, we'll need the word *your*, because this is the attitude that belongs to *you*, thus eliminating (B) and (D). Then the choice is between *entirely sympathetic*, which is fine, and between *sympathetically entire*, which is really weird, so (C) is no good either. Choice (A) must be the one.

Remember, NO CHANGE is right sometimes! Some people pick it too much. Some people don't pick it enough, but if you've done the other steps in the process and have eliminated all the other choices, go ahead and pick (A)!

HOW TO ACE THE WRITING AND LANGUAGE SECTION: A STRATEGY

- Check what's changing in the answer choices.
- Figure out what the question is testing and let the differences reveal potential errors.
- Use Process of Elimination.
- If you haven't eliminated three answers, pick the shortest one that is most consistent with the rest of the sentence.

In the next few chapters, we'll get into some of the more technical issues in Writing and Language, but we'll be using this strategy throughout. Try the drill on the next page to get some of the basics down.

Writing and Language Drill

The purpose of this drill is to get a basic idea of what each question is testing from only the answer choices. Check your answers on page 228.

1

A) NO CHANGE
B) singers' preferred songwriters
C) singer's preferred songwriter's
D) singers' preferred songwriters'

What's changing in the answer choices?

_____

What is this question testing?

_____

2

A) NO CHANGE
B) had
C) has
D) has had

What's changing in the answer choices?

_____

What is this question testing?

_____

3

A) NO CHANGE
B) Even though
C) If
D) Since

What's changing in the answer choices?

_____

What is this question testing?

_____

4

A) NO CHANGE
B) seem attractive for their
C) seems attractive for its
D) seems attractive for their

What's changing in the answer choices?

_____

What is this question testing?

_____

5

A) NO CHANGE
B) smooth, as in completely lumpless.
C) smooth, like talking not a single lump.
D) smooth.

What's changing in the answer choices?

_____

What is this question testing?

_____

DRILL ANSWERS

1. Apostrophes; apostrophes and where they go
2. Verbs; verb tense and number
3. Words; transition words (direction)
4. Was/were and their/its; verb number and pronoun number
5. Number of words; conciseness

Chapter 10
Punctuation

WAIT; THE PSAT WANTS ME TO KNOW HOW TO USE A SEMICOLON?

Kurt Vonnegut once wrote, "Here is a lesson in creative writing. First rule: Do not use semicolons… All they do is show you've been to college." Unfortunately, the writers of the PSAT don't quite agree. They want you to know how to use the semicolon and a few other types of weird punctuation besides. In this chapter, we're going to talk about the varieties of punctuation that the PSAT wants you to know how to use. Learn these few simple rules, and you'll be all set on the punctuation questions.

First and foremost, remember how you can spot a question that's asking about punctuation.

Start by asking *What's changing in the answer choices?*

If you see punctuation marks—commas, periods, apostrophes, semicolons, colons—changing, then the question is testing punctuation. Then, as you work the problem, make sure to ask the big question:

Does this punctuation need to be here?

The particular punctuation mark you are using—no matter what it is—must have a specific role within the sentence. You wouldn't use a question mark without a question, would you? Nope! Well, all punctuation works that way, and in what follows, we'll give you about seven basic instances in which you would use some type of punctuation. Otherwise, let the words do their thing unobstructed!

STOP, GO, AND THE VERTICAL LINE TEST

Let's get the weird ones out of the way first. Everyone knows that a period ends a sentence, but even particularly nerdy grammarians can get lost when things get more complicated. Because of this confusion, we've come up with a basic chart that summarizes the different times you might use what the PSAT calls "end-of-sentence" and "middle-of-sentence" punctuation.

When you are linking ideas,

STOP
- Period
- Semicolon
- Comma + FANBOYS
- Question mark
- Exclamation Mark

HALF-STOP
- Colon
- Long dash

GO
- Comma
- No punctuation

> STOP punctuation can link *only* complete ideas.
>
> HALF-STOP punctuation must be *preceded* by a complete idea.
>
> GO punctuation can link anything *except* two complete ideas.

Let's see how these work. Here is a complete idea:

> *Samantha studied for the PSAT.*

Notice that we've already used one form of STOP punctuation at the end of this sentence: a period.

Now, if we want to add a second complete idea, we'll keep the period.

> *Samantha studied for the PSAT. She ended up doing really well on the test.*

In this case, the period is linking these two complete ideas. But the nice thing about STOP punctuation is that you can really use any of the punctuation in the list to do the same thing, so we could also say this:

> *Samantha studied for the PSAT; she ended up doing really well on the test.*

What the list of STOP punctuation shows us is that essentially, a period and a semicolon are the same thing. We could say the same for the use of a comma plus one of the FANBOYS.

> *Samantha studied for the PSAT, and she ended up doing really well on the test.*

In the right margin:

FANBOYS stands for **F**or, **A**nd, **N**or, **B**ut, **O**r, **Y**et, and **S**o.

You can also use HALF-STOP punctuation to separate two complete ideas, so you could say

> *Samantha studied for the PSAT: she ended up doing really well on the test.*

Or

> *Samantha studied for the PSAT—she ended up doing really well on the test.*

There's a subtle difference, however, between STOP and HALF-STOP punctuation: For STOP, both ideas have to be complete, but for HALF-STOP, only the first one does.

Let's see what this looks like. If we want to link a complete idea and an incomplete idea, we can use HALF-STOP punctuation as long as the complete idea is first. For example,

> *Samantha studied for the PSAT: all three sections of it.*

Or

> *Samantha studied for the PSAT: the silliest test in all the land.*

When you use HALF-STOP, there has to be a complete idea before the punctuation, so these examples wouldn't be correct:

> ~~*Samantha studied for: the PSAT, the SAT, and every AP test in between.*~~

> ~~*The PSAT—Samantha studied for it and was glad she did.*~~

When you are not linking two complete ideas, you can use GO punctuation. So you could say, for instance,

> *Samantha studied for the PSAT, the SAT, and every AP test in between.*

Or

> *Samantha studied for the PSAT, all three sections of it.*

These are the three types of mid-sentence or end-of-sentence punctuation: STOP, HALF-STOP, and GO. You'll notice that there is a bit of overlap between the concepts, but the writers of the PSAT couldn't possibly make you get into the minutiae of choosing between, say, a period and a semicolon. If you can figure out which of the big three (STOP, HALF-STOP, and GO) categories you'll need, that's all you need to be able to do.

In the following exercise, choose the type of punctuation that will go in the blank. Some questions have more than one answer! Check your answers on page 232.

	STOP	HALF-STOP	GO
The other day I went to the stadium _____ and bought a ticket.			
I had saved up all week _____ I couldn't think of anything better to spend the money on!			
Some of my favorite sports include _____ hockey, baseball, and tennis.			
There's always something _____ for me to see at the stadium.			
When I arrived _____ I was thrilled to see that I had bought great seats.			
Some people from my school were sitting next to me _____ we're all in the same math class.			
The game was exciting _____ a goal in the first five minutes!			
The crowd was extremely diverse _____ men, women, and children in the stands.			
I didn't want to go home _____ even though I had school the next day.			
You can be sure of one thing _____ I'll be back as soon as I can.			

	STOP	HALF-STOP	GO
The other day I went to the stadium _____ and bought a ticket.			X
I had saved up all week _____ I couldn't think of anything better to spend the money on!	X	X	
Some of my favorite sports include _____ hockey, baseball, and tennis.			X
There's always something _____ for me to see at the stadium.			X
When I arrived _____ I was thrilled to see that I had bought great seats.			X
Some people from my school were sitting next to me _____ we're all in the same math class.	X	X	
The game was exciting _____ a goal in the first five minutes!		X	X
The crowd was extremely diverse _____ men, women, and children in the stands.		X	
I didn't want to go home _____ even though I had school the next day.			X
You can be sure of one thing _____ I'll be back as soon as I can.	X	X	

Let's see what this will look like on the PSAT.

———————◯———————

Noah took the PSAT way more seriously than many of his **1** friends he was almost certain he would get a National Merit honor of some kind.

1

A) NO CHANGE
B) friends, he was almost
C) friends he was almost,
D) friends; he was almost

Here's How to Crack It

As always, check what's changing in the answer choices. In this case, the words all stay the same. All that changes is the punctuation, and notice the types of punctuation that are changing: STOP and GO.

Now, when you see STOP punctuation changing in the answer choices, you can do a little something we like to call the Vertical Line Test.

Draw a line where you see the punctuation changing—in this case, between the words *test* and *he*. Then, read up to the vertical line: *Noah took the PSAT way more seriously than many of his friends*. That's Complete. Now, read after the vertical line: *he was almost certain he'd get a National Merit honor of some kind*. That's also Complete.

By the time you're done, your page should look like this.

Complete | Complete

Noah took the PSAT way more seriously than many of his **1** friends | he was almost certain he would get a National Merit honor of some kind.

So let's think, we've got two complete ideas here. What kind of punctuation do we need? STOP or HALF-STOP. It looks like STOP is the only one available, so let's choose (D).

———————◯———————

Let's try another.

───────────────○───────────────

He really wanted to make sure he had balanced **2** scores. Over 700 for both.

2

A) NO CHANGE

B) scores; over

C) scores: over

D) scores, he wanted over

Here's How to Crack It

Check the answer choices. What's changing? It looks like the punctuation is changing, and some of that punctuation is STOP. Let's use the Vertical Line Test. Draw a vertical line where you see the punctuation: between *scores* and *over* or *scores* and *he*.

What's before the vertical line? *He really wanted to make sure he had balanced scores* is complete. Then, *over 700 for both* is not. Therefore, because we have one complete idea (the first) and one incomplete idea (the second), we can't use STOP punctuation, thus eliminating (A) and (B).

Now, what's different between the last two? Choice (C) contains HALF-STOP punctuation, which can work, so we'll keep that. Choice (D) adds some words, with which the second idea becomes *he wanted over 700 for both*, which is complete. That makes two complete ideas separated by a comma, but what do we need when we're separating two complete ideas? STOP punctuation! Eliminate (D)! Only (C) is left.

───────────────○───────────────

Let's see one more.

───────────────○───────────────

Every day after Noah got home from baseball **3** practice—he hit the books.

3

A) NO CHANGE

B) practice; he

C) practice, he,

D) practice, he

Here's How to Crack It

The punctuation is changing in the answer choices, and there's some STOP punctuation, so let's use the Vertical Line Test. Put the line between *moment* and *he*. The first idea, *Every day after Noah got home from baseball practice*, is incomplete, and the second idea, *he hit the books*, is complete. Therefore, we can't use STOP (which needs two complete ideas) or HALF-STOP (which needs a complete idea before the punctuation), thus eliminating (A) and (B). Then, because there is no good reason to put a comma after the word *he*, the best answer must be (D).

A SLIGHT PAUSE FOR COMMAS

Commas can be a little tricky. In the last question (#3), we got down to two answers, (C) and (D), after having completed the Vertical Line Test. But then, how do you decide whether to keep a comma in or not? It seems a little arbitrary to say that you use a comma "every time you want to pause," so let's make that thought a little more concrete.

If you can't cite a reason to use a comma, *don't use one.*

On the PSAT, there are only four reasons to use a comma:
- in STOP punctuation, with one of the FANBOYS.
- in GO punctuation, to separate incomplete ideas from other ideas.
- in a list of three or more things.
- in a sentence containing unnecessary information.

We've already seen the first two concepts, so let's look at the third and fourth.

Try this one.

His favorite classes were **4** English, physics and history.

4

A) NO CHANGE
B) English, physics, and history.
C) English, physics, and, history.
D) English physics and history.

Here's How to Crack It

First, check what's changing in the answer choices. It looks like the commas in this list are changing. Because there's not any obvious STOP or HALF-STOP punctuation, the Vertical Line Test won't do us much good.

Then, it will help to know that that the PSAT wants a comma after every item in a series. Think of it this way. There's a potential misunderstanding in this sentence:

I went to the park with my parents, my cat Violet and my dog Stuart.

Without a comma, it sure sounds like this guy has some interesting parents. If there's no comma, how do we know that this sentence isn't supposed to say his parents are *my cat Violet and my dog Stuart*? The only way to remove the ambiguity would be to add a comma like this:

I went to the park with my parents, my cat Violet, and my dog Stuart.

Keep that in mind as we try to crack number 4. In this problem, *English, physics, and history* form a list or series, so they should be set off from one another by commas as they are in (B).

Let's try another.

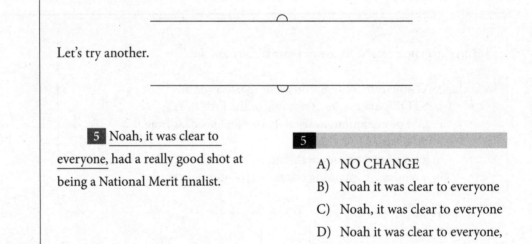

[5] Noah, it was clear to everyone, had a really good shot at being a National Merit finalist.

5

A) NO CHANGE
B) Noah it was clear to everyone
C) Noah, it was clear to everyone
D) Noah it was clear to everyone,

Here's How to Crack It

First, check what's changing in the answer choices. Just commas. And those commas seem to be circling around the words *it was clear to everyone*. When you have a few commas circling around a word, phrase, or clause like this, the question is usually testing necessary vs. unnecessary information.

A good way to test whether the idea is necessary to the meaning of the sentence is to take it out. Read the original sentence again. Now read this one: *Noah had a really good shot at being a National Merit finalist.*

Is the sentence still complete? Yes. Has the meaning of the sentence changed? No, we just lost a little extra thing. Therefore, the idea is *unnecessary* to the meaning of the sentence and should be set off with commas as it is in (A).

Let's try a few more. Try to figure out whether the word or idea in italics is necessary to the meaning of the sentence.

i. The student *with the highest score* has a good chance at a National Merit scholarship.
ii. Katie wants to go to Yale *which has a really good theater program.*
iii. The team *that scored five touchdowns* won the game in a landslide.
iv. The National Merit competition *which began in 1955* had over 1.25 million applicants in 2005.
v. Rising senior *Liam* is hoping to be one of the chosen few this year.

Answers are on page 241.

Let's put it all together in this question.

All his teachers [6] believed, he had a real shot, when he sat down to take the test.

6

A) NO CHANGE
B) believed, he had a real shot, when he sat down,
C) believed, he had a real shot when he sat, down,
D) believed he had a real shot when he sat down

Here's How to Crack It

Check what's changing in the answer choices. There are varying numbers of commas in varying places. Remember, the rule of thumb with commas is that if you can't cite a reason to use a comma, *don't use one.*

It looks like *he had a real shot* is being set off by commas. Let's see whether it's necessary or unnecessary information. Read the original sentence; then read the sentence again without that piece of information: *All his teachers believed when he sat down to take the test.* It looks like the sentence has changed meaning and is not really complete anymore. Therefore, that bit of information is necessary to the meaning of the sentence, so it doesn't need commas. Then, there are no good reasons to put commas around or in the word *down*.

In the end, there aren't reasons to put commas anywhere in this sentence. The best answer is (D). Sometimes the PSAT will test unnecessary punctuation explicitly, so make sure you have a good reason to use commas when you use them!

―――――――――――○―――――――――――

YOUR GOING TO BE TESTED ON APOSTROPHE'S (AND INTERNET SPELLING IS A TERRIBLE GUIDE!)

As with commas, apostrophes have only a very limited set of applications. Apostrophes are a little trickier, though, because you can't really hear them in speech, so people misuse them all the time. Think about the header of this section. The apostrophes are wrong there. Here's the correct way of punctuating it: *You're going to be tested on apostrophes.* Can you hear the difference? Neither can we.

Therefore, as with commas, if you can't cite a reason to use an apostrophe, don't use one. There are only two reasons to use apostrophes on the PSAT.

If you can't cite a reason to use an apostrophe, *don't use one.*

On the PSAT, there are only two reasons to use an apostrophe:

- Possessive nouns (NOT pronouns)
- Contractions

Let's see some examples.

―――――――――――○―――――――――――

Some recognition from National Merit would help strengthen [7] his application's, especially for the high-end school's.

7

A) NO CHANGE

B) his applications, especially for the high-end schools'.

C) his application's, especially for the high-end schools.

D) his applications, especially for the high-end schools.

Here's How to Crack It

Check what's changing in the answer choices. In this case, the words are all staying the same, but the apostrophes are changing. Remember: We don't want to use apostrophes at all if we can't cite a good reason to do so.

Does anything belong to *schools* or *applications*? No! Are they forming contractions like *school is* or *application is*? No! Therefore, there's no reason to use apostrophes, and the only possible answer is (D), which dispenses with the apostrophes altogether.

As in the previous question, there's no need for any punctuation, and in a question like this, the PSAT is testing whether you can spot unnecessary punctuation.

But sometimes the apostrophes will be necessary. Let's have a look at another.

8 It's not easy to get you're score high enough for National Merit.

8

A) NO CHANGE

B) Its not easy to get your

C) Its not easy to get you're

D) It's not easy to get your

Here's How to Crack It

Check what's changing in the answer choices. The main changes have to do with apostrophes, particularly on the words *its/it's* and *your/you're*.

The first word, *its/it's*, needs an apostrophe: It creates the contraction *it is*. Therefore, because this one needs an apostrophe, get rid of (B) and (C). As for the other, this word is possessive (as in, the *score* belonging to *you*), but remember! Possessive *nouns* need an apostrophe, but possessive *pronouns* don't. Therefore, because *you* is a pronoun, this word should be spelled *your*, as it is in (D).

Phew! These apostrophes can get a little tricky, so let's try a few more. On these (as on many parts of the PSAT), you'll find that using your ear, sounding things out, doesn't really help all that much.

Circle the option that works. The big question is this: apostrophes or no apostrophes?

   i.   *Salims/Salim's* teacher said *hes/he's* allowed to miss next *Tuesdays/Tuesday's* exam.

   ii.   *Its/It's* really not going to hurt my feelings if you don't want to go to *they're/their* party with me.

   iii. *Whatever the *justification's/justifications* for *your/you're* attitude, *there/they're* is no reason to be so obnoxious about it.

   iv. *Were/We're* going to get back to you as soon as your *application's/applications* processed.

   v.   *They're/Their they're/their* nachos, but they *wont/won't* share any unless *its/it's* absolutely necessary or we share *ours/our's*.

Answers are on page 241.

CONCLUSION

In sum, we've looked at all the punctuation you'd ever need on the PSAT. It's really not so much, and you probably knew a lot of it already. In general, checking what's changing in the answer choices can help reveal mistakes that you may not have heard, and POE can help you narrow those answers down.

Punctuation rules are easy to learn, as is the biggest rule of all about punctuation.

> Know why you are using punctuation, whether that punctuation is STOP, HALF-STOP, GO, commas, or apostrophes. If you can't cite reasons to use these punctuation marks, don't use them!

In the last few pages of this chapter, try out these skills on a drill.

Answers to Questions on Page 237:

i. NECESSARY to the meaning of the sentence (no commas). If you remove the italicized part, the sentence is not adequately specific.

ii. UNNECESSARY to the meaning of the sentence (commas). If you remove the italicized part, the sentence is still complete and does not change meaning.

iii. NECESSARY to the meaning of the sentence (no commas). If you remove the italicized part, the sentence is not adequately specific.

iv. UNNECESSARY to the meaning of the sentence (commas). If you remove the italicized part, the sentence is still complete and does not change meaning.

v. NECESSARY to the meaning of the sentence (no commas). If you remove the italicized part, the sentence is no longer complete.

Answers to Questions on Page 240:

i. Salim's, he's, Tuesday's
ii. It's, their
iii. justifications, your, there
iv. We're, application's
v. They're, their, won't, it's, ours

Drill

Time: 5-6 minutes

There is no question that the United States is a country of 1 immigrants, the original countries of those immigrants varies so much that it can be tough to know who has contributed what. Moreover, different groups have come at 2 different time's for they're different reason's. In the late 1980s and 3 early 1990s, for instance, those, from the former Soviet Union arrived in large numbers on American shores.

1
A) NO CHANGE
B) immigrants, and the
C) immigrants and the
D) immigrants. And the

2
A) NO CHANGE
B) different time's for their different reason's.
C) different times for they're different reasons.
D) different times for their different reasons.

3
A) NO CHANGE
B) early 1990s, for instance those
C) early 1990s, for instance, those
D) early 1990s for instance those

This may seem a bit late, given that most of the USSR and USSR-affiliated empires fell around 1990 (starting with East Germany and [4] it's Berlin Wall in 1989) in fact the largest migrations of Soviets and ex-Soviets happened just *after* the Union had fallen. Indeed, whatever the shortcomings of the socialist republic, the real [5] poverty, depression and deprivation, began in earnest when the government was no longer tasked with providing basic necessities. As a result, while there had been a somewhat steady flow of immigration from the USSR since [6] the 1970s, the largest numbers came to the United States in the early 1990s.

4

A) NO CHANGE
B) its Berlin Wall in 1989), in fact,
C) it's Berlin Wall in 1989). In fact,
D) its Berlin Wall in 1989); in fact,

5

A) NO CHANGE
B) poverty, depression, and deprivation began
C) poverty, depression, and, deprivation began
D) poverty, depression, and deprivation, began

6

A) NO CHANGE
B) the 1970s the
C) the 1970s—the
D) the 1970s. The

Whether we realize it or not, the contributions of these Russian expatriates are with us everywhere. The [7] co-founder, of Google, Sergey Brin, came to the United States from Moscow at the age of 6 in 1979. Singer-songwriter Regina Spektor moved at the age of 9 in 1989, the same year that historian Artemy Kalinovsky arrived [8] with his parents. These and other children of the Soviet Union continue to shape the American experience in all kinds of positive and enlightening ways.

7

A) NO CHANGE
B) co-founder of Google. Sergey Brin,
C) co-founder of Google, Sergey Brin,
D) co-founder, of Google, Sergey Brin,

8

A) NO CHANGE
B) with his parents, today, these
C) with his parents. Today, these
D) with his parents today; these

In the same year and at the same age as Brin, **9** a writer, named David Bezmozgis, moved, with his family, from Riga, Latvia, then under Soviet control. While he has undoubtedly been one of the great success stories of Soviet immigration to North America (Canada in this case), he has found that success in detailing the difficult and often conflicting motivations that many people had for leaving the Soviet Union. While we have become comfortable believing that the Soviets came to North America looking for **10** freedom, whatever that term may mean. Bezmozgis shows that this was not always the case and that "freedom" could remain an elusive dream even for those who made the trip successfully. His first **11** novel *The Free World*, was published in 2011 to great critical acclaim.

As we think about the fact that ours is a nation of immigrants, we would be severely limited if we believed that people came from all over the world to assimilate to the American way of life. In fact, the peoples of the world may have become American, but they have done so while shaping and reshaping the meaning of that term in ever richer ways.

9

A) NO CHANGE

B) a writer, named David Bezmozgis moved with his family, from Riga,

C) a writer named, David Bezmozgis, moved, with his family, from Riga,

D) a writer named David Bezmozgis moved with his family from Riga,

10

A) NO CHANGE

B) freedom, whatever that term may mean: Bezmozgis

C) freedom, whatever that term may mean, Bezmozgis

D) freedom, whatever that term may mean; Bezmozgis

11

A) NO CHANGE

B) novel: *The Free World*,

C) novel—*The Free World*,

D) novel, *The Free World*,

DRILL ANSWERS

1. B
2. D
3. C
4. A
5. B
6. A
7. C
8. C
9. D
10. B
11. D

Chapter 11
Words

THE WORDS CHANGE, BUT THE SONG
REMAINS THE SAME

In the last chapter, we looked at what to do when the PSAT is testing punctuation. In this chapter, we're going to look at what to do when the PSAT is testing the parts of speech—mainly verbs, nouns, and pronouns.

Our basic strategy, however, has remained the same. As we saw in the previous two chapters, when faced with a PSAT Writing and Language question, we should always

> Check what's changing in the answer choices and use POE.

As you will notice, throughout this chapter, we talk a lot about certain parts of speech, but we don't really use a lot of grammar terms. That's because we find that on the PSAT, the best answers across a lot of different parts of speech can be summed up more succinctly with three basic terms: Consistency, Precision, and Concision.

You don't need to know a ton of grammar if you can remember these three basic rules.

> **CONSISTENCY:** Correct answers are consistent with the rest of the sentence and the passage.
>
> **PRECISION:** Correct answers are as precise as possible.
>
> **CONCISION:** Barring other errors, correct answers are as concise as possible.

Let's look at some examples of each.

CONSISTENCY

────────────○────────────

The purveyors of the philosophy known as **1** Pragmatism is part of a long and complex movement.

A) NO CHANGE

B) Pragmatism has been

C) Pragmatism are

D) Pragmatism being

Here's How to Crack It

First, as always, check what's changing in the answer choices. In this case, *Pragmatism* stays the same, but the forms of the verb *to be* change. Therefore, because the verbs change, we know that the question is testing verbs.

When you see verbs changing in the answer choices, the first thing to check is the subject of the sentence. Is the verb consistent with the subject? In this case, it's not. The subject of this sentence is *purveyors*, which is plural. Therefore, (A) and (B) have to be eliminated, and (D) creates an incomplete idea. Only (C) can work in the context.

Thus, when you see verbs changing in the answer choices, check the subject first. Subjects and verbs need to be consistent with each other.

────────────○────────────

Let's have a look at another.

────────────○────────────

Pragmatism has entered the popular language as a kind of synonym for "realistic" or "cynical," but William James, perhaps the greatest of the American Pragmatists, **2** show that the movement can in fact be much more human and adaptable.

2

A) NO CHANGE

B) showed

C) will show

D) has shown

Here's How to Crack It

Check what's changing in the answer choices. The verbs are changing. Remember from the first question that whenever you see verbs changing, you want to make sure the verb is consistent with the subject. Because the subject of this part of the sentence is *William James*, a singular noun, you can eliminate (A), which isn't consistent.

Then, because all the others are consistent with the subject, make sure they are consistent with the other verbs. It looks like the other main verb in this sentence is *has been*, so the underlined verb should be in this form, as it is in (D). Choices (B) and (C) could work in some contexts, but not this one!

As you can see, verbs are all about consistency.

> When you see verbs changing in the answer choices, make sure those verbs are
>
> - CONSISTENT with their subjects
> - CONSISTENT with other verbs in the sentence and surrounding sentences

Let's try one that has a little bit of everything.

Reading James and the other theorists **3** reveal that as we make the big decisions in our lives, we think about those decisions in interestingly pragmatic ways.

3

A) NO CHANGE

B) reveal that we made the decisions in our lives, we have thought

C) reveals that as we make the big decisions in our lives, we could have been thinking

D) reveals that as we make the big decisions in our lives, we think

Here's How to Crack It

Check what's changing in the answer choices. It looks like lots of verbs!

Let's start with the first. See which one, *reveal* or *reveals*, is consistent with the subject. That subject is *Reading*, which is singular, thus eliminating (A) and (B).

Then, we have to choose between *think* and *could have been thinking*. Since both of these are consistent with the subject *we*, let's try to pick the one that is most consistent with other verbs. The only other verbs are *reveals* and *make*, both of which are in the present tense and don't use the odd *could have been...* form. Therefore, if we have to choose between (C) and (D), (D) is definitely better.

———————————○———————————

Consistency applies across the test. Let's see another question in which the idea of Consistency might help us.

———————————○———————————

The early Pragmatists and **[4]** their follower suggest that the big decisions in life should be measured by their possible outcomes alone.

4

A) NO CHANGE

B) they're followers suggest

C) their followers suggest

D) their follower suggests

Here's How to Crack It

Check the answer choices first. It looks like pretty much everything is changing here: *they're/their*, *followers/follower*, and *suggest/suggests*. Let's look at the ones we have done already.

We can't cite a good reason to use an apostrophe, so let's get rid of (B). Then, the verb changes, so let's check the subject. That subject is *The early Pragmatists and their follower/followers*, which is plural regardless of the word *follower* or *followers*. Keep the verb consistent with the plural subject and eliminate (D).

Then, we have to choose between *follower* and *followers*, two nouns. As with verbs, nouns are all about consistency. When you see nouns changing in the answer choices, make sure they are consistent with the other nouns in the sentence. In this case, we are talking about *The early Pragmatists*, all of them, who must have many *followers* as well, as (C) suggests.

———————————○———————————

Noun consistency can show up in other ways as well. Let's have a look at #5.

The logical processes of the Pragmatists are much different from [5] other schools of thought.

5
A) NO CHANGE
B) other school's
C) those of other schools
D) schools that are otherwise

Here's How to Crack It

Look at what's changing in the answer choices. It looks like the main change is between the nouns—*schools* and *those*. We saw in the last problem that when nouns are changing in the answer choices, we want to make sure those nouns are consistent with other nouns in the sentence.

In this case, the nouns are being compared. *The logical processes of the Pragmatists* are being compared with the logical processes of people from other schools. Choices (A), (B), and (D) suggest that the *processes* are being compared with the *schools*, so both (B) and (D) are inconsistent. Only (C) is left.

SAT calls this concept "faulty comparison," but we don't have to know that name. Instead, we can just remember that *nouns have to be consistent with other nouns.* When the answer choices show a change in nouns, look for the sentence's other nouns. They'll provide the clue!

Pragmatism may be rooted in the German philosophers Immanuel Kant and Georg Friedrich Hegel, but it has found more popularity in Anglo-American communities than in [6] German or French ones.

6
A) NO CHANGE
B) German or French.
C) other ones.
D) European.

Here's How to Crack It

Check what's changing in the answer choices. There's a fairly significant change between *German or French* and *German or French ones*. As in the previous sentence, let's make sure this is consistent. The part of the sentence right before the underlined portion refers to *Anglo-American communities*, so we should make our part of the sentence consistent: *German or French communities*, not merely *German or French* or *European*, as in (B) and (D).

Then, we are down to (A) and (C). The difference here comes between the words *German or French* and *other*. While we do want to be concise when possible, we need to make sure first and foremost that we are being *precise*. Choice (A) is more precise than (C) in that it has a clearer relation to the *Anglo-American communities* with which it is being contrasted. Therefore, (A) is the best answer in that it is the most *consistent* with the rest of the sentence and the most *precise* of the remaining possible answers.

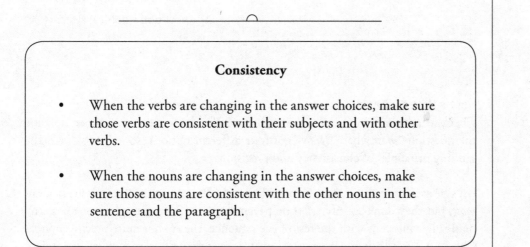

Consistency

- When the verbs are changing in the answer choices, make sure those verbs are consistent with their subjects and with other verbs.

- When the nouns are changing in the answer choices, make sure those nouns are consistent with the other nouns in the sentence and the paragraph.

PRECISION IS...

Consistency is probably the most important thing on the Writing and Language section of the PSAT, but precision is a close second. Once you've made sure that the underlined portion is consistent with the rest of the sentence, make sure that the underlined portion is as precise as possible. Perfect grammar is one thing, but it won't matter much if no one knows what the writer is talking about!

Let's hear that one more time.

> Once you are sure that a word or phrase is consistent with the non-underlined portion of the sentence, make that word or phrase as precise as you can.

Although purporting to be systems of universal truth, [7] most are bound to their countries of origin.

7
A) NO CHANGE
B) most of them
C) most from philosophy
D) most philosophical systems

Here's How to Crack It

Check what's changing in the answer choices. The changes could summed up with the question "*most* what?" We've got four different options, so let's use our main guiding principles of consistency and precision.

Let's be as precise as possible. Choices (A) and (B) are very similar in that they say *most*, but they don't specify *what* that *most* refers to. Even though these are grammatically consistent with the rest of the sentence, they're not quite precise enough. Choice (C) is a little more precise, but it doesn't actually clarify what *most* refers to. With these answers out of the way, we can see that (D) is the best of the bunch because it is the only one that is sufficiently precise.

As question #7 shows, pronouns can be a bit of a challenge. They can appear in otherwise grammatically correct sentences. Still, precision is key when you're dealing with pronouns. See what you can do with these sentences. Circle the potentially imprecise pronouns and rewrite the sentences.

i.   Certain philosophers can be confusing, but it's still an important endeavor.
ii. Each of us uses some of this philosophical logic in their everyday life.
iii. Whether Anglo-American or Continental models, it can all tell us something important about how to live.
iv. A philosopher's life cannot help but influence their work.
v.   Self-help, psychology, economics are the cornerstones: it is each in a way part of the philosophical tradition.

Answers are on page 257.

Precision can show up in some other ways as well. Have a look at this question.

The Continental school's **8** approach has a tendency to problems to be far more abstract than the Anglo-American school's.

8

A) NO CHANGE

B) approach has a tendency to be far more abstract to problems

C) approach to problems has a tendency to be far more abstract

D) approach has a tendency to be to problems far more abstract

Here's How to Crack It

Check what's changing in the answer choices. This step is crucial here because there are no obvious grammatical errors, so the answer choices are essential to figuring out exactly what the question is asking you to do.

In the end, the only difference among the answer choices is that the phrase *to problems* is in different places. In the end, we will just need to put that phrase in the most precise place, hopefully right next to whatever it is modifying.

In this case, we can choose from among *approach*, *tendency*, *be*, and *abstract*. Which of these would have the most precise need for the phrase *to problems*? Because *problems* seem to have something to do with how those problems are solved, it would go best with *approach*, creating the phrase *approach to problems*, particularly because the other combinations don't make a lot of sense. What does it mean to be *abstract to problems*? Nothing!

Let's have a look at some more of these modifiers. Rewrite the sentence so the modifier makes the *precise* sense that it should.

i.   Given all its logical twists and turns, many people struggle with philosophy.

ii.   Readers in different times tend to gravitate toward different philosophers and places.

iii.   Once cracked, you can find incredible guidance and solace in philosophy.

iv.   I first learned about Pragmatism from a professor in college at 20.

v.   Boring and uninteresting, Jack didn't care much for the work of William James.

Answers are on page 258.

CONCISION. PERIOD.

This is not to say, however, that more words always mean more precision. In fact, a lot of the time less is more. If you were to ask for directions, which answer would you rather receive?

> *Turn right at Main Street and walk four blocks.*

Or

> *Since this street, Elm Street, is facing in a northerly direction, and your destination is due northeast, go east when you arrive at the intersection of Elm and Main. Going east will entail making a right turn in quite that easterly direction. After having made this turn and arrived on the perpendicular street...*

The first one. Obviously.

And that's because concision is key when you want to communicate meaning. Really, as long as everything else is in order—as long as the grammar and punctuation are good to go—the best answer will almost always be the shortest.

Let's see an example.

I find Pragmatism to be one of the most **9** interesting and fascinating of the philosophical schools.

9

A) NO CHANGE
B) interesting
C) fascinatingly interesting
D) interestingly fascinating

Here's How to Crack It

Check what's changing in the answer choices. In this case, the word *interesting* appears in all the answer choices, and in some it is paired with the word *fascinating*. Typically, if you see a list of answer choices wherein one answer is short and the rest mean the same thing but are longer, the question is testing concision.

What, after all, is the difference between the words *interesting* and *fascinating*? There really isn't a very significant one, so there's no use in saying both of them, as in (A), or pairing them awkwardly, as in (C) and (D). In fact, the shortest answer, (B), does everything the other answers do, but it does so in the fewest words. Choice (B) is therefore the best answer.

Let's see one more.

---

10 Maybe it's just me but for me, Pragmatism in my view has the most applications to the most different kinds of problems.

10

A) NO CHANGE

B) Really and truly, Pragmatism

C) In my humble opinion, Pragmatism

D) Pragmatism

Here's How to Crack It

As always, check what's changing in the answer choices. The changes could be summed up like this: There's a bunch of stuff before the word *Pragmatism*. Does any of that stuff contribute in a significant way to the sentence? No. Does the word *Pragmatism* alone help the sentence to fulfill its basic purpose? Yes. Therefore, the best answer is (D).

As we have seen in this chapter, when the PSAT is testing *words* (i.e., any time the words are changing in the answer choices), make sure that those words are

- **Consistent.** Verbs, nouns, and pronouns should agree within sentences and passages.
- **Precise.** The writing should communicate specific ideas and events.
- **Concise.** When everything else is correct, the shortest answer is the best.

Answers to Questions on Page 254:

i.   *it* is the problem. *Certain philosophers can be confusing, but the pursuit of philosophical knowledge can still be an important endeavor.*

ii.   *their* is the problem. *Each of us uses some of this philosophical logical in his or her everyday life.*

iii. *it* is the problem. Take it out! *Anglo-American and Continental models can all tell us something important about how to live.*

iv.   *their* is the problem. *A philosopher's life cannot help but influence that philosopher's work.*

v.   *it* is the problem. *Self-help, psychology, economics are the cornerstones: each of these is part of the philosophical tradition.*

Answers to Questions on Page 255:

i. Many people struggle with philosophy given all its logical twists and turns.

ii. Readers in different times and places tend to gravitate toward different philosophers.

iii. Once cracked, philosophy can provide incredible guidance and solace.

iv. I first learned about Pragmatism from a college professor when I was 20 years old.

v. Jack didn't care much for the work of William James, which he found boring and uninteresting.

Drill

Time: 7-8 minutes

William James's *Pragmatism* (1907) has been called the **1** greatest and best book of American philosophy. The series of lectures that were to become *Pragmatism* **2** encompasses James's adaptation of the great Pragmatists, such as Charles Peirce, who came before and adds a uniquely human element. **3** His work in psychology and religion laid the foundation for how theoretical work intersects with the concrete work of living.

In a way, pragmatism turns the philosophical endeavor on its head and **4** attacked the importance of its big questions. Philosophy is traditionally concerned with the big questions: what is the meaning of life? Are there many worlds like this one or only this one? What if none of us exist? Pragmatism is concerned with these questions as well, but it is equally concerned with another question: so what? Pragmatism is concerned, with what difference a particular truth means in the world **5** with *practice.*

1

A) NO CHANGE
B) best and truly greatest
C) greatly best
D) greatest

2

A) NO CHANGE
B) encompass
C) does encompass
D) are encompassing

3

A) NO CHANGE
B) James's
C) Their
D) Some

4

A) NO CHANGE
B) has been attacking
C) attacks
D) could be said to attack

5

If the punctuation were adjusted accordingly, the best placement for the underlined portion would be
A) where it is now.
B) after the word *Pragmatism.*
C) after the word *concerned.*
D) after the word *truth.*

Let's consider a basic example. Say you are stressed about an upcoming math test. You're afraid you might not get the grade you want, and the fear of it **6** keeps you up at night. Rather than asking, "Will you do well on this test?", the Pragmatists will want to know instead "What difference does it make whether you do well or poorly on the test?" If your answer is, "Well, no difference, I guess," then you've got **7** one. If your answer is, "I won't be able to get an A in the class!" then you've got another and a whole other series of questions. By constantly asking "So what?", the pragmatic approach helps to situate problems in their practice and their consequences rather than **8** abstracting.

6
- A) NO CHANGE
- B) keeping you up
- C) awakens
- D) kept you up

7
- A) NO CHANGE
- B) something.
- C) one approach.
- D) approaching.

8
- A) NO CHANGE
- B) abstractly.
- C) in their abstraction.
- D) by a process of abstraction.

The approach is especially interesting for life's big questions. One of James's particular favorites was, "Is life fated or free?" In other words, do we make our own choices, or are our lives completely predetermined? Well, for James, the question is an interesting but fundamentally irrelevant one. **9** Whether there is a cosmic order to our lives or not, we still have to live them responsibly, so it doesn't **10** differ whether our lives are "fated or free," because the distinction won't create practical differences.

These are two relatively simple examples of the pragmatic method in action, but give it a try yourself. Next time something is really stressing you out, ask the simple question: what difference does it make if that does happen? You may find that the real consequences are what help you to see through the problem, establish a plan, or **11** forgot about the issue entirely.

9

The writer is considering deleting the phrase *but fundamentally irrelevant*. Should the phrase be kept or deleted?

A) Kept, because it shows James's sense of humor as displayed in his writings.

B) Kept, because it sets up the subject of the remainder of the paragraph.

C) Deleted, because it dismisses the importance of Pragmatism as a movement.

D) Deleted, because the paragraph as a whole is focused on relevant subjects.

10

A) NO CHANGE

B) concern us or anyone else

C) count

D) make a significant difference

11

A) NO CHANGE

B) forget about them

C) forget about the issue

D) forget about the issues

DRILL ANSWERS

1. D
2. B
3. B
4. C
5. C
6. A
7. A
8. C
9. B
10. D
11. C

Chapter 12
Questions

AND THEN THE PSAT WAS LIKE, "HEY, CAN I ASK YOU A QUESTION?"

In the previous two chapters, we saw most of the concepts that the PSAT will test. In this chapter, we're not going to learn a lot of new stuff in the way of grammar. Instead, we'll look at some of the questions that the PSAT asks.

As we've seen, a lot of the questions don't have questions at all. They're just lists of answer choices, and we start the process of answering them by asking a question of our own: "What's changing in the answer choices?" Because you need to move quickly through this test, you may fall into the habit of not checking for questions. Even when you do read the questions, you may read them hastily or vaguely. Well, we are here to tell you that neither of these approaches will work.

> The most important thing about Writing and Language questions is that you *notice* those questions and then *answer* those questions.

This may seem like just about the most obvious advice you've ever been given, but you'd be surprised how much less precise your brain is when you're working quickly.

Here's an example. Do these next 10 questions as quickly as you can.

1. $2 + 1 =$

2. $1 + 2 =$

3. $3 + 1 =$

4. $3 + 2 \neq$

5. $1 + 2 =$

6. $2 - 1 <$

7. $2 \pm 2 =$

8. $3 + 1 =$

9. $3 + 2 =$

10. $3 + 3 \neq$

Now check your answers.

1. 3

2. 3

3. 4

4. Anything but 5

5. 3

6. Any number greater than 1 (but not 1!)

7. 0 or 4

8. 4

9. 5

10. Anything but 6

Now, it's very possible that you got at least one of those questions wrong. What happened? It's not that the questions are hard. In fact, the questions are about as easy as can be. So why did you get some of them wrong? You were probably moving too quickly to notice that the signs changed a few times.

This is a lot like the Writing and Language section. You might miss some of the easiest points on the whole test by not reading carefully enough.

As we will see throughout this chapter, most of the questions will test concepts with which we are already familiar.

WORDS AND PUNCTUATION IN REVERSE

Many of the concepts we saw in the Punctuation and Words chapters show up explicitly with questions, but usually there's some kind of twist.

Here's an example.

It is well known that the film industry has largely eclipsed the once-booming theater business in the United [1] States: once the silver screen came along, audiences were more interested in the new medium.

1
Which of the following alternatives to the underlined portion would NOT be acceptable?

A) States; once

B) States. Once

C) States, for once

D) States, once

Here's How to Crack It

First and foremost, it's important to notice the question. This one is asking for the alternative that would NOT be acceptable, so we'll need to find an answer that doesn't work.

In the meantime, let's go through the steps. What's changing in the answer choices? STOP, HALF-STOP, and GO punctuation. Use the Vertical Line Test between the words *States* and *once*. The idea before the line, *It is well known that the film industry has largely eclipsed the once-booming theater business in the United States*, is complete. The idea after the line, *once the silver screen came along, audiences were more interested in the new medium*, is also complete. Therefore, we need either STOP or HALF-STOP punctuation.

Choices (A) and (B) definitely provide the punctuation we want. Choice (C) doesn't look like it does, but remember! *For* is one of the FANBOYS, and comma+FANBOYS is one of the forms of STOP punctuation! The only one, therefore, that doesn't work in the context is (D), so it is the alternative that would NOT be acceptable.

Notice how important that word NOT was in this question. If you missed it, you might have thought the question had three correct answers!

Let's try another.

---○---

The [2] wonder that a beautiful film can inspire would seem to be unsurpassable.

2

Which of the following substitutions would be LEAST acceptable?

A) amazement

B) curiosity

C) awe

D) stupefaction

Here's How to Crack It

Again, the question asks for the LEAST acceptable, so find and eliminate answers that work. In this case, we need something similar in meaning to the word *wonder* as it is used in this sentence. All four words mean something similar to *wonder* in different contexts, but we want something that refers to just how *breathtaking* a beautiful film is, so (A), (C), and (D) would work.

Choice (B) does give a synonym for the word *wonder*, but it means something more like *pondering* than *breathtaking*, so it is the LEAST acceptable of the substitutions.

---○---

Even if you're not sure what *stupefaction* is (*astonishment* or *shock*), you can see that *curiosity* is clearly in a different category altogether. POE is your friend!

Let's look at another that deals with some of the topics we've seen earlier.

What many have forgotten, however, is that the theater remains a vibrant medium. The vibrancy of the medium comes partly from the particular intimacy of the connection between actors and audience. **3**

3

Which of the following gives the best way to combine these two sentences?

A) What many have forgotten, however, is that the theater remains a vibrant medium; the vibrancy of the medium comes partly from the particular intimacy of the connection between actors and audience.

B) What many have forgotten, however, is that the theater remains a vibrant medium, particularly given the intimacy of the connection between actors and audience.

C) A lot of people forget, however, about the vibrancy of theater as a medium when they don't think about how intimate the connection is between the actors in the theater and the audience in the seats.

D) What many have forgotten, however, is that the theater remains a vibrant medium. The connection between actors and audience is so intimate.

Here's How to Crack It

The question asks us to combine the two sentences. Your eyes were probably drawn immediately to (D), which is the most concise of the choices. There's just one problem: (D) doesn't answer the question! The question asks to *combine* the sentences, and while (D) shortens them, it doesn't combine them.

Choice (B) is therefore the best option. It combines the sentences and shortens them a bit, unlike (A) and (C), which combine the sentences, but don't really do much beyond changing the punctuation or adding a bunch of words.

———————○———————

Questions like #3 are why…

> The most important thing about Writing and Language questions is that you *notice* those questions and then *answer* those questions.

PRECISION QUESTIONS

Not all questions will just be applications of punctuation and parts of speech. Some questions will ask you to do more specific things. Remember the three terms we kept repeating in the Words chapter: Consistency, Precision, and Concision. We'll start with the Precision-related questions. Even in those where Precision is not asked about directly, or when it is mixed with Consistency or Concision, remember this:

> Answer the question in the most precise way possible. Read literally!

Let's try one.

In fact, the history of the theater in the United States provides as riveting a story as the greatest stage drama. **4**

4

The writer is considering deleting the phrase *of the theater in the United States* from the preceding sentence. Should this phrase be kept or deleted?

A) Kept, because removing it would remove a crucial piece of information from this part of the sentence.

B) Kept, because it stirs the reader's national sentiments and might generate extra interest in the story.

C) Deleted, because it wrongly implies that stage plays are not interesting on their own terms.

D) Deleted, because it gives information that has no bearing on this particular essay.

Here's How to Crack It

This question asks whether we should keep or delete the phrase *of the theater in the United States*. Without that phrase, the sentence reads: *In fact, the history provides as riveting a story as the greatest stage drama.* Because nothing in this sentence or any of the previous ones specifies what this *history* might be, we should keep the phrase. We want to be as precise as possible!

And, as (A) says, we want to keep the phrase because it is crucial to clarifying precisely what *the question* is. Choice (B) is a little too grandiose and vague a reason to keep the phrase. Choice (A) is therefore the best answer.

Let's try another.

The history of the theater in the United States is part of Revolutionary history. **5** The early provisional government banned all theaters during the War for Independence.

5

At this point, the writer is considering adding the following true statement:

> William Shakespeare was a British playwright, but his stature extends to all parts of the English-speaking world.

Should the writer make this addition here?

A) Yes, because it names an important figure in theatrical history.

B) Yes, because it shows that theater can bring nations together rather than drive them apart.

C) No, because it does not contribute in a significant way to the discussion of the history of the theater in the United States.

D) No, because other playwrights have had a large impact in the United States as well.

Here's How to Crack It

The proposed sentence does contain an interesting bit of information, but that piece of information has no clear place either in these few sentences or in the passage as a whole. Therefore, it should not be added, thus eliminating (A) and (B).

Then, because it does not play a significant role in the passage, the sentence should not be added for the reason stated in (C). While (D) may be true in a way, it does not reflect anything clearly relating to the role the sentence might play in the passage as a whole. Read literally, and answer as literally and precisely as you can.

CONSISTENCY QUESTIONS

Just as questions should be answered as *precisely* as possible, they should also be answered with information that is *consistent* with what's in the passage.

When answering consistency questions, keep this general rule in mind:

> Writing and Language passages should be judged on what they *do* say, not on what they *could* say. When dealing with Style, Tone, and Focus, make sure to work with the words and phrases the passage has already used.

Let's look at two questions that deal with the idea of consistency.

---

[1] The status of the theater was especially controversial in the pre-Revolutionary era. [2] These writings may have even influenced Shakespeare himself. [3] In particularly religious places, like Boston, the theater **6** has become a popular and respected profession in the twentieth century. [4] In Philadelphia, too, theater could have only a marginal influence over and above religious protests. [5] It was really in the southern colonies, especially around Virginia, that the real English love of the theater came through. [6] In fact, John Smith's writings of his trip to this early colony are full of imagery from the theater. **7**

6

Which of the following choices would best complete the idea presented in this sentence?

A) NO CHANGE

B) was thought to encourage unrighteous behavior in the audience and the actors.

C) may have hosted one of the first performances of the temperance play *The Drunkard.*

D) could be a pleasant way to spend a Sunday afternoon after church.

7

The best placement for sentence 2 would be

A) where it is now.

B) before sentence 1.

C) after sentence 5.

D) after sentence 6.

Here's How to Crack Them

Let's look at #6 first. In this case, the question tells us exactly what to look for: something that would *complete the idea* in the sentence, an idea about how religious places were less likely to allow the theater. Choices (A) and (C) may be true, but they don't have anything to do with religion. Choice (D) addresses religion, but not in the way that the rest of the sentence or surrounding ideas do. Only (B) discusses religion in an appropriate way by noting how religious authorities saw the theater as promoting *unrighteous* behavior.

Now, as for #7, we need to find some very literal way to make sentence 2 consistent with the rest of the paragraph. Look for words and phrases that will link sentence 2 to other sentences. Remember, it's not what the passage *could* say; it's what the passage *does* say. Sentence 2, we should note, starts with *These writings*, thus clearly referring to writings that have been mentioned before it. As such, sentence 2 belongs definitively after sentence 6, which discusses the *writings* of John Smith. This is answer (D).

As we have seen, these questions are not difficult, but they do require very specific actions on your part. Make sure you read the questions carefully and that you answer those questions as precisely and consistently as you can.

The same goes for Charts and Graphs on the Writing and Language section. Don't let the strangeness of the charts throw you off! Just read the graphs with as much precision as you can and choose the most precise answers possible.

Let's have a look at one.

For all the interest of its history, however, the theater has seen a remarkable decline in popularity. A recent study showed that in 2002 just 17.1%, 12.3%, and 3.2% of adults had seen a performance of an opera, a musical, or a non-musical play within the previous year. **8**

8

The writer wants the information in the passage to correspond as closely as possible with the information in the chart. Given that goal and assuming that the rest of the previous sentence would remain unchanged, in which sequence should the three cultural activities be listed?

A) NO CHANGE
B) opera, non-musical, musical
C) non-musical, musical, opera
D) musical, non-musical, opera

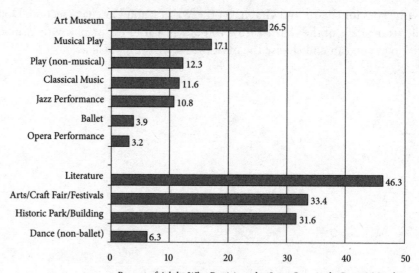

Participation in Arts and Cultural Activities – 2002

Percent of Adults Who Participated at Least Once in the Past 12 Months

Here's How to Crack It

This question is asking for what agrees with the graph. From what we have seen, these questions are usually pretty straightforward. You don't have to do anything overly complex with the graphs, and that is certainly the case here.

There are three activities: opera, non-musical plays, and musical plays. Notice how the numbers are listed in the passage and match each of these numbers with the graph. The graph shows "Musical Play" at 17.1%, "Play (non-musical)" at 12.3%, and "Opera Performance" at 3.2%. This should therefore be the order in which the activities are listed, as in (D).

In general, graphs on the PSAT Reading and Writing and Language sections are very straightforward, and the fundamental question they ask is this: "Can you read a graph?" These are easy points as long as you read the graphs carefully and use POE.

CONCLUSION

As we have seen in this chapter, the PSAT can ask a lot of different kinds of questions, but the test won't throw throw anything really crazy at you. The biggest things to remember, aside from the punctuation rules, are *PRECISION* and *CONSISTENCY*. If you pick answers that are precise and consistent with other information in the passage, you should be good to go. Just make sure to answer the question!

Drill

Time: 10 minutes

[1]

1 In the 1980s and 1990s, cultural critics had begun to express concern that Americans watched too much television. The numbers varied, but it was widely touted that Americans spent anywhere from three to five hours a day in front of the tube. **2** Whether this was true, it certainly did present a startling finding, especially to those who were interested in promoting other media and activities.

1

Which of the following choices would best introduce the essay by identifying a way that a historical period understood a particular medium?

A) NO CHANGE

B) If you don't own a TV today, it's not considered that weird anymore.

C) It's very possible that the only thing you listen to on the radio is music.

D) The old cathode-ray-tube TVs are relics of the past by this point.

2

The writer is considering deleting the phrase *in front of the tube* and ending the sentence with a period after the word *day*. Should the phrase be kept or deleted?

A) Kept, because the meaning of the sentence is unclear without the phrase.

B) Kept, because it shows what the viewers of television find so compelling.

C) Deleted, because it does not clarify whether the number was closer to three or five.

D) Deleted, because this kind of slangy language should be avoided at all costs.

[2]

Therefore, in today's world, where the internet seems to be the new medium of choice, we should not be so quick to criticize it in these terms. Still, as a recent survey has shown, American consumers spend more time online than they have on any other media platform in the last five years. **3** Spending more time on the internet as of 2012, **4** American consumers in 2013 spent an average of over 5 hours a day on the internet.

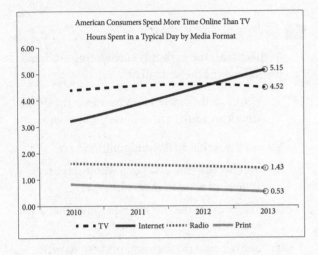

American Consumers Spend More Time Online Than TV
Hours Spent in a Typical Day by Media Format

3

The writer is considering replacing the word *spend* in the preceding sentence with the word *pay out*. Should the writer make the change or keep the sentence as it is?

A) Make the change, because the words *pay out* are more relatable to readers.

B) Make the change, because the words *pay out* provide a more direct indication of the action of the sentence.

C) Keep the sentence as it is, because the words *pay out* change the meaning in a way inconsistent with the passage as a whole.

D) Keep the sentence as it is, because the word *spend* hides the fact that the use of media platforms varies widely by socioeconomic status.

4

Which of the following gives information consistent with the graph?

A) NO CHANGE

B) the world's consumers in 2013 spent an average of over 3 hours a day on the internet.

C) American consumers only a year earlier spent an average of as few as 2 hours a day on the internet.

D) American consumers decided that the internet was a better place to watch shows than was the television.

5 All the while, TV is as good now as it has ever been in its 60-year history. Political theorists warned that too much time in front of the television would dampen people's political awareness. Nutrition activists feared that such a sedentary activity would spur an obesity epidemic. **6** Movie-theater owners cautioned that the lower-quality television could destroy the high-end film industry. Lovers of literature fretted that people no longer had the time or attention span to read the great works.

5

Which of the following choices would offer the most effective transition between the previous paragraph and the current one?

A) NO CHANGE

B) In addition, this general movement toward the television seemed to bode ill for society at large.

C) The first televised presidential debate came during the 1960 election.

D) The technology of new TVs has improved by leaps and bounds even in the last ten years.

6

At this point, the author is considering adding the following true statement:

A 2015 study showed that over two-thirds of American adults are overweight or obese.

Should the writer make this addition here?

A) Yes, because the essay as a whole has very little hard statistical data like this.

B) Yes, because the obesity rate shows that TV was truly a destructive medium.

C) No, because the mention of these statistics is cruel to those who are overweight.

D) No, because the essay as a whole is focused on a different subject.

[4]

7 While each of these criticisms certainly has its merits, each was in a way following in a long path of conservative skepticism at new media developments. Movies were controversial in the 1920s. The National Association of Librarians wrote a report in the 1940s. In this report, radio was excoriated for distracting children from life's real pursuits. **8** The criticisms went even further back. The printing press, even early in its history as mainly a printer of Bibles, was thought to give religious messages to too many who couldn't properly **9** understand the messages. Even newspapers, now a mainstay of the serious American consumer, were once considered politically subversive.

7

Which of the following alternatives to the underlined portion would NOT be acceptable?

A) Although each

B) However, each

C) Even if each

D) However, while each

8

Which of the following gives the most effective way to combine the previous two sentences, reproduced below?

The National Association of Librarians wrote a report in the 1940s. In this report, radio was excoriated for distracting children from life's real pursuits.

A) (keep the sentences as they are)

B) The National Association of Librarians wrote a report in the 1940s. It was about the following: radio, they said, should be excoriated for distracting children from life's real pursuits.

C) In a 1940 report from the National Association of Librarians, radio was excoriated for distracting children from life's real pursuits.

D) The National Association of Librarians was so upset about radio's excoriating influence that they wrote a report on children in 1940.

9

Which of the following alternatives to the underlined portions would be LEAST acceptable?

A) comprehend

B) grasp

C) appreciate

D) intuit

[5]

Is this a troubling change? Well, history would seem to say that it's not. **10** After all, the internet has the advantage of being significantly more active than all those other media. In short, effective use of the internet requires your participation in a way that TV does not. Even so, upwards of six hours a day is a tremendous amount. There must at least be some kind of change, even if it's not necessarily for the worse.

10

At this point, the writer wants to insert an idea that will support the idea given in the previous sentence ("Well, history…not"). Which of the following true statements would offer that support?

A) The rate of literacy remains at an all-time high, despite the introduction of the radio in the 1930s.

B) The number of creative-writing majors may soon eclipse the number of English majors, which will lead to an odd imbalance.

C) Then-candidate Richard Nixon looked really bad on TV in 1960, and how else would people have known his big scandal was coming?

D) The printing press, the newspapers, the radio, and even the television have all been integrated effectively into American culture.

11

The best placement for paragraph 2 would be

A) where it is now.

B) after paragraph 3.

C) after paragraph 4.

D) after paragraph 5.

DRILL ANSWERS

1. A
2. A
3. C
4. A
5. B
6. D
7. B
8. C
9. D
10. D
11. C

Part III
Drill Answers
and
Explanations

CHAPTER 5

Drill 1 Answers

1.   c   Examples: −7, 0, 1, 8

2.   d   Examples: .5, 2, 118

3.   g   Examples: −.5, −2, −118

4.   f   Examples: −4, 0, 10

5.   b   Examples: −5, 1, 17

6.   a   Examples: *Factors* of 12 are 1, 2, 3, 4, 6, and 12. Factors of 10 are 1, 2, 5, and 10.

7.   i   Examples: *Multiples* of 12 include −24, −12, 0, 12, 24, and so on. Multiples of 10 include −20, −10, 0, 10, 20, 30, and so on.

8.   h   Examples: 2, 3, 5, 7, 11, and so on. There are no negative *prime numbers*, and 1 is not prime.

9.   e   Examples: 3 and 4 are *distinct* numbers. −2 and 2 are also distinct.

10.   j   Examples: In the number 274, 2 is the *digit* in the hundreds place, 7 is the digit in the tens place, and 4 is the digit in the ones place.

11.   p   Examples: −1, 0, 1, and 2 are *consecutive* numbers. Be careful—sometimes you will be asked for *consecutive even* or *consecutive odd* numbers, in which case you would use just the odds or evens in a consecutive list of numbers.

12.   n   Examples: 6 is *divisible* by 2 and 3, but not by 4 or 5.

13.   l   Examples: When you divide 26 by 8, you get 3 with a *remainder* of 2 (2 is left over). When you divide 14 by 5, you get 2 with a remainder of 4 (4 is left over).

14.   k   Examples: When you add 2 and 3, you get a *sum* of 5. When you add −4 and 1, you get a sum of −3.

15.   r   Examples: When you multiply 2 and 3, you get a *product* of 6. When you multiply −4 and 1, you get a product of −4.

16.   m   Examples: When you subtract 2 from 3, you get a *difference* of 1. When you subtract −4 from 1, you get a difference of 5.

17.   q   Examples: When you divide 2 by 3, you get a quotient of $\frac{2}{3}$. When you divide −4 by 1, you get a quotient of −4.

18.   o   Examples: The absolute value of −3 is 3. The absolute value of 41 is 41.

Drill 2 Answers

a. 3^5

b. 3^1

c. 3^6

d. x^8

e. x^4

f. x^{12}

g. $2\sqrt{2}$

h. -4

i. $7\sqrt{3}$

j. $y\sqrt{y}$

k. $-y$

l. $6x\sqrt{y}$

3.   **A**   If $3^4 = 9^x$, then $81 = 9^x$. Therefore, $x = 2$. You could also rewrite 3^4 as $3 \times 3 \times 3 \times 3 = 9 \times 9$.

5.   **B**   If $(3x)^3 = 3^{15}$, then by the rules of MADSPM, $3x = 15$, and $x = 5$.

11.   **D**   Let's take the two equations separately, using the rules of MADSPM. If $x^y \times x^6 = x^{54}$, then $y + 6 = 54$, and $y = 48$. If $(x^3)^z = x^9$, then $3z = 9$, and $z = 3$. Now you know that $y = 48$ and $z = 3$, so $y + z = 51$.

4.   **D**   Add 3 to both sides to get $\sqrt{s} = 12$. Square both sides of the equation to get $s = 144$.

9.   **A**   Start with applying the root to the coefficient: $\sqrt[4]{81} = 3$. Therefore, eliminate (C) and (D) because these answer choices have the wrong coefficient. To find the fourth root of an exponent, divide the exponent by 4. Therefore, $\sqrt[4]{81b^3c} = 3b^{\frac{3}{4}}c^{\frac{1}{4}}$. The correct answer is (A).

10.   **B**   When you simplify the fractional exponent, you get $\sqrt{x^5} = 8x$. Squaring both sides gives you $x^5 = 64x^2$. You can divide by x^2 on each side to get $x^3 = 64$ (remember your MADSPM rules!). Finally, taking the cube root of both sides gives you $x = 4$, which is (B).

Drill 3 Answers

3. **C** This is a translation question. Translate the English to math one step at a time to get $x = 3 + 7x$. Now you can subtract $7x$ from both sides to leave you with $-6x = 3$. Divide both sides by -6 and you find that x is equal to 3 divided by -6, which equates to (C).

5. **D** Currently Ann has $32 + 18 = 50$ recipes. Given that the book will include up to 98 recipes, Ann can include at most $98 - 50 = 48$ recipes. Therefore, $r \leq 48$. Solve for r in (A) to get $r \geq 148$. Eliminate (A). Solve for r in (B) to get $r \leq 148$. Eliminate (B). In (C), $98 - 50 - r \leq 0$, so $48 - r \leq 0$. Solve for r to get $-r \leq 48$ or $r \leq -48$. Eliminate (C). In (D), $98 - 50 - r \geq 0$, so $48 - r \geq 0$. Solve for r to get $-r \geq -48$ or $r \leq 48$. The correct answer is (D).

4. **C** Cross-multiply to get $3a \times 6d = 4b \times 5c$. Simplify both sides of the equation to get $18ad = 20bc$. Solve for bc to get $\dfrac{18ad}{20} = bc$. Reduce to get $\dfrac{9ad}{10} = bc$. The correct answer is (C).

8. **C** Start with the easier equation and use Process of Elimination. The easier equation is related to the total number of skis and snowboards, $s + b$, the ski resort rented. According to the problem the following number of skis and snowboards were rented:

	Total Skis and Snowboards rented
Friday	40
Saturday	55
Sunday	85
Total	**180**

Therefore $s + b = 180$. Eliminate (A) and (D) because neither of these answers includes this equation. The other equation in the set is related to the amount of money the ski resort collected in rental fees. According to the question the following amounts were collected:

	Rental Fees Collected
Friday	$1,100
Saturday	$1,400
Sunday	$2,100
Total	**$4,600**

Eliminate (B) because the total in the money equation is wrong. The correct answer is (C).

12. **B** First, get rid of the fractions by multiplying both sides of the equation by 21. The equation becomes $\dfrac{21(m + 9)}{3} + 21(2) = \dfrac{21(m - 2)}{7} + 21(3)$, which simplifies to $7(m + 9) + 42 = 3(m - 2) + 63$. Multiply it out to get $7m + 63 + 42 = 3m - 6 + 63$ or $7m + 105 = 3m + 57$. Subtract $3m$ and 105 from both sides, resulting in $4m = -48$; then divide both sides by 4. The result is $m = -12$, so the correct answer is (B).

23.   **C**   Let s represent snickerdoodle cookies and c represent cinnamon cookies. Translate the two equations given in the problem as $2s + 7c = 14$ and $8s + 3c = 17.5$. To solve for one of the variables, try to make the coefficient for one of the variables the same and then add or subtract the two resulting equations from each other to get rid of that variable. In this case, take the first equation and multiply it by -4 to get $-8s - 28c = -56$. Place the two equations on top of each other and add:

$$-8s - 28c = -56.00$$
$$+ \underline{8s + 3c = 17.50}$$
$$-25c = -38.50$$

Solve for c to get $c = 1.54$. Plug 1.54 in for c in the first equation to get $2s + 7(1.54) = 14$. Solve for s to get $2s + 10.78 = 14$, or $2s = 3.22$, so $s = 1.61$. Plug 1.61 in for s and 1.54 in for c in the answers to see which answer works. Choice (A) becomes $2(1.61) + 3(1.54) = 8.00$. Solve the left side of the equation to get $3.22 + 4.62 = 8.00$ or $7.84 = 8.00$. This is not true, so eliminate (A). Choice (B) becomes $4(1.61) + 6(1.54) = 16.25$. Solve the left side of the equation to get $6.44 + 9.24 = 16.25$ or $15.68 = 16.25$. Eliminate (B). Choice (C) becomes $6(1.61) + 5(1.54) = 17.36$. Solve the left side of the equation to get $9.66 + 7.70 = 17.36$ or $17.36 = 17.36$. The correct answer is (C).

Drill 4 Answers

a.   6

b.   6

c. -1

d. -1

e.   1

f. $6\sqrt{2}$

g. $(0, 1)$

2.   **B**   The slope-intercept form of the equation of a line is $y = mx + b$, where m is the slope and b is the y-intercept. So the slope of the line given by the first equation is 6. To find the slope of a perpendicular line, you would take the negative reciprocal. So $c = \dfrac{1}{6}$, which is (B).

3.   **A**   The slope-intercept form of the equation of a line is $y = mx + b$, where m is the slope, and b is the y-intercept. So you would manipulate this equation to solve for y. Subtracting $2x$ from both sides of the equation and then dividing both sides by 3 gives you $y = -\dfrac{2}{3}x + 4$, so the y-intercept is 4.

12. **D** The x–intercept of a line is where the line crosses the x-axis. The line in the graph has a positive x-intercept, so you can eliminate (A) and (B). To find the x–intercept, first find the slope of the line and then use one of the points given to determine the value of x. The slope of a line is determined by the equation $\dfrac{y_2 - y_1}{x_2 - x_1}$. The slope of the line shown is $\dfrac{-4 - (-2)}{-6 - (-2)} = \dfrac{-2}{-4} = \dfrac{1}{2}$. At the x-intercept, $y = 0$, so the coordinates for the x-intercept are $(x, 0)$. To find x, plug point $(x, 0)$ and $(-2, -2)$ into the slope equation and solve for x. $\dfrac{-2 - 0}{-2 - x} = \dfrac{1}{2}$, so $\dfrac{-2}{-2 - x} = \dfrac{1}{2}$. Cross-multiply to get $-2 - x = -4$, or $-x = -2$. Therefore, $x = 2$, and the correct answer is (D).

15. **A** The line shown crosses the y-axis at -2; this point is also known as the y-intercept. The answers are all in the slope-intercept form, $y = mx + b$, where m is the slope and b is the y-intercept. You can eliminate (B) right away because the y-intercept in (B) is 2 not -2. Next, calculate the slope of the line with the two given points. The slope of a line is determined by the equation $\dfrac{y_2 - y_1}{x_2 - x_1}$. Therefore, the slope of the line shown can be calculated as follows: $\dfrac{2a - a}{\dfrac{9}{2}a - 3a} = \dfrac{a}{\dfrac{3}{2}a} = \dfrac{1}{\dfrac{3}{2}} = \dfrac{2}{3}$. The only remaining answer that has a slope equal to $\dfrac{2}{3}$ is (A), so that is the correct answer.

Drill 5 Answers

28. **0.833 or $\dfrac{5}{6}$**

Take the number of contracted users, 225, and divide it by the total number of users in 2008, 270:

$\dfrac{225}{270} = 0.\overline{833}$ or $\dfrac{5}{6}$.

14. **625** Because $5x^2 = 125$, you know that $x^2 = 25$ and $x = -5$ or 5. Since you can grid in only positive numbers, assume $x = 5$. Therefore, $5x^3 = 5 \times 125 = 625$.

29. **9** Start by squaring both sides of the equation to get $\left(5 - \sqrt{z}\right)\left(5 - \sqrt{z}\right) = z - 5$. Expand the right side of the equation to get $25 - 10\sqrt{z} + z = z - 5$. Subtract z from both sides to get $25 - 10\sqrt{z} = -5$. Solve for z to get $-10\sqrt{z} = -30$, so $\sqrt{z} = 3$. Square both sides of the equation to get $z = 9$. The correct answer is 9.

16. **6** Whenever you have two equations with the same two variables, think Simultaneous Equations. The goal with simultaneous equations is to create a common coefficient for one of the variables and then add or subtract the two equations from each other to get rid of that variable. To get rid of a, multiply the first equation by 7 to get $21a + 14b = 259$ and multiply the second equation by -3 to get $-21a - 12b = -255$. Place the two equations on top of each other and subtract them from each other.

$$
\begin{array}{rcr}
21a + 14b &=& 259 \\
\underline{-21a - 12b} &=& \underline{-255} \\
2b &=& 4
\end{array}
$$

Solve for b to get $b = 2$. Therefore, $b^2 + 6b - 10 = 2^2 + 6(2) - 10 = 4 + 12 - 10 = 6$. The correct answer is 6.

CHAPTER 6

Drill 1 Answers

12. **D** Let's pick numbers for a, b, and c such that $a = \dfrac{b}{c^2}$. We can pick $4 = \dfrac{16}{2^2}$. Now the question becomes, what is $\dfrac{1}{b^2}$ or $\dfrac{1}{16^2}$? The answer is $\dfrac{1}{256}$. When you work through all of the answer choices using $a = 4$, $b = 16$, and $c = 2$, which choice says this? Choice (D) does.

13. **A** Let's pick a number for p. How about 2? Now the problem reads $\dfrac{\frac{1}{8}}{2(2)} = \dfrac{1}{32}$. When you plug $p = 2$ into the answers, (A) turns out to be right.

18. **D** Variables in the answer choices? Absolutely! So let's plug in our own numbers: For x (Jodi's account), plug in \$18 (hey, who said Jodi had to be rich?). With \$18 in her account, $\dfrac{1}{6}$ for rent is \$3 and the car payment is also \$3. Subtract that from the \$18, and Jodi has \$12 left in her account. Now we have to plug in for y (the amount Jodi deposits); let's make that \$8, bringing her account balance to \$20. Well, she now purchases a set of knives for \$10 ($\dfrac{1}{2}$ the amount in her account) and has \$10 left. Go through all of the answer choices, using $x = 18$ and $y = 8$, and see which one gives you \$10. The only one that works is (D).

29. **92.3** You don't know how many students are in the incoming freshman class, so Plug In. Because you're taking percentages of the class, make the total number of students 100. That means that there are 15 left-handed students in the class. There are also 65 female students and 35 male students. If $\frac{2}{3}$ of the left-handed students are male, then $\frac{2}{3} \times 15 = 10$ of the left-handed students are male, leaving 5 female left-handed students. If 5 of the 65 female students are left-handed, then the other 60 female students are right-handed. To find the percentage of female students who are right-handed, divide: $\frac{60}{65} = 0.923 = 92.3\%$. Remember to multiply a decimal by 100 to get the equivalent percentage.

Drill 2 Answers

3   **D**   Start with (B). If $n = 3$, then the equation becomes $2(3 + 5) = 3(3 - 2) + 8$. Work the equation: $2(8) = 3(1) + 8$; $16 = 11$. This isn't true, so eliminate (B). You might not know whether you need a bigger or smaller number, so try a larger number. With (C), make $n = 4$. Now work the equation: $2(4 + 5) = 3(4 - 2) + 8$; $2(9) = 3(2) + 8$; $18 = 14$. Not quite; eliminate (C) and try (D). $2(8 + 5) = 3(8 - 2) + 8$; $2(13) = 3(6) + 8$; $26 = 26$. This works, so pick (D).

8.   **C**   Start by trying (C), 3, for x. Does $3^5 = 243$? Yes! So the answer is (C).

10.   **D**   If we try plugging in (C), $\frac{1}{4}$, for x, the equation becomes $\frac{6}{4} + 4 = 5$, which is false. If we try plugging in (D), $\frac{1}{2}$, for x, the equation becomes $\frac{12}{4} + 2 = 5$, which is true.

Drill 3 Answers

a.   90

b.   320

c.   6

d. $x = 8$

e.   5

f.   3

g.   10

h.   120%

i.   108

j.   10%

k. $\dfrac{2,600}{18,600}$ = approximately 14%

The amount of money in a savings account after m months is modeled by the function $f(m) = 1,000(1.01)^m$.

l. $1,000

m.   1%

n.   40

o.   1.5

p.   5 kPa

2.   **D**   This question is asking us to compare pecks and bushels, so let's make a proportion: $\dfrac{10 \text{ pecks}}{2.5 \text{ bushels}} = \dfrac{x \text{ pecks}}{4 \text{ bushels}}$. Then we can cross-multiply and solve for x, which results in $x = 16$.

24. **C**   Consider each Roman numeral one at a time. The last two tests have an average of 90. If the student scored the same on both tests, his score would be 90 on each of those two tests. The two tests have a total of 180 points (2 × 90), so he could have also scored 0 on one test and 180 on the other test, or anything in between. No matter what, there's at least one test on which the student scored more than 85, so I must be true. Eliminate (B) and (D). Now you only need consider II (because there's no option remaining which includes III). You already determined that the last two tests have a total of 180 points. If the first three tests were an average of 80, then the total for those tests would be 3 × 80 = 240. The total points over all 5 tests would be 180 + 240 = 420, and the average would be 420 ÷ 5 = 84, which is less than 85. II is true, so choose (C).

28. **45**   If Marcia types 18 pages per hour, and David can type 14 pages per hour, then together they will be able to type 18 + 14, or 32 pages per hour. To see what fraction of an hour it will take them to type 24 pages, we can set up a proportion: $\dfrac{32 \text{ pages}}{1 \text{ hour}} = \dfrac{24 \text{ pages}}{x \text{ hours}}$.

If we solve for x, we can see that they can type 24 pages in .75 of an hour. But that isn't our answer! The question asks for the answer in minutes. Three-quarters of an hour is equal to 45 minutes, so the answer is 45.

CHAPTER 7

Drill 1 Answers

15. **3** Since the problem tells us that $f(a) = 10$, and that $f(x) = x^2 - x + 4$, we can plug a into the function for x so $f(a) = a^2 - a + 4$, and $10 = a^2 - a + 4$. Now we need to factor to solve for a. If we subtract 10 from both sides of the equation, we get $a^2 - a - 6 = 0$ which we can factor as $(a - 3)(a + 2) = 0$. The value of a could be 3 or –2, but since the question tells us that a is non-negative, the value of a must be 3.

21. **D** Negative exponents mean to take the reciprocal of the positive exponent. For example, $y^{-2} = \dfrac{1}{y^2}$, and $2^{-3} = \dfrac{1}{2^3}$. For fractional exponents, the denominator tells us what root of the number to take and the numerator acts as a normal exponent. So, $f(x)$ is $\dfrac{1}{\sqrt[3]{x^2}}$. First, let's find $f(8)$: $\dfrac{1}{\sqrt[3]{8^2}} = \dfrac{1}{\sqrt[3]{64}} = \dfrac{1}{4}$. Next, let's find $f(3)$: $\dfrac{1}{\sqrt[3]{3^2}} = \dfrac{1}{\sqrt[3]{9}}$. Put these values in for $\dfrac{f(8)}{f(3)}$. So, $\dfrac{\frac{1}{4}}{\frac{1}{\sqrt[3]{9}}} = \dfrac{1}{4} \div \dfrac{1}{\sqrt[3]{9}} = \dfrac{1}{4} \times \sqrt[3]{9} = \dfrac{\sqrt[3]{9}}{4}$. Remember to look at the answer choices so you don't keep trying to simplify when there's no need to.

Drill 2 Answers

4. **B** You could solve this one by expanding the squared binomial, setting it equal to zero, factoring, and solving, but look for a faster way. When the question asks for a specific value and there are numbers in the answer choices, think Plugging In the Answers. In (A), if $t = -9$, the equation becomes $12 - (-9 + 2)^2 = 3$ or $12 - (-7)^2 = 3$. This becomes $12 - 49 = 3$, which is not true, so eliminate (A). In (B), if $t = -5$, $12 - (-5 + 2)^2 = 3$ or $12 - (-3)^2 = 3$. This becomes $12 - 9 = 3$, which is true, so (B) is the correct answer.

6. **B** The equations in the answer choices are factored, making it easy to see the roots. The correct answer will have roots at –3 and 1, as shown on the graph. For (A), the roots are $x - 3 = 0$ or $x = 3$ and $x + 1 = 0$ or $x = -1$, which are the right numbers but the wrong signs. For (B), though, the roots are –3 and 1, so (B) is the correct answer. Another approach would be to plug the given points into the answer choices to see which one works for both points.

14. **3** The maximum profit will occur at the vertex of the parabola. The equation is in vertex form, so the vertex is (3, 2,000). The x-coordinate is the price, so the shop should charge \$3. If you forget the form, you can use a sort of plugging in. To maximize its profit, the donut shop needs to make the

negative part of the equation, $-4(x-3)^2$, either positive or 0. Because $(x-3)^2$ is always either positive or 0, it is not possible to make $-4(x-3)^2$ positive. Therefore, the maximum profits will occur when $-4(x-3)^2 = 0$. Solve for x by dividing both sides by -4 to get $(x-3)^2 = 0$. Solve for x to get $x = 3$. The correct answer is 3.

23. **B**   Whenever there are variables in the question and numbers in the answers, think Plugging In the Answers. In (A), $c = 33$ and the equation becomes $x^2 + 24x + 33 = (x+9)(x+p)$. This means that 33 would equal $9p$ once the right side was multiplied out. Eliminate (A) since 33 is not divisible by 9. In (B), $c = 135$ and the equation becomes $x^2 + 24x + 135 = (x+9)(x+p)$. Divide 135 by 9 to get $x^2 + 24x + 135 = (x+9)(x+15)$. Test whether this is the right answer by using FOIL to expand $(x+9)(x+15)$ to get $(x+9)(x+15) = x^2 + 24x + 135$. The middle term is in fact $24x$, and the correct answer is therefore (B).

Drill 3

6. **A**   Notice that the 40 is being subtracted from the rest of the equation, which means that there is a $40 reduction in the driver's net pay. Look for other information in the question that suggests some type of reduction. The only information on any type of reduction is that the shipping company "deducts a separate fee daily for the use of the company's delivery truck." Therefore, it is reasonable to assume that the 40 represents this fee. The correct answer is (A).

10. **D**   For this question, you have to find the slope of the best-fit line, which will represent the average yearly change. The formula for slope is $\dfrac{y_2 - y_1}{x_2 - x_1}$, so find two points to use. On the graph, the number of carp in 2010 was 25,000 and in 2011, the number of carp was 22,500. You can substitute these x and y values from the graph to get $\dfrac{25,000 - 22,500}{2010 - 2011}$. Simplify to get $\dfrac{2,500}{-1}$, or $-2,500$. However, because the question asks for the yearly decrease, it should be a positive number. Therefore, the answer is (D).

8. **C**   The equation includes a $-0.40c$. A minus sign indicates some type of reduction. According to the question, the only deduction to the net proceeds is the cost of paying for cleaning supplies. It is logical to assume that the students pay 0.40 in cleaning supplies for each car that they wash. Therefore, the correct answer is (C).

12. **C**   Consider each answer and use Process of Elimination. Choice (A) is not supported by the graph because one employee had a linear decrease in energy while the other employee's energy increased and decreased in an exponential fashion; eliminate (A). Choice (B) is also not supported; one employee had low energy after lunch (and may be drowsy), but the other employee had the highest energy level immediately after lunch. Eliminate (B). Choice (C) fits the employee who started with high energy and decreased throughout the afternoon; keep (C). Choice (D) fits neither employee:

One employee decreased throughout the afternoon, and the other employee increased and then rapidly decreased. Eliminate (D) and choose (C).

11. **D**   Whenever there are variables in the question and in the answer choices, think Plugging In. Plug in values that should work and values that shouldn't work and use Process of Elimination. If $t = 37$, the correct answer will provide a statement that is true. Plug 37 in for t in the answers and eliminate any answers that are not true. Choice (A) becomes $|37 + 7| \leq 37$ or $|44| \leq 37$. Since this statement is false, eliminate (A). Choice (B) becomes $|37 - 3.5| \leq 33.5$ or $|33.5| \leq 33.5$. Since this statement is true, keep (B). Choice (C) becomes $|37 - 30| \leq 7$, or $|7| \leq 7$. Since this statement is true, keep (C). Choice (D) becomes $|37 - 33.5| \leq 3.5$, or $|3.5| \leq 3.5$. Since this statement is true, keep (D). Next try a value that should not work such as $t = 29$ in the remaining answer choices and eliminate any answers that provide a true statement. Choice (B) becomes $|29 - 3.5| \leq 33.5$ or $|25.5| \leq 33.5$. Since this statement is true, eliminate (B). Choice (C) becomes $|29 - 30| \leq 7$ or $|-1| \leq 7$. Since this statement is true eliminate (C). Therefore, the correct answer must be (D).

CHAPTER 8

Drill 1 Answers

a.   36

b.   24

c. $x = 10, y = 5$

d.   30

e.   22

4.   **D**   Because this is a square, the two sides are equal. Therefore, $2x + 1 = x + 3$. Solve for x, and you get that x must be 2. Therefore, a side equals $x + 3$ or $2x + 1 = 5$, so the area equals 25.

3.   **D**   Here are four lines; a and b are parallel, d intersects a and b, and c does not intersect both parallel lines. In statement I, angles 1 and 5 do not have to be equal because a side of angle 1 is line c, which has nothing to do with the parallel lines. Thus, the angles in statement I do not have to be equal, and you can eliminate (A). The angles in statement II have to be equal because angles 2 and 7 are opposite angles (two angles made up of the same two lines) and opposite angles must be equal. Eliminate (C). The angles in statement III must be equal because angles 3 and 9 are made up of the same line (line d) and one of the parallel lines. In fact, 3, 6, 5, and 9 are all the same "small angle," so eliminate (B). Therefore, statements II and III are true, and the correct answer is (D).

Drill 2 Answers

a.   24

b.   10

c. $\dfrac{6}{10}, \dfrac{3}{5}$, or 0.6

d.   20

e. $20\sqrt{5}$

f. $\dfrac{20}{20\sqrt{5}}, \dfrac{1}{\sqrt{5}}$, or $\dfrac{\sqrt{5}}{5}$

14. **100**   Because the triangle is isosceles, with $AB = BC$, you know that angles A and C must have the same measure. So angle A must also be 40°. Angles A and C have a combined measure of 80°, and you need a total of 180° in the triangle. Therefore, x must measure 100°.

8. **C**   The problem tells you that the triangle is isosceles, and you see there is a right angle present in the figure. This tells you that the base angles are 45° each. Since the length of side AB is 5, that means that the length of side BC is 5 as well. Using the relationships for a 45°-45°-90° right triangle, you can infer than the length of AC is $5\sqrt{2}$. To find the perimeter, add all three sides together: 5 + 5 + $5\sqrt{2}$ = 10 + $5\sqrt{2}$. The correct choice is (C).

10. **D**   Since these two triangles are right triangles and share another angle, then all three angles must be congruent, and the triangles are therefore similar. You need to determine which sides correspond in order to set up a proportion. Since the only value given in the large triangle is the base, you need to determine the base of the smaller triangle in order to form your proportion. You may recognize the smaller triangle as a Pythagorean triple (5-12-13), but if you do not, you can use the Pythagorean theorem to solve for the base, which is 12. Using this value, you can then set up a proportion: $\dfrac{5}{12} = \dfrac{x}{24}$. Solving this for x will yield 10. Be careful though, the question did not ask for AD; it asked for BD. So you need to subtract 5 (the length of AB) from this to get $BD = 5$, which is (D).

Drill 3 Answers

a. 16π

b. 8π

16. **A** Angle AOB is 60 degrees, which is $\frac{1}{6}$ of 360 degrees. Since arc AB is 2π, it is $\frac{1}{6}$ of the total circumference. The circumference then is $6 \times 2\pi$, which comes to 12π. The diameter of the circle is 12, making the radius 6. The area of the circle then is 36π, (A).

18. **C** Since there is no figure given, you should draw one according to the directions. The figure should look like the following:

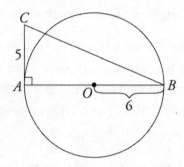

Given that the area of the circle is 36π, the radius is 6. That means that the diameter is 12. The point where a tangent hits the circle makes a 90 degree angle, so angle OAC is 90 degrees. Now that you have a right triangle, you can use the Pythagorean theorem to find that the length of BC is 13. Adding 5 + 12 + 13 gives you 30, (C).

Drill 4 Answers

3. **B** There are variables in the answer choices, so plug in a number for a. How about 90, just to make the math easy? If $a = 90$, then the other angle inside the triangle must be equal to 60. Therefore, b must be equal to 120. What choice says 120, remembering that $a = 90$? Choice (B) does.

7. **B** This is another great example of Plugging In. Make 3 the radius of Cone A and 4 the radius of Cone B. Set the height to 3. The volume of Cone A is therefore 9π, and the volume of Cone B is 16π. Divide both sides by π to get a ratio of 9 : 16. Choice (B) is correct.

22. **A**   Plug in for x, choosing 18 to make the math easier. Since $A = \pi r^2$ and $r = 18$, the total area is 324π.

Since $C = 2\pi r$, the total circumference is 36π. Minor arc PQ takes up $\dfrac{\pi x}{18}$ or π of 36π, which is

$\dfrac{1}{36}$. Sector POQ must therefore take up $\dfrac{1}{36}$ of the area, which is $\left(\dfrac{1}{36}\right)324\pi = 9\pi$. This is the tar-

get answer, so plug $x = 18$ into the answer choices to see which one equals 9π. Choice (A) becomes

$\dfrac{\pi(18)^2}{36} = \dfrac{324\pi}{36} = 9\pi$. This matches the target. Since all the other answers have the same numera-

tor and different denominators, only (A) will work.

Part IV
The Princeton Review Practice Tests and Explanations

Chapter 13
Practice Test 1

Reading Test

60 MINUTES, 47 QUESTIONS

Turn to Section 1 of your answer sheet to answer the questions in this section.

Questions 1-9 are based on the following passage.

The following is an excerpt from a novel by Thomas Hardy published in 1878. This portion speaks about a man named Clym Yeobright who has recently returned to his hometown, Egdon Heath.

In Clym Yeobright's face could be dimly seen the typical countenance of the future. The observer's eye was arrested, not by his face as a picture, but by his face
Line as a page; not by what it was, but by what it recorded.
5 His features were attractive in the light of symbols, as sounds intrinsically common become attractive in language, and as shapes intrinsically simple become interesting in writing.

He had been a lad of whom something was
10 expected. Beyond this all had been chaos. That he would be successful in an original way, or that he would go to the dogs in an original way, seemed equally probable. The only absolute certainty about him was that he would not stand still in the
15 circumstances amid which he was born.

Hence, when his name was casually mentioned by neighbouring yeomen, the listener said, "Ah, Clym Yeobright—what is he doing now?" When the instinctive question about a person is, What is
20 he doing? it is felt that he will be found to be, like most of us, doing nothing in particular. There is an indefinite sense that he must be invading some region of singularity, good or bad. The devout hope is that he is doing well. The secret faith is that he is making
25 a mess of it. Half a dozen comfortable market-men, who were habitual callers at the Quiet Woman as they

passed by in their carts, were partial to the topic. In fact, though they were not Egdon men, they could hardly avoid it while they sucked their long clay tubes
30 and regarded the heath through the window. Clym had been so inwoven with the heath in his boyhood that hardly anybody could look upon it without thinking of him. So the subject recurred: if he were making a fortune and a name, so much the better for him; if he
35 were making a tragical figure in the world, so much the better for a narrative.

The fact was that Yeobright's fame had spread to an awkward extent before he left home. "It is bad when your fame outruns your means," said the Spanish Jesuit
40 Gracian. At the age of six he had asked a Scripture riddle: "Who was the first man known to wear breeches?" and applause had resounded from the very verge of the heath. At seven he painted the Battle of Waterloo with tiger-lily pollen and black-currant juice,
45 in the absence of water-colours. By the time he reached twelve he had in this manner been heard of as artist and scholar for at least two miles round. An individual whose fame spreads three or four thousand yards in the time taken by the fame of others similarly situated
50 to travel six or eight hundred, must of necessity have something in him. Possibly Clym's fame, like Homer's, owed something to the accidents of his situation; nevertheless famous he was. He grew up and went to London; and thence, shortly after, to Paris, where he
55 had remained till now.

Something being expected of him, he had not been at home many days before a great curiosity as to why he stayed on so long began to arise in the heath.

CONTINUE ▶

The natural term of a holiday had passed, yet he still
60 remained.
    Was Yeobright's mind well-proportioned? No.
A well-proportioned mind is one which shows no
particular bias; its usual blessings are happiness and
mediocrity. It enables its possessors to find their way
65 to wealth, to wind up well, to step with dignity off the
stage, to die comfortably in their beds, and to get the
decent monument which, in many cases, they deserve.
It never would have allowed Yeobright to do such a
ridiculous thing as throw up his business to benefit his
70 fellow-creatures.
    He walked along towards home without attending
to paths. If anyone knew the heath well it was Clym.
He was permeated with its scenes, with its substance,
and with its odours. He might be said to be its product.
75 His eyes had first opened thereon; with its appearance
all the first images of his memory were mingled, his
estimate of life had been coloured by it: his toys had
been the flint knives and arrow-heads which he found
there, wondering why stones should "grow" to such
80 odd shapes; his flowers, the purple bells and yellow
furze: his animal kingdom, the snakes and croppers;
his society, its human haunters. He gazed upon the
wide prospect as he walked, and was glad.

The passage most strongly suggests that which of the
following is true of Clym?

A) The locals support him, which has bolstered his
   achievement.

B) He is not going to return to Paris because his fame
   was all accidental.

C) His religious upbringing prepared him well for
   prosperity.

D) He was expected to either prosper or fail but not
   to be mired in anything banal.

Which choice provides the best evidence for the
answer to the previous question?

A) Lines 10-15 ("That he . . . born")

B) Lines 40-43 ("At the age . . . heath")

C) Lines 51-55 ("Possibly . . . now")

D) Lines 61-64 ("Was . . . mediocrity")

As used in line 3, "arrested" most nearly means

A) indicted.

B) forced.

C) engaged.

D) charged.

The author uses the quote ("It is bad . . . your means")
in lines 38-39 primarily to suggest that

A) Clym may not live up to the people of his
   hometown's expectations, despite relatively
   widespread fame.

B) Clym has used his fame to his advantage for too
   long and now people are beginning to bore of
   him.

C) Clym has run out of money and can no longer
   support his luxurious European lifestyle.

D) Clym can never live up to his own notoriety.

The fifth paragraph (lines 56-60) primarily serves to

A) show the townspeople's frustration that Clym
   won't go back to Paris.

B) underscore that Clym's extended return is
   incongruous with someone of his potential.

C) provide an example of the locals' intrusive
   presence in Clym's life.

D) prove that Clym's illustriousness has spread to an
   awkward extent.

As used in line 52, "accidents" most nearly means

A) predecessors.

B) fate.

C) chance.

D) trauma.

7

Based on the information in the passage, Yeobright is known chiefly for his

A) vast wealth and reputation overseas.

B) sweeping acclaim and abundant promise.

C) unique aesthetic features and tragic circumstances.

D) aptitude as a scholar and preacher.

8

Which choice provides the best evidence for the answer to the previous question?

A) Lines 1-4 ("In Clym . . . recorded")

B) Lines 45-47 ("By the time . . . round")

C) Lines 47-51 ("An individual . . . in him")

D) Lines 53-55 ("He grew . . . now")

9

The comparison in lines 6-8 ("as sounds . . . writing") is most similar to which of the following?

A) The allure of the color yellow becoming stronger in a painting of a sunrise versus on the palette

B) A beautiful dress that looks beautiful worn and on the hanger

C) A phrase in another language causing confusion until it is translated

D) Diamond rings that are more attractive than ruby rings

CONTINUE

No Test Material On This Page

Questions 10-18 are based on the following passage.

This passage is adapted from Michael Pollan, *The Botany of Desire.* © 2001 by Michael Pollan.

The modern tulip has become such a cheap and ubiquitous commodity that it's hard for us to recover a sense of the glamour that once surrounded the flower. That glamour surely had something to do with
5 its roots in the Orient—Anna Pavord speaks of the "intoxicating aura of the infidels" that surrounded the tulip. There was, too, the preciousness of the early tulips, the supply of which could be increased only very slowly through offsets, a quirk of biology that kept
10 supply well behind demand. In France in 1608, a miller exchanged his mill for a bulb of Mère Brune. Around the same time a bridegroom accepted a single tulip as the whole of his dowry—happily, we are told; the variety became known as "Marriage de ma fille."
15   Yet tulipomania in France and England never reached the pitch it would in Holland. How can the mad embrace of these particular people and this particular flower be explained?

For good reason, the Dutch have never been
20 content to accept nature as they found it. Lacking in conventional charms and variety, the landscape of the Low Countries is spectacularly flat, monotonous, and swampy. "An universall quagmire" is how one Englishman described the place; "the buttock of
25 the world." What beauty there is in the Netherlands is largely the result of human effort: the dikes and canals built to drain the land, the windmills erected to interrupt the unbroken sweep of wind across it. In his famous essay on tulipomania, "The Bitter Smell of
30 Tulips," the poet Zbigniew Herbert suggests that the "monotony of the Dutch landscape gave rise to dreams of multifarious, colorful, and unusual flora."

Such dreams could be indulged as never before in seventeenth-century Holland, as Dutch traders
35 and plant explorers returned home with a parade of exotic new plant species. Botany became a national pastime followed as closely and avidly as we follow sports today. This was a nation, and a time, in which a botanical treatise could become a best-seller and a
40 plantsman like Clusius a celebrity.

Land in Holland being so scarce and expensive, Dutch gardens were miniatures, measured in square feet rather than acres and frequently augmented with mirrors. The Dutch thought of their gardens as jewel

45 boxes, and in such a space even a single flower—and especially one as erect, singular, and strikingly colored as a tulip—could make a powerful statement.

To make such statements—about one's sophistication, about one's wealth—has always been
50 one of the reasons people plant gardens. In the seventeenth century the Dutch were the richest people in Europe and, as the historian Simon Schama shows in *The Embarrassment of Riches*, their Calvinist faith did not keep them from indulging in the pleasures of
55 conspicuous display. The exoticism and expense of tulips certainly recommended them for this purpose, but so did the fact that, among flowers, the tulip is one of the most extravagantly useless. Up until the Renaissance, most of the flowers in cultivation had
60 been useful as well as beautiful; they were sources of medicine, perfume, or even food. In the West flowers have often come under attack from various Puritans, and what has always saved them has been their practical uses. It was utility, not beauty, that earned the
65 rose and lily, the peony and all the rest a spot in the gardens of monks and Shakers and colonial Americans who would otherwise have had nothing to do with them.

When the tulip first arrived in Europe, people
70 set about fashioning some utilitarian purpose for it. The Germans boiled and sugared the bulbs and, unconvincingly, declared them a delicacy; the English tried serving them up with oil and vinegar. Pharmacists proposed the tulip as a remedy for
75 flatulence. None of these uses caught on, however. "The tulip remained itself," Herbert writes, "the poetry of Nature to which vulgar utilitarianism is foreign." The tulip was a thing of beauty, no more, no less.

10

The passage suggests that in seventeenth-century Europe, tulips were prized primarily for their

A) intoxicating scent.

B) exotic botany.

C) extravagant beauty.

D) medicinal qualities.

CONTINUE

11

Which choice provides the best evidence for the answer to the previous question?

A) Lines 4-7 ("That glamour . . . tulip")

B) Lines 55-58 ("The exoticism . . . useless")

C) Lines 74-75 ("Pharmacists . . . flatulence")

D) Lines 77-78 ("The tulip . . . less")

12

As used in line 16, "pitch" most nearly means

A) throw.

B) angle.

C) level.

D) promotion.

13

The author uses the word "spectacularly" (line 22) in order to

A) emphasize the beauty to be found in the flat landscape of the Low Countries.

B) highlight the monotonous nature of the Dutch landscape.

C) maintain the tone of irony used to describe the Dutch attitude towards their land.

D) underscore the importance of human efforts to make the Low Countries beautiful.

14

The primary purpose of the fourth paragraph (lines 33-40) is to

A) illustrate the widespread popularity of botany in seventeenth-century Holland.

B) indicate that the Dutch landscape is as flat as a baseball field.

C) provide an example to show the relative lack of fame of Dutch traders and plantsmen.

D) introduce a metaphor supporting the idea that the Dutch obsession for tulips was unusually strong.

15

It can be inferred from the passage that seventeenth-century Dutch gardens were

A) as small as jewel boxes.

B) indicators of wealth and sophistication.

C) full of exotic and expensive flowers.

D) often adorned by only a single flower.

16

Which choice provides the best evidence for the answer to the previous question?

A) Lines 41-44 ("Land . . . mirrors")

B) Lines 48-50 ("To make . . . gardens")

C) Lines 69-71 ("When . . . it")

D) Lines 74-75 ("Pharmacists . . . however")

17

As used in line 70, "utilitarian" most nearly means

A) practical.

B) industrial.

C) culinary.

D) decorative.

18

It can reasonably be inferred from the passage that the characteristic that makes the tulip most different from a rose or a lily is its

A) price.

B) exoticism.

C) beauty.

D) uselessness.

Questions 19-28 are based on the following passage.

This passage is adapted from Harriet H. Robinson, "Early Factory Labor in New England," in Massachusetts Bureau of Statistics of Labor, *Fourteenth Annual Report* (Boston: Wright & Potter, 1883). Robinson was a mill-worker, writer, and social activist who played a prominent role in the labor and women's suffrage movements in the United States.

In 1832, Lowell was little more than a factory village. Five "corporations" were started, and the cotton mills belonging to them were building. Help was in
Line great demand and stories were told all over the country
5 of the new factory place, and the high wages that were offered to all classes of workpeople; stories that reached the ears of mechanics' and farmers' sons and gave new life to lonely and dependent women in distant towns and farmhouses. Troops of young girls came from
10 different parts of New England, and from Canada, and men were employed to collect them at so much a head, and deliver them at the factories.

At the time the Lowell cotton mills were started, the caste of the factory girl was the lowest among the
15 employments of women. In England and in France, particularly, great injustice had been done to her real character. She was represented as subjected to influences that must destroy her purity and self-respect. In the eyes of her overseer she was but a brute,
20 a slave, to be beaten, pinched and pushed about. It was to overcome this prejudice that such high wages had been offered to women that they might be induced to become millgirls, in spite of the opprobrium that still clung to this degrading occupation.

25 The early millgirls were of different ages. Some were not over ten years old; a few were in middle life, but the majority were between the ages of sixteen and twenty-five. The very young girls were called "doffers." They "doffed," or took off, the full bobbins from the
30 spinningframes, and replaced them with empty ones. These mites worked about fifteen minutes every hour and the rest of the time was their own. When the overseer was kind they were allowed to read, knit, or go outside the millyard to play. They were paid
35 two dollars a week. The working hours of all the girls extended from five o'clock in the morning until seven in the evening, with one halfhour each, for breakfast and dinner. Even the doffers were forced to be on duty nearly fourteen hours a day. This was the greatest
40 hardship in the lives of these children. Several years

later a tenhour law was passed, but not until long after some of these little doffers were old enough to appear before the legislative committee on the subject, and plead, by their presence, for a reduction of the hours of
45 labor.

Those of the millgirls who had homes generally worked from eight to ten months in the year; the rest of the time was spent with parents or friends. A few taught school during the summer months. Their life in
50 the factory was made pleasant to them. In those days there was no need of advocating the doctrine of the proper relation between employer and employed. Help was too valuable to be ill-treated.

The most prevailing incentive to labor was to
55 secure the means of education for some male member of the family. To make a gentleman of a brother or a son, to give him a college education, was the dominant thought in the minds of a great many of the better class of millgirls. I have known more than one to give
60 every cent of her wages, month after month, to her brother, that he might get the education necessary to enter some profession. I have known a mother to work years in this way for her boy. I have known women to educate young men by their earnings, who were not
65 sons or relatives. There are many men now living who were helped to an education by the wages of the early millgirls.

The table below shows the daily schedule for workers at the Lowell Mills in 1851.

	TIME TABLE OF THE LOWELL MILLS, To take effect on and after October 21st, 1851.											
The Standard time being that of the meridan of Lowell, as shown by the regulator clock of JOSEPH RAYNES, 43 Central Street												
	From 1st to 10th inclusive				From 11th to 20th inclusive				From 21st to last day of month			
	1st Bell	2d Bell	3d Bell	Eve. Bell	1st Bell	2d Bell	3d Bell	Eve. Bell	1st Bell	2d Bell	3d Bell	Eve. Bell
January	5.00	6.00	6.50	*7.30	5.00	6.00	6.50	*7.30	5.00	6.00	6.50	*7.30
February	4.30	5.30	6.40	*7.30	4.30	5.30	6.25	*7.30	4.30	5.30	6.15	*7.30
March	5.40	6.00		*7.30	5.20	5.40		*7.30	5.05	5.25		6.35
April	4.45	5.05		6.45	4.30	4.50		6.55	4.30	4.50		7.00
May	4.30	4.50		7.00	4.30	4.50		7.00	4.30	4.50		7.00
June												
July												
August												
September	4.40	5.00		6.45	4.50	5.10		6.30	5.00	5.20		*7.30
October	5.10	5.30		*7.30	5.20	5.40		*7.30	5.35	5.55		*7.30
November	4.30	5.30	6.10	*7.30	4.30	5.30	6.20	*7.30	5.00	6.00	6.35	*7.30
December	5.00	6.00	6.45	*7.30	5.00	6.00	6.50	*7.30	5.00	6.00	6.50	*7.30

*Escaping on Saturdays from Sept. 21st to March 20th inclusive, when it is rung at 20 minutes after sunset.

19

The perspective from which Robinson writes is best described as that of

A) a disinterested observer.

B) a passionate advocate.

C) an irate troublemaker.

D) a carefree eyewitness.

20

In lines 3-12 ("Help . . . factories"), Robinson explicitly cites which of the following as a reason that women moved to Lowell to work in the cotton mills?

A) The opportunity to live in a more appealing climate

B) The appeal of generous vacation time

C) The chance to enjoy the company of a diverse array of coworkers

D) The promise of attractive remuneration

21

In the context of the passage as a whole, the author most likely mentions the working conditions of England and France (beginning in line 15) in order to

A) demonstrate the superiority of European factory work.

B) provide a historical overview of the Industrial Revolution.

C) draw a contrast between those conditions and the conditions promised to workers in the Lowell mills.

D) argue that American factories should follow the European model.

22

Which choice provides the best evidence for the answer to the previous question?

A) Lines 1-2 ("In . . . village")

B) Lines 9-12 ("Troops . . . factories")

C) Lines 20-24 ("It . . . occupation")

D) Lines 46-48 ("Those . . . friends")

23

As used in line 23, "opprobrium" most nearly means

A) disgrace.

B) praise.

C) benevolence.

D) trauma.

24

The passage suggests which of the following about the youngest girls employed at the Lowell mills?

A) They had complete freedom to spend their time as they chose.

B) They spent the majority of their time in educational settings.

C) They ranged in age from 10-16 years old.

D) They were afforded more leisure time than were the older girls and adult women.

25

Which choice provides the best evidence for the answer to the previous question?

A) Lines 29-30 ("They . . . ones")

B) Lines 31-34 ("These . . . play")

C) Lines 48-49 ("A few . . . months")

D) Lines 54-56 ("The most . . . family")

26

The information in the table provided most supports which of the following claims made in the passage?

A) Women working in the mills were forced to be on duty nearly fourteen hours per day.

B) There were five growing corporations in Lowell in 1832.

C) Many of the mill girls gave some or all of the wages that they earned to male family members.

D) The idea of working in the mills gave new life to girls and women living in isolated towns across North America.

27

As used in line 54, "prevailing" most nearly means

A) conquering.

B) current.

C) predominant.

D) rare.

28

Which of the following best represents the main idea of the last paragraph (lines 54-67)?

A) The early female mill-workers in Lowell were universally contemptuous of their male relatives.

B) Providing financial resources for their male relatives' education was commonplace among the early female mill-workers in Lowell.

C) A college education is the surest way to achieve the status of a gentleman.

D) The primary reason that middle-aged women worked in the Lowell mills was to provide financial resources for their daughters.

CONTINUE ➤

No Test Material On This Page

Questions 29-37 are based on the following passage.

This passage is adapted from Laurel Woodruff and George Bedinger, "Titanium: Light, Strong, and White" in the U.S. Geological Survey's 2013 Fact Sheet.

Titanium (Ti) is a strong silver-gray metal that is highly resistant to corrosion and is chemically inert. It is as strong as steel but 45 percent lighter, and it
Line is twice as strong as aluminum but only 60 percent
5 heavier. Titanium dioxide (TiO_2) has a very high refractive index, which means that it has high light-scattering ability. As a result, TiO_2 imparts whiteness, opacity, and brightness to many products.

Titanium was first discovered in 1791 by the British
10 clergyman and amateur geologist William Gregor, who produced a white metallic oxide from black magnetic sands. In 1795, the German chemist Martin Klaproth named the oxide "titanium" after the Greek *Titans*, a mythical race of immortal giants with incredible
15 strength and stamina. Pure titanium metal was first isolated in 1910 by chemist Matthew Hunter. Hunter's difficult isolation process made titanium metal mainly a laboratory curiosity until 1938 when William Kroll developed a method (known as the Kroll method)
20 to produce titanium metal in commercial quantities. Because of the unique physical properties of titanium metal and the whiteness provided by TiO_2, titanium is now used widely in modern industrial societies.

Most titanium ore is refined into TiO_2 to impart a
25 durable white color to paint, paper, rubber, wallboard, and plastic. The paint industry began using TiO_2 because of concerns about the environmental hazards related to the use of lead in paint. Because TiO_2 is relatively inert, it can also be used as coloring in
30 such products as toothpaste, skim milk, candy, and sunscreen.

Only about 5 percent of the world's annual production of titanium minerals goes to make titanium metal. The high strength-to-weight ratio and corrosion
35 resistance of titanium metal and its alloys make them particularly valuable to the aerospace industry. Because titanium metal is nonreactive in the human body, it is also used to make artificial hip joints, pins for setting bones, and other types of biological implants.
40 Titanium is the ninth most abundant element in the Earth's crust and can be found in nearly all rocks. The economic viability of a titanium deposit is determined by the grade and available tonnage, as well as the deposit type and titanium mineralogy.

45 The most economically important titanium minerals are ilmenite (which is a titanium-iron oxide that crystallizes at high temperatures from magma) and two TiO_2 polymorphs, rutile and anatase (which have the same chemical composition but different
50 crystal structures). Ninety percent of the world's titanium is accounted for by ilmenite, but because rutile has a very high index of refraction, it is the most desirable mineral for the pigment industry.

Economic high-grade magmatic ilmenite
55 deposits are found in particular rock types. These deposits develop by crystallization of ilmenite from titanium- and iron-enriched magmas. Segregation and emplacement of these early ilmenite-laden liquids are likely related to dynamic magmatic processes
60 accompanying the emplacement of anorthosite (a plagioclase-rich rock) and related mafic rocks. Magmatic ilmenite is currently being mined at the Lac Tio mine in Quebec, Canada, and at Tellnes, a large open pit mine in southern Norway.

The table below shows the percent distribution of titanium pigment in various U.S. industries.

Estimated U.S. Distribution of Titanium Pigment Shipments, Titanium Dioxide Content, by Industry[1] (Percent)		
Industry	2011	2012
Paint, varnish, lacquer	58.5	59.8
Paper	8.6	10.6
Plastics and rubber	27.9	24.6
Other[2]	5.0	5.0
Total	100.0	100.0

[1] Excludes exports.

[2] Includes agricultural, building materials, ceramics, coated fabrics and textiles, cosmetics, food, and printing ink. Also includes shipments to distributors.

CONTINUE

29

The authors state that which of the following characteristics of titanium accounts for its ability to impart white coloring and brightness to objects?

A) Its resistance to corrosion

B) Its relatively light weight

C) Its natural abundance

D) Its high refractive index

30

Which choice provides the best evidence for the answer to the previous question?

A) Lines 5-8 ("Titanium . . . products")

B) Lines 15-20 ("Pure . . . quantities")

C) Lines 32-36 ("Only . . . industry")

D) Lines 40-44 ("Titanium . . . mineralogy")

31

As used in line 18, "curiosity" most nearly means

A) oddity.

B) inquisitiveness.

C) eagerness.

D) desire.

32

The information presented in the table above supports which of the following claims made in the passage?

A) High-grade magmatic ilmenite deposits are developed by magma crystallization in particular rock types.

B) Titanium dioxide imparts opacity and brightness to many products.

C) Most titanium dioxide is used in products such as paint, paper, rubber, wallboard, and plastic.

D) The economic viability of a titanium deposit is determined primarily by quality and weight.

33

The authors claim that the use of titanium in certain products is preferable to that of lead because of lead's dangerous health effects. Do the authors support the idea that titanium is safe for human use with specific reasons and/or examples?

A) Yes, because the authors note that titanium was first discovered in 1791 and that pure titanium metal was first isolated in 1901.

B) Yes, because the authors note that titanium's relative inertness makes it safe for use in toothpaste, milk, and sunscreen and that its non-reactiveness in the human body makes it safe for use in medical procedures.

C) No, because the authors describe a large open pit mine in Norway and imply that mining titanium in such conditions is potentially hazardous to human health.

D) No, because the authors claim that titanium is safe for use in certain products used by humans but do not support that claim with any reasons or examples.

34

As used in line 35, "resistance" most nearly means

A) strident refusal.

B) fierce opposition.

C) lack of vulnerability.

D) psychological defense mechanism.

35

The authors compare titanium metal to steel and aluminum in order to

A) show a specific way in which titanium imparts brightness and opacity to objects.

B) prove that titanium is stronger than all other metals.

C) provide an illustration of titanium's strength and lightness relative to certain other metals.

D) highlight the particularly abundant nature of titanium as a renewable resource that can be easily mined.

36

It can be inferred from the passage that the form of titanium most useful to the manufacturing of paint products is

A) rutile.

B) ilmenite.

C) anatase.

D) titanium metal.

37

Which choice provides the best evidence for the answer to the previous question?

A) Lines 1-5 ("Titanium . . . heavier")

B) Lines 50-53 ("Ninety . . . industry")

C) Lines 54-55 ("Economic . . . types")

D) Lines 62-64 ("Magmatic . . . Norway")

CONTINUE

No Test Material On This Page

Questions 38-47 are based on the following passage.

A new experiment and a psychological study show that a wandering mind can impart a distinct cognitive advantage. Passage 1 is adapted from "A Wandering Mind Reveals Mental Processes and Priorities." © 2012 by the University of Wisconsin-Madison. Passage 2 is adapted from "Neuroscientists Literally Change the Way We Think: Advantages of a Wandering Mind." © 2015 by Bar-Ilan University.

Passage 1

In an experiment—designed and executed by Prof. Bar's post-doctoral researcher Dr. Vadim Axelrod—participants were treated with transcranial direct
Line current stimulation (tDCS), a procedure that uses low-
5 level electricity to stimulate specific brain regions. "We focused tDCS stimulation on the frontal lobes because this brain region has been previously implicated in mind wandering, and also because it is a central locus of the executive control network that allows us to
10 organize and plan for the future," Bar explains.

The researchers used tDCS to stimulate the occipital cortex—the visual processing center in the back of the brain. They also conducted control studies where no tDCS was used.

15 While the self-reported incidence of mind wandering was unchanged in the case of occipital and sham stimulation, it rose considerably when this stimulation was applied to the frontal lobes. "Our results demonstrate that the frontal lobes play a causal
20 role in the production of mind wandering behavior."

In an unanticipated finding, the present study demonstrated how the increased mind wandering behavior produced by external stimulation not only does not harm subjects' ability to succeed at an
25 appointed task, it actually helps. Bar believes that this surprising result might stem from the convergence, within a single brain region, of both the "thought controlling" mechanisms of executive function and the "thought freeing" activity of spontaneous, self-directed
30 daydreams.

"Over the last 15 or 20 years, scientists have shown that mind wandering involves the activation of a gigantic default network involving many parts of the brain," Bar says. "This cross-brain involvement may
35 be involved in behavioral outcomes such as creativity and mood, and may also contribute to the ability to

stay successfully on-task while the mind goes off on its merry mental way."

While it is commonly assumed that people have a
40 finite cognitive capacity for paying attention, Bar says that the present study suggests that the truth may be more complicated. "Interestingly, while our study's external stimulation increased the incidence of mind wandering, rather than reducing the subjects' ability
45 to complete the task, it caused task performance to become slightly improved. The external stimulation actually enhanced the subjects' cognitive capacity."

Passage 2

A new study investigating the mental processes underlying a wandering mind reports a role for
50 working memory, a sort of a mental workspace that allows you to juggle multiple thoughts simultaneously.

Imagine you see your neighbor upon arriving home one day and schedule a lunch date. On your way to add it to your calendar, you stop to turn off the drippy
55 faucet, feed the cat, and add milk to your grocery list. The capacity that allows you to retain the lunch information through those unrelated tasks is working memory.

The new study, published online March 14 in the
60 journal *Psychological Science,* reports that a person's working memory capacity relates to the tendency of their mind to wander during a routine assignment.

Throughout the tasks, the researchers checked in periodically with the participants to ask if their minds
65 were on task or wandering. At the end, they measured each participant's working memory capacity, scored by their ability to remember a series of letters given to them interspersed with easy math questions.

In both tasks, there was a clear correlation. "People
70 with higher working memory capacity reported more mind wandering during these simple tasks," says Levinson, though their performance on the test was not compromised.

The result is the first positive correlation found
75 between working memory and mind wandering and suggests that working memory may actually enable off-topic thoughts." What this study seems to suggest is that, when circumstances for the task aren't very difficult, people who have additional working memory
80 resources deploy them to think about things other than what they're doing," Smallwood says.

CONTINUE ➡

Interestingly, when people were given a comparably simple task but filled with sensory distractors (such as lots of other similarly shaped letters), the link between
85 working memory and mind wandering disappeared. "Giving your full attention to your perceptual experience actually equalized people, as though it cut off mind wandering at the pass," Levinson says.

Working memory capacity has previously been
90 correlated with general measures of intelligence, such as reading comprehension and IQ score.

"Our results suggest that the sorts of planning that people do quite often in daily life—when they're on the bus, when they're cycling to work, when they're in the
95 shower—are probably supported by working memory," says Smallwood. "Their brains are trying to allocate resources to the most pressing problems."

38

Based on the information in Passage 1, it can be reasonably inferred that mind wandering

A) is caused by the occipital lobes.

B) depends on interaction among all parts of the brain.

C) reacts to a sham stimulation.

D) is initiated by the frontal lobes.

39

Which choice provides the best evidence for the answer to the previous question?

A) Lines 1-5 ("In an . . . regions")

B) Lines 11-13 ("The researchers . . . brain")

C) Lines 18-20 ("Our . . . behavior")

D) Lines 25-30 ("Bar . . . daydreams")

40

As used in line 8, "locus" most nearly means

A) operation.

B) position.

C) introspection.

D) circumference.

41

The author of Passage 2 mentions to "turn off the drippy faucet, feed the cat, and add milk to your grocery list" (lines 54-56) primarily in order to

A) stimulate your visual cortex with an image.

B) integrate mundane activities into a scientific article.

C) establish a baseline for working memory.

D) explain a cognitive concept using real-world activities.

42

As used in line 74, "correlation" most nearly means

A) relationship.

B) advancement.

C) discovery.

D) pathway.

43

The passage suggests that mind wandering

A) has an inverse relationship with working memory capacity.

B) increases one's IQ.

C) requires minimal sensory distractors.

D) is not measurable.

44

Which choice provides the best evidence for the answer to the previous question?

A) Lines 65-68 ("At . . . questions")

B) Lines 69-73 ("People . . . compromised")

C) Lines 86-88 ("Giving . . . says")

D) Lines 89-91 ("Working . . . score")

45

The passages differ in that Passage 1, but not Passage 2, specifically

A) correlates mind wandering with intelligence.

B) lists everyday activities that people do while mind wandering.

C) delineates the regions of the brain activated during mind wandering.

D) addresses the capacity of working memory.

46

The authors of both passages would most likely agree with which of the following?

A) Outside stimuli inevitably leads to mind wandering.

B) Mind wandering doesn't impede the completion of certain tasks.

C) Mind wandering elicits creativity and passion.

D) Intelligent people have exclusively internally driven thoughts.

47

Is the conclusion in the last paragraph of Passage 2 consistent with the findings of the study in Passage 1?

A) Yes, because the study in Passage 1 showed that people can be affected by sensory distractors.

B) Yes, because the study in Passage 1 shows mind wandering doesn't necessarily interfere with external activities.

C) No, because the study in Passage 2 focuses on specific tasks and not on brain function.

D) No, because the study in Passage 2 concludes that mind wandering involves many parts of the brain.

STOP
**If you finish before time is called, you may check your work on this section only.
Do not turn to any other section.**

No Test Material On This Page

Writing and Language Test

35 MINUTES, 44 QUESTIONS

Turn to Section 2 of your answer sheet to answer the questions in this section.

Questions 1-11 are based on the following passage.

Supply and Demand

Many parents and students have become concerned that exorbitant college university tuitions are not worth the investment. [A] In response, colleges have not lowered tuitions (quite the contrary), but they have become more sensitive to the connection between university education and eventual employment. **1** Schools are beginning to answer the call for job skills and hire-ability rather than the traditional hallmarks of university education.

1

If the writer were to delete the parenthetical phrase *quite the contrary* from the previous sentence, the sentence would primarily lose

A) an indication on the part of the author that his college tuition was relatively low.

B) a reminder that college tuitions have in fact been rising.

C) a troubling reminder that college is simply too expensive for many who want to go.

D) nothing at all, because the information is given elsewhere in the paragraph.

Graphs like the one shown below measure college success by the attainment of employment, and **2** Business majors are over 10% more likely to have jobs that require college degrees after college than are Humanities majors. As a result, **3** there have been a sharp rise in more practical majors, like SCM, or supply-chain management.

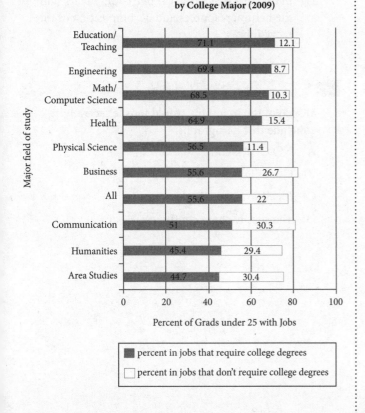

Percent of Young College Grads with Jobs, by College Major (2009)

The term "supply chain management" was coined by Keith Oliver in a 1982 interview. **4** However it happened, when the term began to take hold, the practice of supply-chain management came to be more and more clearly defined. [B] The most general definition holds that SCM is the strategic, systematic coordination of how a business works. For **5** instants, when you buy a new car, your purchase comes at the end of a complex supply chain—the last step of which is the factory sending **6** they're road-ready vehicle to the dealership.

2

Which of the following gives information consistent with the chart?

A) NO CHANGE

B) less than 50% of those with Area Studies majors are currently employed.

C) the Health Professions provide the safest bet for those entering college now.

D) the national average shows that only about 50% of all college grads are currently employed.

3

A) NO CHANGE

B) there've been

C) there has been

D) they're has been

4

Which of the following would best maintain the focus established in the first sentence of this paragraph?

A) NO CHANGE

B) By the mid-1990s,

C) One afternoon,

D) To get down to "business,"

5

A) NO CHANGE

B) instant's,

C) instances,

D) instance,

6

A) NO CHANGE

B) it's

C) its

D) their

Before this step, however, hundreds or thousands of other, smaller processes have to take place first. [C] Each of these has to be imported from other suppliers, **7** which is one could say a process from mining to recycling of the vehicle or its decomposition in the process. After all, when you're done with your car, it doesn't just disappear. [D] You might sell it to someone else, back to a dealer, or to a junkyard for parts. **8** Make sure you get a good price!

7

A) NO CHANGE

B) a process that one could say goes all the way from the mining of natural resources to the eventual decomposition or recycling of the vehicle.

C) from natural resources mining to the decomposition of vehicle recycling in the process one could say.

D) in the life cycle of the car one could say it's both the natural resources and decomposition of the recycling.

8

Which of the following would most effectively conclude this paragraph?

A) NO CHANGE

B) Goodnight, sweet prince!

C) It's all so interesting!

D) The supply chain continues!

A supply-chain manager can't manage every single step of this process, but he or she can oversee the supply-chain for a specific company. A supply-chain manager, then, can provide a major financial benefit to the company for which he or she works. Efficient processes are generally cheaper **9** processes—and not just for manufacturing. SCM practices can also be applied to customer-service, especially to experiences that involve a number of employees. In **10** this way, like any college major, SCM is narrow enough to be an actual major but broad enough to be applicable to a number of industries and actual jobs.

9

A) NO CHANGE

B) processes; and not

C) processes. And not

D) processes—and, not

10

A) NO CHANGE

B) this way, like any college major

C) this way, like, any college major,

D) this way like any college major

11

Upon reviewing the essay and concluding that some information has been left out, the author composes the following sentence:

> The automaker doesn't make the metals that go into the car, or the fluids that power its various functions, or the rubber on the tires.

The best placement for this sentence would be at point

A) A in Paragraph 1.

B) B in Paragraph 2.

C) C in Paragraph 3.

D) D in Paragraph 3.

Questions 12-22 are based on the following passage.

Millard Fillmore's Presidency: Feel More Strongly About It?

Everyone knows who the first President of the United States was, but it takes a real expert to know that the thirteenth was Millard Fillmore. **12** As Zachary Taylor's Vice President, Fillmore took over in 1850 after Taylor's sudden death. Fillmore belonged to the Whig party. With Fillmore's departure in 1853, the Whig party fell out of national politics, **13** but make no mistake, a lot of old guys were wearing wigs back then. If the American people have forgotten that there ever was a true third party, that is likely because **14** they simply faded away at a time when the national conversation was more concerned with the events that would lead up to the Civil War. Millard Fillmore, however, is more than just **15** a funny name that can make us chuckle—like all presidents, he had some influence on life as we live it today.

12

At this point in the essay, the writer is considering adding the following true statement:

> Rutherford B. Hayes, born in 1822, was the nineteenth.

Should the writer make the addition here?

A) Yes, because it provides another obscure fact that readers might like to know.

B) Yes, because more readers have heard of Hayes than of Millard Fillmore.

C) No, because it does not advance the main point that this paragraph is making.

D) No, because Hayes's presidency was far too controversial to deserve mention here.

13

Which of the following would best support the statement made in the first part of this sentence?

A) NO CHANGE

B) though the party's life span in England followed a different trajectory.

C) but Fillmore came back again in 1856 as the candidate for the Know-Nothing party.

D) and every president has been a Democrat or a Republican ever since.

14

A) NO CHANGE

B) they all

C) we

D) the Whig party

15

A) NO CHANGE

B) a funny name that can wash away all our tears—

C) a guffaw-inducing handle, or sobriquet,

D) a funny name—

CONTINUE

Fillmore's influence has been especially strong in international affairs. Relations between Japan and the United States began to open up around this time, after Japan's long history of 16 isolating. 17 After the British opened relations with China, Fillmore and his cabinet took inspiration in trying to open relations with Japan. This was an early step in the productive (and often fraught) relationship between the two nations.

16

A) NO CHANGE

B) isolationism.

C) isolation of itself.

D) isolationism of the nation.

17

Which of the following would best explain the use of the word *inspiration* in the later part of this sentence?

A) NO CHANGE

B) While there were plenty of other things to do at the White House,

C) In the land that would eventually produce Toyota and Nintendo,

D) Totally unrelated to the conflicts the nations would have in World War II,

The best-known, and perhaps most-reviled, of Fillmore's "accomplishments" is his passing of the Fugitive Slave Act in 1851. This Act made slavery a national, **18** the whole United States, problem, as it forbade those in non-slave states from protecting escaped slaves. An escaped slave, because he was considered "property," was committing an act of theft by escaping, and the person who harbored that escapee **19** will be then considered an accessory to that crime. The Fugitive Slave Act is a major scar on American **20** history, nevertheless, it is at least partly responsible for spurring the Civil War. The Fugitive Slave Act held back civil rights **21** forever because it demonstrated that the American government was not the progressive force, especially for African-Americans, that its constitution promised it would be.

Millard Fillmore was at the center of many of these things. While it may not be time to list him among our greatest presidents (in fact, he is routinely listed among the worst), Fillmore certainly provides the essential reminder that history is complex and the **22** presidency, even in its worst form, is a uniquely influential position in the history of the contemporary world.

18

Which of the following would best maintain the focus of this sentence by contributing to the main idea of the paragraph?

A) NO CHANGE

B) like as it related to everyone,

C) rather than merely a southern,

D) and at times international,

19

A) NO CHANGE

B) was

C) is

D) could of been

20

A) NO CHANGE

B) history, therefore,

C) history, and

D) history, but

21

A) NO CHANGE

B) for many years

C) for an eternity

D) for too darn long

22

A) NO CHANGE

B) presidency. Even in its worst form is a uniquely influential position in the history of the contemporary world.

C) presidency: even in its worst form, is a uniquely influential position in the history of the contemporary world.

D) presidency, even in its worst form, is a, uniquely, influential position, in the history of the contemporary world.

CONTINUE

Questions 23-32 are based on the following passage.

The *Noir* Side of Classic American Literature

[1] Film director Robert Siodmak once said, "Hollywood has given the world two kinds of motion pictures which are typically American. [2] They are the western and the gangster film." [3] In 23 that way, Dashiell Hammett and Raymond Chandler are considered the gold standard for great hardboiled fiction by authors from many nations. [4] The same might be said for American literary contributions. [5] With such fantastic authors working in the genre of detective 24 fiction, we can begin to see how these mystery novels come to be so much more than mere entertainment. [6] As Siodmak's quote implies, there is more than meets the eye to certain works in the "entertainment" genres. 25

23

A) NO CHANGE
B) those,
C) genres,
D) the "gangster" genre,

24

A) NO CHANGE
B) fiction. We can
C) fiction we can
D) fiction: we can

25

The best placement for Sentence 4 would be
A) where it is now.
B) after Sentence 2.
C) after Sentence 5.
D) after Sentence 6.

[26] No one can match the intricacy and cleverness of Raymond Chandler's great novels. Macdonald was born Kenneth Millar in Canada in 1915, and he spent most of his formative years there. In his 20s, Millar attended the University of [27] Michigan, when he earned a Ph.D. in English literature, writing a dissertation on the works of Romantic poet Samuel Taylor Coleridge. Millar finished the degree in 1946, but in 1944, he published his first novel, *The Dark Tunnel*. While it may seem that Millar was being pulled in two different directions— [28] toward the "high" Coleridge and the "low" detective novel—Millar's later work under the pseudonym Ross Macdonald shows that he never took the separation very seriously.

26

Which of the following would most effectively introduce this paragraph by linking it to the previous paragraph?

A) NO CHANGE

B) Robert Siodmak had finished most of his career before Ross MacDonald became famous.

C) One proponent of this high-end of crime fiction is Ross Macdonald.

D) This is not to say, however, that there isn't a lot of garbage out there, too.

27

A) NO CHANGE

B) Michigan, which

C) Michigan, where

D) Michigan which

28

Which of the following choices would best maintain the focus of this sentence?

A) NO CHANGE

B) Samuel Taylor Coleridge was most famous for his poem "The Rime of the Ancient Mariner"

C) toward movies and toward books, which both placed demands on his time

D) as to whether he liked Raymond Chandler or Dashiell Hammett better

It is, after all, Macdonald's **29** sophistication that puts his work in a category separate from that of his "pulp" contemporaries. While studying literature, Millar engaged closely not only with words but also with ideas, and the emergent discourses of psychoanalysis and Marxist economics did a good deal to inform how his characters operated. After all, **30** Macdonalds texts remind us that even the foulest murders are committed by **31** people who have a very human motivation. Macdonald was able to get inside the heads of his characters and to humanize some of the most horrendous and inhumane activities. No one is ever forgiven or rewarded for doing bad in a Macdonald novel, but neither is anyone ever portrayed as a purely evil monster.

Although murders, **32** thefts, and kidnappings may propel the plots of his books as they would in less self-conscious works, Macdonald treats them with a literary touch and uses the mystery form to show the depths of life's very mysteriousness. Following **33** to the detective novel in the footsteps of Hammett and Chandler, Macdonald brings something that literary fiction has known all along: human beings are the greatest mystery of all.

29

Which of the following alternatives to the underlined portion would NOT be acceptable?

A) refinement

B) intellect

C) elegance

D) superciliousness

30

A) NO CHANGE

B) Macdonald's

C) Macdonalds's

D) Macdonalds'

31

A) NO CHANGE

B) those who have a very human motivation.

C) someone who has a very human motivation.

D) people who have very human motivations.

32

A) NO CHANGE

B) thefts and kidnappings

C) thefts and, kidnappings

D) thefts, and kidnappings,

33

The best placement for the underlined portion would be

A) where it is now.

B) after the word *Chandler* (and before the comma).

C) after the word *brings*.

D) after the word *are*.

Questions 34-44 are based on the following passage.

Space: The Next Dimension (of Natural Resources)

At a time when the scientific community the world over **34** do all they can to warn the public about the effects of global warming, the idea of "resources" can get **35** lost in the big message. The contemporary dialogue is much more concerned with use and effectiveness than with **36** resourcefulness. We should not forget, however, the age-old concern that resources will, at some point, simply run out. There have been many alternatives presented: solar, wind, and hydrogen power are the day's particularly hot topics. It has become clear, though, that these new resources will not cure us fully of energy dependency, especially with as large as that dependency is on fossil fuels. **37**

34

A) NO CHANGE
B) does all it can
C) do all it can
D) does all they can

35

A) NO CHANGE
B) lost in the mix.
C) lost amid the noise.
D) lost.

36

A) NO CHANGE
B) themselves.
C) the resources themselves.
D) them.

37

Which of the following, if added here, would provide the most effective conclusion to this paragraph and the most effective transition to the next?

A) The solution to Earth's problems may finally have come, however, from a seemingly unlikely source: space.

B) World leaders are finally starting to take seriously the idea that there is a climate-change problem.

C) Some believe that climate change is either not happening or not caused by human activity.

D) Space, the final frontier, has captured the hearts and minds of Americans since the early twentieth century.

CONTINUE

The new, and currently hypothetical, solution to the problem is called "asteroid mining." As 38 fantastic as it may sound, asteroid mining is exactly what it sounds like. It refers to mining asteroids and other near-Earth objects for their raw materials, as these materials dwindle on Earth. Mining data show that 39 discoveries of new nickel sources in 2009 were less than half of what they were only ten years before. Scientists believe that the asteroids could contain a variety of minerals—including iron, nickel, and titanium. The practice may also enable astronauts to gather supplies for space journeys without overstocking or 40 getting new supplies on Earth. This practice, called "in-situ resource utilization," could change both space travel and exploration to be much safer and much more predictable 41 than currently.

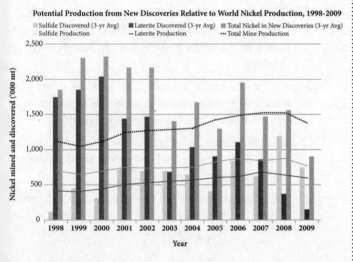

Potential Production from New Discoveries Relative to World Nickel Production, 1998-2009

Note: Potential production in new discoveries is calculated using a 75% resources-to-reserves conversion rate and subtracting 10% for sulfide processing losses and 25% for laterite processing losses; a running three-year average of the annual totals is shown.

Data source: MEG's Strategies for Nickel Reserves Replacement study.

38

Which of the following alternatives to the underlined portion would NOT be acceptable?

A) outlandish

B) wonderful

C) extraordinary

D) unconventional

39

Which of the following choices gives information consistent with the graph?

A) NO CHANGE

B) sulfide production, from 1998 to 2009, was consistently lower than laterite production.

C) for the first time in history, total nickel production in 2009 was lower than the three-year average of total nickel in new discoveries.

D) the total nickel found in new discoveries has decreased steadily since 1998.

40

A) NO CHANGE

B) getting supplies a second time

C) resupplying

D) having resupplied

41

A) NO CHANGE

B) than now.

C) than in the present.

D) than they currently are.

Scientists are confident in the potential results of asteroid mining precisely because they do not consider it all that distinct from Earth-bound mining. In fact, many resources exist in their relative abundance on Earth because of the rain of asteroids that hit the Earth after its surface [42] cooled, although the Earth and many of the asteroids were formed from similar proto-planetary material, Earth was much larger and pulled the many smaller asteroids into [43] its orbit and eventually onto its surface billions of years ago. Therefore, despite the obvious difficulty of capturing an in-flight asteroid, scientists are fairly certain of what they will find on these asteroids if and when they do.

Still, many are concerned that the infinitude of space may be a stopgap solution. First and foremost, the cost of extracting minerals from asteroids and then returning those minerals to Earth far outstrips the value of the minerals themselves. [44] Then, obviously, if we have depleted the vast (and once seemingly infinite) resources of Earth, there is no reason to believe that we will not deplete those of space as well. As a result, asteroid mining may have to remain "a" solution rather than "the" solution to our current energy woes.

42

A) NO CHANGE
B) cooled; although
C) cooled, although,
D) cooled although

43

A) NO CHANGE
B) their
C) it's
D) one's

44

At this point, the author wants to add a detail that will support the claim made in the previous sentence. Which of the following would most effectively achieve that goal?

A) NASA already uses a large amount of public funds, so the venture would have to be privately funded.

B) Astronauts are highly skilled individuals, often respected scientists, so it's tough to imagine an entire industry of adequately skilled people.

C) The exorbitant cost of each of these expeditions would have to bring back an unreasonable amount of mined ore to be profitable.

D) Sometimes it makes you wonder if we should just give up on the whole thing.

STOP
**If you finish before time is called, you may check your work on this section only.
Do not turn to any other section.**

No Test Material On This Page

Math Test – No Calculator

25 MINUTES, 17 QUESTIONS

Turn to Section 3 of your answer sheet to answer the questions in this section.

DIRECTIONS

For questions **1-13**, solve each problem, choose the best answer from the choices provided, and fill in the corresponding circle on your answer sheet. For questions **14-17**, solve the problem and enter your answer in the grid on the answer sheet. Please refer to the directions before question 14 on how to enter your answers in the grid. You may use any available space in your test booklet for scratch work.

NOTES

1. The use of a calculator **is not permitted**.

2. All variables and expressions used represent real numbers unless otherwise indicated.

3. Figures provided in this test are drawn to scale unless otherwise indicated.

4. All figures lie in a plane unless otherwise indicated.

5. Unless otherwise indicated, the domain of a given function f is the set of all real numbers x for which $f(x)$ is a real number.

REFERENCE

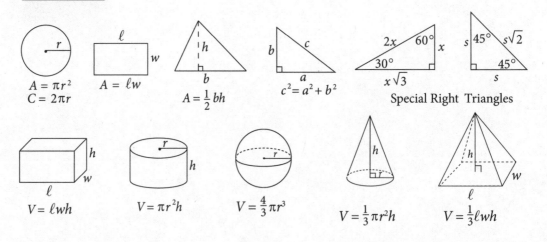

$$A = \pi r^2$$
$$C = 2\pi r$$

$$A = \ell w$$

$$A = \frac{1}{2}bh$$

$$c^2 = a^2 + b^2$$

Special Right Triangles

$$V = \ell wh$$

$$V = \pi r^2 h$$

$$V = \frac{4}{3}\pi r^3$$

$$V = \frac{1}{3}\pi r^2 h$$

$$V = \frac{1}{3}\ell wh$$

The number of degrees of arc in a circle is 360.
The number of radians of arc in a circle is 2π.
The sum of the measures in degrees of the angles of a triangle is 180.

CONTINUE →

1

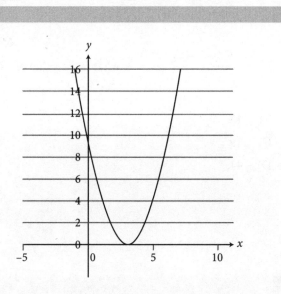

Which of the following functions is represented in the graph above?

A) $y = (x - 3)^2$

B) $y = (x + 3)^2$

C) $y = x - 3$

D) $y = x^2 + 3$

2

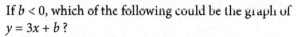

If $b < 0$, which of the following could be the graph of $y = 3x + b$?

A)

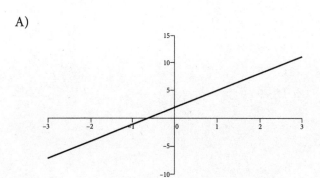

B)

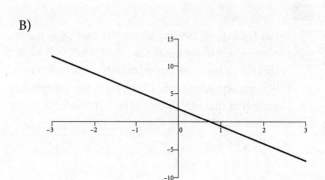

C)

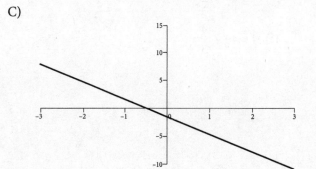

D)

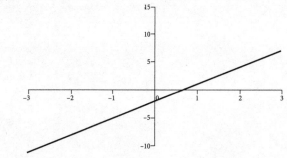

3

If $\dfrac{x^2 - 4x + 3}{3} = 2(x - 1)$, what is the value of x ?

A) 3

B) 5

C) 6

D) 9

4

From January of 1993 to January of 1999, the median income of US households rose from 49,000 to 57,000. If this trend had continued linearly, which of the following equations could have been used to predict the median income, in thousands, in the US x years after January 1999 ?

A) $I = 49 + 8x$

B) $I = 57 + 8x$

C) $I = 57 + \dfrac{4}{3}x$

D) $I = 49 + \dfrac{4}{3}x$

5

If $\dfrac{3(z + 3)}{4} - \dfrac{2(z - 2)}{3} = 2$, what is the value of z ?

A) −19

B) 13

C) 19

D) 41

6

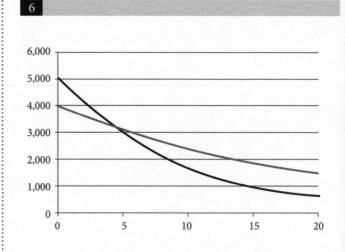

Medical researchers are trying to determine whether a new antibiotic is effective, so they measured the populations of bacteria in a petri dish after treatment with the new antibiotic as well as in a petri dish that was untreated but cultivated under the same conditions. The graph above plots the populations of bacteria over 20 hours in both the treated petri dish and the control dish. Based on these results, researchers determined that the antibiotic was effective. Which of the following expressions shows the difference in population between the treated petri dish and the control dish t hours after treatment?

A) $5,000(.95)^t - 4,000(.9)^t$

B) $4,000(.95)t - 5,000(.9)t$

C) $5,000(.9)^t - 4,000(.95)^t$

D) $5,000(1.1)^t - 4,000(1.05)^t$

CONTINUE

If $\dfrac{a^3}{\sqrt{ba}} = b$ and $ab > 0$, which of the following statements must be true?

A) $a = b^3$

B) $a^5 = b^3$

C) $a^2 = b^2$

D) $a^2 = b$

At the farmer's market, a bag of apples and 3 cartons of strawberries cost \$18 total. If a bag of apples costs 50% more than a carton of strawberries, how much does a bag of apples cost?

A) \$4.00

B) \$4.50

C) \$5.13

D) \$6.00

The number of visitors, V, a website receives doubles every 3 months. If 6 months ago the website received 24,500 visitors, how many visitors, in thousands, will it receive t years from now?

A) $V = 24.5(2^{4t})$

B) $V = 98(2^t)$

C) $V = 98(2^{4t})$

D) $V = 49\left(2^{\frac{t}{3}}\right)$

Carl is 2 inches taller than Sophia. If Sophia grows half an inch per year and Carl grows at 75% of Sophia's rate, then how many years will it take Sophia to reach Carl's height?

A) 4

B) 8

C) 12

D) 16

11

David is a criminology student and wants to determine the effect of several population parameters on the murder rate in a city. He collects data from hundreds of US cities and determines that the number of murders can be approximated with a formula:

$$M = P\left(\frac{100 - (A - 30)^2 - I\sqrt{L}}{25}\right)$$, in which P is the

population in thousands, A is the median age, I is the median income, and L is the literacy rate expressed as a decimal. Given that the median age of a city is 37, which of the following expresses I in terms of M, P, and L ?

A) $\frac{1}{\sqrt{L}}\left(51 - \frac{25M}{P}\right)$

B) $\frac{1}{\sqrt{L}}\left(\frac{25M}{P} - 49\right)$

C) $\frac{M}{P} - 2 - \frac{49}{25} + \sqrt{L}$

D) $\sqrt{L}\left(51 - \frac{25M}{P}\right)$

12

The equation of circle O (not shown) is $(x - 2)^2 + (y + 3)^2 = 16$, and the radian measure of central angle AOB is between $\frac{3\pi}{4}$ and $\frac{5\pi}{4}$. Which of the following could be the length of the arc AB ?

A) 3π

B) 4π

C) 5π

D) 8π

13

In an online shopping rebate program, customers receive a rebate of a given percent of their purchase amount until they reach a certain minimum threshold in a month. They receive a larger percentage rebate on any additional purchases beyond this threshold. If a customer spends more than his minimum threshold in a month, his total rebate is given by the function $R = 4x + (x+5)(.01z - 4)$. Which of the following statements is true?

A) The initial threshold is 1,000.

B) x represents the total amount the customer spends

C) x represents the percentage discount for the purchases over the threshold

D) The initial threshold is 400.

CONTINUE

DIRECTIONS

For questions 14-17, solve the problem and enter your answer in the grid, as described below, on the answer sheet.

1. Although not required, it is suggested that you write your answer in the boxes at the top of the columns to help you fill in the circles accurately. You will receive credit only if the circles are filled in correctly.

2. Mark no more than one circle in any column.

3. No question has a negative answer.

4. Some problems may have more than one correct answer. In such cases, grid only one answer.

5. **Mixed numbers** such as $3\frac{1}{2}$ must be gridded as 3.5 or 7/2. (If 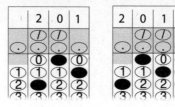 is entered into the grid, it will be interpreted as $\frac{31}{2}$, not as $3\frac{1}{2}$.)

6. **Decimal Answers:** If you obtain a decimal answer with more digits than the grid can accommodate, it may be either rounded or truncated, but it must fill the entire grid.

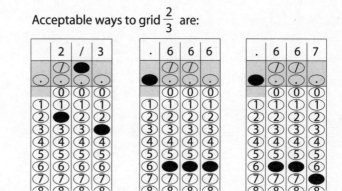

Acceptable ways to grid $\frac{2}{3}$ are:

Answer: 201 – either position is correct

NOTE: You may start your answers in any column, space permitting. Columns you don't need to use should be left blank.

14

If $f(x) = 3x$ and $g(x) = x - 3$, what is the value of $f(4) - g(2)$?

15

There are 8 more males in Sara's class than females. If $\frac{3}{5}$ of the students are male, how many students are in Sara's class?

16

For positive integers c and d, the value of c is at least 3 times the value of d. If the difference between c and d is no more than 8, what is the largest possible value of d ?

17

The distance an object in motion travels is given by the following equation: $Displacement = V_i t + 0.5at^2$, in which V_i, a, and t represent initial velocity, acceleration, and time, respectively. The final velocity of the object is calculated with the equation $V_f = V_i + at$. How long does an object travel, in seconds, if it has a displacement of 22 meters, an initial velocity of 15 meters per seconds, and a final velocity of 5 meters per second?

STOP
**If you finish before time is called, you may check your work on this section only.
Do not turn to any other section.**

No Test Material On This Page

Math Test – Calculator

45 MINUTES, 31 QUESTIONS

Turn to Section 4 of your answer sheet to answer the questions in this section.

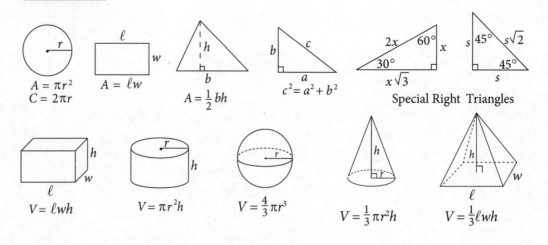

CONTINUE

1

A physicist was studying the velocity of a proton fired through a circular tube filled with different mediums. A proton fired through the circular tube filled with medium *A* traveled 100,000 meters in 5 milliseconds. The velocity of a proton was halved when fired through the circular tube filled with medium *B*. What is the velocity of a proton fired through the circular tube filled with medium *B* ?

A) 10,000 meters per millisecond

B) 20,000 meters per millisecond

C) 40,000 meters per millisecond

D) 50,000 meters per millisecond

2

If $6x - 5 < 2 + 15x$, which of the following must be true?

A) $x < -\dfrac{7}{9}$

B) $x < -\dfrac{1}{3}$

C) $x > -\dfrac{7}{9}$

D) $x > \dfrac{1}{3}$

3

Which of the following values of *r* is a solution for the equation $r + 22 = 3r - 26 + r^2$?

A) −8

B) −6

C)   4

D)   8

4

To be eligible for Spartanville's Super Service Award, a resident must complete at least 2,000 hours of community service through a designated program. There are two designated programs this year: volunteering at the Community Center for 7.5 hours per day and removing street litter for 4 hours per day. Which of the following inequalities represents the possible number of days spent volunteering at the Community Center *c* and days removing street litter *l* needed to be eligible for this year's Spartanville Super Service Award?

A) $\dfrac{7.5}{c} + \dfrac{4}{l} > 2,000$

B) $\dfrac{7.5}{c} + \dfrac{4}{l} \geq 2,000$

C) $7.5c + 4l > 2,000$

D) $7.5c + 4l \geq 2,000$

5

6, 9, 9, 36, 39, x

If the set above has a median of 15, then what is its mean?

A) 15

B) 16.5

C) 19

D) 20

6

A certain gold coin has a volume of 5 cubic centimeters. The density of gold is 19.3 grams per cubic centimeter. If 1 ounce is equal to 28.3 grams, what is the approximate mass of the coin in ounces? (Note: Density is mass divided by volume.)

A) 3.41

B) 7.33

C) 32.16

D) 2,730.95

7

Three months before the presidential election, a polling agency randomly selected 2,500 registered voters from the list of all registered voters in the United States. The selected voters were asked, "Do you plan to vote for Candidate A or for Candidate B?" The polling agency calculated that 44.2% of the voters plan to vote for Candidate A and 55.8% for Candidate B, with a 6.3% margin of error. If the polling agency plans to conduct the survey again two months before the election, which of the following would result in a smaller margin of error?

A) 100 randomly selected registered voters from each of the 10 most populous states

B) 1,000 randomly selected registered voters from all voters in the United States

C) 300 randomly selected registered voters from each of the 10 most populous states

D) 15,000 randomly selected registered voters from all voters in the United States

8

A computer chip factory currently has 50 employees and has an output of 385 computer chips per day. A manager determined that for each additional employee hired the output of the factory would increase by 42 computer chips. Which of the following functions, $C(e)$, expresses the total output of the factory for e employees when $e \geq 50$?

A) $C(e) = 42^{(e - 50)} + 385$

B) $C(e) = (e)^{42} + 385$

C) $C(e) = 42e + 385$

D) $C(e) = 385 + 42(e - 50)$

CONTINUE

9

$$\frac{3(t + 2)}{4} = \frac{100 - 5t + 44}{8}$$

In the equation above, what is the value of t ?

A) -69

B) 4

C) 12

D) 36

10

In the xy-plane, the graph of $y = (3x - 6)(x - 6)$ represents a parabola. If the x- and y-coordinates of the parabola's vertex are to be expressed as constants or coefficients, which of the following forms of the equation is appropriate?

A) $y = (3x - 6)(x - 6)$

B) $y = 3x^2 - 24x + 36$

C) $y = 3(x^2 - 8x + 12)$

D) $y = 3(x - 4)^2 + (-12)$

11

Taylor is preparing to write his next novel, which will be 700 pages long. While typing, Taylor types at a constant rate of 23 words per minute. If each page contains 800 words, which of the following functions p models the number of pages Taylor has left to type after typing for m minutes?

A) $p(m) = \dfrac{700 - 800m}{23}$

B) $p(m) = \dfrac{700 - 23m}{800}$

C) $p(m) = 700 - \dfrac{23m}{800}$

D) $p(m) = 700 - \dfrac{800}{23m}$

12

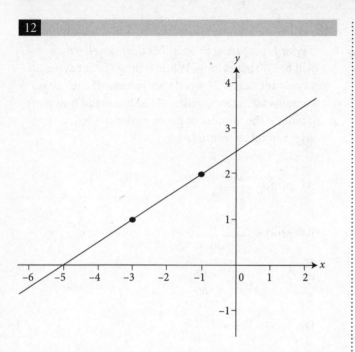

Line *b* is shown above. Line *c* is created by reflecting line *b* across the *y*-axis. What is the slope of line *c* ?

A) −2

B) $-\dfrac{1}{2}$

C) $\dfrac{1}{2}$

D) 2

13

In State Q, the number of people in poverty halved each year from 2008 to 2012. There were 50,000 people in poverty in State Q in 2008, and *m* represents the number of months since January 2008, where $0 \le m \le 48$. Which of the following functions $f(m)$ could be used to estimate the number of people in poverty in State Q m months after January 2008 ?

A) $f(m) = 50{,}000 - \left(\dfrac{1}{2}\right)m$

B) $f(m) = 50{,}000 - \left(\dfrac{1}{2}\right)\left(\dfrac{m}{12}\right)$

C) $f(m) = 50{,}000 \times \left(\dfrac{1^{\frac{m}{12}}}{2}\right)$

D) $f(m) = 50{,}000 - m^{\frac{1}{2}}$

CONTINUE ▸

14

A local charity enrolled 50 people in a job training program. Before enrolling in the program, all of the 50 people were under-nourished. The charity tracked both the increase in participants' weekly wage and their level of nourishment over a two-year period. The participants' weekly wage can be modeled by the function $w(x) = \dfrac{x}{4}$. The participants' level of nourishment can be modeled by the function $n(x) = -(.3x)^2 + 50$, where $w(x)$ is the increase in the weekly wage in dollars, $n(x)$ is the number of people who are under-nourished, and x is the number of months since the job training program began. Which of the following is the graphical representation of the charity's findings?

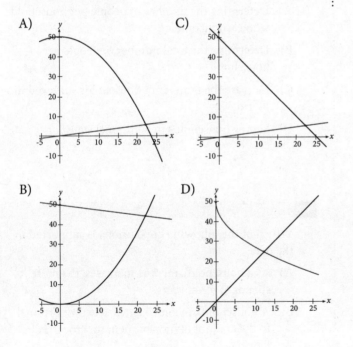

A)

B)

C)

D)

15

If $y = x^2 + x - 20$ and $z = x^2 + 10x + 25$, what is $\dfrac{y^2}{z}$ in terms of x?

A) $\dfrac{x^4 - 8}{10x}$

B) $\dfrac{x^4 + x^2 - 400}{x^2 + 10x + 25}$

C) $x^2 - 8x - 15$

D) $x^2 - 8x + 16$

16

The Squared Up framing store charges $61 to frame a customer's picture. The owner of the store calculated that the cost to frame each picture is $38 in materials plus $5 in the labor cost. The store must also pay $720 each month in general operating costs. Squared Up is profitable when the income from framing customers' picture exceeds the total cost of framing the picture plus the general operating cost. If p is the number of pictures framed in a month, which of the following gives all possible values of p for which Squared Up is profitable during that month?

A) $p < 12$

B) $p < 40$

C) $p > 12$

D) $p > 40$

Questions 17-18 refer to the following information.

A nonprofit group wanted to determine whether there is an association between a household's income and the amount of money spent on groceries. After surveying 800 randomly selected households in Florida, the nonprofit found that as the household's income increased, its spending on groceries decreased.

17

If the nonprofit wanted to determine whether an association exists between a household's income and the average amount of money spent on groceries per person, which of the following changes to the survey would be most appropriate?

A) Determine the number of people per household who earn income.

B) Determine the total number of people per household.

C) Increase the number of households surveyed in Florida.

D) Survey households in additional states.

18

Which of the following conclusions is supported by the data?

A) As a household's income increases, the more it spends at restaurants.

B) A household's income is inversely proportional to the amount of money spent on groceries in Florida.

C) Having a lower household income causes the household to spend more on groceries.

D) There is a positive correlation between a household's income and the amount of money spent on groceries in the United States.

CONTINUE →

19

$$2x - 96 = 4y - x$$
$$3y + 10x = y + 90$$

Based on the system of equations above, what is the value of $\dfrac{x}{y}$?

A) $-\dfrac{4}{5}$

B) $-\dfrac{3}{4}$

C) $-\dfrac{1}{5}$

D) $\dfrac{4}{3}$

20

Larissa uploaded 40,000 songs from her computer to her web storage. The mean file size of a song is 0.022 gigabytes, and the total time to upload all the files was 7.5 hours. If 1 gigabyte is equal to 1,024 megabytes, what is the upload rate for the files in megabytes per second, rounded to the nearest hundredth?

A) 1.48

B) 3.00

C) 33.37

D) 250.28

21

$$\frac{1}{12} + \frac{1}{6} = \frac{1}{x}$$

A water tank is to be filled to capacity by two hoses. The output of the first hose is 4 gallons per hour, and the output of the second hose is twice that of the first. The capacity of the tank is 48 gallons. If the equation above represents the situation described, what could the value of x represent?

A) The fraction of the tank filled after 1 hour

B) The number of gallons of water in the tank after 1 hour

C) The total time required for both hoses to fill the tank to capacity

D) The combined output of both hoses, in gallons per hour

22

Number of Cars	Bronx	Brooklyn	Manhattan	Queens	Staten Island
Zero	960	1,120	1,280	720	80
One	640	560	480	600	40
Two	320	160	320	240	100
Three	0	160	80	80	60

The New York City Department of Motor Vehicles compiled the data for the number of cars owned in each of the city's five boroughs. There are 8 million residents in all five boroughs. The table above shows the number of residents, in thousands, from each of the five boroughs who own the specified number of cars. What percent of the New York City residents own more than the median number of cars per person and live in Manhattan?

A)   5%

B)   11%

C)   27%

D)   48%

23

If $8s = 4t + 17$ and $6t - 5s = 4$, what is the value of $6s + 4t$?

A)   13

B)   15

C)   21

D)   42

24

Circle C is defined by the equation $x^2 + y^2 - 8x + ky = 172$, and parabola P is defined by the equation $y = x^2 - 8x + 22$. For which value of k will circle C be centered at the vertex of parabola P ?

A)   −12

B)   −4

C)   6

D)   8

25

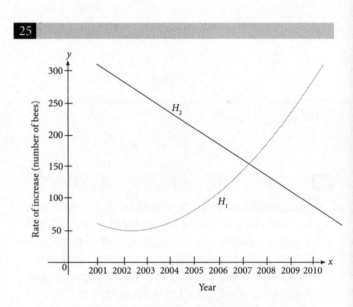

An entomologist analyzed the populations of two bee colonies, H_1 and H_2. She documented the rate of increase, which is the number of bees added to a colony in that year, for each colony over a 10-year period starting in the year 2000. The findings are modeled in the graph above. Which of the following conclusions can be drawn based on the entomologist's findings?

A)   The population of H_2 decreased at a constant rate for each of the 10 years.

B)   In 2007, the populations of H_1 and H_2 were equal.

C)   In 2005, the population of H_2 was increasing at a faster rate than was the population of H_1.

D)   The population of H_1 doubled from 2001 to 2005.

CONTINUE

26

In 2007, a biologist introduced a colony of phytoplankton into Great Blue Fish Lake, which had never contained phytoplankton before. The number of phytoplankton y in Great Blue Fish Lake can be estimated using the equation $y = \left(6.23^{\frac{k}{12}} \right)$, where k represents the number of months since the population was introduced. Which of the following is a proper interpretation of the elements of the equation?

A) 8,564,600 represents the number of phytoplankton after 1 year.

B) 8,564,600 represents the number of phytoplankton prior to 2007.

C) 6.23 represents the rate of increase on phytoplankton each month.

D) 6.23 represents the rate of increase on phytoplankton each year.

27

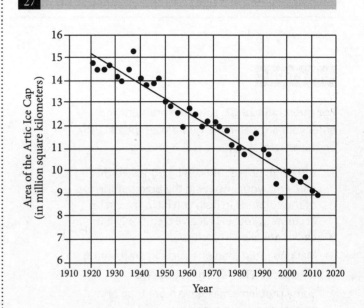

The scatterplot above show the size of the Arctic Ice Cap as observed from 1920 to 2015. Which of the following is the closest approximation of the average annual decrease in the area of the Arctic Ice Cap as indicated by the line of best fit?

A) 1 square kilometers

B) 6.6 square kilometers

C) 100,000 square kilometers

D) 66,000 square kilometers

For questions 28-31, solve the problem and enter your answer in the grid, as described below, on the answer sheet.

1. Although not required, it is suggested that you write your answer in the boxes at the top of the columns to help you fill in the circles accurately. You will receive credit only if the circles are filled in correctly.

2. Mark no more than one circle in any column.

3. No question has a negative answer.

4. Some problems may have more than one correct answer. In such cases, grid only one answer.

5. **Mixed numbers** such as $3\frac{1}{2}$ must be gridded as 3.5 or 7/2. (If 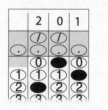 is entered into the grid, it will be interpreted as $\frac{31}{2}$, not as $3\frac{1}{2}$.)

6. **Decimal Answers:** If you obtain a decimal answer with more digits than the grid can accommodate, it may be either rounded or truncated, but it must fill the entire grid.

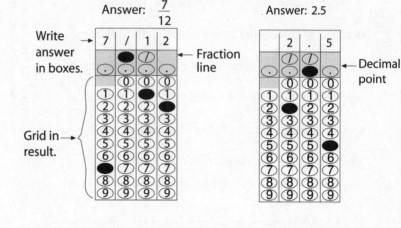

Answer: $\frac{7}{12}$ Answer: 2.5

Write answer in boxes.
Fraction line
Grid in result.
Decimal point

Acceptable ways to grid $\frac{2}{3}$ are:

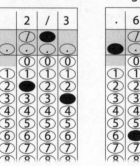
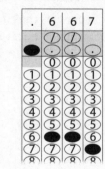

Answer: 201 – either position is correct

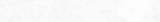

NOTE: You may start your answers in any column, space permitting. Columns you don't need to use should be left blank.

CONTINUE

28

$$(x - 2)^2 + (y + 8)^2 = 154$$

The equation of a circle in the *xy*-plane is shown above. For which value of *x* will the *y*-coordinate be the greatest?

29

$$p(x) = \frac{(x^2 - 16)(\sqrt{-x})}{x + 4}$$

For how many values of *x* does $p(x) = 0$?

Questions 30-31 refer to the following information.

A new car dealership offers a choice of two different compensation packages to its salespeople. With Package A, a salesperson is paid an annual salary of $10,000 plus a commission as a percentage of the sale price of each car sold that year. With Package B, a salesperson is not paid any salary but earns a fixed fee for each car sold that year. A salesperson must choose one of the packages at the time of hire and has the option to switch packages only on January 1 of each year.

30

On January 1, 2003, Jason chose compensation Package A. Jason sold 110 cars with a mean sales price of $30,000 that year. If Jason had chosen compensation Package B, his total compensation for the year would have been $1,550 more. If the commission percentage of Package A was 1%, what was the fixed fee per car, in dollars, for compensation Package B in 2003 ?

31

In 2005, the commission percentage of Package A was 1.5%, and the fixed fee per car of Package B was $725. Jason sold 80 cars that year and determined that his total compensation would be the same under both Package A and Package B. What is the mean price, in thousands of dollars, of the cars that Jason sold in 2005 ?

STOP

**If you finish before time is called, you may check your work on this section only.
Do not turn to any other section.**

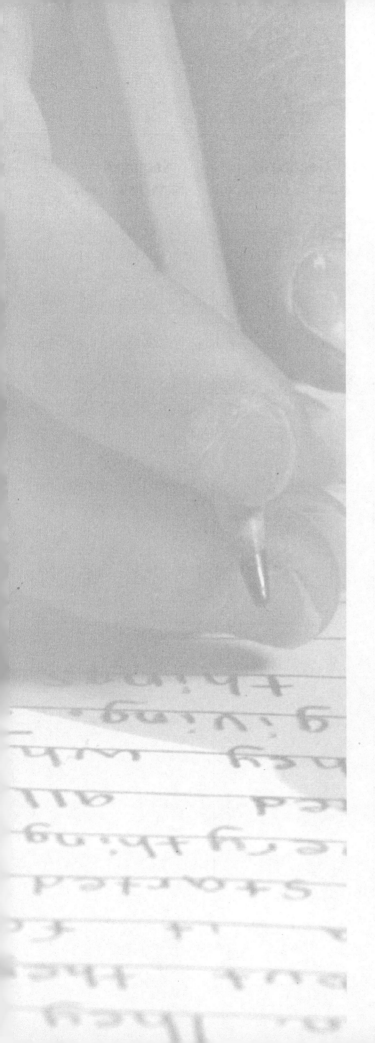

Chapter 14
Practice Test 1:
Answers and
Explanations

PRACTICE TEST 1 ANSWER KEY

Section 1: Reading

1.	D	25.	B
2.	A	26.	A
3.	C	27.	C
4.	A	28.	B
5.	B	29.	D
6.	C	30.	A
7.	B	31.	A
8.	C	32.	C
9.	A	33.	B
10.	C	34.	C
11.	D	35.	C
12.	C	36.	A
13.	B	37.	B
14.	A	38.	D
15.	B	39.	C
16.	B	40.	B
17.	A	41.	D
18.	D	42.	A
19.	B	43.	C
20.	D	44.	C
21.	C	45.	C
22.	C	46.	B
23.	A	47.	B
24.	D		

Section 2: Writing and Language

1.	B	23.	D
2.	A	24.	A
3.	C	25.	B
4.	B	26.	C
5.	D	27.	C
6.	C	28.	A
7.	B	29.	D
8.	D	30.	B
9.	A	31.	D
10.	A	32.	A
11.	C	33.	C
12.	C	34.	B
13.	D	35.	D
14.	D	36.	C
15.	D	37.	A
16.	B	38.	B
17.	A	39.	A
18.	C	40.	C
19.	B	41.	D
20.	C	42.	B
21.	B	43.	A
22.	A	44.	C

Section 3: Math (No Calculator)

1.	A	11.	A
2.	D	12.	B
3.	D	13.	D
4.	C	14.	13
5.	A	15.	40
6.	C	16.	4
7.	B	17.	2.2
8.	D		
9.	C		
10.	D		

Section 4 : Math (Calculator)

1.	A	16.	D
2.	C	17.	B
3.	A	18.	B
4.	D	19.	A
5.	D	20.	C
6.	A	21.	C
7.	D	22.	B
8.	D	23.	D
9.	C	24.	A
10.	D	25.	C
11.	C	26.	D
12.	B	27.	D
13.	C	28.	2
14.	A	29.	1
15.	D	30.	405
		31.	40,000

EXPLANATIONS

Section 1—Reading

1. **D** Use POE! Although there doesn't seem to be any animosity, there also is no evidence of the townspeople supporting Clym, so eliminate (A). Choice (B) can also be eliminated because it is not supported in the passage. Clym's fame was built over years in his youth, and there is no reason given for why he is not going to return to Paris. We don't even know for sure whether he will return or not! Choice (C) is not stated in the passage. The passage mentions Clym telling a *Scripture riddle*, but this does not mean his upbringing was religious. Eliminate (C). Choice (D) is the correct answer because the passage states that *the only absolute certainty about him was that he would not stand still in the circumstances amid which he was born.*

2. **A** The answer to the previous question is best supported by (A) because this portion of the passage discusses that something was expected of Clym regardless of whether it was good or bad, and he would not simply stagnate. None of the other answer choices are parts of the passage that support this idea.

3. **C** The *observer's eye* is being *arrested* by Clym's face which is later described as *attractive*. This is obviously not a criminal type of arrest, so (A) and (D) can be eliminated. This sentence is discussing an onlooker's glance being captured by Clym's features, so (B) doesn't make sense because nothing is forcing this. Choice (C) is the correct answer.

4. **A** Use POE! Choice (B) can be eliminated because we have no support that people are beginning to bore of him. Choice (C) can be eliminated because the passage doesn't say anything about the state of Clym's finances or how fancy his lifestyle is. Choice (D) can be eliminated because we don't know for sure that he never COULD live up to his renown. We don't know precisely if the quote was originally about Clym, but it doesn't matter. The author uses this quote to plant the idea of disappointment. Later in the passage, suspicions continue when a *curiosity as to why he stayed on so long* arises. We know that Clym went off to London and Paris, but now he is back and for longer than a holiday.

5. **B** This paragraph suggests that Clym has stayed in town longer than a normal vacation which causes *curiosity* because he is someone who has *something being expected of him*. These two ideas seem to be at odds with each other, which is best summarized in (B). There is no evidence to support the idea that the townspeople want him to return to Paris or that they are intrusive in his life, so (A) and (C) can be eliminated. The word *prove* in (D) is too strong because this paragraph doesn't even discuss awkward spreading of Clym's fame, so (D) can be eliminated as well. Choice (B) is the correct answer.

6. **C** This sentence is contrasting the idea that comes before it which says that Clym *must of necessity have something in him* by saying that it is possible his fame possibly *owed something to the accidents of his situation*. In context the word *accidents* means "luck" or "happenstance." The answer that best summarizes this is (C). Choice (A) is incorrect because no predecessors are mentioned. Choice (B) is the opposite of the intended meaning. Choice (D) plays off the idea of an accident like a car accident, but is incorrect in this context.

7. **B** Use POE! The passage doesn't say anything about Clym being wealthy or having reputation overseas, so eliminate (A). The passage does mention his facial features but not any sort of tragic circumstances, so eliminate (C). Clym is never said to have any skill as a preacher, so eliminate (D). Only (B) correctly characterizes him because he is known to be *famous* and *a lad of whom something was expected*.

8. **C** The answer to the previous question is best supported by (C). In these lines, Clym is described as *An individual whose fame has spread* and therefore must *have something in him*. None of the other answer choices support this idea of fame and potential.

9. **A** The comparison being made in the first paragraph is one of something prosaic (sounds and shapes) becoming *attractive* and *interesting* when used in conjunction with others to create language or writing. This relationship is best mirrored in (A). The color yellow by itself on the palette is commonplace, but painted with other colors into something such as a sunrise makes it more appealing. Choice (B) describes two things being equally appealing. Choice (C) is about something not being beautiful until it is understood. Choice (D) is comparing two different types of gems.

10. **C** The passage says that the tulip was useless but beautiful. The passage makes no mention of the tulip's scent. Therefore, (A) is not the best answer. Though the tulip is called exotic, the author does not ascribe the flower's popularity to its exotic botany. Therefore, (B) is not the best answer. Because (C) mentions the flower's beauty, (C) is the best answer. Choice (D) is not the best answer because it contradicts the passage, which specifically states that the tulip had no medicinal qualities.

11. **D** The answer to the previous question was that the tulip was prized for its beauty. Only (D) mentions the tulip's beauty. Therefore, (D) is the best answer.

12. **C** In context, the word *pitch* refers to the *mad embrace* of the tulip by the Dutch. Therefore, the correct answer should mean something like "frenzy." *Throw, angle,* and *promotion* mean completely different things, while *level* can mean "intensity," which most closely matches the meaning of *pitch*. Therefore, (C) is correct.

13. **B** In context, the word *spectacularly* emphasizes how very flat, monotonous, and swampy Holland is. Choice (A) is not the best answer because the Low Countries are never described as beautiful. Choice (B) is the best answer because the Dutch landscape is described as monotonous. Choice (C) is not the best answer because there is no tone of irony in the passage. Choice (D) is not the best

answer because the efforts to make the Low Countries beautiful are not mentioned until later in the paragraph. The best answer is (B).

14. **A** The fourth paragraph describes the popularity of botany in seventeenth-century Holland. This matches (A). Choice (B) is not the best answer because there is no mention of a baseball field. Choice (C) contradicts the passage, which says that Dutch botanists were extremely famous. Choice (D) is not the best answer because there is nothing that says the Dutch obsession was unusually strong.

15. **B** The passage states that Dutch gardens were used to make statements about one's sophistication and wealth. Choice (A) is incorrect because it takes an overly literal interpretation of the statement that the Dutch saw their gardens as being like jewel boxes. Choice (B) is correct because the passage states that flowers were a status symbol for the Dutch. Choice (C) says that all Dutch gardens were full of exotic and expensive flowers, which is not supported by the text. Choice (D) says that Dutch gardens had only one flower in them, which is not supported by the text, which states only that that one flower could make a powerful statement.

16. **B** The answer to the previous question states that the flowers were used as a status symbol for the Dutch. Therefore, our answer will match that. Choice (A) is not the right answer because it emphasizes how tiny and prized Dutch gardens were, but does not mention social status. Choice (B) is the best answer because it states "*To make such statements—about one's sophistication, about one's wealth—has always been one of the reasons people plant gardens,*" which matches question 15. Choices (C) and (D) are incorrect because they do not discuss status or wealth in relation to the flower.

17. **A** In context, *utilitarian* means "useful." Only *practical* matches this meaning. The best answer is (A).

18. **D** The passage contrasts the useful rose and lily with the useless tulip. There is no indication of the price of roses or lilies; therefore, (A) is not the best answer. There is no indication of whether or not roses or lilies are exotic, so (B) is not the best answer. There is no indication that roses and lilies are not beautiful, so (C) is not the best answer. Choice (D) is supported by the text's claim that roses and lilies were originally prized for how useful they are, but that the tulip is *extraordinarily useless*.

19. **B** The blurb indicates that the author of this passage *was a mill-worker, writer, and social activist* and played an important role in *the labor and women's suffrage movements*. Therefore, *disinterested* would not describe Robinson's perspective, so (A) can be eliminated. Choice (B) is a good match because she is a social activist, and the final sentence of the passage expresses her strong belief that *many men…were helped to an education by the wages of the early millgirls*. Choice (C) is incorrect because Robinson never expresses anger nor is she trying to cause trouble. Choice (D) is not the best answer because *carefree* does not capture the way she proudly and positively portrays the hard work of the women she describes in this passage. Therefore, (B) is the best answer.

20. **D** In the first paragraph, the author states that *women* and *troops of young girls* came from all over to take advantage of the cotton mills that were looking for help and the *high wages that were offered to all classes of work-people*. Therefore, the reason that the women moved to Lowell was because

they wanted these jobs with high wages. Choices (A) and (B) are incorrect because the author never discussed the climate or any vacation time in this paragraph. Choice (C) is tempting because the women and girls were coming from *distant towns*, *different parts of New England*, and *Canada*. However, the author does directly cite working in a diverse atmosphere as the reason for them wanting to work in the cotton mills. This leaves (D). Even if you're unsure about what *remuneration* means, you can confidently pick (D) because of POE. However, if you do know what *remuneration* means (money paid for work or service), then (D) is clearly the correct answer.

21. **C** This question is really asking, "Why does the author mention the working conditions of England and France?" In the second paragraph, the author states that, at the time, being a factory girl was the lowest employment position a woman could hold. This view—that working as a millgirl was a *degrading occupation*—was established due to the treatment of women in factories in countries like England and France. In order to overcome this prejudice, high wages were offered to entice women to work as millgirls. Thus, the author uses the reference of working conditions in England and France to illustrate how the working conditions at the Lowell mills would be different. Choice (C) is a good match. Eliminate (A) and (D) because the author says exactly the opposite. The conditions in these two European countries were not superior nor were they a model that the author was advocating the Americans should follow. The author has given an example of working conditions elsewhere during this time period but has not provided a historical overview of the Industrial Revolution, so (B) in incorrect. The best answer is (C).

22. **C** The answer to the previous question was that the working conditions in England and France were mentioned in order to *draw a contrast between those conditions and the conditions promised to workers in the Lowell mills*. Because being a factory girl was a *degrading occupation*, the corporations in Lowell needed a way to convince women to take these positions, so they offered high wages. The lines that best support this answer are lines 20–24 (C). Eliminate (A) and (B) because neither choice offers a contrast between the conditions in European factories to those in the Lowell mills. Choice (D) provides information about working conditions only in the Lowell mills but provides no information about the working conditions in England and France. Therefore, (C) is the best answer.

23. **A** The corporations were trying to find ways to *overcome a prejudice* by offering them high wages to work in a role that had a negative association still clinging to *this degrading occupation*. Work that is degrading would cause humiliation or shame, so *opprobrium* means something similar to "shame." Eliminate (B) and (C) because those choices have positive meanings. Choice (D) is a possibility because *trauma* (a disturbing or distressing event) could cause shame; however, the word itself does not mean "shame" so this answer should be eliminated. Choice (A) is *disgrace*, which is a synonym for "shame." Therefore, the best answer is (A).

24. **D** In the third paragraph, the author describes the youngest girls employed at the Lowell mills. While they might have some free time, they were responsible for taking off the *full bobbins from the spinning-frames* and replacing *them with empty ones*, so they did not have "complete freedom," which makes (A) incorrect. There is no mention of the youngest girls spending their time in an educa-

tional setting in this paragraph or the passage, so (B) is not correct. Choice (C) is incorrect because the doffers were aged under 10 years old. This leaves (D), which can be supported by information earlier in the third paragraph. In lines 31–34, the author lists activities that the girls might occupy their free time with when they weren't replacing empty bobbins. The correct answer is (D).

25. **B** The answer to the previous question was that the youngest girls were afforded more leisure time than were the older girls and adult women. The best evidence for this answer is found in lines 31–34 (B). Because the youngest girls worked only 15 minutes every hour, this left 45 minutes to fill, which they sometimes did by reading, knitting, or playing outside if they had a kind overseer. Choice (A) is incorrect because these lines describe only what the youngest girls were called and what they did in the mills, not that they had more leisure time than the older girls and women. Choice (C) is incorrect because those lines are not specifically referring to the youngest girls. All the millgirls had an opportunity for some time off during the year. Choice (D) includes lines that make no mention of the youngest girls working in the mills, so it cannot providence supporting evidence for the previous question. The correct answer is (B).

26. **A** The table provided in this passage *shows the daily schedule for the workers at the Lowell Mills in 1851.* Choice (A) is a good match because this answer references the amount of time the women were required to be at the mills and the table contains the daily schedule for the year. The table does not indicate that there are five corporations (eliminate (B)) or how the millgirls spent their wages (eliminate (C)). Choice (D) is incorrect because the daily schedule provided in the table in no way connects to the claim made in this answer choice. The information in the table best supports the claim made in (A).

27. **C** In the last paragraph, the author explains that the main incentive for women who wanted these jobs was to *secure the means of education for some male member of the family.* The money for the men's education was the most important reason to take these jobs. In context, *prevailing* means something similar to "main" or "most important." Eliminate (A), (B), and (D) because they do not mean the same thing as "main" or "most important." *Predominant* does mean the same thing as "main" or "most important," so (C) is the best answer.

28. **B** The fifth paragraph discusses the idea that the money the millgirls earned often went to *secure the means of education for some male member of the family.* Lines 56–59 indicate that the importance of a college education for the men was a *dominant thought* in the minds of many of the millgirls. The author also gives examples of women who provided men the means to earn their education. The author never indicates that the women were *contemptuous* (scornful) of the men, so (A) should be eliminated. Choice (B) is a good match for the main idea of this paragraph because it was common for the women to use their earnings to pay for their male relatives' education, and the author gives examples of women who did so. Choice (C) could be true, but that claim is never directly made in the passage, but more importantly it is not the main idea of the fifth paragraph (eliminate (C)). Choice (D) is incorrect because the women were not earning money for their daughters; they were using to the money to pay for the male relatives' education. Therefore, the best answer is (B).

29. **D**   The authors mention titanium's ability to impart white coloring and brightness to objects at the end of the first paragraph. In lines 5–7, the authors state that the *very high refractive index* of titanium dioxide means that it *has high light-scattering ability*. The phrase *as a result* lets the reader know that this quality is what allows titanium dioxide to impart *whiteness, opacity, and brightness to many products*. While the authors do state in the first paragraph that titanium is *highly resistant to corrosion* (A) and *45% lighter than steel* (B), these facts are not mentioned in relation to titanium's ability to impart whiteness and brightness to objects. Choice (C) is mentioned in lines 40–41, but there is no reference to whiteness or brightness in this paragraph. Therefore, the correct answer is (D).

30. **A**   The answer to the previous question was that titanium's "high refractive index" accounts for its ability to impart white coloring and brightness to objects. Lines 5–8 directly state this, so (A) provides the best evidence for the answer to the previous question. Choices (B) and (C) do not make any reference to titanium's ability to impart whiteness and brightness to objects, so neither choice could support the answer to the previous question. If the answer to the previous question had been "its natural abundance," then (D) could work for the answer to this question. However, the fact titanium is naturally abundant does not account for its ability to impart whiteness or brightness to objects. Choice (A) is the correct answer.

31. **A**   Matthew Hunter was the first person to isolate titanium metal. However, because the process was so difficult, the metal was considered a laboratory *curiosity*. Once William Kroll developed a method to produce the metal in commercial quantities, titanium was used more widely. In context, the word *curiosity* means something similar to "peculiar" or "unusual" because, at first, it could not be made into commercial quantities because of the difficult isolation process—it was only something found in a laboratory. Choices (C) and (D) do not mean "peculiar" or "unusual," so eliminate both of them. Choice (B) is a definition often associated with *curiosity*; however, this word does not match unusual and would not make sense in context because the metal itself cannot be inquisitive, so eliminate this answer. Only *oddity* in (A) has a similar meaning to "peculiar" or "unusual" and is, therefore, the best answer.

32. **C**   Use POE and compare each answer choice to the information provided in the table. The table presents the percentage of titanium dioxide and the distribution by industry for 2011 and 2012. Choice (A) does not contain any information that is listed in the table, so this answer is incorrect. The table does not include information about opacity and brightness, so the table cannot support (B). Choice (C) could work because the products listed in the answer are found in the table and would account for more than 75% of titanium dioxide's distribution, which supports that *most* titanium dioxide is used in these products. The table does not provide information on quality or weight, so the table cannot support (D). The best answer is (C).

33. **B**   In lines 26–28, the authors mention that the paint industry began using titanium dioxide because of the environmental hazards associated with lead paint. Then in lines 28–31, the authors list several products that titanium is used in for coloring because it is *relatively inert*. In lines 36–39, the authors mention that titanium is also used in biological implants because the metal is *nonreactive*

in the human body. The authors do support the idea that titanium is safe for human use and give specific examples and reasons, so (C) and (D) can be eliminated. Choice (A) is incorrect because it does not provide the correct reasons/examples to answer this question. The correct answer is (B) because it includes the information from lines 28–31 and lines 36–39.

34. **C** In lines 34–36, the authors state that titanium metal has a *high strength-to-weight ratio* and high *corrosion resistance*—because it's strong, light, and able to withstand damage, its alloys are used in the aerospace industry. In context, *resistance* has a similar meaning "able to withstand" in terms of its ability to not be physically damaged. Choices (A), (B), and (D) do not have a similar meaning to "able to withstand" in a physical sense, so they should be eliminated. This leaves (C). *Lack of vulnerability* can mean that the metal is not susceptible to physical damage and is the answer most similar in meaning to "able to withstand." Therefore, the best answer is (C).

35. **C** The authors mention steel and aluminum in the first paragraph. Titanium is compared to steel—*It is as strong as steel but 45 percent lighter*—and aluminum—*it is twice as strong as aluminum but only 60 percent heavier*. So the authors are comparing the three metals to give the reader a sense of titanium's strength and weight compared to those qualities in steel and aluminum. Choice (C) is a good match. The authors discuss titanium's ability to impart brightness and opacity to objects later in this paragraph but not compared in any way to steel or aluminum, so (A) should be eliminated. While titanium is stronger than aluminum, it is only as strong as steel, so titanium is not *stronger than all other metals*. Eliminate (B). The natural abundance of titanium is never mentioned in this paragraph. When it is mentioned later in the passage, steel and aluminum are not, so (D) is not the reason for the authors' comparison. Therefore, the best answer is (C).

36. **A** In lines 52–53, the authors state that *rutile has a very high index of refraction* and *is the most desirable in the pigment industry*. Because rutile is the most desirable form of titanium for the pigment industry, it is likely the most useful for manufacturing paint products (A). Ilmenite accounts for 90% of the world's titanium, but the authors do not state that it is used by the pigment industry or for paint products (eliminate (B)). The specific economic importance of anatase is never directly stated, so eliminate (C). Titanium metal was mentioned earlier in the passage as being useful for biological implants and to the aerospace industry, not to the pigment industry (eliminate (D)). The correct answer is (A).

37. **B** Because the answer to the previous question was *rutile*, (B), (lines 50–53) would best support this answer. The lines in (A) make no reference to rutile. Choices (C) and (D) discuss ilmenite, which is not the correct answer to the previous question. Therefore, the answer that provides the best evidence for the answer to the previous question is (B).

38. **D** The question asks what can be inferred from Passage 1, and each answer choice relates to mind wandering. Choice (A) is not the best answer since the occipital lobes are not involved in mind wandering. Choice (B) sounds good, but it's extreme—the author doesn't say all parts of the brain are involved. The passage states that *sham simulation caused no changes in mind wandering,* so (C) is incorrect. Thus, (D) is the best answer.

39. **C** Choice (C) states that the *results demonstrate that the frontal lobes play a causal role in the production of mind wandering behavior.* Thus, the passage says mind wandering is initiated in the frontal lobes, so (C) is the correct answer, and you can eliminate (A), (B), and (D).

40. **B** The word *locus* means "location." Thus, (B) is the best answer. Choice (A) means "procedure" or "task," while (C) means "contemplation" or "deep thought," neither of which matches the meaning of *locus* in the passage. Choice (D) means the "perimeter of a circle," which can contain a locus, but it's not the same as the "locus"—the location itself.

41. **D** The author of Passage 2 describes a list of activities that people commonly do in order to explain how we can do several different things, but still remember to do something we discussed earlier due to working memory. Thus, (D) is the best answer. While we may see in our minds the activities the author mentions, the purpose is to show a real example, not just stimulate the visual cortex—making (A) wrong. Choice (B) is true in that the author wanted to use mundane examples, but the overall purpose was not just to include them in the article. Choice (C) is incorrect because it's too vague.

42. **A** Line 74 and the surrounding lines discuss how working memory relates to mind wandering. A word meaning *connection* or *relationship* works the best in this context. Choice (A) is the best answer.

43. **C** The passage states that mind wandering is positively correlated with working memory capacity, which is the opposite of an inverse relationship. So (A) is not the best answer. While the passage does say that working memory is correlated with IQ, this does not mean that mind wandering increases one's IQ. Choice (B) can be eliminated. The passage states that in one study the presence of sensory distractors *cut off mind wandering at the pass,* which supports (C). Mind wandering is measurable because it was measured in several studies described in the passage; therefore, (D) is not the best answer. Choice (C) is the best answer.

44. **C** The answer to the previous question indicates that mind wandering requires minimal sensory distractors. Choice (A) describes measuring working memory, and so does not support this conclusion. While (B) does describe a study that involves mind wandering, it doesn't mention sensory distractors. Choice (C) describes how sensory distractors can inhibit mind wandering, which supports the previous answer. Choice (D) doesn't mention mind wandering or sensory distractors. Choice (C) is the best answer.

45. **C** The best answer is (C) because Passage 1 mentions the parts of the brain involved in mind wandering, while Passage 2 does not. Only Passage 2 correlates mind wandering with intelligence and lists everyday activities people do while mind wandering, so eliminate (A) and (B), respectively. Both passages address the issue of whether working memory has limits, so (D) is incorrect.

46. **B** Choice (B) is the best answer because both studies showed that mind wandering didn't hurt but even helped participants succeed on certain tasks. Choice (A) is too strong due to *inevitably,* and (D) is too strong due to *exclusively.* Only Passage 1 mentions creativity and mood, so (C) is incorrect.

47. **B** The conclusion reached in the last paragraph of Passage 2 is that mind wandering is a way for our brains *to allocate resources to the most pressing problems*. In Passage 1 it says that *This cross-brain involvement …may also contribute to the ability to stay successfully on-task while the mind goes off on its merry mental way*. Thus, Passage 1 does support the last paragraph of Passage 2—making (B) correct. Choice (A) is incorrect because the sensory distractors were used in the study in Passage 2. Choice (C) is also incorrect because Passage 2 does discuss brain function. Choice (D) is incorrect because Passage 1 concludes that mind wandering involves many parts of the brain, not Passage 2.

Section 2—Writing and Language

1. **B** The phrase *quite the contrary* in meant to emphasize that tuition costs are not only not decreasing, they are increasing. The answer that best matches this is (B). Choice (A) is not supported by the text—the author does not mention his or her tuition costs. Choice (C) goes too far; although the phrase does indicate that tuition costs have increased, it does not support the claim that it is too expensive for many who wish to attend college. There is no indication elsewhere in the paragraph that tuition has increased, so (D) is not correct. The best answer is (B).

2. **A** The sentence in question states that *Business majors are over 10% more likely to have jobs that require college degrees…than are Humanities majors*. According to the graphic, this statement is true. Business majors holding jobs that require college degrees are counted at 55.6%, while Humanities majors holding jobs that require college degrees are counted at 45.4%. Choice (B) is incorrect; more than 50% of Areas studies majors are employed in both jobs that do and do not require a college degree. Choice (C) is not supported by the graphic as it demonstrates only the current rate of employment for certain areas of studies by college degree requirement; it does not indicate future trends. Choice (D) is not relevant to the point being made in the paragraph. Also, because the focus is on specific types of majors that are more likely to lead to employment for graduates, (D) is too vague. The only answer that is supported by the graphic and expresses this point is (A).

3. **C** The underlined portion *there have been* refers to the *sharp rise* later in the sentence. Because a *sharp rise* is a singular subject, it needs to have a singular verb. Because both (A) and (B) are plural (and they have the exact same meaning), they can be eliminated. Choice (D) corrects the agreement error between the subject and verb but includes an apostrophe error with "they're." The correct answer is (C), as it corrects the agreement error with the word "has" and does not contain any additional errors.

4. **B** The first sentence of this paragraph describes when the phrase "supply-chain management" was introduced. The second sentence describes the progression of how that term and practice became defined. The choice that stresses this progression over time is (B), as it clearly establishes a timeline by referencing a specific era. Choice (C) references time but is too vague. Choices (A) and (D) are both awkward and are not related to the progression of the term. The best answer is (B).

5. **D** In this sentence, the author is introducing an example to support his or her argument. The idiomatic phrase used should be "For instance." The only choice that contains the correct phrasing is (D).

6. **C** Expand out the contraction. *They're* is the same as *they are*, which is not correct in this context. Eliminate (A). The remaining answer choices contain both plural and singular pronouns. Because the noun earlier in the sentence that is being replaced is *factory*, which is singular, a singular pronoun is needed. Eliminate (D) as well. Expanding (B) results in "it is," which is incorrect. The *its* in (C) is singular and demonstrates the factory's possession of the *road-ready vehicles*, so it is the correct answer.

7. **B** As it is currently written, the sentence is very awkward. Because the introductory phrase is describing the process of supply-chain management, that process needs to be placed closely to that phrase in the sentence. Only (B) does this. Choice (C) has *natural resources* being described by the introductory phrase and is also awkward. Choice (D) has *the life cycle of the car* being described by the introductory phrase rather than the process and would create a comma splice. Choice (B) is the best answer.

8. **D** The central idea of this paragraph is the multi-step process that supply-chain management goes through. The most effective conclusion to the paragraph will relate to that process in some way or other. Choice (A) refers to making personal profit, which is not directly related to the process. Choice (B) refers to a prince, which does not make sense with the topic of this paragraph. Choice (C) indicates that the topic of the paragraph is interesting but does not refer to it directly. Rather, *it* could refer back to a number of singular pronouns used in the previous sentence. Because this answer would create ambiguity, (C) is not a very effective conclusion. Choice (D) directly refers to the supply chain mentioned in the paragraph, which makes it the most effective conclusion to this paragraph.

9. **A** Punctuation is what is changing in the answer choices. As the sentence is written in the passage, a complete idea comes before the single dash. As long as a complete idea comes before a single dash, it is grammatically correct, regardless of what comes after. Keep (A). Because the second part of the sentence is not a complete idea, neither a period nor a semicolon can be used, so eliminate both (B) and (C). In (D), the use of the single dash is grammatically correct, but the comma is unnecessary. Therefore, the best answer is (A).

10. **A** Two commas should be used around unnecessary information. Because the phrase *like any college major* is not necessary in this sentence, the two commas are correct as written. Eliminate (B) and (D). Choice (C) should be eliminated because it adds an extra comma after *like*, which is not needed. Therefore, the correct answer is (A).

11. **C** The additional sentence refers to aspects of manufacturing a car. Because the only parts of the passage that discussed car manufacturing were paragraphs 2 and 3, eliminate (A). Choice (B) places the discussion of different aspects of car manufacturing before the example of car manufacturing is mentioned, so it is not the best answer. Choice (C) places the additional sentence after a reference to *hundreds or thousands of other, smaller processes* and before *Each of these has to be....* Because there

is nothing mentioned in the first sentence of paragraph 3 that *Each* is clearly referring to, the additional sentence not only connects these two ideas but also corrects that ambiguity error. Choice (D) would place the additional sentence later in the paragraph, where the discussion is focused on the selling of the car rather than the manufacturing of it. The best answer is (C).

12. **C** The central idea of the first paragraph is who Millard Fillmore is and the background of his presidency. Because the addition is referring to a completely unrelated president who took office years after Fillmore and does not relate to Fillmore or his presidency directly, the best answer choice is (C). Choice (D) is not supported by the text in the passage, so it can be eliminated. Choices (A) and (B) are incorrect because the addition would take the focus away from the topic being discussed rather than bring any benefit to the reader.

13. **D** As it is written, the second part of the sentence does not support the first part. The first part of the sentence indicates that Fillmore's presidency marked the end of the Whig Party's popularity in the United States. Currently, the sentence is speaking about wigs, not the Whig Party. Eliminate (A). Among the remaining choices, the only one that references the lack of the Whig Party in presidential politics is (D), which indicates there were no more Whig Party Presidents. Choice (B) refers to England, which is not relevant. Choice (C) focuses on Fillmore specifically, rather than the absence of the Whig Party. The best answer is (D).

14. **D** The pronoun *they* in the underlined portion is plural. The previous sentence mentions that the *Whig party fell out of national politics,* so *they* is referring to the Whig party, which is singular. Eliminate (A) and (B) because both contain plural pronouns. Between (C) and (D), only (D) clearly indicates what noun is being discussed and is the correct answer.

15. **D** Because there is nothing grammatically incorrect with any of the answer choices, the most concise choice that maintains the meaning of the sentence will be the best answer. Choices (A), (B), and (C) all contain superfluous information that is not necessary to the sentence. The most concise answer is (D).

16. **B** This sentence is discussing the growing relationship between the United States and Japan. The underlined portion is referring to the previous approach taken by Japan to foreign relations. Japan's approach would be better described by a noun rather than a verb, so (A) is incorrect. *Itself* is redundant in (C); the sentence refers to Japan's own history of isolation. Choice (D) is both wordy and ambiguous; the word *nation* could refer to either of the nations listed at the beginning of the sentence. The most concise and grammatically correct answer is (B).

17. **A** The second part of this sentence states that the *inspiration* led Fillmore and others to try to *open relations with Japan.* The word *inspiration* should therefore refer to a similar instance of this happening. Choice (A) gives the example of the British and Chinese opening relations, which is a similar instance of what happened with the United States and Japan. Choice (B) refers to an aspect only of American life, not two countries increasing relations, so it can be eliminated. Similarly, (C) refers to aspects only of Japan, so it too can be eliminated. Choice (D) is completely off topic,

discussing conflicts that would come later in history rather than an opening up of relations. The best answer is (A).

18. **C** The sentence is discussing slavery as a national problem. As the sentence is currently written, the phrase *the whole United States* is redundant with the word *national*. Eliminate (A). Choice (B) is awkward and contains redundant language with the word *everyone*, so it can be eliminated as well. The sentence refers to *non-slave states*, which indicates the different approaches taken by the North and the South of the United States towards slavery. Choice (C) indicates the shift that was made by Fillmore to making slavery a national concern, rather than just a southern one. As there is no evidence that slavery was an international concern, only an American one, (D) cannot be correct. The best answer is (C).

19. **B** This question is testing verb tense. Because both the non-underlined portion of the sentence and the underlined portion are discussing how the Fugitive Slave Act worked when it was enacted, both portions should be in the past tense. Choice (A) should be eliminated because it uses the future tense. Choice (C) is in the present tense and can also be eliminated. Choice (D) incorrectly uses the word *of* instead of have after *could* and should be eliminated. The only answer choice that correctly contains the past tense is (B).

20. **C** The answer choices contain various conjunctions, which are meant to link ideas. Since STOP punctuation is used in the answer choices, use the Vertical Line Test. Both ideas are complete, so (A) and (B) should be eliminated since *nevertheless* and *therefore* are not FANBOYS (a semicolon would be needed in place of the first comma to be correct punctuation). The difference between (C) and (D) is the type of FANBOYS used. The first part of the sentence discusses the negative side of the Fugitive Slave Act, and the second part of the sentence discusses how it helped spur—or cause—the Civil War. Therefore, a word that indicates a similarity in thought should be used, which makes (C) the best answer.

21. **B** The word *forever* is not accurate as civil rights began to be addressed in the mid-twentieth century in the United States. Furthermore, *forever* and *eternity* are synonyms. Both (A) and (C) cannot be correct, so eliminate them. Between (B) and (D), (B) is the factually accurate and less opinionated choice, whereas (D) is informal and doesn't match the academic tone of this passage (nor does the author state his or her personal opinion about how long civil rights were held back). Choice (B) is the correct answer.

22. **A** Because STOP punctuation appears in the answer choices, use the Vertical Line Test. Because the part before the punctuation is incomplete and the part after the punctuation is incomplete, (B) and (C) can be eliminated. Choice (D) adds unnecessary commas around *uniquely* and after *position*, so this choice is incorrect. This leaves (A), which correctly places commas around *even in its worst form* and is therefore the correct answer.

23. **D** It is unclear what the phrase *that way* at the beginning of the sentence is referring to. Choice (B) switches from *that way* to "those," which does not make anything clearer in the sentence. Choice (C)

replaces *that way* with "genres." Although "genres" is more specific than (A) and (B), it does not refer to any specific type or types and so is still highly vague. Choice (D) provides the most detailed answer "the 'gangster' genre," which not only makes the underlined portion clearer, but also matches the topic of the paragraph and passage. Therefore, the best answer is (D).

24. **A** This question is testing punctuation. The first part of the sentence is an incomplete idea, while the second part is a complete idea. Because a period can link only two complete ideas, (B) cannot be correct. Also, because a complete idea must come before a colon, (D) is wrong. Compare (A) and (C). Because the first part of the sentence constitutes an introductory phrase, a comma should follow the phrase. Choice (A) is the best answer.

25. **B** Pay attention to where there is a shift in the paragraph that seems out of place. The first two sentences give a quote from a film director about American film, while the remainder of the paragraph discusses American literature. As this shift comes between sentences 2 and 3, moving sentence 4 between those two would provide a link between the discussion of American film and literary genres. All other answer choices place this sentence between sentences discussing American literature, which do not need to be linked. The correct answer is (B).

26. **C** The second paragraph discusses the background and work of Ross Macdonald. The best introduction to this paragraph is one that is focused on Ross Macdonald specifically. Choice (A) refers to a different author who was mentioned earlier in the passage, so it is not the correct answer. Choice (B) is also focused on another author as compared to just focusing on Ross Macdonald, so that choice is incorrect as well. Choice (C) introduces who Ross Macdonald is, which effectively introduces the subject of the paragraph. Choice (D) does not mention authors at all but rather is merely negative about writing in general, so it is not the most effective introduction of the topic of the paragraph. The best answer is (C).

27. **C** The answer choices are switching which "wh" word is used: "when," "which," and "where." *When* is used to refer to time; *which* is used to refer to things other than people, places, and time; and *where* is used to refer to places. In this sentence, the thing being referred to is *University of Michigan*. Because the University of Michigan is a place, the correct answer should have "where." Choice (C) is the correct answer.

28. **A** The first part of the sentence discusses the two different directions it appeared that Millar was being pulled in, so the best choice to maintain the focus of the sentence will relate that topic. As it is currently written, the underlined portion gives an example of those two directions. Choice (B) discusses the most famous work of Coleridge, which does not maintain the focus of the sentence since the sentence is about Millar. Choice (C) mentions both movies and books, but there is no indication in this sentence or paragraph that Millar was at all involved with movies. Choice (D) discusses Millar's preference between two different writers, but the authors are not *directions* he was being pulled in. The only answer that maintains the focus of this sentence is (A).

29. **D** Because the underlined portion must be correct, any words that match *sophistication* are correct grammatically can be eliminated. Because "refinement" and "elegance" match *sophistication*, both (A) and (C) can be eliminated. This leaves (B) and (D). Looking back at the text of the passage, the author discusses Millar's use of words and ideas and the academic depths he went to when writing his characters. This best matches (B) *intellect*, so that answer can be eliminated as well. Choice (D) most closely means behaving as if you are superior to others, which is not how Millar is described. Choice (D) is the answer that does NOT work in the underlined portion.

30. **B** Based on the answer choices, this question is testing apostrophe usage. The text refers to the text of Macdonald, which indicates possession, so eliminate (A). Because Macdonald does not end in an "s," eliminate (C) and (D). To show possession, an apostrophe + "s" should be added to the end of the name. The only choice that contains this correct construction is (B).

31. **D** As it is currently written, the underlined portion contains a noun agreement error. Many *people* cannot have a single *motivation* between them all. Eliminate (A). Choice (B) repeats this error, as "those" is plural and "motivation" is singular, so it is also incorrect. Choice (C) corrects the agreement error by replacing *people* with "someone," but this creates an agreement error with the *murders* earlier in the sentence. Choice (D) correctly addresses the noun agreement error by retaining "people" and changing "motivation" to "motivations," while not creating any new errors. Choice (D) is the best answer.

32. **A** The sentence contains a list of things. In lists, all items must be separated by a comma. The items in this list are *murders*, *thefts*, and *kidnappings*. As there is a comma after *thefts* in the underlined portion, this sentence is correct as written. Choice (B) omits the comma after *thefts*, which is incorrect (remember to include the comma before the word "and"). Choice (C) omits the comma after *thefts* but includes a comma after *and*, which is also incorrect. And (D) adds a comma after the last item in the list *kidnapping*, so it is also incorrect. The best answer is (A).

33. **C** The current placement of the underlined phrase creates an error since the underlined portion separates the correct idiomatic phrase: *Following in the footsteps of….* Therefore, eliminate (A). Choice (B) is incorrect as it creates a sentence that sounds as though Hammett and Chandler are literally walking towards the detective novel, so it can be eliminated. Choice (D) does not make any sense, as humans are not anything *to* the detective novel. Only (C) expresses the author's intended meaning—that it is Macdonald who is bringing something to the detective novel—making it the best answer.

34. **B** There are verb changes in the answer choices, so the first thing to do is to check if the subject and verb are consistent. The subject earlier in the sentence is *the scientific community*, which is singular. The verb in the underlined portion is *do*, which is plural. Eliminate both (A) and (C). Choices (B) and (D) both correct the subject-verb agreement error with "does" but contain different pronouns. Because *the scientific community* is singular, it must be replaced by a singular pronoun. Because (D) contains "they," which is plural, it can be eliminated. The correct answer is (B).

35. **D** Choices (A), (B), and (C) are all very similar as they include extraneous words. Choice (D) is the most concise answer which also maintains the meaning of the sentence. Choice (D) is, therefore, the best answer.

36. **C** There are pronoun and noun changes in the answer choices, so the first thing to do is check what noun these pronouns are replacing. There is some ambiguity in the passage as to the original word, so using a noun is the safer choice. Choices (B) and (D) can be eliminated. *Resources* makes sense in the context of the passage, while *resourcefulness* does not. Choice (C) is the correct answer.

37. **A** This paragraph ends by mentioning a problem: *that these new resources will not cure us fully of energy dependency*. The next paragraph introduces a solution to the problem: "asteroid mining" in space. To conclude this paragraph and introduce the next paragraph, the best choice will connect these two ideas. Choice (A) is a good match. Choices (B) and (C) can be eliminated because neither answer mentions space. Choice (D) can be eliminated because it doesn't reference the problem discussed in the first paragraph. Therefore, the best answer is (A).

38. **B** Because this question is asking which answer choice is NOT acceptable, the underlined word is correct. Therefore, anything that matches that word's meaning in the context of the sentence can be eliminated. *Fantastic* is used in this context to mean "bizarre" or "unbelievable." The answers that best match these meanings are (A), (C), and (D). The only word that does not match is *wonderful*, (B). Therefore, (B) is the answer that is NOT acceptable.

39. **A** Compare the answer choices with the provided graphic. Choice (A) is true based on the graph; new nickel discoveries in 2009 were under 1,000 mt, while new nickel discoveries in 1999 were over 2,000 mt. Choice (B) is incorrect; sulfide production was consistently higher than laterite production from 1998 to 2009. Choice (C) is also incorrect, as total nickel production was lower than the three-year average of total nickel in new discoveries from 1998 to 2004, 2006, and 2008. Choice (D) is also incorrect; the total nickel found since 1998 has fluctuated over time according to the graphic. The only possible answer is (A).

40. **C** The point of the underlined portion of the sentence is that the ship will not need to restock supplies. The most concise way of saying this while maintaining the meaning of the sentence is (C), *resupplying*. Choices (A), (B), and (D) all say the same thing but are wordier and are not the best answers. The correct answer is (C).

41. **D** The underlined portion is referring to both *space travel* and *exploration*, but that is not clear as the sentence is currently written. Choices (A), (B), and (C) are all ambiguous as they do not directly refer to *space travel* and *exploration*, so none completes the comparison being made. Choice (D) corrects this error by including the pronoun "they" to refer to the subjects earlier in the sentence, which completes the comparison, making (D) the best answer.

42. **B** The answer choices contain changes in punctuation. Using the Vertical Line Test, it is apparent that the first part of the sentence is a complete idea and the second part of the sentence is a complete idea. Because a comma by itself cannot link two complete ideas together, (A) and (C)

are incorrect. Two complete ideas also cannot be linked without punctuation, so (D) is incorrect as well. Because two complete ideas can be linked by a semicolon, (B) is the correct answer.

43. **A** There are apostrophes in the answer choices, so check for the need of an apostrophe first. The word *its* refers to the Earth, which is correct without the apostrophe (*it's* is the contraction form of "it is"), so (C) can be eliminated. Because the Earth is a singular object, (B) can be eliminated as it is a plural pronoun. Because there is no reason to change from "it" to "one" when referring to the Earth, (A) is the best answer.

44. **C** The claim in the previous statement focuses on the belief that the cost of asteroid mining is far greater than the worth of what is being mined. The question asks for an addition that best supports this claim, so eliminate any answer choices that do not relate to this topic. Choice (B) is focused on the skill of astronauts, not on the cost of asteroid mining, so it can be eliminated. Choice (D) is too general of a statement and does not relate specifically to the cost of asteroid mining, so it too can be eliminated. Choice (A) refers to money by noting the types of funding NASA receives but does not specifically relate that funding to asteroid mining. Choice (C) does bring up the exorbitant costs of "these expeditions," which is a direct reference to the mining in the previous sentence. Therefore, (C) is the only answer that supports the previous sentence.

Section 3—Math (No Calculator)

1. **A** Use Process of Elimination to eliminate (C) because the equation in (C) is a straight line. Remember the rules of graph transformations. If the number is inside the parentheses, the graph moves left or right in the opposite direction of the sign. In this case, the graph has been moved 3 units in the positive direction and therefore the correct answer is (A). An alternate way to approach this question is to plug in the point (0, 3) into each of the equations to see which equation works.

2. **D** The equation of a line is $y = mx + b$ where m stands for slope and b stands for the y-intercept. In the given equation the slope is a positive 3. Use Process of Elimination to eliminate (B) and (C) since both of these lines have a negative slope. According to the question, the y-intercept is negative. Use this information to eliminate (A) which has a positive y-intercept. The correct answer is (D).

3. **D** Whenever there are variables in the question and numbers in the answers think Plugging In the Answers. Start with (B). If $x = 5$, then the equation becomes $\dfrac{5^2 - (4)(5) + 3}{3} = 2(5 - 1)$. Solve both sides of the equation to get $\dfrac{25 - 20 + 3}{3} = 2(4)$, $\dfrac{8}{3} = 8$. Because this is not a true statement, eliminate (B). It may not be clear which direction to go so just pick a direction. Choice (C) becomes $\dfrac{6^2 - (4)(6) + 3}{3} = 2(6 - 1)$. Solve both sides of the equation to get $\dfrac{36 - 24 + 3}{3} = 2(5)$, $\dfrac{15}{3} = 10$, and 5 = 10. Eliminate (C). Choice (D) becomes $\dfrac{9^2 - (4)(9) + 3}{3} = 2(9 - 1)$. Solve both sides of the equation to get $\dfrac{81 - 36 + 3}{3} = 2(8)$, $\dfrac{48}{3} = 16$, and 16 = 16. Therefore, the correct answer is (D).

4. **C** According to the question, the median income rose $8,000 in a 6 year period. If the trend continues linearly, then the median income would rise again in 6 years. Whenever there are variables in the question think Plugging In. If $x = 6$, then the median income would be 57,000 + 8,000 = 65,000. Plug in 6 for x in the answer choices to see which answer equals 65. Choice (A) becomes $I = 49 + (8)(6) = 97$. Eliminate (A). Choice (B) becomes $I = 57 + (8)(6) = 105$. Eliminate (B). Choice (C) becomes $I = 57 + \left(\frac{4}{3}\right)(6) = 57 + 8 = 65$. Keep (C), but check (D) just in case. Choice (D) becomes $I = 49 + \left(\frac{4}{3}\right)(6) = 49 + 8 = 57$. Eliminate (D). Therefore, the correct answer is (C).

5. **A** Whenever there are variables in the question and numbers in the answer choices, think Plugging In the Answers. Start with (B). If $z = 13$, the equation becomes $\frac{3(13+3)}{4} - \frac{2(13-2)}{3} = 2$. Simplify the left side of the equation to get $\frac{3(16)}{4} - \frac{2(11)}{3} = 2$, $12 - 7.\overline{3} = 2$, and $4.\overline{6} = 2$. Eliminate (B). It may not be clear which direction to go from here, so just pick a direction. If we try (A), $z = -19$, and the equation becomes $\frac{3(-19+3)}{4} - \frac{2(-19-2)}{3} = 2$. Simplify the right side of the equation to get $\frac{3(-16)}{4} - \frac{2(-21)}{3} = 2$, $3(-4) - \left[2(-7)\right] = 2$, $-12 - [-14] = 2$, $-12 + 14 = 2$, and $2 = 2$. Therefore, the correct answer is (A).

6. **C** The decay rate is not linear; therefore, you can eliminate (B). Because the percentages in (D) are increasing (greater than 1), you can eliminate (D). The black line starts at a count of 5,000 and is decreasing at a bigger rate than the grey line. Therefore, the black decay rate (starting at 5,000) must be larger. Therefore, the answer is (C) because it is decreasing at a rate of 10% (0.9 = 1.0 − 0.1), and the grey would be decreasing at a lower rate of 5% (0.95 = 1.0 − 0.05).

7. **B** Start by multiplying both sides of the equation by $\sqrt{ba}$ to get $a^3 = b \times \sqrt{ba}$. Square both sides of the equation to get $a^6 = b^2 \times ba$. Combine like terms to get $a^6 = b^3 a$ and $a^5 = b^3$. Therefore, the correct answer is (B).

8. **D** According to the question, a bag of apples and 3 cartons of strawberries cost $18. If a = a bag of apples and c = a carton of strawberries, then $a + 3c = 18$. According to the question, a bag of apples cost 50% more than a carton of strawberries, which can be written as $a = 1.5c$. Substitute this into the first equation to get $1.5c + 3c = 18$. Solve for c to get $4.5c = 18$, and $c = 4$. Therefore, $a = 1.5 (4) = 6$. The correct answer is (D).

9. **C** If the website received 24,500 visitors 6 months ago, then three months ago the website received $24,500 \times 2 = 49,000$ visitors, and today the website is receiving $49,000 \times 2 = 98,000$ visitors. Whenever there are variables in the question and in the answers, think Plugging In. Every year the number of visitors will increase by a factor of $2^4 = 16$. So, if $t = 2$, then the population would

increase $16 \times 16 = 2^8$. Therefore, in 2 years the population would be $98,000 \times 2^8$ which when expressed in thousands would simply be 98×2^8. Eliminate (A) and (D) because neither of these answers include 98. In (B), the equation becomes $V = 98(2^2)$. Eliminate (B). The correct answer is therefore (C).

10. **D** Whenever there is an unknown and the answers are numbers, think Plugging In the Answers. According to the question, Sophia grows $\frac{1}{2}$ inch per year and Carl grows $\frac{3}{4} \times \frac{1}{2} = \frac{3}{8}$. Start with (B). In 8 years, Carl will have grown $\frac{3}{8} \times 8 = 3$ inches and Sophia will have grown $\frac{1}{2} \times 8 = 4$. Given that Carl starts off 2 inches taller, he will still be an inch taller than Sophia. Eliminate (B) because it is too short a time period. Eliminate (A) for the same reason. Try (C). In 12 years, Carl will have grown $\frac{3}{8} \times 12 = \frac{9}{2} = 4.5$ inches and Sophia will have grown $\frac{1}{2} \times 12 = 6$. Given that Carl started off 2 inches taller, he will still be 0.5 inches taller than Sophia at the end of 12 years. Eliminate (C). Therefore, the correct answer must be (D).

11. **A** Use POE to solve this problem. Start by plugging in 37 for A. The resulting equation is $M = P\left(\dfrac{100 - (37 - 30)^2 - I\sqrt{L}}{25} \right)$. Multiply both sides by 25 to get $25M = P\left(100 - (37 - 30)^2 - I\sqrt{L}\right)$. Because M is now multiplied by 25, eliminate (C). Simplify the right side of the equation to get $25M = P\left(100 - (7)^2 - I\sqrt{L}\right)$, $25M = P\left(100 - 49 - I\sqrt{L}\right)$ and $25M = P\left(51 - I\sqrt{L}\right)$. The correct answer will include 51 in it, so eliminate (B). Divide both sides by P to get $\dfrac{25M}{P} = 51 - I\sqrt{L}$. Subtract 51 from both sides to get $\dfrac{25M}{P} - 51 = -I\sqrt{L}$. In order to isolate I, both sides will need to be divided by $\sqrt{L}$. Choice (D) multiplies by $\sqrt{L}$ instead. Eliminate (D). The correct answer is (A).

12. **B** Start by converting the radians to degrees by multiplying the radian values by $\dfrac{180}{\pi}$: $\dfrac{3\pi}{4} \times \dfrac{180}{\pi} = 135$ and $\dfrac{5\pi}{4} \times \dfrac{180}{\pi} = 225$. Therefore, the central angle AOB is between 135 and 225 degrees. The formula of a circle is $(x - h)^2 + (y - k)^2 = r^2$, where r stands for the radius. Therefore, the radius of circle O is 4. The formula for the circumference of a circle is $C = 2\pi r$. Therefore, the full circumference of circle O can be calculated as $C = 2\pi(4) = 8\pi$. If the central angle were 135 degrees, then the length

of arc AB would be $\dfrac{135}{360} \times 8\pi = 3\pi$. If the central angle were 225 degrees, the length of arc AB would be $\dfrac{225}{360} \times 8\pi = 5\pi$. Only (B) lies between these two values.

13. **D** According to the question, the discount is greater on later purchases. Looking at the variables, x must be the discount on the initial threshold because it is the number that increases to $x + 5$. Based on this, eliminate (B) and (C). The initial discount is therefore given by $4x$. Because x is a percentage discount and the customer spent more than the initial threshold, the discount on the initial amount would be $\dfrac{x}{100}I$, in which I is the initial discount. Therefore, $\dfrac{x}{100}I = 4x$, and $I = 400$. The correct answer is (D).

14. **13** Plug in the numbers given in the function to get $f(4) = 3(4) = 12$ and $g(2) = 2 - 3 = -1$. Therefore, $f(4) - g(2) = 12 - (-1) = 13$. The correct answer is 13.

15. **40** According to the question, males make up $\dfrac{3}{5}$ of the class, which means that females make up $\dfrac{2}{5}$ of the class. The difference between males and females is 8, which is equal to $\dfrac{3}{5} - \dfrac{2}{5} = \dfrac{1}{5}$ of the class. Therefore, the number of students in the class can be calculated as $\dfrac{1}{5}(total) = 8$. Solve for the total to get a total of 40 students. The correct answer is 40.

16. **4** According to the question, c is at least 3 times the value of d. This can be translated as $c \geq 3d$, and the difference between c and d is no more than 8, which can be translated as $c - d \leq 8$. To find the greatest value of d, plug in values for d. It helps to create a chart like the following:

d	$c \geq 3d$	$c - d \leq 8$ (plug in the smallest value of c).
1	$c \geq 3$	$3 - 1 = 2$
2	$c \geq 6$	$6 - 2 = 4$
3	$c \geq 9$	$9 - 3 = 6$
4	$c \geq 12$	$12 - 4 = 8$

Therefore, the smallest possible value of d is 4. The correct answer is 4.

17. **2.2** First, put the values given in the problem into the equations. Because displacement is 22 meters and initial velocity is 5 meters, the first equation becomes $22 = 15t + 0.5at^2$. The second equation becomes $5 = 15 + at$. Working with the second equation, subtract 15 from both sides to get $-10 = at$, which means that $a = \dfrac{-10}{t}$. Next, substitute this value for a into the first equation to get $22 = 15t + 0.5\left(\dfrac{-10}{t}\right)(t^2)$. Simplify the equation to get $22 = 15t + 0.5(-10t)$. Distribute the 0.5 to get $22 = 15t - 5t$. Solve for t to get $22 = 10t$, *and* $t = 2.2$. The correct answer is 2.2.

Section 4—Math (Calculator Allowed)

1. **A** According to the question the proton travelled through the tube filled with medium A at 100,000 meters in 5 milliseconds, which is equal to a velocity of 20,000 meters per millisecond. Therefore, the velocity through medium B can be calculated as $20,000 \div 2 = 10,000$ meters per millisecond. The correct answer is therefore (A).

2. **C** Add 5 to both sides to get $6x < 7 + 15x$. Subtract $15x$ from both sides to get $-9x < 7$. Remember when dividing by a negative number, flip the inequality sign. Solve for x to get $x > -\dfrac{7}{9}$. The correct answer is (C).

3. **A** Whenever the question includes variables and the answers are numbers, think Plugging In the Answers. Start with (B). If $r = -6$, the equation becomes $-6 + 22 = 3(-6) - 26 + 6^2$. Simplify the equation to get $16 = -18 - 26 + 36$ and $16 = -8$. Eliminate (B). It may not be clear which direction to go, so pick a direction. In (A), $r = -8$ and the equation becomes $-8 + 22 = 3(-8) - 26 + (-8)^2$. Simplify the equation to get $14 = -24 - 26 + 64$ and $14 = 14$. The correct answer is (A).

4. **D** Use POE. The term *at least* means $\geq$. On this basis, eliminate, (A) and (C). To calculate the total number of hours worked at the community center, multiply the number of hours worked per day by the number of days. This calculation is $7.5c$. Likewise, to calculate the total number of hours spent removing street litter, multiply the number of hours worked per day by the number of days. This calculation is $4l$. Therefore, eliminate (B). The correct answer is (D).

5. **D** The median is the middle number when the numbers are listed in order from low to high. In order for the median to be 15, x must be in the middle of the list of numbers. So, lined up from low to high, the numbers are 6, 9, 9, x, 36, 39 and $\dfrac{9+x}{2} = 15$. Solve for x to get $9 + x = 30$ and $x = 21$. To find the mean, add all of the numbers together and divide by 6: $\dfrac{6+9+9+21+36+39}{6} = 20$. The correct answer is (D).

6. **A** According to the question, $density = \dfrac{mass}{volume}$. Substitute the numbers given into the equation to get $19.3 = \dfrac{mass}{5}$. Solve for mass and get 96.5 grams. Use the following proportion to convert mass into ounces: $\dfrac{1}{28.3} = \dfrac{x}{96.5}$. Cross-multiply to get $28.3x = 96.5$. Solve for x to get $x \approx 3.41$. The correct answer is (A).

7. **D** The larger the polling population, the smaller the potential margin of error. According to the question, the poll selected 2,500 registered voters of all registered voters in the US. Only (D) provides a larger pool of registered voters.

8. **D** Whenever there are variables in the question and in the answer choices, think Plugging In. If $e = 52$, then the output $= 385 + 2(42) = 385 + 84 = 469$ computer chips. Plug 52 in for e in the answers to see which answer equals 469. Choice (A) becomes $C(d) = 42^{(52-50)} + 385 = 42^2 + 385 = 2,149$. Eliminate (A). Choice (B) becomes $C(d) = 52^{42} + 385$. This number is huge! Eliminate (B). Choice (C) becomes $C(d) = 42(52) + 385 = 2,184 + 385 = 2,569$. Eliminate (C). Therefore, the answer must be (D).

9. **C** Multiply the right side of the equation by $\dfrac{2}{2}$ to get $\dfrac{6(t+2)}{8} = \dfrac{100 - 5t + 44}{8}$. Because the denominators are now the same, $6(t + 2) = 100 - 5t + 44$. Distribute the 6 to get $6t + 12 = 100 - 5t + 44$. Combine like terms to get $6t + 12 = 144 - 5t$ and $11t + 12 = 144$. Solve for t to get $11t = 132$ and $t = 12$. The correct answer is (C).

10. **D** The question is asking about changing the format of the equation for a parabola to the vertex form of the equation. The vertex form of a parabola is $y = a(x - h)^2 + k$, where (h, k) denotes the vertex of the parabola. Only (D) is written in this format.

11. **C** Whenever there are variables in the question and in the answers, think Plugging In. If $m = 2$, then Taylor has written $23 \times 2 = 46$ words. Given that each page has 800 words, Taylor has written far less than a page, which means he has 699 page plus a fraction of a page left. Plug in 2 for m in the answers to see which answer yields 699 plus a fraction. Choice (A) becomes $p(m) = \dfrac{700 - 800(2)}{23} = \dfrac{700 - 1600}{23} = \dfrac{-900}{23}$. Eliminate (A). Choice (B) becomes $p(m) = \dfrac{700 - 23(2)}{800} = \dfrac{700 - 46}{800} = \dfrac{654}{800}$, which is less than a page. Eliminate (B). Choice (C) becomes $p(m) = 700 - \dfrac{23(2)}{800} = 700 - \dfrac{46}{800} = 699.9425$. This is possible. Keep (C), but check (D) just in case. Choice (D) becomes $p(m) = 700 - \dfrac{800}{23(2)} = 700 - \dfrac{800}{46} \approx 700 - 17.39 \approx 682.61$. Eliminate (D), and you're left with (C).

12. **B** The line shown includes the points $(-3, 1)$ and $(-1, 2)$. The equation for the slope of a line is $m = \dfrac{y_2 - y_1}{x_2 - x_1}$, which for the line shown can be calculated as $m = \dfrac{1 - 2}{-3 - (-1)} = \dfrac{-1}{-3 + 1} = \dfrac{-1}{-2} = \dfrac{1}{2}$. To find the slope of the line reflected across the y-axis flip the sign to $-\dfrac{1}{2}$. The correct answer is (B).

13.   **C**   A quick look at the answer choices shows that the population of people in poverty in 2008 must have been 50,000. Whenever there are variables in the question and in the answers, think Plugging In. If $m = 12$, then the population of those in poverty should be $50,000 \div 2 = 25,000$. Plug 12 in for m in the answers to see which answer equals 25,000. Choice (A) becomes $f(m) = 50,000 - \frac{1}{2}(12) = 50,000 - 6 = 49,994$. Eliminate (A). Choice (B) becomes $f(m) = 50,000 - \left(\frac{1}{2}\right)\left(\frac{12}{12}\right) = 50,000 - 0.5 = 49,999.5$. Eliminate (B). Choice (C) becomes $f(m) = 50,000\left(\frac{1^{\frac{12}{12}}}{2}\right) = 50,000\left(\frac{1}{2}\right) = 25,000$. Keep (C), but check (D) just in case. Choice (D) becomes $f(m) = 50,000 - 12^{\frac{1}{2}} \approx 50,000 - 3.45 = 49,996.55$. Eliminate (D), and you're left with (C).

14.   **A**   Use POE. Start with the linear equation first. The equation of a line is $y = mx + b$, where m stands for the slope, and b stands for the y–intercept. Therefore, in the equation $w(x) = \frac{x}{4}$ the slope is $\frac{1}{4}$, and the y-intercept is 0. On this basis, eliminate (B), which depicts a line with a negative slope, and (D), which depicts a line with a slope greater than $\frac{1}{4}$. The equation $n(x) = -(.3x)^2 + 50$ is a parabola. On this basis, eliminate (C), which depicts two linear equations. The correct answer is (A).

15.   **D**   Whenever there are variables in the question and in the answers, think Plugging In. If $x = 4$, then $y = 4^2 + 4 - 20 = 4 + 2 - 20 = 0$ and $\frac{y^2}{z} = \frac{0^2}{z} = 0$. Plug 4 in for x in the answers to see which answer equals 0. Choice (A) becomes $\frac{4^4 - 8}{10(4)} = \frac{256 - 8}{40} = \frac{248}{40}$. Eliminate (A). Choice (B) becomes $\frac{4^4 + 4^2 - 400}{4^2 + 10(4) + 25} = \frac{256 + 16 - 400}{16 + 40 + 25} = \frac{-128}{81}$. Eliminate (B). Choice (C) becomes $4^2 - (8)(4) - 15 = 16 - 32 - 15 = -31$. Eliminate (C), and you're left with (D).

16.   **D**   Start by using POE. The more pictures Squared Up frames, the greater its profits will be. Therefore, the correct answer must include a > symbol. Eliminate (A) and (B). Start with the remaining answers. According to (C), Squared Up would turn a profit if it framed 13 pictures. Profit = Revenue – Expenses. On 13 pictures, Squared Up would make $13 \times 61 = 793$ in revenue. The expenses to frame these pictures can be calculated as $13(38 + 5) + 720 = 13(43) + 720 = 559 + 720 = 1,279$. Because expenses exceed revenues, Squared Up will not make a profit if it framed only 13 pictures. Eliminate (C), and you're left with (D).

17. **B** The average amount spent per person in a household can be calculated as the total amount spent on groceries divided by the number of people in the household. The survey provided no data on the number of people in each household. Therefore, the correct answer is (B).

18. **B** Use Process of Elimination to solve. Because no data is provided on meals had at restaurants, eliminate (A). According to the question as household income increased, grocery spending decreased. So, (B) is a possible answer. While there is a connection between household income and grocery spending, it is not clear from the data that it is a causal connection. Therefore, eliminate (C). The data focuses just on Florida and therefore no inferences can be made about grocery spending in the United States. Eliminate (D), and you're left with (B).

19. **A** Whenever there are two equations with the same variables, think Simultaneous Equations. First, rewrite both equations so that the variables are on one side of the equation. The first equation becomes $3x - 96 = 4y$ and $3x - 4y = 96$. The second equation becomes $10x + 2y = 90$. Multiply this second equation by 2 to get $20x + 4y = 180$. Place the two equations on top of each other and add them:

$$\begin{array}{r} 20x + 4y = 180 \\ + \ (3x - 4y = 96) \\ \hline 23x \quad\quad = 276 \end{array}$$

Solve for x to get $x = 12$. Plug 12 in for x in the second equation to get $3(12) - 4y = 96$. Solve for y to get $36 - 4y = 96$, $-4y = 60$, and $y = -15$. Therefore, $\dfrac{x}{y} = -\dfrac{12}{15} = -\dfrac{4}{5}$. The correct answer is (A).

20. **C** The mean file size of a single song is $0.022 \times 1,024 = 22.528$ megabytes. The file size of all the songs Larissa uploaded is $40,000 \times 22.528 = 901,120$ megabytes. The upload time in seconds is $7.5 \times 60 \times 60 = 27,000$ seconds. Therefore, the upload time in megabytes per second is $\dfrac{901,120}{27,000} \approx 33.37$. The correct answer is (C).

21. **C** The output of the first hose is 4 gallons per hour, and the capacity of the tank is 48 hours. That means the first hose will fill the tank in $\dfrac{48}{4} = 12$ hours. The first fraction in the equation therefore represents the fraction of the tank the first hose fills in one hour. Given that the output of the second hose is twice the first, the $\dfrac{1}{6}$ in the equation must be the fraction of the tank the second hose fills in one hour. The $\dfrac{1}{x}$ in the equation most therefore be connected to the time both hoses take to fill the tank. Eliminate (B) and (D) because neither of these answers is related to time. Eliminate (A) because the fraction of the tank filled after 1 hour is $\dfrac{1}{x}$ not x. Therefore, the correct answer is (C).

22. **B** Start by figuring out the median number of cars owned in all 5 boroughs. To do this find the total number of cars and then see where the middle of the list is:

Number of Cars	Total in All 5 Boroughs
Zero	4,160
One	2,320
Two	1,140
Three	380

The median number is at 4 million cars, which is 0 cars. Next, add up the number of residents who live in Manhattan and own more than 0 cars:

Number of Cars	Manhattan
One	480
Two	320
Three	80
Total	**880**

The question can be translated as 880,000 is what percent of 8,000,000? Do math translation to get the following equation: $880,000 = \dfrac{x}{100} \times 8,000,000$. Solve for x to get $x = 11$. The correct answer is (B).

23. **D** Whenever there are two equations with two variables, think Simultaneous Equations. Rewrite the first equation as $8s - 4t = 17$ and the second equation as $-5s + 6t = 4$. Stack the two equations on top of each other and add them:

$$8s - 4t = 17$$
$$\underline{+(-5s + 6t = 4)}$$
$$3s + 2t = 21$$

Multiply the entire equation by 2 to get $6s + 4t = 42$. The correct answer is (D).

24. **A** The vertex form of a parabola is $y = a(x - h)^2 + k$, where (h, k) stands for the vertex. Start by converting the parabola equation into its vertex form by completing the square. The equation becomes $y - 6 = x^2 - 8x + 22 - 6$. Simplify the equation to get $y - 6 = x^2 - 8x + 16$. Factor the right side of the equation to get $y - 6 = (x - 4)^2$. Move the 6 over to get $y = (x - 4)^2 + 6$. Therefore, the vertex of the parabola is (4, 6). The equation of a circle is $(x - h)^2 + (y - k)^2 = r^2$, where the center of the circle is (h, k). Therefore, the equation of a circle centered at (4, 6) is $(x - 4)^2 + (y - 6)^2 = r^2$. Expand the circle equation to get $x^2 - 8x + 16 + y^2 - 12y + 36 = r^2$. Rewrite the equation of the circle given in the problem as $x^2 - 8x + y^2 + ky = 172$. Therefore, $ky = -12y$ and $k = -12$. The correct answer is (A).

25. **C** Use POE. Be careful in reading the y-axis. The information provided is related to the rate of increase not the population. Given that no information on the actual population is given, eliminate (B) and (D). Looking at the graph, the population of H_2 increased by 300 bees in 2001, but only increased by 250 bees in 2003. In other words, the population increased albeit at a slower rate during the 10 years. For this reason eliminate (A). The correct answer is (C).

26. **D** Use POE to solve this question. Given that y is the number of phytoplankton over time, eliminate (A). According to the question, prior to 2007 there were no phytoplankton in the lake, so eliminate (B). According to the problem, k represents the number of months the population was introduced. Therefore, the rate of increase in a month would be equal to $6.23^{\frac{1}{12}}$. Eliminate (C). The correct answer is (D).

27. **D** Look for years where the line of best fit gives an easy-to-approximate number for the area of square miles. 1970 correlates with approximately 12 million for the decrease in area of square miles, and 2000 correlates with 10 million. Subtract these values for a difference of 2 million. Then divide by 30, because there is a 30-year difference between 1970 and 2000. The answer is roughly 66,000 which is (D).

28. **2** To maximize the value of y, make $(x-2)^2 = 0$. Solve for x to get $x = 2$. The correct answer is 2.

29. **1** In order for $p(x)$ to equal 0, the numerator must equal 0. If $x^2 - 16 = 0$, then $x^2 = 16$ and $x = \pm 4$. However, x cannot equal -4 because that would make the denominator 0. And x cannot equal 4 because the square root of a negative 4 is an imaginary number. Therefore, the only value that will make the function 0 is when $x = 0$ which makes $\sqrt{-x} = \sqrt{0} = 0$. The correct answer is 1.

30. **405** Under Package A, Jason earned $10,000 + (.01)(110)(30,000) = \$43,000$. The question tells us that had Jason chosen Package B, he would have earned $43,000 + 1,550 = 44,550$. Given that Package B is comprised of a fixed price per car $\times$ the number of cars sold, and Jason sold 110 cars, the fixed amount earned for each car can be calculated as $44,500 \div 110 = 405$. The correct answer is 405.

31. **40,000** There is enough information given to see how much Jason would earn with Package B. Multiply the amount he earns per car by the number of cars: $750 \times 80 = 60,000$. Now write an equation for Package A: $A = \$10,000 + (.015)(80)x$, where x is the number of cars. We can set this equation equal to 60,000 because Package A equals Package B. The answer is $40,000.

Chapter 15
Practice Test 2

Reading Test

60 MINUTES, 47 QUESTIONS

Turn to Section 1 of your answer sheet to answer the questions in this section.

Questions 1-9 are based on the following passage.

This passage is adapted from Henry James, "The Beast in the Jungle," originally published in 1903. The passage describes the meeting, after many years, of John Marcher and May Bertram.

"You know you told me something I've never forgotten and that again and again has made me think of you since; it was that tremendously hot day when we
Line went to Sorrento, across the bay, for the breeze. What I
5 allude to was what you said to me, on the way back, as we sat under the awning of the boat enjoying the cool. Have you forgotten?"

He had forgotten and was even more surprised than ashamed. But the great thing was that he saw
10 in this no vulgar reminder of any "sweet" speech. The vanity of women had long memories, but she was making no claim on him of a compliment or a mistake. With another woman, a totally different one, he might have feared the recall possibly even of some
15 imbecile "offer." So, in having to say that he had indeed forgotten, he was conscious rather of a loss than of a gain; he already saw an interest in the matter of her mention. "I try to think—but I give up. Yet I remember that Sorrento day."

20 "I'm not very sure you do," May Bertram after a moment said; "and I'm not very sure I ought to want you to. It's dreadful to bring a person back at any time to what he was ten years before. If you've lived away from it," she smiled, "so much the better."

25 "Ah, if *you* haven't why should I?" he asked.
"Lived away, you mean, from what I myself was?"

"From what *I* was. I was of course [a boor]," Marcher went on; "but I would rather know from you just the sort of [boor] I was than—from the
30 moment you have something in your mind—not know anything."

Still, however, she hesitated. "But if you've completely ceased to be that sort—?"

"Why I can then all the more bear to know. Besides,
35 perhaps I haven't."

"Perhaps. Yet if you haven't," she added, "I should suppose you'd remember. Not indeed that *I* in the least connect with my impression the invidious name you use. If I had only thought you foolish," she explained,
40 "the thing I speak of wouldn't so have remained with me. It was about yourself." She waited as if it might come to him; but as, only meeting her eyes in wonder, he gave no sign, she burnt her ships. "Has it ever happened?"

45 Then it was that, while he continued to stare, a light broke for him and the blood slowly came to his face, which began to burn with recognition. "Do you mean I told you—?" But he faltered, lest what came to him shouldn't be right, lest he should only give himself
50 away.

"It was something about yourself that it was natural one shouldn't forget—that is if one remembered you at all. That's why I ask you," she smiled, "if the thing you then spoke of has ever come to pass?"

55 Oh then he saw, but he was lost in wonder and found himself embarrassed. This, he also saw, made her sorry for him, as if her allusion had been a mistake. It took him but a moment, however, to feel it hadn't

CONTINUE

been, much as it had been a surprise. After the first
60 little shock of it her knowledge on the contrary began,
even if rather strangely, to taste sweet to him. She was
the only other person in the world then who would
have it, and she had had it all these years, while the fact
of his having so breathed his secret had unaccountably
65 faded from him. No wonder they couldn't have met
as if nothing had happened. "I judge," he finally said,
"that I know what you mean. Only I had strangely
enough lost any sense of having taken you so far into
my confidence."

1

The point of view from which the passage is written
can best be described as

A) a first-person narrator telling his life story.

B) a disinterested reporter listing objective facts.

C) a critical observer who judges Marcher's actions.

D) a sympathetic chronicler who relates to Marcher's
feelings.

2

Over the course of the passage, the emotions of John
Marcher shift from

A) incredulity to begrudging acceptance.

B) confusion to disconcerted recognition.

C) disdain to unrequited love.

D) amazement to painful embarrassment.

3

Information in the passage suggests that John
Marcher and May Bertram are

A) comforting one another over mistakes made
during the previous ten years.

B) trusting one another with sensitive personal
information.

C) reminiscing about former times and
conversations.

D) expressing their true feelings for one another.

4

Which choice provides the best evidence for the
answer to the previous question?

A) Lines 1-6 ("You know . . . cool")

B) Lines 22-24 ("It's dreadful . . . better")

C) Lines 55-57 ("Oh then . . . mistake")

D) Lines 61-65 ("She was . . . him")

5

As used in line 12, "claim" most nearly means

A) application.

B) remark.

C) appeal.

D) demand.

6

In the second paragraph, the "loss" (line 16) Marcher
feels most likely refers to

A) a connection over an interest he has in common
with May.

B) a missed opportunity to compliment May.

C) his longing to return to the warm weather in
Sorrento.

D) May's rejection of his speech declaring love for
her.

7

The conversation between Marcher and May Bertrand
suggests that Marcher had previously told May about
which of the following?

A) A troublesome puzzle

B) A romantic confession

C) A forgotten trifle

D) A personal inclination

8

Which choice provides the best evidence for the answer to the previous question?

A) Lines 13-15 ("With . . . 'offer'")

B) Lines 22-23 ("It's dreadful . . . before")

C) Line 41 ("It was . . . yourself")

D) Lines 55-56 ("Oh then . . . embarrassed")

9

As used in line 57, "allusion" most nearly means

A) reference.

B) image.

C) quotation.

D) apparition.

CONTINUE

No Test Material On This Page

Questions 10-18 are based on the following passage.

This passage is adapted from a speech delivered by Winston Churchill on May 13, 1940. Churchill became Prime Minister of Britain on May 10. This speech was his first address to the House of Commons, in which he asks the House to support his new administration.

I beg to move,

That this House welcomes the formation of a Government representing the united and inflexible
Line resolve of the nation to prosecute the war with
5 Germany to a victorious conclusion.

On Friday evening last I received His Majesty's commission to form a new Administration. It [w]as the evident wish and will of Parliament and the nation that this should be conceived on the broadest possible basis
10 and that it should include all parties, both those who supported the late Government and also the parties of the Opposition. I have completed the most important part of this task. A War Cabinet has been formed of five Members, representing, with the Opposition
15 Liberals, the unity of the nation. The three party Leaders have agreed to serve, either in the War Cabinet or in high executive office. The three Fighting Services have been filled. It was necessary that this should be done in one single day, on account of the extreme
20 urgency and rigour of events. A number of other positions, key positions, were filled yesterday, and I am submitting a further list to His Majesty to-night. I hope to complete the appointment of the principal Ministers during to-morrow. The appointment of the
25 other Ministers usually takes a little longer, but I trust that, when Parliament meets again, this part of my task will be completed, and that the administration will be complete in all respects.

I considered it in the public interest to suggest
30 that the House should be summoned to meet today. Mr. Speaker agreed, and took the necessary steps, in accordance with the powers conferred upon him by the Resolution of the House. At the end of the proceedings today, the Adjournment of the House will
35 be proposed until Tuesday, 21st May, with, of course, provision for earlier meeting, if need be. The business to be considered during that week will be notified to Members at the earliest opportunity. I now invite the House, by the Motion which stands in my name, to
40 record its approval of the steps taken and to declare its confidence in the new Government.

To form an Administration of this scale and complexity is a serious undertaking in itself, but it must be remembered that we are in the preliminary
45 stage of one of the greatest battles in history, that we are in action at many other points in Norway and in Holland, that we have to be prepared in the Mediterranean, that the air battle is continuous and that many preparations, such as have been indicated
50 by my hon. Friend below the Gangway, have to be made here at home. In this crisis I hope I may be pardoned if I do not address the House at any length today. I hope that any of my friends and colleagues, or former colleagues, who are affected by the political
55 reconstruction, will make allowance, all allowance, for any lack of ceremony with which it has been necessary to act. I would say to the House, as I said to those who have joined this government: "I have nothing to offer but blood, toil, tears and sweat."
60 We have before us an ordeal of the most grievous kind. We have before us many, many long months of struggle and of suffering. You ask, what is our policy? I can say: It is to wage war, by sea, land and air, with all our might and with all the strength that God can
65 give us; to wage war against a monstrous tyranny, never surpassed in the dark, lamentable catalogue of human crime. That is our policy. You ask, what is our aim? I can answer in one word: It is victory, victory at all costs, victory in spite of all terror, victory, however
70 long and hard the road may be; for without victory, there is no survival. Let that be realised; no survival for the British Empire, no survival for all that the British Empire has stood for, no survival for the urge and impulse of the ages, that mankind will move forward
75 towards its goal. But I take up my task with buoyancy and hope. I feel sure that our cause will not be suffered to fail among men. At this time I feel entitled to claim the aid of all, and I say, "come then, let us go forward together with our united strength."

10

Over the course of the speech, Churchill's focus shifts from

A) defeating Germany to reconstructing the government.

B) forming a War Cabinet to establishing war policy.

C) appointing an Administration to bolstering spirits.

D) reconciling differences to accepting defeat.

CONTINUE ▶

11

As used in line 4, "prosecute" most nearly means

A) fight.

B) litigate.

C) accuse.

D) enforce.

12

In the speech, Churchill claims that his administration must be formed more quickly than usual because

A) the king has told him to act with haste.

B) Parliament has been united under three party leaders.

C) the British Empire is in danger of losing the war.

D) the international political situation requires unusual measures.

13

Which choice provides the best evidence for the answer to the previous question?

A) Lines 6-7 ("On Friday . . . Administration")

B) Lines 18-20 ("It was . . . events")

C) Lines 53-57 ("I hope . . . to act")

D) Lines 71-75 ("Let that . . . goal")

14

It can be inferred from the passage that Churchill's administration

A) is likely to be controversial.

B) will meet with approval from all members of the House of Commons.

C) is dominated by Opposition Liberals.

D) has some unfilled positions.

15

Which choice provides the best evidence for the answer to the previous question?

A) Lines 13-15 ("A war . . . nation")

B) Lines 24-28 ("The appointment . . . respects")

C) Lines 31-33 ("Mr. Speaker . . . House")

D) Lines 60-62 ("We have . . . suffering")

16

Churchill makes the statement "I have nothing to offer but blood, toil, tears and sweat" (lines 58-59) primarily to

A) convey his deep level of commitment to the war effort.

B) indicate that he believes Britain has little hope of winning the war.

C) suggest that there is not much he can offer in support of the military.

D) offer evidence of his dedication to a governing coalition.

17

The primary rhetorical effect of the repetition of the words "victory" and "no survival" in the last paragraph is to

A) emphasize the hopeless nature of Britain's struggle.

B) clarify the administration's war strategy.

C) underscore the long-term implications of the outcome of the war.

D) maintain the sense of optimism introduced earlier in the speech.

18

As used in line 76, "suffered" most nearly means

A) endured.

B) allowed.

C) tolerated.

D) endorsed.

Questions 19-28 are based on the following passage.

This passage is adapted from Alex Kotlowitz, *Never a City So Real*. © 2004 by Alex Kotlowitz.

Fourteen miles southeast of the Loop, at the base of Lake Michigan, the city's easternmost corner, one finds a fistful of neighborhoods with hearty names
Line like Irondale, Hegewisch, The Bush, and Slag Valley.
5 This is South Chicago. Apart from Altgeld Gardens—a vast public housing complex virtually hidden from the rest of the world by towering mountains of garbage and often referred to as Chicago's Soweto—South Chicago is the city's most isolated community, its most
10 removed. The labor lawyer and author Tom Geoghegan has called it "a secret city." The vast majority of Chicagoans have never set foot here, and as if to ensure such detachment, above the compact redbrick bungalows with postage-stamp-size yards looms the
15 Chicago Skyway, a highway on stilts, which takes the prosperous to their cottages along the Indiana and Michigan shorelines. The neighborhoods below are modest in appearance, a collection of small homes and small taverns and diners with simple names like Steve's,
20 Pete's Hideaway, Who Cares?, Small World Inn, and Maria's Den. There's nothing fanciful about this area. As one observer wrote: "Streets named Commercial and Exchange offer testimony that people came here to make a buck, not admire the scenery."
25 And yet the scenery, so to speak, is awe-inspiring, the man-made equivalent of the Rockies. Dark, low-to-the-ground muscular structures, some three times the size of a football field, sprawl across the landscape, sprouting chimneys so tall that they're equipped
30 with blinking lights to alert wayward aircraft. These chimneys shoot full-bodied flames thirty feet into the sky; at night they appear almost magical, like giant torches heating the moon. Billows of smoke linger in the air like phantom dirges. It used to be, when the
35 steel mills were going strong, that these smokestacks spat out particles of graphite that would dust the streets and cars and rooftops like snow, catching the sun and setting the neighborhood aglitter. Suspended conveyor belts, pipes, and railroad overpasses weave in, out, and
40 over the behemoth buildings. The noise is crushing, the stench of sulfur so powerful that not even a closed car window can keep it at bay. Had Rube Goldberg lost his sense of humor, this is, I imagine, what he would have produced.

45 This is the heart of American industrial might, or what's left of it. The first of the mills was built in the 1850s, and within a hundred years more steel was produced in this stretch of land than anywhere else in the world. The freighters delivered iron ore
50 from Minnesota's Mesabi Range, and the mills turned the mineral into steel, shipping it west by rail and eventually east by the St. Lawrence Seaway. By the 1960s, the mills employed eighty thousand men and women; they cascaded in from Poland, from
55 Yugoslavia, from Mexico, and from the American South. Steel mills and refineries lined up along the dredged Calumet River and along the Lake Michigan shoreline, extending twenty-two miles from South Chicago to Gary, Indiana. This stretch of boiling steel
60 was the equivalent of an industrial mountain stream, the source for can openers and knives, refrigerators and cars, bridges and skyscrapers. It fed this country's insatiable hunger for consumption and comfort. It was, in short, the nation's lifeblood.

65 The local population is still so dependent on the mills that the daily newspaper in Hammond, Indiana, which is just over the Chicago border, runs a box score every Wednesday of the region's steel tonnage and capacity. Nonetheless, there are only fifteen
70 thousand working in the mills now; the owners grew complacent, so accustomed to their oligopoly that they forgot how to compete. Between the mills that still roll steel, there are hundreds of acres of vacant land littered with abandoned factory buildings stripped
75 of their exteriors, brick coke houses collapsing in on themselves, and railroad tracks and bridges that have turned a muddy brown from rust.

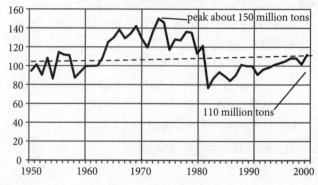

Domestic Steel Production, 1950-2000

Source: American Iron and Steel Institute

CONTINUE

19

The author of the passage most likely believes South Chicago

A) should be a more popular vacation destination.

B) will soon have no working steel mills.

C) is very isolated from the rest of the city.

D) embodies the dirty, smelly nature of American industry.

20

Which choice provides the best evidence for the answer to the previous question?

A) Lines 5-10 ("Apart . . . removed")

B) Lines 25-26 ("And yet . . . Rockies")

C) Lines 40-42 ("The noise . . . bay")

D) Lines 45-46 ("This is . . . of it")

21

The author includes a list of restaurant names (lines 19-21) primarily to

A) emphasize the modest nature of the neighborhood.

B) recommend places for visitors to have a meal.

C) suggest that there is little variety in the eating establishments.

D) explain why most people never visit South Chicago.

22

As used in line 38, "suspended" most nearly means

A) drooping.

B) hanging.

C) slumbering.

D) fixed.

23

In the context of the passage, steel mills are compared to

A) the Rockies.

B) wayward aircraft.

C) a football field.

D) phantom dirges.

24

Which choice provides the best evidence for the answer to the previous question?

A) Lines 1-4 ("Fourteen . . . Valley")

B) Lines 11-17 ("The vast . . . shorelines")

C) Lines 26-30 ("Dark . . . aircraft")

D) Lines 49-52 ("The freighters . . . Seaway")

25

As used in line 63, "consumption" most nearly means

A) eating.

B) expenditure.

C) corrosion.

D) burning.

26

In the context of the passage as a whole, the primary purpose the last paragraph is to

A) criticize the steel mill owners.

B) lament the state of abandoned property.

C) explain the current status of the steel mills.

D) suggest changes to the steel industry.

Which claim about domestic steel production is supported by the graph?

A) Production increased only from 1950 to 2000.

B) Production was stagnant between 1950 and 2000.

C) Production peaked in the 1960s, followed by a steep decline in the 1970s.

D) Net production increased slightly from 1950 to 2000.

28

It can reasonably be inferred from the passage and the graph that

A) South Chicago steel mills reached their greatest productivity in the mid-1970s.

B) US steel production in areas other than South Chicago has increased since the 1960s.

C) all domestic steel mills cut their workforces by over 75% between 1950 and 2000.

D) air pollution in communities surrounding steel mills was worse in the 1970s than in 2000.

CONTINUE

No Test Material On This Page

Questions 29-37 are based on the following passage.

This passage is adapted from E. Gene Towne and Joseph M. Craine, "Ecological Consequences of Shifting the Timing of Burning Tallgrass Prairie." © 2014 by E. Gene Towne and Joseph M. Craine. A forb is an herbaceous flowering plant.

Periodic burning is required for the maintenance of tallgrass prairie. The responses of prairie vegetation to fire, however, can vary widely depending upon
Line when the fires occur. Management and conservation
5 objectives such as biomass production, livestock performance, wildlife habitat, and control of specific plant species, often influence when grasslands are burned. In some prairie regions, timing of seasonal burns have been used to manipulate the balance of C_3
10 and C_4 species, control woody species, stimulate grass flowering, and alter the proportion of plant functional groups. Most grassland fire research, however, has focused on either burn frequency or comparing growing season burns with dormant season burns,
15 and there are few studies that differentiate effects from seasonal burning within the dormant season. In the Kansas Flint Hills, when prairies are burned is an important management issue, but the ecological consequences of burning at different times are poorly
20 understood.

The Flint Hills are one of the last remaining regions supporting extensive native tallgrass prairie in North America and frequent burning is integral to its preservation and economic utilization. Since
25 the early 1970's, recommendations have been to burn Kansas Flint Hills grasslands annually in late spring, typically once the dominant grasses have emerged 1.25–5 cm above the soil surface. Although frequent late-spring burning has maintained the Flint Hills
30 grassland, the resultant smoke plumes from en masse burning often leads to air quality issues in nearby cities. Concentrated smoke from grass fires produces airborne particulates, volatile organic compounds, and nitrogen oxides that facilitate tropospheric ozone
35 production. Burning in late spring also generates more ozone than burning in winter or early spring due to the higher air temperatures and insolation.

If the Flint Hills tallgrass prairie, its economic utilization, and high air quality are all to be
40 maintained, a good understanding of the consequences of burning at different times of the year is necessary. Burning earlier in spring has been regarded as

undesirable because it putatively reduces total biomass production, increases cool-season [grasses] and
45 undesirable forbs, is ineffective in controlling woody species, and lowers monthly weight gains of steers compared to burning in late spring. Consequently, burning exclusively in late spring has become ingrained in the cultural practices of grassland
50 management in the Flint Hills, and local ranchers often burn in unison when weather conditions are favorable.

Despite long-standing recommendations that tallgrass prairie be burned only in late spring, the data supporting this policy is equivocal. Total biomass
55 production was lower in plots burned in early spring than plots burned in late spring, but the weights included grasses, forbs, and shrubs. It was not known if [grass] biomass was reduced by early-spring burning or if the differences were a site effect rather than a
60 treatment effect. Burning in early spring also shifted community composition in a perceived negative pattern because it favored cool-season grasses and forbs. This shift in community composition, however, may actually be desirable because many cool-season
65 grasses have higher production and nutritional quality than warm-season grasses at certain times of the year, and many forb species are beneficial to the diet of grazers. Burning in late spring has been considered the most effective time to control invasive shrubs,
70 but *Symphoricarpos orbiculatus* was the only woody species that declined with repeated late spring burning. Finally, average weight gain of steers was lower in an unburned pasture than in burned pastures, but there was no significant difference in monthly weight gain
75 among cattle grazing in early-, mid-, or late-spring burned pastures.

The historical studies that formed the foundation for time of burning recommendations in tallgrass prairie are inconclusive because none had
80 experimental replications and most were spatially limited to small plots. All of these studies were interpreted as suggesting that shifting the time of burning by only a few weeks would negatively influence the plant community. A more recent large-
85 scale replicated study that compared the effects of annual burning in autumn, winter, and late spring found that the timing of burning had no significant effect on grass production and no reductions in the composition of desirable warm-season grasses.

CONTINUE →

Grass

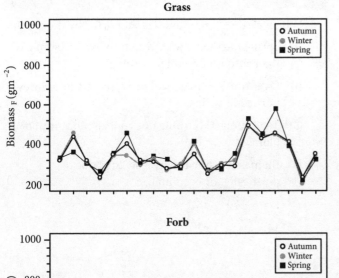

Forb

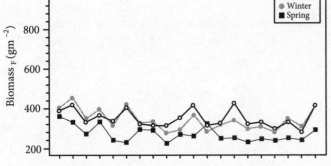

Figure 1. Changes in upland and lowland grass (a) and forb (b) productivity over time for Autumn-, Winter-, and Spring-burned watersheds

---

29

The authors of the passage most likely believe that

A) burning should be done on a semi-annual basis.

B) no burning should happen in the late spring.

C) late spring may not be the best time for burning.

D) changing burning schedules will negatively influence plants.

30

According to the passage, which of the following does NOT influence decisions on the timing of seasonal burns?

A) Biomass production

B) Control of specific plant species

C) Tropospheric ozone production

D) Weather

31

The passage suggests that the Kansas Flint Hills

A) are an ecologically sensitive area that must be treated with extreme caution.

B) must be regularly burned to remain economically viable.

C) have a unique composition of grasses and forbs that must be studied further.

D) will not support healthy livestock if the burning schedule changes.

32

Which choice provides the best evidence for the answer to the previous question?

A) Lines 21-24 ("The Flint . . . utilization")

B) Lines 38-41 ("If the Flint . . . necessary")

C) Lines 42-47 ("Burning . . . spring")

D) Lines 54-57 ("Total . . . shrubs")

33

As used in line 49, "practices" most nearly means

A) traditions.

B) rehearsals.

C) accomplishments.

D) chores.

34

As used in line 54, "equivocal" most nearly means

A) wrong.

B) misleading.

C) ambivalent.

D) unclear.

Based on the passage, it can be inferred that *Symphoricarpos orbiculatus* is

A) a forb species beneficial to grazers.

B) an invasive shrub.

C) a woody warm-season grass.

D) a late spring grass.

Which choice provides the best evidence for the answer to the previous question?

A) Lines 21-24 ("The Flint . . . utilization")

B) Lines 54-57 ("Total . . . shrubs")

C) Lines 63-68 ("This . . . grazers")

D) Lines 68-71 ("Burning . . . burning")

Which claim about grasses is supported by the graph?

A) Spring burning always results in higher biomass than autumn or winter burning.

B) Over time, biomass will increase only in prairies burned in spring.

C) The timing of burning does not significantly affect biomass.

D) Biomass declined sharply in 2012 due to drastically lower rainfall.

CONTINUE

No Test Material On This Page

Questions 38-47 are based on the following passage.

These passages are adapted from KU Leuven, "Bacterium counteracts 'coffee ring effect.'" ©2013 and University of Pennsylvania, " Physicists undo the 'coffee ring effect'". © 2011 Science Daily.

Passage 1

A team of University of Pennsylvania physicists has shown how to disrupt the "coffee ring effect"— the ring-shaped stain of particles leftover after coffee
Line drops evaporate—by changing the particle shape. The
5 discovery provides new tools for engineers to deposit uniform coatings.

The research was conducted by professor Arjun Yodh, director of the Laboratory for Research on the Structure of Matter; doctoral candidates Peter Yunker
10 and Matthew Lohr; and postdoctoral fellow Tim Still.

"The coffee ring effect is very common in everyday experience," Yunker said. "To avoid it, scientists have gone to great lengths designing paints and inks that produce an even coating upon evaporation. We found
15 that the effect can be eliminated simply by changing the shape of the particle."

University of Chicago physicists Sidney Nagel, Thomas Witten and their colleagues wrote an influential paper about this process in 1997, which
20 focused mainly on suspended spherical particles, but it was not until the Yodh team's recent experiments that the surprising role played by suspended particle shape was discovered.

Yodh's team used uniformly sized plastic particles
25 in their experiments. These particles were initially spherical but could be stretched into varying degrees of eccentricity, to ensure the experiments only tested the effect of the particle's shape on the drying pattern. The researchers were surprised at how big an effect particle
30 shape had on the drying phenomenon.

"Different particle geometries change the nature of the membrane at the air-water interface," Yodh said. "And that has big consequences." Spherical particles easily detach from the interface, and they flow past one
35 another easily because the spheres do not substantially deform the air-water interface. Ellipsoid particles, however, cause substantial undulation of the air-water interface that in turn induces very strong attractions between the ellipsoids. Thus the ellipsoids tend to get
40 stuck on the surface, and, while the stuck particles

can continue to flow towards the drop's edges during evaporation, they increasingly block each other, creating a traffic jam of particles that eventually covers the drop's surface.

45 After experimenting with suspended particle shape, the researchers added a surfactant, essentially soap, into the drops to show that interactions on the drop's surface were responsible for the effect. With the surfactant lowering the drop's surface tension, ellipsoid
50 particles did not get stuck at the interface and flowed freely to the edge.

"We were thinking it would be useful if you could just sprinkle in a few of these ellipsoid particles to remove the coffee ring effect," Yodh said, "and we
55 found that sometimes this idea works and sometimes it doesn't."

Passage 2

Researchers from the Departments of Chemical Engineering and Chemistry at KU Leuven have now discovered how to counteract coffee rings with
60 'surfactants', i.e. soap. The key to the discovery was not a kitchen towel, but a bacterium that counteracts the coffee ring effect at the microscopic level.

When a coffee ring dries, its edges become noticeably darker and thicker. This occurs because the
65 coffee particles move toward the edge of the stain while the water in the liquid evaporates. At a microscopic level, this coffee ring effect can also be seen in liquids with particles of other materials such as plastic and wood.

70 In various industrial applications—applying an even coat of paint or varnish, for example—the coffee ring effect can be particularly troublesome and scientists have long been seeking ways to counteract it. Raf De Dier and Wouter Sempels (Departments
75 of Chemical Engineering and Chemistry) have now described a solution based on examples found in nature. De Dier and Sempels carried out experiments and calculations on nanomaterials as well as on a particularly promising bacterium, *Pseudomonas*
80 *aeruginosa*.

Pseudomonas aeruginosa is a dangerous bacterium that can cause infections in open wounds. "A *Pseudomonas aeruginosa* bacteria colony wants to find as large a breeding ground as possible. To avoid
85 overconcentration on the edges of a wound when spreading itself during the drying-out process, the

CONTINUE ➤

bacterium produces substances that counteract the coffee ring effect."

These surface-tension-disrupting substances are
90 called surfactants. Detergents such as soap are also surfactants. "Add soap to a stain—a coffee stain or any other stain—and you will still get a coffee ring effect. But at the same time the soap causes a counterflow from the edge back towards the centre of the stain
95 in such a way that the small particles—material or bacteria—end up in a kind of whirlwind. In this way, you get a more uniform distribution of particles as evaporation occurs."

38

Passage 1 most strongly suggests that Professor Yodh's team at the University of Pennsylvania assumed which of the following before their experiments?

A) The shape of the particles leads to detachment from the interface.

B) The shape of the particles has a minimal effect on drying patterns.

C) The shape of a spherical particle can't be changed to ellipsoid.

D) The shape of the particles is the only factor that affects the membrane.

39

The author of Passage 1 refers to a paper by University of Chicago physicists Sidney Nagel and Thomas Witten (lines 17-23) primarily to

A) imply that Nagel and Witten could have discovered the impact of ellipsoid particles.

B) describe an impediment to research on suspended spherical particles.

C) suggest that the study done by Nagel and Witten influenced the research by Yodh's team.

D) contrast the results of earlier, flawed research with the useful data obtained more recently.

40

Based on the passage, which choice best describes the relationship between Nagel and Witten's and Yodh's research?

A) Yodh's research challenges Nagel and Witten's.

B) Yodh's research builds on Nagel and Witten's.

C) Nagel and Witten's research contradicts Yodh's.

D) Nagel and Witten's research supports Yodh's.

41

As used in line 37, "undulation" most nearly means

A) attraction.

B) evaporation.

C) undertow.

D) ripple.

42

In lines 84-90 ("To avoid . . . surfactants"), what is the most likely reason the author of Passage 2 compares detergents and bacterium?

A) To justify research into surfactants from bacterium, since the surfactants in soap may not serve industrial needs

B) To alert companies that want surfactants for paint and varnish to the dangers of bacterium

C) To show that soap can help reduce the movement of particles to the edge of a stain, but can't stop it

D) To contend that soap is a better surfactant so it's best to avoid using *Pseudomonas aeruginosa* until further studies have been done

---

43

What does Passage 2 most strongly suggest about the coffee ring effect?

A) It generates many studies on ways to thwart it.

B) It sends microscopic particles into a whirlwind.

C) It can be eliminated with the use of surfactants.

D) It has various industrial applications.

44

Which choice provides the best evidence for the answer to the previous question?

A) Lines 57-60 ("Researchers . . . soap")

B) Lines 60-62 ("The key . . . level")

C) Lines 66-69 ("At a . . . wood")

D) Lines 70-74 ("In various . . . counteract it")

45

As used in line 97, "uniform" most nearly means

A) spread thin.

B) similarly shaped.

C) evenly distributed.

D) wiped clean.

46

Is the main conclusion presented by the author of Passage 2 consistent with the properties of the coffee ring effect, as described in Passage 1?

A) No, since Passage 1 shows that surfactants can increase the coffee ring effect if ellipsoids are present.

B) No, since the study in Passage 1 describes how oblong spheres diminish the coffee ring effect.

C) Yes, since the study in Passage 2 explains that surfactants have an effect on the movement of particles.

D) Yes, since the study in Passage 2 concludes that bacteria can be genetically modified in order to produce surfactants.

47

One difference between the studies described in the two passages is that unlike the researchers discussed in Passage 1, the researchers in Passage 2

A) stretch the *Pseudomonas aeruginosa* until they become surfactants.

B) utilize biological organisms to disrupt the surface tension.

C) experiment on nanomaterials in order to breed *Pseudomonas aeruginosa* .

D) explore ways to increase evaporation speed and particle flow.

STOP
**If you finish before time is called, you may check your work on this section only.
Do not turn to any other section.**

No Test Material On This Page

Writing and Language Test

35 MINUTES, 44 QUESTIONS

Turn to Section 2 of your answer sheet to answer the questions in this section.

Each passage below is accompanied by a number of questions. For some questions, you will consider how the passage might be revised to improve the expression of ideas. For other questions, you will consider how the passage might be edited to correct errors in sentence structure, usage, or punctuation. A passage or a question may be accompanied by one or more graphics (such as a table or graph) that you will consider as you make revising and editing decisions.

Some questions will direct you to an underlined portion of a passage. Other questions will direct you to a location in a passage or ask you to think about the passage as a whole.

After reading each passage, choose the answer to each question that most effectively improves the quality of writing in the passage or that makes the passage conform to the conventions of standard written English. Many questions include a "NO CHANGE" option. Choose that option if you think the best choice is to leave the relevant portion of the passage as it is.

Questions 1–11 are based on the following passage.

Getting a CLOe

Imagine you go to a restaurant you've never tried before. Now, let's say you **1** had a bad experience. What next? For many, the answer is **2** simple, get on social media and tell the world. Aside from telling all your

1

A) NO CHANGE
B) have had
C) were having
D) have

2

A) NO CHANGE
B) simple get on
C) simple: get on
D) simple, hop on

CONTINUE

friends and followers about the experience on Twitter and Facebook, **3** you would probably decide not to return to that restaurant. In fact, you might have used these services to find the restaurant in the first place. And really, if a place has two out of five stars on Yelp when you look it up, what's the chance you'll go there in the first place?

Companies, not just restaurants, are starting to see that their biggest business generators are not TV or internet ads anymore. **4** Today, "buzz" gets created on social media, and it is more important than ever for companies to **5** insure that they are showing the best possible face to the world on social media. Maintaining that public face has created a new job: Chief Listening Officer. Where a Social Media Manager might be in charge of a **6** companies output on Facebook and other sites, a Chief Listening Officer is on the other side. A CLO scours blogs, Pinterest, tumblr, Facebook, Twitter, Google, Yelp, and whatever new site will be hot when you read this to make sure that a company's public image is under control.

3

Which of the following would best maintain the focus of this sentence and paragraph?

A) NO CHANGE

B) you might also go to a consumer-review site, such as Yelp, to tell future patrons.

C) it might make you feel better to tell your friends and relatives about the experience over the phone.

D) you could take the edge off by watching videos of animals doing funny stuff.

4

The author is considering deleting the phrase *not just restaurants* from the preceding sentence and adjusting the punctuation accordingly. Should the phrase be kept or deleted?

A) Kept, because it clarifies that the practice described in the essay is not limited to one industry.

B) Kept, because it encourages companies other than restaurants to hire Chief Listening Officers.

C) Deleted, because it incorrectly implies that patrons of other businesses discuss their experiences on social media.

D) Deleted, because the previous paragraph is all about restaurants, and this one is not.

5

A) NO CHANGE

B) assure the public

C) ensure

D) make insurance

6

A) NO CHANGE

B) companies'

C) company's

D) companys'

If a CLO sees a bad review on someone's blog, for instance, the CLO might contact a customer-service representative 7 and make it better to see if the situation can be remedied. On the other hand, if a company 8 unfurls a new advertising campaign and the ads are getting buzz on Twitter or many views on YouTube, the CLO might tell his marketing team to keep up the good work. The incredible 9 thing about this is that it is more detailed than market research has ever been before. People share their entire lives on social media, and a single post can reveal not only someone's positive or negative reaction but also 10 their age, gender, location, social status, friends, and so on.

7

A) NO CHANGE
B) and improve things
C) and say, "Get on it!",
D) DELETE the underlined portion.

8

A) NO CHANGE
B) rolls out
C) unrolls
D) roles out

9

A) NO CHANGE
B) thing about this kind of "market research"
C) thing
D) reality

10

A) NO CHANGE
B) they're
C) your
D) his or her

CONTINUE

Some criticize the CLO position as a fad, suggesting that companies are overreacting to the power of social media. [11] The fact of the matter is, however, CLOs will be needed as long as social media are around. After all, consumers are realizing that social-media reviews are often the purest of the pure—neither that of an overrefined food critic or tech geek nor that of someone in the pay of this or that company. The people are talking, and companies have at last made their "listening" official.

[11]

Which of the following most directly answers the criticism presented in the previous sentence?

A) NO CHANGE

B) They see social media as temporarily popular but not likely to endure.

C) Teachers say that students spend too much time on social media.

D) They say that some social media outlets are more effective than others.

Questions 12–22 are based on the following passage.

Gimme Fever… Actually, Please Don't

Medical science has created some modern miracles, but it can be difficult to appreciate just how miraculous some of them are. The Spanish Flu hit the United States in the 1910s, and **12** polio rocked the foundations of America in the 1930s and 1940s, but it is difficult to imagine an epidemic like the Philadelphia Yellow Fever Epidemic of 1793. The official register listed over 5,000 deaths between August 1st and November 9th of that year. These figures are staggering when we consider that Philadelphia city, **13** the largest city in the country today, had a population of over 1.5 million, and its surrounding areas had only about 50,000.

Rank	Place	Population
1	New York city, NY *	33,131
2	Philadelphia city, PA*	28,522
3	Boston town, MA*	18,320
4	Charleston city, SC	16,359
5	Baltimore town, MD	13,503
6	Northern Liberties township, PA*	9,913
7	Salem town, MA	7,921
8	Newport town, RI	6,716
9	Providence town, RI*	6,380
10	Marblehead town, MA	5,661
10	Southwark district, PA*	5,661
12	Gloucester town, MA	5,317
13	Newbury town, MA	4,837
14	Portsmouth town, NH	4,720
15	Sherburne town (Nantucket), MA*	4,620
16	Middleborough town, MA	4,526
17	New Haven city, CT*	4,487
18	Richmond city, VA	3,761
19	Albany city, NY	3,498
20	Norfolk borough, VA	2,959
21	Petersburg town, VA	2,828
22	Alexandria town, VA*	2,748
23	Hartford city, CT*	2,683
24	Hudson city, NY	2,584
* See Notes for Indiviudual Places.		
Source: U.S. Bureau of the Census		
Internet Release date: June 15, 1998		

Table 2. Population of the 24 Urban Places: 1790

12

Which of the following would provide a detail that would best maintain the focus of this paragraph?

A) NO CHANGE

B) many people died from this flu, especially soldiers in World War I,

C) it's possible to get flu vaccinations at your local drug store now,

D) it just faded away even though doctors could never cure it,

13

Which of the following gives information consistent with the chart?

A) NO CHANGE

B) the second largest city in the country at that time, had a population of only about 28,000,

C) second only to New York and Boston, had a population of over 28,000 at the time,

D) was larger than its neighboring New York City by nearly 10,000 people,

It was not ultimately medical science that saved the day during this epidemic. Doctors tried various **14** treatments, but they were stalled by their inability to figure out both how the disease originated and how **15** it was spreading. It therefore seemed a godsend when the frost came in November, and the number of deaths tapered off. Medical historians now know that the disease was spread by mosquitoes, but this was **16** pretty shady until nearly a century after the disease had come and gone.

14

Which of the following alternatives to the underlined portion would NOT be acceptable?

A) strategies

B) procedures

C) tactics

D) maintenance

15

A) NO CHANGE

B) it spread.

C) it had been spread.

D) its spread.

16

A) NO CHANGE

B) stupid idiocy

C) not verified

D) downright wrong

[1] In 1793, Philadelphia was the second largest city in the new nation of the United States. [2] As a result, all of the quarantine and curfew measures that **17** they tried to impose had failed. [3] Panicked politicians blamed immigration. [4] The city's College of Physicians published a letter in the city newspapers that spoke to the confusion. [5] They recognized the epidemic for what it was, but their eleven measures for prevention were haphazard and confused and included the avoidance of **18** alcohol, hot sun, and night air. [6] Philadelphia didn't know what had hit it. Dr. Benjamin Rush, one of the earliest and most brilliant physicians in all of American history, blamed a rotten shipment of coffee that had come into Philadelphia's port. **19**

17

A) NO CHANGE

B) one

C) city authorities

D) some

18

A) NO CHANGE

B) alcohol, hot sun and night air.

C) alcohol, hot sun, and also night air.

D) alcohol, hot sun, and the air of the night.

19

The best placement for Sentence 6 would be

A) where it is now.

B) at the beginning of the paragraph.

C) after Sentence 1.

D) after Sentence 3.

CONTINUE

It's difficult to imagine an epidemic on this kind of scale today. Moreover, Philadelphia's relative prominence and sophistication in that era should give us pause. The medical establishment sat **20** back helplessly: as the disease ravaged the city. The recent outbreak of **21** the Ebola virus, in West Africa, provides a terrifying reminder, of just how deadly certain diseases can be, when they are unchecked or inadequately understood. **22** By the same token, the Yellow Fever Epidemic provides a remarkable instance of a city's resilience in the face of adversity. As the population of the city was literally decimated, and other yellow-fever epidemics continued to ravage the city, Philadelphia persisted, and with it, the new nation grew stronger, just as it has in the face of crisis ever since.

20

A) NO CHANGE

B) back helplessly, as the disease

C) back helplessly as the disease

D) back helplessly; as the disease

21

A) NO CHANGE

B) the Ebola virus in West Africa provides a terrifying reminder of just how deadly certain diseases can be when

C) the Ebola virus, in West Africa provides a terrifying reminder, of just how deadly certain diseases can be when

D) the Ebola virus, in West Africa, provides a terrifying reminder of just how deadly certain diseases can be, when

22

A) NO CHANGE

B) On the other hand,

C) Therefore,

D) Thus,

Questions 23–33 are based on the following passage.

The Singing Brakeman

[1]

The early days of recorded music can be hazy. Many people find it difficult to believe that artists recording before the radio boom in the 1940s, or even before the rock and roll boom in the 1950s, could have had any success at all **23** seems doubtful. Despite this misconception, there is a treasure trove of recorded music from that era, and not only by the greats of bebop and swing. **24**

[2]

The circumstances of **25** Rodgers's birth is obscure, but legend has it that he was born in Meridian, Mississippi in 1897. Little is known **26** for sure, but his father was a foreman on the Mobile and Ohio Railroad in Meridian. Jimmie eventually became a brakeman, but **27** a health issue cut his career short. He stayed alive for a few years after his dismissal in 1927, but he could no longer work the rails.

23

A) NO CHANGE

B) strikes us as odd.

C) appears improbable.

D) DELETE the underlined portion and end the sentence with a period.

24

Which of the following would most effectively conclude this paragraph by introducing the main subject of the essay as a whole?

A) It takes a real music connoisseur to know who was famous before Elvis Presley.

B) Most of the best known names from the 1930s and 1940s are those of jazz singers.

C) One of these greats was Jimmie Rodgers, one of the first megastars of country music.

D) Some of the greats were Robert Johnson, Mississippi John Hurt, and Jimmie Rodgers.

25

A) NO CHANGE

B) Rodgers's birth are

C) Rodgers's birth has been

D) Rodgers's birth was

26

A) NO CHANGE

B) for certain,

C) for sure about his family,

D) for sure about his mother, father, and siblings,

27

At this point, the writer wants to include a detail that provides specific information about Rodgers's illness. Which of the following would best fulfill that goal?

A) NO CHANGE

B) problems with his health

C) a bout of tuberculosis

D) one of the current diseases

CONTINUE ▶

[3]

The recording had moderate success, and it sparked Rodgers to pursue his music career in earnest. In October of that year, after Rodgers chased his dream, Victor released "Blue Yodel," better known as "T for Texas," which sold **28** all the way to New York City half a million copies. Rodgers quickly became a household name, and his trademark yodel would be known the world over. By this **29** time, Rodgers had become the famous "Singing Brakeman," and his influence would be felt for many generations to come.

[4]

This influence would not be felt only in country music either: blues singer Howlin' Wolf cited Rodgers as an early **30** influence, like Elvis Presley. Ultimately losing his battle with tuberculosis at age 33, Rodgers may have lived a short life, but if the history of American music is an indication, his influence is still alive and well.

28

If the punctuation were to be adjusted accordingly, the best placement for the underlined portion would be

A) where it is now.

B) after the word *year*.

C) after the word *dream*.

D) after the word *copies*.

29

A) NO CHANGE

B) time, when Rodgers

C) time, as Rodgers

D) time: Rodgers

30

A) NO CHANGE

B) influence, as did Elvis Presley.

C) influence, similar to Elvis Presley.

D) influence, much like that of Elvis Presley.

[5]

This inability to work, however, proved to be <u>31</u> <u>fortuitous</u> for Rodgers's great passion—music. At age 13, Rodgers had already secretly organized two traveling shows, only to be recovered and brought back to Meridian by his father. Once Jimmie could no longer work the <u>32</u> <u>rails, however, he</u> pursued his musical career in earnest. In Bristol, Tennessee, Rodgers organized his first band. That same year, the band was asked to record some songs for Ralph Peer of the Victor Talking Machine Company. The recordings survive today, though they feature a solo Jimmie Rodgers rather than his whole band, as a pre-recording quarrel led them to break up. <u>33</u>

31

Which of the following alternatives to the underlined portion would NOT be acceptable?

A) chancy

B) opportune

C) fortunate

D) lucky

32

A) NO CHANGE

B) rails however he

C) rails; however, he

D) rails, however he

33

The best placement for Paragraph 5 would be

A) where it is now.

B) before Paragraph 1.

C) before Paragraph 2.

D) before Paragraph 3.

Questions 34–44 are based on the following passage.

Whale Grandmothers Know Best

We don't often think to apply gender differences to the animal kingdom. Certainly, males and females have **34** a distinct role, but these seem to be largely determined by biology and by the propagation of the species. As a result, many females do not live much beyond menopause, the phase after which females can no longer reproduce. The data below show that **35** only a handful of animals, such as the black-tailed prairie dog, have any post-reproductive life span at all. Some species, however, like humans, short-finned pilot whales, and killer whales, have females who typically live two or more decades after

34

A) NO CHANGE

B) a distinction,

C) a role that is distinct,

D) distinct roles,

35

Which of the following gives accurate data based on the graph?

A) NO CHANGE

B) most animals, including homo sapiens, tend to have some post-reproductive life span.

C) the common bottlenose dolphin has one of the shortest pre-reproductive life spans relative to other animals.

D) no rodent species has any post-reproductive life span at all.

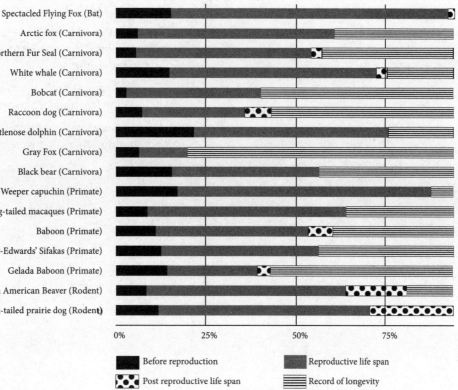

menopause. Scientists have long wondered why evolution has determined **36** <u>they</u> should live so much longer, sometimes to be as old as 90, than their counterparts in other species.

37 It seems that the social forces that define gender may apply to the animal kingdom as well, even though we consider animal behavior to be determined almost entirely by nature rather than nurture. After watching over 750 hours of video and observing the behaviors of pods of whales, **38** <u>whale grandmothers were observed to have teaching behaviors by the scientists.</u>

36

A) NO CHANGE

B) any of them

C) themselves

D) the female whales

37

Which of the following would provide the most effective transition from the previous paragraph to this paragraph?

A) The answer may have come from a recent study of killer whales.

B) Killer whales are some of the most fascinating marine species.

C) Pretty much everyone knows by now that whales are mammals, not fish.

D) Scientists will experiment and try new things until they find something interesting.

38

A) NO CHANGE

B) scientists observed that many of the teaching behaviors were performed by whale grandmothers.

C) whale grandmothers were the most likely to exhibit teaching behaviors.

D) teaching behaviors were observed from whale grandmothers that were shown to scientists.

CONTINUE

39 This knowledge is particularly useful for whale pods because the abundance of salmon is typically what determines whale life-cycles, both reproduction and mortality.

The scientists ascribe this behavior to what they refer to as the grandmothers' roles as "repositories of ecological **40** knowledge" in other words. Sharpened memories and long experience of learned behaviors make the older females extremely valuable to future generations. Without this knowledge, the younger whales would not be able to make the transition to maturity, and the species would not continue to propagate. The elder females have evolved this longevity because the species, simply put, needs it. **41**

39

At this point, the writer is considering adding the following true statement:

> The older female whales were the most likely to lead younger whales to salmon feeding grounds, particularly in the periods where the usually plentiful salmon were sparse.

Should the writer make this addition here?

A) Yes, because it clarifies some of the teaching behaviors mentioned in the previous sentence.

B) Yes, because it gives some credit to older whales, who were otherwise ignored in the study.

C) No, because the information conflicts with other information given later in the passage.

D) No, because the scientists' observations are not given as conclusive.

40

A) NO CHANGE

B) knowledge" in other words; sharpened

C) knowledge," in other words, sharpened

D) knowledge." In other words, sharpened

41

The writer is considering replacing the word *longevity* with the word *life* in the previous sentence. Should the writer make the change or keep the sentence as it is?

A) Keep the sentence as is, because "longevity" provides a more formal way of saying the same thing.

B) Keep the sentence as is, because the sentence refers to the length of whale life, not only the life itself.

C) Make the change, because "life" provides a more general way of articulating the point.

D) Make the change, because readers may not know the meaning of the word "longevity."

42 From a gender perspective, these findings further break down the idea that gender roles are biologically determined. From an age perspective, the findings also show that societies that value youth and middle age to the detriment of old age may do so at **43** there own peril. Anyone with grandparents knows that these older relatives have experienced enough of life to know a thing or two. In whale pods as well as human communities, it seems, life may depend on the accrued knowledge **44** about the secrets of life that have been gathered by the old people who know about it.

42

Which of the following choices would introduce this paragraph most effectively?

A) Gender discrimination does not really exist in whale communities.

B) Whale grandmothers know things other than where to find the salmon.

C) There is a beautiful scene in Herman Melville's *Moby Dick* featuring whale families.

D) The findings are interesting to non-scientists as well.

43

A) NO CHANGE

B) their

C) it's

D) its

44

A) NO CHANGE

B) of some of the secret-knowing people whose long lives are long enough.

C) of those who have lived long enough to know the secrets of long life.

D) the longer-lived people who are more secret oricntcd.

STOP

If you finish before time is called, you may check your work on this section only.
Do not turn to any other section.

No Test Material On This Page

Math Test – No Calculator

25 MINUTES, 17 QUESTIONS

Turn to Section 3 of your answer sheet to answer the questions in this section.

DIRECTIONS

For questions **1-13**, solve each problem, choose the best answer from the choices provided, and fill in the corresponding circle on your answer sheet. For questions **14-17**, solve the problem and enter your answer in the grid on the answer sheet. Please refer to the directions before question 14 on how to enter your answers in the grid. You may use any available space in your test booklet for scratch work.

NOTES

1. The use of a calculator **is not permitted**.

2. All variables and expressions used represent real numbers unless otherwise indicated.

3. Figures provided in this test are drawn to scale unless otherwise indicated.

4. All figures lie in a plane unless otherwise indicated.

5. Unless otherwise indicated, the domain of a given function f is the set of all real numbers x for which $f(x)$ is a real number.

REFERENCE

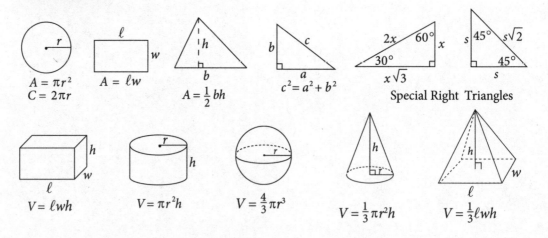

The number of degrees of arc in a circle is 360.
The number of radians of arc in a circle is 2π.
The sum of the measures in degrees of the angles of a triangle is 180.

CONTINUE

1

If $3(x^2 + 2x + 5) = 4$, what is the value of $3x^2 + 6x$?

A) −11

B) −1

C) 7

D) 19

2

If $\dfrac{2x + 2}{3} > x$, which of the following describes all possible values of x ?

A) $x < -2$

B) $x > -2$

C) $x < 2$

D) $x > 2$

3

At a store the cost of a shirt and two pairs of equally priced socks is $24, and the cost for three of the same shirt and two pairs of the same socks is $32. What is the cost of the shirt and one pair of socks?

A) 4

B) 10

C) 14

D) 56

4

$$\frac{2\sqrt{3}}{\sqrt{x}} = \frac{\sqrt{x}}{\sqrt{3}}$$

Based on the equation above, what is the value of x ?

A) 2

B) $2\sqrt{3}$

C) $3\sqrt{2}$

D) 6

5

The value of John's baseball card collection decreases exponentially over time, and the value of his silver collection increases exponentially over time. If the value of John's two collections combined t years from now is given by the function $V = 500(1.05)^t + 600(.95)^{\frac{t}{2}}$, which of the following statements must be true?

A) John's silver collection is more valuable currently than his baseball collection.

B) John's baseball card collection decreases in value by 10% every six months.

C) The value of John's silver collection changes at a faster rate than the value of John's baseball card collection.

D) The total value of the two collections remains constant over time.

6

In a certain city, x % of the voters strongly support a bill and 40% strongly oppose it. Three-fifths of the remaining voters slightly support the bill and the rest slightly oppose it. Which of the following equations shows the total percentage of voters, S, who either strongly or slightly support the bill?

A) $S = \dfrac{3(60 - x)}{5}$

B) $S = 60 - \dfrac{2x}{5}$

C) $S = \dfrac{2(60 - x)}{5}$

D) $S = 36 + \dfrac{2x}{5}$

7

The square of the sum of x and y is equal to 8 more than the square of the difference between x and y. What is x in terms of y ?

A) $x = \dfrac{2}{y}$

B) $x = 2y$

C) $x = \dfrac{4}{y}$

D) $x = y$

8

Given that $\left(\dfrac{\sqrt{x} - 3}{x - 9} \right) B = 1$, what is the value of B in terms of x ?

A) $x - 9$

B) $x + 3$

C) $\sqrt{x} + 3$

D) $\sqrt{x} - 3$

CONTINUE

9

Two-thirds *m* is greater than *n* and the sum of *n* and *m* is greater than 10. Which of the following expresses all possible values of *m* ?

A) $m > 2$

B) $m < 5$

C) $m < 6$

D) $m > 6$

10

A saleswoman receives a commission of 15% for the first \$100 in sales that she makes, and then 20% for the next \$200, and then 25% for all remaining sales in a month. How much commission, in dollars, does the saleswoman earn for selling *a* dollars if $a > 300$?

A) $.35a + .25(a - 300)$

B) $.25a - 20$

C) $.60a$

D) $55 + .25a$

11

Rachel is studying the suburbanization of her city and determines that the suburbs are growing exponentially, and the population can be modeled by the equation $P = S\left(\dfrac{t}{4}\right)^2$, in which *S* is the starting population now and *t* is the time in years that passes. The population in the urban areas is decreasing by 50,000 per year and is currently 50% greater than the population of the suburbs. Which of the following equations could be used to solve for the time before the suburbs and urban areas have equal populations?

A) $S\left(\dfrac{t}{4}\right)^2 = 1.5S - 50,000t$

B) $S\left(\dfrac{t}{4}\right)^2 = .5S - 50,000t$

C) $1.5S\left(\dfrac{t}{4}\right) = S + 50,000t$

D) $S\left(\dfrac{t}{4}\right)^2 = 1.5S + 50,000t$

12

Michonne is studying the metabolic rates of rats and determines that, for every degree above room temperature (20° C), the rats burn an extra 3 calories per hour above their normal metabolic rate, and their normal metabolic rate is directly proportional to their weights, represented by w, in grams. If the number of calories burned by a rat, E, when the temperature, t, is at or above room temperature is given by the equation $E = (0.017w)t + (t - 20)(0.017w + 3)t$, which of the following statements is true?

A) The number of calories a rat burns per hour at room temperature is 0.017.

B) At 20 degrees Celsius a rat burns 0.017 calories per gram of body weight per hour.

C) A rat that weighs 100 grams will burn 17 calories per hour.

D) The base metabolic rate of a rat is 20 calories per hour.

13

While testing the effects of various conditions on memory recall, Dr. Jones determines that memory recall, represented by M, is directly proportional to the square of the number of hours of sleep a participant received the night before and inversely proportional to the square root of the calories the participant has consumed that morning. The variable h denotes the hours of sleep the participant received, and c represents the number of calories consumed. If k is a constant, which of the following could express h in terms of c ?

A) $h = \dfrac{\sqrt{c}M}{k}$

B) $h = cM^2k$

C) $h = \dfrac{\sqrt[4]{c}\sqrt{M}}{k}$

D) $h = \dfrac{\sqrt[4]{c}M}{k}$

CONTINUE

DIRECTIONS

For questions 14-17, solve the problem and enter your answer in the grid, as described below, on the answer sheet.

1. Although not required, it is suggested that you write your answer in the boxes at the top of the columns to help you fill in the circles accurately. You will receive credit only if the circles are filled in correctly.

2. Mark no more than one circle in any column.

3. No question has a negative answer.

4. Some problems may have more than one correct answer. In such cases, grid only one answer.

5. **Mixed numbers** such as $3\frac{1}{2}$ must be gridded as 3.5 or 7/2. (If [3 1 / 2] is entered into the grid, it will be interpreted as $\frac{31}{2}$, not as $3\frac{1}{2}$.)

6. **Decimal Answers:** If you obtain a decimal answer with more digits than the grid can accommodate, it may be either rounded or truncated, but it must fill the entire grid.

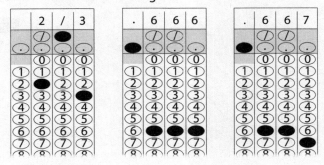

Acceptable ways to grid $\frac{2}{3}$ are:

Answer: 201 – either position is correct

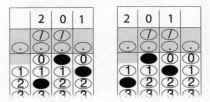

NOTE: You may start your answers in any column, space permitting. Columns you don't need to use should be left blank.

14

If $2x + y = 16$ and $y - 3x = 6$, what is the value of x?

15

If one-fourth z is four less than twice the value of z, what is z?

16

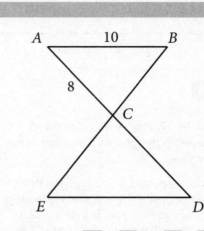

In the figure above, $\overline{AD} \perp \overline{CE}$ and $\overline{AB} \parallel \overline{ED}$. If the perimeter of triangle ABC is $\dfrac{2}{3}$ of the perimeter of $\triangle CDE$, what is $\overline{CE}$?

17

If $6x^2 + 4x = 2$, and $x > 0$, what is x?

STOP

If you finish before time is called, you may check your work on this section only.
Do not turn to any other section.

No Test Material On This Page

Math Test – Calculator

45 MINUTES, 31 QUESTIONS

Turn to Section 4 of your answer sheet to answer the questions in this section.

DIRECTIONS

For questions **1-27**, solve each problem, choose the best answer from the choices provided, and fill in the corresponding circle on your answer sheet. For questions **28-31**, solve the problem and enter your answer in the grid on the answer sheet. Please refer to the directions before question 28 on how to enter your answers in the grid. You may use any available space in your test booklet for scratch work.

NOTES

1. The use of a calculator **is permitted**.
2. All variables and expressions used represent real numbers unless otherwise indicated.
3. Figures provided in this test are drawn to scale unless otherwise indicated.
4. All figures lie in a plane unless otherwise indicated.
5. Unless otherwise indicated, the domain of a given function f is the set of all real numbers x for which $f(x)$ is a real number.

REFERENCE

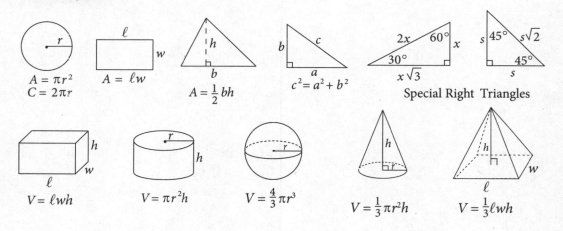

$A = \pi r^2$
$C = 2\pi r$

$A = \ell w$

$A = \frac{1}{2} bh$

$c^2 = a^2 + b^2$

Special Right Triangles

$V = \ell wh$

$V = \pi r^2 h$

$V = \frac{4}{3}\pi r^3$

$V = \frac{1}{3}\pi r^2 h$

$V = \frac{1}{3}\ell wh$

The number of degrees of arc in a circle is 360.
The number of radians of arc in a circle is 2π.
The sum of the measures in degrees of the angles of a triangle is 180.

CONTINUE ➡

1

Arno must write x pages to successfully complete his paper on the French Revolution. If $2x + 17 = 39$, then what is the value of x ?

A) 11

B) 17

C) 22

D) 28

2

Dr. Yi wishes to construct a rectangular frame to display his world-renowned butterfly collection. He wants the frame to have dimensions of 36 inches by 24 inches. How much wood, in feet, will Dr. Yi need to construct the perimeter of this rectangular frame?

A) 12

B) 10

C) 6

D) 5

3

If a colony of mice contains 4 mice at the end of the first week, 6 mice at the end of the second week, and 8 mice at the end of the third week, which of the following best describes the colony of mice?

A) The colony of mice will contain 16 mice by the end of fourth week.

B) The colony of mice is losing an average of two mice per week.

C) The colony of mice is gaining an average of two mice per week.

D) The colony of mice will cease to grow after the third week.

4

Based on the scatterplot graph below, which of the following best describes the relationship between the number of hours the Omega High School lacrosse team practices in a given week and the number of goals scored in that week's game?

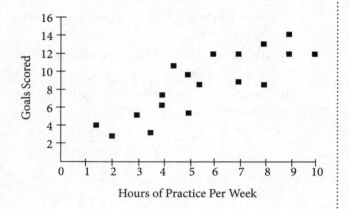

A) The more hours the lacrosse team practices, the fewer goals they score in a game.

B) The fewer hours the lacrosse team practices, the more goals they score in a game.

C) The more hours the lacrosse team practices, the more goals they score in a game.

D) There is no relationship between the hours the team practices and the goals scored in a game.

5

If $(x + 4)(x - 7) = 0$, which of the following must be true?

A) $2x^2 + 56 = 0$

B) $x^2 - 3x - 28 = 0$

C) $x^2 - 121 = 0$

D) $3x^2 + 3x + 3 = 0$

6

Dr. Seeker, a noted paleontologist, polls colleagues around the world asking for the their theory on what caused the mass extinction of most dinosaur species and brought about the end of the Cretaceous Period. After polling 200,000 of his colleagues, 151,394 of them reply that they believe the mass extinction to be caused by the Chicxulub Asteroid impact. The remaining 48,606 reply with alternative theories. From this data, which is the best conclusion that Dr. Seeker could make?

A) Approximately 10% of all scientists polled believe the mass extinction to be caused by the Chicxulub Asteroid impact.

B) Approximately 25% of all scientists polled believe the mass extinction to be caused by the Chicxulub Asteroid impact.

C) Approximately 50% of all scientists polled believe the mass extinction to be caused by the Chicxulub Asteroid impact.

D) Approximately 75% of all scientists polled believe the mass extinction to be caused by the Chicxulub Asteroid impact.

CONTINUE

Adam is hoping to make his high school's varsity football squad. As part of the tryout, Adam must run the length of the football field, and his time will be compared to the other candidates' times. Adam has run 240 feet and hopes to put on one last burst of speed to improve his time. If a football field is exactly 100 yards, how many *more* feet must Adam run to complete the tryout drill?

A) 340

B) 300

C) 140

D) 60

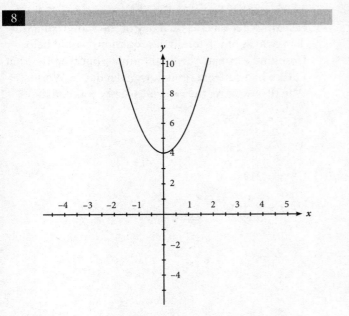

Which of the following functions could be the equation of the graph of *f(x)*, shown above?

A) $x + 4$

B) $2x + 8$

C) $2x^2 + 4$

D) $4x^2 - 20$

Questions 9-10 refer to the information below.

John, a sophomore at Boulder Canyon High School, is asked to chart his friends' after-school activities as part of an experiment for his sociology elective. He polls 50 of his close friends, and notes the following.

**After-School Activities of
50 Boulder Canyon Sophomores**

Activity	Sport	Club	Job	Volunteer	Home
Percentage	44%	32%	14%	8%	2%

According to the information above, which of the following is the ratio of those who go to an after-school sport to those who do not go to an after-school sport?

A) 11:25

B) 11:14

C) 11:10

D) 11:2

Based on the information presented, how many of John's friends have an after-school job?

A) 4

B) 7

C) 8

D) 14

11

If twice a number minus 15 is equal to seven times that number, what is the value of the number?

A) −5

B) −3

C) 3

D) 5

12

List A: [2, 5, 5, 7, 9, 13, x]

The median of List A, shown above, is 7. If List A has two distinct modes, which of the following must be true about the value of x?

A) $x \geq 7$

B) $x < 7$

C) $x = 0$

D) $x =$ all real numbers

13

If $a^3 - 7 = 20$, which of the following equations must also be true?

A) $a^3 = 3$

B) $a^2 = 3$

C) $a = \sqrt[3]{3}$

D) $\sqrt[3]{a} = \sqrt[3]{3}$

14

For his European History project, Desmond is evaluating the total number of casualties suffered by France in x number of days of World War II. He estimates that France suffered an average of 259 casualties per day for each day of the war. Using this data, which of the following equations would help Desmond estimate the total number of casualties that France had suffered up to any given day in World War II, assuming the rate of casualty was constant?

A) $y = x + 259$

B) $y = x - 259$

C) $y = 259x$

D) $y = \dfrac{1}{259}x$

CONTINUE

15

Chef Gordon is preparing a recipe for his private client, Bobby. Gordon needs 4 cups of milk and 3 cups of water as the primary liquid ingredients for a gourmet mac and cheese that Bobby has requested. While shopping for these ingredients, Gordon discovers that milk and water are only sold in gallons at the local market. He decides to purchase one gallon each of both milk and water and make multiple portions of the mac and cheese dish for Bobby. If Gordon uses only the gallon of milk and gallon of water purchased at the market, and uses all of the available milk, how much water, in ounces, should Gordon have left over?
(Note: 1 gallon = 128 ounces and 1 cup = 8 ounces)

A) 128

B) 96

C) 32

D) 8

16

If $f(x) = 17$ and $f(x) = x^2 + 1$, which of the following is the correct series of steps to find the value of $g(x)$ if $g(x) = 7x - 4$?

A) Substitute 17 for the value of x into the function $f(x)$ and substitute the resulting value for the value of x into the function $g(x)$.

B) Set $x^2 + 1 = 17$ and solve for x; then substitute the resulting value for the value of x into the function $g(x)$.

C) Set $7x - 4 = 17$ and solve for x; then substitute the resulting value for the value of x into the function $f(x)$.

D) Substitute 17 for the value of x into the function $g(x)$ and substitute the resulting value for the value of x into the function $f(x)$.

17

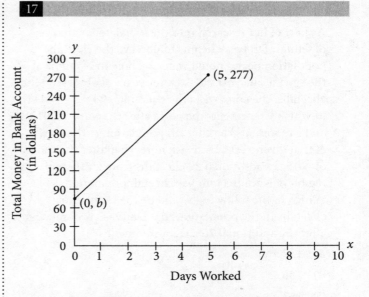

In the graph above, x represents the number of days Chris has worked his part-time job and y represents the total amount of money in his bank account. If the graph has a slope of 40, what is the value of b, assuming Chris does not spend any of the money in his bank account?

A) 117

B) 77

C) 40

D) 37

18

Geology experts at Black University receive a shipment of assorted rare stones from their scientists out at a local dig site. In the first month, they receive x rare stones. In the second month, they receive $2x + 18$ rare stones. In the third month, they receive $4x - 30$ rare stones. If they receive as many rare stones in the third month as they had received in the first two months combined, how many total rare stones did the experts at Black University receive over the entire three-month period?

A) 48

B) 114

C) 162

D) 324

19

As part of her research into the social behaviors of felines, Dr. Ivask begins to observe the cheetah population near a noted watering hole in Namibia at the start of the year 2012. After years of observing the cheetahs, she constructs the equation $c(y) = 17y + 112$, in which y represents the years after the start of 2012 and c represents the cheetah population at the start of that given year. Dr. Ivask notes that after the start of 2015, an additional 20 cheetahs from a different region of Namibia join her cheetah population. Which of the following would be the number of cheetahs in the population that Dr. Ivask is observing after the additional 20 cheetahs joined?

A) 132

B) 166

C) 163

D) 183

20

Right triangles *ABC* and *DEF* (not shown) are similar with hypotenuses *AC* and *DF*, respectively. If $AB = 3$, $BC = 4$, and $EF = 8$, what is the value of $2(DF - AC)$?

A) 10

B) 8

C) 6

D) 4

21

A certain polynomial is in the form $ax^2 + bx + c = 0$. If $a = 1$ and the polynomial has zeros of 3 and −4, which of the following could be the graph of the polynomial?

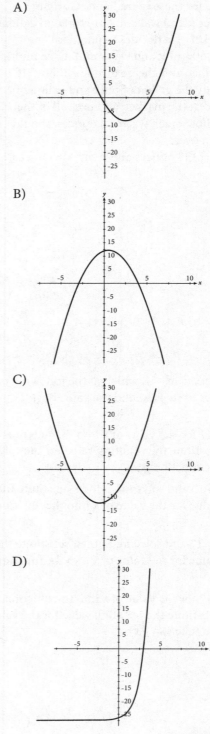

A)

B)

C)

D)

CONTINUE

22

Kristine wants to determine the effectiveness of her junior year high school instructors. She polls each of the 19 students who share the exact same five instructors as her by asking them to list out their final grades in junior year. Kristine makes sure to include her own grades as part of the results. She compiles the following data:

Final Grades by Class of 20 Students at Victory High School

Final Grade	Ms. Fisher (English)	Mr. Murphy (History)	Mr. Cuda (Math)	Mrs. Flores (Spanish)	Ms. Jones (Science)
A	5	4	3	2	6
B	8	7	3	3	1
B+	3	4	7	3	2
C	2	3	5	7	5
C+	2	2	2	4	6

Kristine determines that effectiveness is defined by the teacher's total number of A, B, and B+ grades, where the higher the total number is, the more effective the teacher must be. After reviewing the above data, Kristine determines that Ms. Jones is the most effective of her five instructors at Victory High School. Is Kristine's conclusion supported by the data?

A) Yes, Ms. Jones is the most effective instructor because she has the highest total number of A grades.

B) No, Mr. Murphy is the most effective instructor because he has the highest total number of A, B, and B+ grades combined.

C) Yes, Ms. Jones is the most effective instructor because she has the highest total number of A, B, and B+ grades combined.

D) No, Ms. Fisher is the most effective instructor because she has the highest total number of A, B, and B+ grades combined.

23

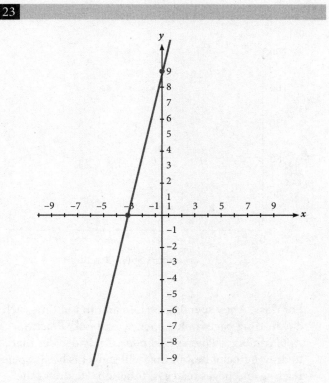

The graph of $f(x)$ is shown above. If $f(x)$ is reflected over the x-axis to create $g(x)$, and then $g(x)$ is reflected over the y-axis to create $h(x)$, which of the following could represent $h(x) - g(x)$?

A) 0

B) $g(x) + f(x)$

C) $f(x) + h(x)$

D) $f(x)$

24

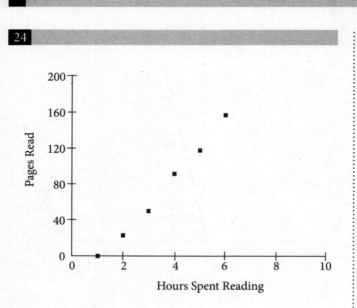

Hours Spent Reading

For class, Andy spends a certain amount of time each day reading pages of his science textbook, *Practical Applications of Physics Formulae*. Andy decides that to draw a line of best fit that will show his hours spent reading and pages read as a function. He draws the line $y = 32x - 32$ as his line of best fit. As Andy spends more time reading his book, he starts to comprehend the content more quickly and will read pages at a faster rate. Based on the information presented, is Andy's line of best fit accurate?

A) Yes, because multiple points on the scatter plot are solutions to the equation $y = 32x - 32$.

B) Yes, because the slope of $32x$ means that Andy will read more quickly as he spends more time reading.

C) No, because the slope of $32x$ means that Andy will read more slowly as he spends more time reading.

D) No, because the faster rate means that the graph must be quadratic or exponential, not linear.

25

If $f(x) = \dfrac{3}{2}x - 6$ and $g(x) = 3^x - 81$, for what value of x does $f(x) = g(x)$?

A) 4

B) 3

C) $\dfrac{2}{3}$

D) 0

26

At Dean's Discount Furniture Store, two sofas and one loveseat cost $1,200. At the same store, one sofa and three loveseats cost $1,350. During a special sale, Dean announces that all furniture in the store will be discounted at 10% off. Matt needs to purchase both sofas and loveseats to furnish a house he just purchased. How much money will Matt spend at Dean's Discount Furniture Store if Matt purchases three sofas and five loveseats during the special sale?

A) $675

B) $750

C) $2,565

D) $2,850

CONTINUE

27

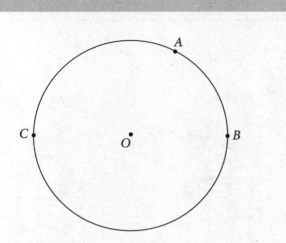

In the figure above, points *A, B,* and *C* lie on circle *O* such that $\overline{BC}$ is a diameter of Circle *O*. If the radius of Circle *O* is 6 and $\overline{AO} = \overline{AB}$, what is the sector area of sector *AOC* ?

A)   6π

B)   12π

C)   18π

D)   36π

DIRECTIONS

For questions 28-31, solve the problem and enter your answer in the grid, as described below, on the answer sheet.

1. Although not required, it is suggested that you write your answer in the boxes at the top of the columns to help you fill in the circles accurately. You will receive credit only if the circles are filled in correctly.

2. Mark no more than one circle in any column.

3. No question has a negative answer.

4. Some problems may have more than one correct answer. In such cases, grid only one answer.

5. **Mixed numbers** such as $3\frac{1}{2}$ must be gridded as 3.5 or 7/2. (If [3 1 / 2] is entered into the grid, it will be interpreted as $\frac{31}{2}$, not as $3\frac{1}{2}$.)

6. **Decimal Answers:** If you obtain a decimal answer with more digits than the grid can accommodate, it may be either rounded or truncated, but it must fill the entire grid.

Answer: $\frac{7}{12}$

Write answer in boxes.
Fraction line
Grid in result.

Answer: 2.5

Decimal point

Acceptable ways to grid $\frac{2}{3}$ are:

Answer: 201 – either position is correct

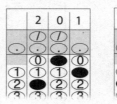

NOTE: You may start your answers in any column, space permitting. Columns you don't need to use should be left blank.

CONTINUE

28

If $\dfrac{3}{2}x + 5y = 72$ and $2x + 10y = 90$, what is the value of $3x + 5y$?

29

Dr. Sopious is a political science professor at Athens Community College. Depending on the term, Dr. Sopious will assign a different number of required essays for his students to read. For instance, during the fall term, the number of required essays will be a two digit prime number less than the square root of 144. In the spring, however, the number of required essays will be the smallest positive odd integer with four distinct prime factors. What is twice the difference between the number of required essays in the fall term and the number of required essays in the spring term?

Questions 30-31 refer to the following information.

Rob is deciding which board game to purchase next. Via a message board, he reaches out to 200 fellow board game enthusiasts and polls their interest in three separate board games: *Fire and Ice, Escape from Marley's Manor,* and *Sands of Devastation.* He asks the enthusiasts to indicate whether they are interested in a certain game, and tells them to feel free to vote for multiple games. The results of the replies are organized in the table below.

	Fire and Ice	*Escape from Marley's Manor*	*Sands of Devastation*
Interested	137	84	168
Not Interested	63	116	32

30

Assume that any individual who responded "interested" for *Escape from Marley's Manor* also responded "interested" for both *Fire and Ice* and *Sands of Devastation.* If this is true, what percent of those who responded "interested" for *Fire and Ice* responded "not interested" for *Escape from Marley's Manor,* rounded to the nearest tenth?

31

After conducting the poll, Rob realizes that he left out one additional game: *Winds of Change.* Since *Winds of Change* is created by the same person as *Sands of Devastation,* Rob sends out an additional email only to those who voted "interested" for *Sands of Devastation,* asking those individuals to vote "interested" or "not interested" for *Winds of Change.* Rob receives replies from everyone polled and is delighted to learn that 87.5% of those interested in *Sands of Devastation* are also interested in *Winds of Change.* What is the difference between those who are not interested in *Escape from Marley's Manor* and those who are not interested in *Winds of Change*?

STOP

If you finish before time is called, you may check your work on this section only. Do not turn to any other section.

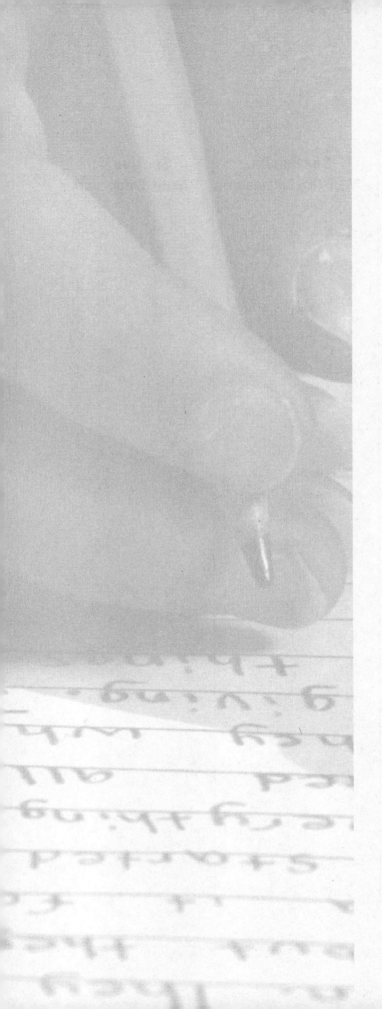

Chapter 16
Practice Test 2:
Answers and
Explanations

PRACTICE TEST 2 ANSWER KEY

Section 1:
Reading

1.	D	25.	B
2.	B	26.	C
3.	C	27.	D
4.	A	28.	B
5.	C	29.	C
6.	A	30.	C
7.	D	31.	B
8.	C	32.	A
9.	A	33.	A
10.	C	34.	D
11.	A	35.	B
12.	D	36.	D
13.	B	37.	C
14.	D	38.	B
15.	B	39.	C
16.	A	40.	B
17.	C	41.	D
18.	B	42.	A
19.	C	43.	A
20.	A	44.	D
21.	A	45.	C
22.	B	46.	C
23.	A	47.	B
24.	C		

Section 2:
Writing and Language

1.	D	23.	D
2.	C	24.	C
3.	B	25.	B
4.	A	26.	C
5.	C	27.	C
6.	C	28.	C
7.	D	29.	A
8.	B	30.	B
9.	B	31.	A
10.	D	32.	A
11.	A	33.	D
12.	A	34.	D
13.	B	35.	A
14.	D	36.	D
15.	B	37.	A
16.	C	38.	B
17.	C	39.	A
18.	A	40.	D
19.	D	41.	B
20.	C	42.	D
21.	B	43.	B
22.	A	44.	C

Section 3:
Math (No Calculator)

1.	A	11.	A
2.	C	12.	B
3.	C	13.	C
4.	D	14.	2
5.	C	15.	$\frac{16}{7}$
6.	D		
7.	A	16.	9
8.	C	17.	$\frac{1}{3}$
9.	D		
10.	B		

Section 4 :
Math (Calculator)

1.	A	16.	B
2.	B	17.	B
3.	C	18.	D
4.	C	19.	D
5.	B	20.	A
6.	D	21.	C
7.	D	22.	D
8.	C	23.	C
9.	B	24.	D
10.	B	25.	A
11.	B	26.	C
12.	A	27.	B
13.	D	28.	153
14.	C	29.	2,288
15.	C	30.	38.7
		31.	95

EXPLANATIONS

Section 1—Reading

1. **D** The reader is presented throughout the passage with John Marcher's inner thoughts as he tries to remember the comment he made to May Bertram many years ago. The narrator describes John in the second paragraph as being *even more surprised than ashamed* and more *conscious of a loss than a gain*. In the eighth paragraph, the narrator says that *the blood slowly came to his face...[and] began to burn with recognition*. Later in the last paragraph, John is described as *embarrassed*. The narrator is not judging him but rather describing his emotions through the course of this interchange with May, so eliminate (C). Choice (D) is a good match. This passage is not told from a first-person perspective, so (A) cannot be the correct answer. The first-person pronouns are used when one of the characters is speaking. The information presented to the reader is not a list of facts but rather details about John's emotions and various questions the two characters ask each other, making (B) incorrect. Therefore, the best answer is (D).

2. **B** In lines 45–47 (*Then it was that...a light broke for him...which began to burn with recognition.*), there is a shift in the emotions of John Marcher. Before this point in the passage, he is not sure what comment he made to May Bertram and is trying to remember. His emotions in this part of the passage can be described as unsure, which matches well with *confusion* in (B). Once the *light broke for him*, he falters and is hesitant to *give himself away* and later feels *embarrassed*. So while he has remembered the comment, he is uncomfortable about the fact that she has known his secret for all these years. This feeling of discomfort and realization matches well with the second part of (B)—*disconcerted recognition*. "*Begrudging*" in (A) doesn't match John's emotions at the end of the passage. "*Amazement*" in (D) is not a good match for John's emotions at the beginning of the passage—he was surprised that he had forgotten what she said but not "amazed" by that fact. Neither part in (C) can be supported by the passage. Therefore, (B) is the best answer.

3. **C** This passage is primarily centered on a secret that John told May long ago, but nothing is indicated that mistakes were made in the past. Eliminate (A). Only John shared a secret with May; both did not share secrets with each other, so (B) is incorrect. They are only discussing this past secret, not their feelings, so (D) is also incorrect. In the first paragraph of the passage, May references a previous outing on a boat, during which John said something that has always remained in her memory. This supports (C) in which they are discussing a former time and conversation.

4. **A** Work both this question and the previous question together by matching answer choices to one another. If you cannot find a match for an answer in question 4, then that cannot be the correct answer. Choice (A) describes a discussion of conversation that took place on a boat ride sometime in the past. This best matches (C) in question 3, so keep it. Choice (B) contains the advice that one should not be reminded of what they were ten years ago. While it seems like this may match with (A) in question 3, there is not actual mention of mistakes that were made. Eliminate (B).

Choice (C) describes a reaction both of the characters have to one character remembering something from the past, which does not match any in question 3. Choice (D) refers to May knowing a secret of John's, which appears to match (B) in question 3. But read carefully! It is only John who trusted May with a secret, not that they both trusted each other. The best match and only pair that is supported by the passage is (A).

5. **C** The sentence in question describes how John Marcher realized that May Bertram was not asking him to remember *a compliment* he had given her nor was she asking him to admit to *a mistake*. May was not making any request of him. In context, *claim* means something similar to "request." Choices (A), (B), and (D) do not mean "request," which leaves (C). *Appeal* in (C) is the most similar word to "request," so it is the best answer.

6. **A** In the first part of the sentence, the author reveals that John Marcher feels that by not remembering what he said to May Bertram, he's lost something rather than gained something. After the semicolon in this sentence, the author writes *he already saw an interest in the matter of her mention.* Therefore, he, too, is interested in learning what May remembers just as she is interested in discovering if he does remember. The two have a shared concern (does he remember what he said), so the *loss* that John feels is referring to this concern that has brought them together (keep (A)). Earlier in the paragraph, John realized that she was not asking him for a compliment or to acknowledge a mistake, so eliminate (B). Sorrento and its weather were mentioned in the first paragraph, but John makes no indication that he wishes to return there, so (C) is incorrect. Neither May nor John have expressed a declaration love for each other, so he has not rejected anything from her—he realized earlier that she was not asking him to admit a mistake, so (D) is also incorrect. The best answer is (A).

7. **D** When John Marcher finally realizes what he thinks he told May Bertram, he starts to bring it up and then falters because he doesn't want to reveal something about himself in case that isn't what he told May in the past. May then says, *It was something about yourself....* Though the reader does not know exactly what John said, it's enough to know that it's something personal about John, so the best description of what he said is (D). Choice (B) is incorrect because there is still no indication that he said anything romantic. Choices (A) and (C) are incorrect because the thing he said to her is no longer a *puzzle* nor is it *forgotten* because now he thinks he knows what he told her. The best answer is (D).

8. **C** The answer to the previous question is that John Marcher told May Bertram something personal about himself, as May reveals when she says, *It was something about yourself.* Therefore, (C) would provide evidence for the answer to the previous question. Choice (A) is incorrect because it would only provide support for where he said it to May, not what he said. Choice (B) would not provide support for what specifically John said to her. Choice (D) provides information about how John feels about what he said but doesn't refer specifically to what he said, so it is not the correct answer either. Choice (C) is the best answer.

9. **A** The sentence in question describes John Marcher noticing that his reaction to May Bertram's last question has *made her feel sorry for him.* Because he became embarrassed, he believes that she feels

it was a mistake to give him hints about what he said. In context, *allusion* means something similar to "hints" about what he said. Choices (B), (C), and (D) do not mean "hints," which leaves (A). *Reference* in (A) is the most similar word to "hint" and is, therefore, the best answer.

10. **C** The passage begins with an explanation of why and how Churchill formed a new government and the bodies and appointments therein. The passage then transitions to speaking of *one of the greatest battles in history* and that the aim of the new government and the country is *victory*, and he urges the new government and country to *go forward together with…united strength*. This best supports (C) because the passage first discusses formation of a new government through appointments and then goes on to rally that government to the shared cause of defeating Germany. Choice (A) also references both of these topics but lists them in the opposite order that they appear in the passage. Choice (B) is too narrow because it focuses only on the formation of the War Cabinet, as opposed to the government as a whole. Choice (D) is incorrect because the passage does not encourage an acceptance of defeat but rather urges a policy dedicated to victory. The best answer is (C).

11. **A** As used in this context, the word *prosecute* is used to mean "pursue" the war with Germany. Choices (B) and (C) are deceptive; they are both words that can be used in the same situation that prosecute is used as it relates to the law, but that is not how prosecute is being used in this context. Eliminate both choices. Between *fight* and *enforce*, "fight" more accurately matches the meaning of pursuing a way. Therefore, (A) is the best answer.

12. **D** After describing the positions in the government that had been filled, Churchill states that *it was necessary that this should be done in one single day, on account of the extreme urgency and rigour of events*. These events, as referenced throughout the passage, are the war-related interactions with Germany. The answer that best matches this statement is (D). Choice (A) is too narrow, and there is no indication in the passage why the King asked for the formation of the new administration or that it had to be hasty. The previous leadership of parliament and the number of parties had nothing to do with why a new government needed to be formed quickly, so (B) can be eliminated. Choice (C) is too extreme; although the war is the reason the new government must be formed so quickly, the war has only just begun. There is no indication that the British Empire is about to lose the war, only that it needs to become better enabled to fight the war effectively. The best answer is (D).

13. **B** As the correct answer to the previous question was (D), the choice that best supports that answer will reference the international political situation. Choice (A) references only the King's orders to form a new government, not why that government needed to be formed, so it is incorrect. Choice (C) references the political reconstruction of parliament and that Churchill hopes those affected by his quick actions will *make allowances…for any lack of ceremony*. However, these lines do not explain *why* his actions had to be quick, so (C) is incorrect as well. Finally, (D) only discusses the need of the British to prevail in their fight, not why Churchill needed to form his administration with haste. The best supported answer is (B)—that line specifically references the larger *events* that prompted the formation of the new government.

14.   **D**   The passage provides a great deal of information regarding Churchill's administration, so approach this question with POE. At no point does Churchill indicate that he believes the new government will be controversial, and he even invites the body before him to *record its approval of the steps taken and to declare its confidence in the new Government*. Because it seems unlikely that Churchill would invite such an action if he believed the majority would not agree, (A) is not a supported answer based on the text. However, despite the fact that Churchill seems confident by calling a vote of approval, (B) is extreme in saying that *all* the members of the House of Commons will approve it. Choice (C) is discredited by the several references made throughout the third paragraph to the various party members appointed to positions of leadership and to the united representation of the country through the new government. At the end of the third paragraph, Churchill does state that not all of the Minister positions have been appointed as they will take longer, but he hopes that task will be soon completed. This supports (D), which mentions that there are some unfilled positions in the government.

15.   **B**   Work both this question and the previous question together in a pair to see if any match, because these answer choices are the references for justifying the answer to question 14. Use Parallel POE to find the answer to both questions. Beginning with the answer choices for question 15, (A) contains a description of the formation of a war cabinet that represents the *unity of the nation*. This matches (B) in question 14 because both reference *unity*, but that answer for question 14 contains extreme language (*all*). Choice (B) refers to the fact that some minister positions are still unfilled, which best matches (D) in question 14. Choice (C) refers to Mr. Speaker and the steps he has taken, which does not match any in question 14. Choice (C) can be eliminated. Choice (D) refers to suffering in the time ahead, which also does not match any choices in question 14, so it can be eliminated as well. The only choices left that match choices from question 14 are (A) and (B). Because this question is open-ended, use your POE rules. While (A) does match an answer in question 14, (B) in question 14 is too extreme and not fully supported by the passage. Because (B) both matches an answer from question 14 and both are explicitly supported by the passage, it is the correct answer.

16.   **A**   This question asks why Churchill makes the statement that he has *nothing to offer but blood, toil, tears, and sweat*. His use of physical imagery serves to show the amount of exertion Churchill is willing to expend on accomplishing the task at hand. The best match to this description is (A)—this statement is meant to convey Churchill's deep level of commitment to the war effort. Choice (B) is refuted by the remainder of the passage, as Churchill strongly speaks of victory, so it cannot be correct. Choice (D) goes against common sense—his statement is a list of what he is ready to offer. This list does not count as "evidence" of his dedication but more as a description of the intense level of dedication he intends to offer. The best answer is (A).

17.   **C**   Churchill repetitively uses the phrases *victory* and *no survival* to stress the importance of these aspects to the battle. Without victory, the British Empire will fundamentally change from what it currently is, or so Churchill believes. His repetitive use of the phrases serves to emphasize that point. Choice (A) cannot be correct because Churchill is urging the country to future victory;

eliminate it. Because these words are used for emphasis rather than to describe any specific strategy, (B) is not supported by the text of the passage and can be eliminated. Although the use of the phrase victory is optimistic, Churchill declares that there would be no survival for the British Empire without victory to stress the importance of what is at stake, so optimism is an overly positive word in (D). The answer that is best supported by the passage is (C); both these terms are used to stress the importance of the outcome of the war for the British Empire.

18. **B** As used in this context, the word *suffered* means "to permit"—Churchill believes that mankind will not permit their cause (victory over tyranny) to fail. Choices (A) and (C) are synonyms—if people endure or tolerate something, they "deal with" it. To not "deal with" their cause failing is not as precise as the prediction: to not "permit" their cause to fail. Additionally, there cannot be two correct answers, so examine the other two answer s. Eliminate (D) because *endorsed* means *approved*, which would go against what Churchill is saying in this context. Choice (B) is a synonym for "permit," so it would work in this context. Churchill is certain that their cause will not be allowed to fail among men. The best answer is (B).

19. **C** The author discusses quite a bit about South Chicago in this passage, so the best approach to this question is POE. The author does not discuss anything about vacation destinations or tourism and references a quote that says no one goes there to admire the scenery, so (A) is not supported by the passage. The author does address the decrease of workers in the steel mills but also states that the local population is still highly dependent on the mills. It says nothing that would indicate all the mills will soon close, so (B) can be eliminated. In the first paragraph, the author describes South Chicago as *isolated, removed, and detached*, which strongly supports (C). Choice (D) is highly negative, and while the author does refer to the unattractive appearances of some buildings and reference ashes from chimneys, this is too sweeping a statement to refer to South Chicago as a whole. The best answer is (C).

20. **A** Because the correct answer to the previous question says that the author believes South Chicago is very isolated from the rest of the city, the correct answer to this question must support that answer. The only answer that does this is (A) because that line refers to South Chicago as the *most isolated community…most removed*. Choice (B) discusses the aesthetics of South Chicago, (C) refers to the noise and smell of South Chicago, and (D) contains a reference to American industry. Because these last three choices do not contain any information related to isolation, (A) is the best answer.

21. **A** The author mentions the names of the restaurants while describing what South Chicago is like. He refers to the appearance of these neighborhoods as *modest* and says the names of the restaurants are *simple*. The point the author is making will match the *modest* and *simple* nature of the area in general. The answer that is best supported by this is (A) because it says that it is the modest aspect of the neighborhood that the author is trying to emphasize.

22. **B** In this sentence, *suspended* is used to describe the *belts, pipes, and railroad* as being up in the air. The answer must therefore match the meaning of "up in the air." The only answer that matches this is (B), *hanging*. Neither (C) nor (D) has any relation to being up in the air, so they can be

eliminated. Although the word *drooping* can mean "hanging," it refers to a certain way something hangs that is not supported by the sentence, so (A) is also wrong. The best answer is (B).

23. **A** This question is asking for a direct comparison being made in the passage, so look back to the second paragraph to find the answer. The first sentence of the second paragraph states that the scenery of South Chicago is *the man-made equivalent of the Rockies.* Because the scenery in South Chicago is comprised of the steel mills, the comparison is likening those mills to the Rockies. This supports (A). Choice (B) refers to why the lights are on the chimneys, (C) refers to the size of some of the structures, and (D) gives a description of the smoke. The best answer is (A).

24. **C** Work both this question and the previous question together in a pair to see if any match; these answer choices are the references for justifying the answer to question 23. You can then use Parallel POE to find the answers to both questions. Beginning with the answer choices in question 24, (A) contains a description of neighborhoods that does not match any of the choices in question 23. Choice (A) can be eliminated. Choice (B) describes a highway and also does not match any of the choices in question 23, so it can be eliminated as well. Choice (C) contains words that match three choices in question 23, so be careful! Although the lines reference *football fields* and *aircrafts*, these are descriptions that are part of the larger comparison that the steel mills are like the Rockies. This best matches (A) in question 23. Choice (D) describes the function of the steel mills and does not match any choice in question 23. Therefore, (C) is the correct answer.

25. **B** In this sentence, *consumption* is referring to all of the things American's consume or purchase, such as the items listed in the previous sentence. The closest thing to the meaning of consume or purchase in the answers is (B). Choice (A) is an alternate definition of consumption that does not work in the context of this sentence, so it is not correct. Neither corrosion nor burning matches the meaning of purchase at all, so (C) and (D) cannot be correct. The best answer is (B).

26. **C** Pay close attention to what this question is asking: It asks not only for the primary purpose of the last paragraph but also how that relates to the whole passage. The last paragraph is focused on the current state of the steel mills of South Chicago and the decrease in production from the mills. This fits with the descriptive approach the passage has taken as a whole to illustrate this area of a city for the reader. Although the author does take a critical view of the owners of mills, (A) is too specific and does not touch on how this paragraph relates to the passage as a whole. Choice (B) goes too far in saying that the author is lamenting the state of South Chicago; the author is only describing the state of that area, not sharing his personal feelings about it. Choice (D) has the same issue; the author is not suggesting changes, only reviewing changes that have taken place. The best answer is (C)—that the author is explaining the current state of the steel mills—this matches the descriptive nature of the last paragraph and the passage as a whole.

27. **D** Compare each answer against the data provided in the graph. Choice (A) can be eliminated because domestic steel production did not increase only from 1950 to 2000. Choice (B) can also be eliminated because the domestic steel production did not remain stagnant during that time period; it fluctuated. Choice (C) can also be eliminated as the peak of domestic steel production occurred

in the 1970s, not the 1960s. Choice (D) is supported by the graph: The domestic steel production was just under 100 million tons in 1950 and just over 100 million tons in 2000, so the net production had only slightly increased from where it started. The correct answer is (D).

28. **B** This question is asking for a synthesis of information between the graph and the passage. Choice (A) could be true, but nowhere on the graph is it indicated that this data represents only South Chicago's steel mill production. Furthermore, the passage does not explicitly state that the mills reached their greatest productivity in the mid-1970s. Eliminate (A). Choice (C) is extreme by saying that *all* domestic steel mills cut their workforces, which is not supported by either the passage or the graph. Choice (D) references air pollution, which is mentioned in the passage but is in no way addressed by the graph, so eliminate it. Choice (B) states that US steel production has increased in areas other than South Chicago. This is supported by the graph in that there has been a general increase in steel production domestically and is also supported by the passage in the last paragraph—there has not been an increase in South Chicago's steel production.

29. **C** In the second paragraph, the authors state that the grasslands are burned *annually in late spring* and then mention some of the air quality issues that have resulted from late spring burning. They acknowledge that *late spring burning has maintained* the grassland, but it comes at a price, which makes (C) a possible answer. The authors never state that burning should be done twice a year, so (A) should be eliminated. Late spring burning has been the recommendation since the early 1970s and does maintain the grassland, so the authors would not agree with (B). The authors discuss the consequences of burning during different times of the year in the following paragraph, and in the last paragraph they include information from historical studies claiming that shifting the burning time *would negatively impact the plant community*. However, they also mention that a recent study *found that the time of burning had no significant effect* and believe the recommendations are *inconclusive*, so (D) is incorrect. The best answer is (C).

30. **C** Pay attention to the word *NOT* in the question. Use POE to eliminate three answer choices that do influence decisions on the timing of seasonal burning. Choices (A) and (B) are found in lines 4–8 (the second sentence of the first paragraph: *Management…are burned.*), so eliminate those two choices because they *do* influence decisions. Lines 47–51 (the last sentence in paragraph three: *Consequently…are favorable.*) indicate that weather influences the timing of seasonal burns, so (D) should be eliminated. This leaves (C). *Tropospheric ozone production* is mentioned as a consequence of late spring burning not as something that influences when burning happens. Therefore, (C) is the correct answer.

31. **B** The authors describe the Kansas Flint Hills at the beginning of the second paragraph as *one of the last remaining regions supporting extensive native tallgrass prairie in North America, and frequent burning is integral to its preservation and economic utilization.* Choice (B) is a good paraphrase of this sentence. The authors never directly say in this paragraph or elsewhere in the passage that this area is *sensitive* or that *extreme caution* be used when dealing with this area, so eliminate (A). While the passage implies that the Flint Hills are a special grassland, one might assume that they

are composed of a unique composition of grasses and shrubs. However, there is no evidence to support that it requires more study, so eliminate (C). Choice (D) is not the best answer, even though it seems feasible at first glance. The article discusses how early spring burning leads to lower weight gain in cattle. However, the passage does not deem the weight gain as being unhealthy. In addition, this option goes against the main idea of the passage. The best answer is (B).

32.　**A**　The answer to the previous question was that burning the Kansas Flint Hills regularly is essential to keep the area economically useful. The best support for this answer can be found in first sentence of the second paragraph (A). The remaining choices can be eliminated because none of these lines mentions that the burning must happen regularly—each focuses on the time of the season when the burning occurs. Therefore, (A) is the correct answer.

33.　**A**　For the sentence in question, the word *practices* is used to refer to something that is done so much that it has become *ingrained* into the culture—*burning exclusively in late spring has become ingrained in the cultural practices*. Thus, burning in late spring has become a custom, so the correct answer should mean something similar to "customs." Eliminate (B), (C), and (D) because they don't have the same meaning as "customs." *Traditions* in (A) is most similar to "customs," so it is the best answer.

34.　**D**　For the sentence in question, the word *equivocal* is used to describe the data supporting the policy that *tallgrass prairie be burned only in late spring*. The rest of the paragraph details the data and reveals results (many which were conflicting or unknown) about burning during various parts of the spring. At the beginning of the last paragraph, the authors state, *The historical studies...for time of burning recommendations in tallgrass prairie are inconclusive*. So *equivocal* should mean something similar to "uncertain." Eliminate (A), (B), and (C) because they don't have the same meaning as uncertain." *Unclear* in (D) is most similar to "uncertain," so it is the best answer.

35.　**B**　This sentence is discussing burning to control *invasive shrubs*. The conjunction *but* lets the reader know that *Symphoricarpos orbiculatus* is in contrast to the first part of the sentence: While burning in late spring has been an effective way to control the shrubs, the only wooded species to decline was this species. Therefore, *Symphoricarpos orbiculatus* is a wooded species of invasive shrub, so (B) is the answer. Forbs and grasses are mentioned earlier in the paragraph as part of early spring burning, so the remaining (A), (C), and (D) can be eliminated. The best answer is (B).

36.　**D**　Work both this question and the previous question together in a pair to see if anything matches; these answer choices are the references for justifying the answer to question 35. You can then use Parallel POE to find the answers to both questions. Beginning with the answer choices for question 36, (A) contains description of the Flint Hills and the type of prairie they support, which requires intermittent burning for survival. This description does not match any choice in question 35, so it can be eliminated. Choice (B) discusses the biomass resulting from burning different types of plants at different times, none of which matches any choice in question 35. Eliminate (B) as well. Choice (C) contains many words seen in the choices in question 35 but be careful! Choice (C) discusses several types of grasses and shrubs, so it does not match any single choice in question 35.

Choice (D) directly references *Symphoricarpos orbicultatus* and explicitly states that it is an *invasive shrub*. This matches completely with (B) in question 35. As this is the only match between the two questions, (D) is the correct answer.

37. **C**   Use POE to check each answer against the graph. Choice (A) is incorrect because spring burning does not always have a higher biomass than that of other seasons. There is not enough information provided in the graph to support (B) or (D)—prairies and rainfall are not represented in the graph. This leaves (C), which can be supported by the figure because the three lines are generally rising and falling together: Regardless of the time of year, there isn't a significant change in biomass. Therefore, the best answer is (C).

38. **B**   The passage states that the *researchers were surprised at how big an effect particle shape had on the drying phenomenon.* Thus, (B) is correct because they had assumed shape wouldn't have a major effect. Choice (A) is incorrect because the detachment from the interface happens when surfactants are added. Choice (C) is the opposite of what they did in the experiment, which is stretch the spheres, so that's incorrect. Choice (D) is incorrect because Passage 1 describes how surfactants affect the membrane, not just the particles.

39. **C**   The passage states that *University of Chicago physicists Sidney Nagel, Thomas Witten, and their colleagues wrote an influential paper about this process in 1997, which focused mainly on suspended spherical particles, but it was not until the Yodh team's recent experiments that the surprising role played by suspended particle shape was discovered.* It's clear that their paper was influential and that they used spherical particles, but Passage 1 gives no other information about their work. Thus, (C) is correct. There's no reason given for why Nagel and Witten didn't experiment with ellipsoid particles, so (A) is incorrect. Passage 1 doesn't state whether Nagel and Witten's work in any way limited other studies, nor does the passage state that their research was flawed, so (B) and (D) are incorrect.

40. **B**   The passage states that *Sidney Nagel, Thomas Witten, and their colleagues wrote an influential paper,* and Yodh's team starts off working with spherical particles, so it's clear that Yodh's research builds on Nagel and Witten's. Choice (B) is the best answer. Choices (C) and (D) are impossible because Nagel and Witten came first. Choice (A) is too strong because it's unclear that Yodh's work in any way proved Nagel and Witten's work wrong. Rather, it appears that Yodh's team tried things that the earlier team had not.

41. **D**   The passage states that *spherical particles easily detach from the interface, and they flow past one another easily because the spheres do not substantially deform the air-water interface. Ellipsoid particles, however, cause substantial undulation of the air-water interface that in turn induces very strong attractions between the ellipsoids.* Because the spheres do not deform the interface, and the ellipsoids behave differently, they must cause the interface to change shape or "ripple." Thus, (D) is correct. For (A) the attraction of the ellipsoids causes the undulation, so this answer is incorrect. Evaporation happens much later in the process, so (B) is incorrect. The word *undertow* could possibly address the movement of the ellipsoid particles, but it does not mean the same as undulation in this context, so (C) is incorrect.

42. **A** Passage 2 mentions that surfactants are in soap and that surfactants can reduce the coffee ring effect, but the passage also states that scientists have been working for many years to find surfactants for industrial applications, so there must be a need for surfactants in forms other than those in soap. Thus, (A) is the best answer for why the author of Passage 2 compares detergents and bacterium. Choice (B) is incorrect because the passage doesn't address the dangers of using the bacterium, nor does the passage state that soap is a better surfactant, so (D) is incorrect as well. Choice (C) is mentioned in the passage, but it doesn't explain why the author of Passage 2 discusses detergents and bacterium together.

43. **A** Passage 2 states that *the coffee ring effect can be particularly troublesome and scientists have long been seeking ways to counteract it.* Thus (A) is correct. Choice (B) is incorrect because that's the effect of surfactants. Choice (C) is incorrect because the passage states that the effect can be reduced, but not completely eliminated—*Add soap to a stain—a coffee stain or any other stain—and you will still get a coffee ring effect.* Choice (D) is incorrect because the coffee ring effect actually hinders industrial applications.

44. **D** Choice (D) explains why the coffee ring effect generates many studies on ways to thwart it: *In various industrial applications—applying an even coat of paint or varnish, for example—the coffee ring effect can be particularly troublesome and scientists have long been seeking ways to counteract it.* Thus, (A), (B), and (C) are incorrect.

45. **C** In the beginning of Passage 2, the author explains how the coffee ring effect works: *The coffee particles move toward the edge of the stain while the water in the liquid evaporates.* When surfactants are added to the particles, *the soap causes a counterflow from the edge back towards the centre of the stain in such a way that the small particles—material or bacteria—end up in a kind of whirlwind.* Thus, the particles are more evenly distributed, so (C) is the best answer. For (A), it's not clear whether they're spread thin or thick, so this is incorrect. Choice (B) doesn't make sense in the context of *distribution of particles as evaporation occurs.* Choice (D) also doesn't address the way the particles are distributed, so it is incorrect.

46. **C** Both passages describe the properties of the coffee ring effect similarly, and both studies look at how to diminish the effect. They have different solutions, but both passages address how surfactants cause particles to move away from the edge of a fluid, thus reducing the coffee ring effect. This makes (C) the best answer. Choice (A) is incorrect because it says the opposite of what the passage says, and (B) is not correct because the results of the study in Passage 1 don't prove that the conclusion of Passage 2 is inconsistent with the properties of the coffee ring effect. Choice (D) is incorrect because the fact that bacterium can be genetically modified to not produce surfactants doesn't change the fact that when the bacterium have surfactants they react as the scientists would expect.

47. **B** In Passage 2, the researchers use a bacterium to counteract the coffee ring effect, so (B) is correct. They do not stretch the *Pseudomonas aeruginosa* bacterium, so (A) is incorrect. They also do not experiment on nanomaterials in order to breed *Pseudomonas aeruginosa*. They more likely breed

Pseudomonas aeruginosa in order to experiment on nanomaterials, so (C) is incorrect. Choice (D) is true of both studies, so it is not the best answer.

Section 2—Writing and Language

1. **D** The answer choices indicate that verb tense is being tested, so let the non-underlined portions guide your choice of verb. Present tense is seen in the first part of this sentence: *Imagine you go....* Eliminate (A) and (B) because both use *had*, which is the wrong tense. Choice (C) is also incorrect since *were having* is not consistent with the verbs in the non-underlined portion: *Imagine* or *go*. Choice (D) uses a present tense verb that is consistent with the verbs in rest of the sentence, so it is the best answer.

2. **C** Look at the answers to see that comma usage is being tested. First, check to see if *For many, the answer is simple* is an introductory idea. Because it is a complete idea and the idea after the comma is a complete idea (in this case, a command), a comma should not be used. Eliminate (A) and (D). Compare (B) and (C). Choice (C) has a colon, and (B) has no punctuation. Because the two ideas are complete, punctuation is needed. Therefore, the correct answer is (C).

3. **B** Notice the question, and use POE to find the best answer that maintains the focus of the sentence and paragraph. The focus of the paragraph is on the relationship between social media and restaurants. As written, the sentence is not focused on social media, but on the decision to not return to a restaurant. Eliminate (A). Choice (B) mentions Yelp, a consumer review website that is mentioned later in the paragraph. Therefore, (B) is a good answer. Choice (C) makes no mention of social media, so eliminate it. Choice (D) mentions neither social media nor restaurants, so eliminate (D). The best answer is (B).

4. **A** Whenever you are given the option to delete, determine whether the portion in question serves a precise role within the passage. In this case, *not just restaurants*, transitions between the first paragraph, which is all about restaurants, and the second paragraph, which is about the behavior of companies in general. This matches (A). Eliminate (B) because the phrase *just restaurants* does not encourage anyone to hire CLOs. Eliminate (C) because this phrase itself does not imply anything about the patrons' discussions. Eliminate (D) because the fact that the previous paragraph is all about restaurants and the current one is in support of keeping the phrase, not eliminating it. Therefore, the best answer is (A).

5. **C** Look at the answers to see that the word *insure* is being tested. *Insure* describes what companies should do, and the next sentence says that companies should maintain public face. Therefore, the best answer will mean something like "make sure." Because *insure* means to arrange for compensation in the event of damage, (A) and (D) can be eliminated. Because *assure* means to dispel doubts, (B) can also be eliminated. Because *ensure* means to make it certain that something will happen, (C) is the best answer.

6. **C** Look at the answers to see that apostrophes are being tested. First, look immediately after the word in question to see if it (*company*) should be possessive. Because the Social Media Manager is in charge of the output of a company, the word is possessive and requires an apostrophe. Eliminate (A). Because *companys'* is not a word, eliminate (D). A difference between (B) and (C) is the placement of the apostrophe. Because the word immediately preceding the underlined word is *a*, the underlined word should be singular. Therefore, the apostrophe must come before the *s*, as is the case in (C). Thus, (C) is the best answer.

7. **D** Whenever you are given the option to delete, determine whether the portion in question serves a precise role within the passage. The sentence ends with the phrase *to see if the situation can be remedied*, so the underlined portion is redundant, as are the options in (B) and (C). Therefore, the best answer is (D).

8. **B** Look at the answers to see that the word *unfurls* is being tested. Because the advertising campaign is described as *new*, the underlined word should mean something like introduces. *Unfurls* means "unfolds," so (A) is not the correct answer. *Rolls out* means introduces, so (B) is a good answer. *Unrolls* means flatten out from a roll, so (C) is not the best answer. A *role* is a part that an actor plays or a position that someone assumes in a certain situation, so (D) should be eliminated. The correct answer is (B).

9. **B** The underlined portion of this sentence contains a pronoun (*this*), so make sure it is consistent with the non-underlined portion by finding the other pronouns and nouns. The partner noun is *market research*, but *this* could partner with any of the singular nouns in the previous sentence. Therefore, *this* is an ambiguous pronoun. Eliminate (A). Next, compare (B) and (C). Whenever you are given the option to be more concise, determine whether the portion in question serves a precise role within the passage. The phrase *about this kind of "market research"* does play a precise role in the passage. It provides a partner noun for the pronoun *it* in the same sentence. Without *this kind of market research*, *it* would be an ambiguous pronoun. Though they are more concise, (C) and (D) do not provide the clarity that (B) does. Therefore, (B) is the best answer.

10. **D** The underlined portion of this sentence is a pronoun, so make sure it is consistent with the non-underlined portion by finding the other pronouns and nouns. The partner noun is *someone*, which is singular. Therefore, the underlined pronoun must also be singular. Eliminate (A) and (B). Because *your* cannot partner with anything other than other forms of *you*, eliminate (C). Choice (D) is correct.

11. **A** The criticism in the previous sentence is that the CLO position is not going to last for long. (A fad is anything that is fashionable for a short amount of time.) Choice (A) directly answers the criticism and is therefore a good answer. Choice (B) agrees with the criticism, so it is not the best answer. Choice (C) has nothing to do with the CLO position, so it is not the best answer. Choice (D) makes no mention of how long social media will last, so it is not the best answer either.

12. **A** Because the paragraph is contrasting the scale of the Yellow Fever Epidemic with that of other diseases, keep (A). Choice (B) provides unnecessary information, namely World War I, and is therefore not the best answer. Choice (C) makes no mention of other diseases, so it is not the best answer. Choice (D) does not support the paragraph's main idea that the Yellow Fever Epidemic was worse than the others mentioned and is not the best answer. Therefore, (A) is the best answer.

13. **B** The chart provides census data from 1790. The underlined portion discusses the population of cities today. Therefore, (A) is not the best answer. The chart indicates that Philadelphia was the second largest city in the country and had a population of 28,522. Therefore, (B) is consistent with the chart. Choice (C) states that Philadelphia was smaller than Boston and is therefore not consistent with the chart. Choice (D) states that Philadelphia was larger than New York and is therefore not consistent with the chart. Choice (B) is the best answer.

14. **D** The underlined portion indicates doctors' efforts to stem the epidemic. Choices (A), (B), and (C) all indicate different ways the doctors could have tried to slow the spread of the disease. Choice (D) is the best answer because doctors do not do maintenance to stop the spread of a disease.

15. **B** The answer choices indicate that verb tense is being tested, so let the non-underlined portions guide your choice of verb. Past tense is seen in *how the disease originated*, so (B) is consistent. Choice (A) uses an -ing verb, which is not consistent with *originated*. Choice (C) uses *had been* which is not consistent with *originated*, so eliminate it. Choice (D) uses *spread* as a noun, so eliminate it as well. The correct answer is (B).

16. **C** Of the four answers, (A), (B), and (D) are too informal to match the academic tone of the rest of the paper. Choice (C) is the best answer.

17. **C** The underlined portion of this sentence is a pronoun, so make sure it is consistent with the non-underlined portion by finding the other pronouns and nouns. There are multiple potential partner nouns in the previous sentence, including *Philadelphia* and *nation*. Therefore, the correct answer should not contain a pronoun. Because (A), (B), and (D) contain pronouns, (C) is the best answer because it clearly specifies who tried to impose quarantine and curfew measures.

18. **A** Look at the answers to see that comma usage is being tested. Because the underlined portion is a list, there must be a comma placed after each item on the list. Choice (B) omits the comma after *hot sun*, so it is incorrect. Choices (C) and (D) add unnecessary words and are therefore not the best answers. The best and most concise answer is (A).

19. **D** Sentence 6 provides an account of the confusion that accompanied the arrival of Yellow Fever in Philadelphia by providing a prominent physician's theory regarding the cause of the disease. Therefore, it should not follow an account of the eleven measures for prevention, so (A) is not the best answer. In addition, such an account should not introduce the paragraph. Therefore, (B) is incorrect. Sentence 6 is too specific to follow a general sentence like sentence 2, so (C) is incorrect. Sentence 3 mentions another party's theory regarding the cause of the disease. Therefore, (D) is the best answer.

20. **C** Look at the answers to see that STOP punctuation is being tested. Perform the Vertical Line Test to see that the semicolon in (D) separates a complete idea from an incomplete idea, so eliminate it. While a comma and a colon can separate a complete idea from an incomplete idea, there is no reason to pause/interrupt the sentence in this case, so eliminate (A) and (B). Because no punctuation is needed, (C) is the best answer.

21. **B** Look at the answers to see that comma usage is being tested. Check to see if the phrases *in West Africa*, *provides a terrifying reminder*, and *of just how deadly certain diseases can be*, are necessary or unnecessary information. If any are removed from the sentence, it does not make sense. Therefore, they are all necessary and should not be set off by commas. Choice (B) is the best answer.

22. **A** *By the same token* means something like "for the same reason" or "in the same way." Because both ideas have to do with the effects of an epidemic, (A) is an appropriate introduction to this sentence. Because (B) indicates that the Yellow Fever Epidemic and the Ebola Virus are somehow opposites, (B) is not the best answer. Because (C) and (D) indicate that the final sentence is the last logical step in an argument, neither is the best answer. Choice (A) is the best answer.

23. **D** Whenever you are given the option to delete, determine whether the underlined portion serves a precise role within the passage. The sentence has already said that *Many people find it hard to believe*, so the phrase *seems doubtful* is redundant. Eliminate (A). Eliminate (B) and (C) as well because they express the same idea as *seems doubtful*. Choice (D) is the best answer.

24. **C** The main subject of the passage as a whole is a musician named *Rodgers*. The best answer will introduce Rodgers, so (A) and (B) should be eliminated. Choice (D) introduces Jimmie Rodgers, but it also introduces two other musicians who are not mentioned again in the passage. Therefore, (C) is the best answer.

25. **B** The underlined portion of this sentence includes a verb, so find the subject to check whether it agrees with the verb. The subject of *is* is *circumstances*, which is plural. Therefore, the verb must be plural. Eliminate (A), (C), and (D). Choice (B) is correct.

26. **C** When you are given the option to add information, determine whether the added information serves a precise role in the passage. As written, the sentence does not say anything about what little was known. Therefore, neither (A) nor (B) is the best answer. Choices (C) and (D) express similar information, but (C) is more concise, so it is the best answer.

27. **C** Notice the question: It is asking for *specific information* about Rodgers's illness. Choices (A), (B), and (D) are vague. None of them name a specific illness. Only (C) names a specific illness, so it is the best answer.

28. **C** Make sure that the phrase has some precise and definable role within the sentence or passage. It serves no role in the current sentence because the clause is about the number of copies the record sold, not where it sold. Choice (A) is not the best answer. It also serves no role when placed after *In October of that year* because that piece of introductory information has nothing to do with place,

only time. Choice (B) is not the best answer. When placed after *after Rodgers chased his dream*, the underlined portion does serve a purpose: It explains where Rodgers chased his dream. Therefore, (C) is a good answer. When placed after *which sold half a million copies*, the underlined portion does not add relevant information. The purpose of the clause is to explain how many copies the record sold. Therefore, (D) is not the best answer. Choice (C) is the best answer.

29.   **A**   Look at the answers to see that comma usage is being tested. A comma can come after introductory information, as it does in the underlined portion, so keep (A). Later in the sentence, a comma plus FANBOYS is used, so the first idea must be complete. Because *when* and *as* make the first idea incomplete, (B) and (C) are incorrect. Because a colon can only follow a complete idea, (D) is incorrect. Choice (A) is the correct answer.

30.   **B**   On proposition questions, make sure the phrase has some precise and definable role within the sentence or passage. The relevant information is that both Howlin' Wolf and Elvis Presley cited Rodgers as an early influence. As it is written, the underlined portion says that Howlin' Wolf also cited Elvis Presley as an early influence. This is incorrect, so (A) is not the best answer. Choices (C) and (D) also indicate that Howlin' Wolf cited Presley as an early influence, so neither is the best answer. Choice (B) is the best answer.

31.   **A**   Because the question is asking for an alternative to the underlined portion that would NOT be acceptable, the word *fortuitous* is correctly used. Find and eliminate any answers that are similar to *fortuitous*, which means "lucky." *Chancy* is the only one that doesn't fit, because it means "risky." Choice (A) is the best answer.

32.   **A**   Because there is a semicolon in the answer choices, use the Vertical Line Test to see if the STOP punctuation is separating two complete ideas. *Once Jimmie could no longer work the rails* is not a complete idea, so (C) should be eliminated. The remaining answer choices indicate that comma usage is being tested. Check to see if *however* is necessary or unnecessary information. If removed from the sentence, it would still make sense, so it's unnecessary information (eliminate (B) and (D)). Commas should always be placed around unnecessary information, so (A) is the best answer.

33.   **D**   The fifth paragraph begins by mentioning Rodgers's illness, and it ends by discussing the beginning of his recording career. Therefore, it should not be where it is now, but between a paragraph that discusses his illness and a paragraph that discusses his music career. Therefore, (A) is incorrect. Because the paragraph should come between two other paragraphs, (B) is incorrect. Because paragraph 1 does not mention his illness, (C) is incorrect. Because paragraph 2 mentions his illness and paragraph 3 mentions his music career, the proper place for paragraph 5 is between those two paragraphs. Choice (D) is the best answer.

34.   **D**   Look at the answer choices to see that noun agreement is being tested. Because the sentence is about males and females, the corresponding noun should be plural. Eliminate (A), (B), and (C) because each uses a singular noun. Choice (D) uses a plural noun. Therefore, (D) is the best answer.

35.   **A**   The question asks for accurate data based on the graph, so check each answer and use POE to eliminate anything that is not consistent with the graph. Choice (A) tells us that only a handful of animals has a post-reproductive life span and gives the black-tailed prairie dog as an example. According to the graph, it is true that the black-tailed prairie dog does have a post-reproductive life span, and only half of the species represented on the graph do as well. Both assertions in (A) are consistent with the graph. Choice (B) states that most animals have some post-reproductive life span, such as humans. Neither of these assertions is consistent with the graph, as only half of the species have some post-reproductive life span, and humans are not represented on the graph. Eliminate (B). Choice (C) is not consistent with the graph because the common bottlenose dolphin has the longest, not the shortest, pre-reproductive life span compared to the only species on the graphic. Choice (D) is also not consistent with the graph because both of the rodent species listed do have substantial post-reproductive life spans. Both (C) and (D) can be eliminated as well, leaving (A) as the only consistent answer.

36.   **D**   The underlined portion of this sentence is a pronoun, so make sure it is consistent with the non-underlined portion by finding the other pronouns and nouns. The partner noun could be *humans, short-finned pilot whales, killer whales,* or *females.* Therefore, the pronoun is ambiguous, and (A) is not the best answer. Choice (C) is incorrect because it uses the wrong case (a subject pronoun is needed). Compare (B) and (D). Choice (B) contains pronouns, whereas (D) is more specific. Because it offers the most clarity to the sentence, (D) is the best answer.

37.   **A**   The previous paragraph ends by discussing the surprising longevity of female whales, and the paragraph in question discusses a study that may have provided a possible explanation. Therefore, (A) is a good answer because it mentions the study and clarifies that it may provide an answer. Choices (B), (C), and (D) make no mention of the study, so eliminate them. Choice (A) is the best answer.

38.   **B**   Look at the answer choices. The main difference among them is word order. To determine which words should come first, look at the modifier that begins the sentence. *After watching over 750 hours of video and observing the behaviors of pods of whales* describes the scientists, so scientists should be immediately after the modifying phrase. Therefore, (B) is the best answer.

39.   **A**   When you are given the option to add information, determine whether the added information would serve a precise and necessary role in the passage. In this case, the information is an example of the teaching behavior mentioned in the previous sentence. Therefore, (A) is the best answer. Choice (B) is incorrect because older whales were not ignored in the study. Rather, they were the subject of the study. Choice (C) is not the best answer because there is no information that conflicts with the proposed sentence. Choice (D) is not the best answer because there is no indication elsewhere in the passage that the scientists' observations should be understood to be conclusive.

40.   **D**   Because there are periods and semicolons in the answer choices, this question is testing STOP punctuation. As written, the STOP punctuation comes between an incomplete idea and a complete idea, so (A) should be eliminated. Choice (B) places STOP punctuation incorrectly between two incomplete ideas and should also be eliminated. Choice (C) creates a comma splice because

the comma after *knowledge* separates two complete ideas, so it should be eliminated. In (D), however, the STOP punctuation comes between two complete ideas. Therefore, (D) is the best answer.

41. **B** First, note that *longevity* means "length of a life." Therefore, the two words do not mean the same thing, so (A) is not the best answer. Because (B) indicates that the words do not have the same meaning, it is a good answer. Because (C) and (D) indicate that the words have the same meaning, both of them can be eliminated. Choice (B) is the best answer.

42. **D** The paragraph in question discusses the wider ramifications of the study's findings. Choice (A) is not the best answer because it makes a claim that is unsupported by the study's findings. Choice (B) is not the best answer because it does not make mention of the wider consequences of the study's findings. Choice (C) is not the right answer because it makes no mention of the study at all. Choice (D) is the best answer because it says that the findings have ramifications beyond the scientific community.

43. **B** The answer choices indicate that this question is testing word choice. Because the underlined word should be a possessive pronoun, (A) and (C) should be eliminated. Because each of the remaining answer choices contains a pronoun, make sure it is consistent with the non-underlined portion by finding the other pronouns and nouns. The partner noun is *societies*, which is plural. Eliminate (D) because *its* is singular. The best answer is (B).

44. **C** Use POE to find the clearest and most concise answer. As written, the sentence is unnecessarily wordy, so it is not the best answer. Choice (B) contains the redundant phrase *long lives are long enough*, so (B) is not the best answer. Choice (C) makes no grammar errors, and is more concise than the sentence as written, so it is the best answer. Choice (D) needs a preposition to link *the accrued knowledge* to *the longer-lived people*, so it is not the correct answer. Therefore, (C) is the best answer.

Section 3—Math (No Calculator)

1. **A** Distribute the 3 to get $3x^2 + 6x + 15 = 4$. Subtract 15 from both sides to get $3x^2 + 6x = -11$. The correct answer is (A).

2. **C** Multiply both sides of the equation by 3 to get $2x + 2 > 3x$. Subtract $2x$ from both sides of the equation to get $2 > x$. The correct answer is (C).

3. **C** If x is the cost of a shirt and y is the cost of a pair of socks, then $x + 2y = 24$ and $3x + 2y = 32$. Whenever there are two equations with the same variables think Simultaneous Equations. Stack the two equations on top of each other and subtract them to get:

$$\begin{array}{r} 3x + 2y = 32 \\ -(\ x + 2y = 24) \\ \hline 2x \quad\quad = 8 \end{array}$$

Solve for x to get $x = 4$. Plug this value of x back into the bottom equation to get $4 + 2y = 24$. Solve for y to get $2y = 20$ and $y = 10$. Therefore, the cost of a shirt and a pair of socks is $4 + 10 = 14$. The correct answer is (C).

4. **D** Cross-multiply to get $\left(2\sqrt{3}\right)\left(\sqrt{3}\right) = \left(\sqrt{x}\right)\left(\sqrt{x}\right)$. Multiply each side to get $(2 \times 3) = x$ and $6 = x$. The correct answer is (D).

5. **C** Because John's baseball card collection decreases in value over time, and his silver collection increases over time, the $500(1.05)^t$ of the equation must be related to his silver collection, and the 600 part of the equation must be related to his baseball card collection. Use POE to find the answer. The current value of his silver collection, at $t = 0$, is 500, and the current value of his baseball card collection is $600(.95)^{\frac{t}{2}}$. For this reason, eliminate (A). Given that t is time in years, the baseball card collection is losing 5% in value every 2 years. For this reason eliminate (B). Eliminate (D) because according to the equation, the silver collection gains 5% every year, and the baseball collection loses 5% every 2 years. Therefore, the total value of the baseball and silver collection will not remain constant over time. The correct answer is therefore (C).

6. **D** Whenever there are variables in the question and answers, think Plugging In. Plug in 100 voters, and $x = 10$. Therefore, 10 voters strongly support the bill, and 40 voters strongly oppose the bill. There are $100 - 40 - 10 = 50$ voters remaining. Of those, $\frac{3}{5} \times 50 = 30$ voters slightly support the bill, leaving $50 - 30 = 20$ voters who slightly oppose the bill. Strongly support + slightly support = $10 + 30 = 40$ voters. Plug 10 in for x in the answers to see which answer equals 40. Choice (A) becomes $S = \frac{3(60 - 10)}{5} = \frac{3(50)}{5} = 3(10) = 30$, so eliminate it. Choice (B) becomes $S = 60 - \frac{2(10)}{5} = 60 - 4 = 56$, so eliminate it. Choice (C) becomes $S = \frac{2(60 - 10)}{5} = \frac{2(50)}{5} = 2(10) = 20$, so eliminate it. The correct answer must therefore be (D).

7. **A** The equation described in the question can be written as $(x + y)^2 = (x - y)^2 + 8$. Expand both sides of the equation to get $x^2 + 2xy + y^2 = x^2 - 2xy + y^2 + 8$. Eliminate the x^2 and y^2 from both sides of the equation to get $2xy = -2xy + 8$. Combine like terms to get $4xy = 8$. Divide both sides by 4 to get $xy = 2$. Solve for x to get $x = \frac{2}{y}$. Therefore, the correct answer is (A).

8. **C** Whenever there are variables in the question and in the answers think Plugging In. If $x = 4$, then the equation becomes $\frac{\sqrt{4} - 3}{4 - 9} B = 1$. Simplify the right side of the equation to get $\frac{2 - 3}{4 - 9} B = 1$, $\frac{-1}{-5} B = 1$, and $\frac{1}{5} B = 1$. Solve for B to get $B = 5$. Plug 4 in for x in the answers to see which answer equals 5. Choice (A) becomes $4 - 9 = -5$, so eliminate it. Choice (B) becomes $4 + 3 = 7$, so eliminate it. Choice (C) becomes $\sqrt{4} + 3 = 2 + 3 = 5$. Keep (C), but check (D) just in case. Choice (D) becomes $\sqrt{4} - 3 = 2 - 3 = -1$, so eliminate it. The correct answer is (C).

9. **D** Whenever there are variables in the question and in the answer choices, think Plugging In. According to the question, the following two inequalities hold true: $\frac{2}{3}m > n$ and $n + m > 10$. Plug $m = 3$ into the first inequality to get $\frac{2}{3}(3) > n$. Solve the left side of the equation to get $2 > n$. Plug both values into the second equation to get *a value less than* $2 + 3 > 10$. This cannot work. Choices (A), (B), and (C) all provide ranges that would include $m = 3$. Therefore, they can be eliminated. The correct answer is (D).

10. **B** Whenever there are variables in the question and in the answer choices, think Plugging In. Let $a = 400$. The value of the sales woman's pay check can be calculated as follows:

First $100	$100 \times 0.15 = 15$
Second $200	$200 \times 0.2 = 40$
Remaining $100	$100 \times 0.25 = 25$

Therefore, her total pay is $15 + 40 + 25 = 80$. Plug 400 in for a in the answers to see which answer equals 80. Choice (A) becomes $.35(400) + .25(400 - 300) = 140 + 25 = 165$, so eliminate it. Choice (B) becomes $.25(400) - 20 = 100 - 20 = 80$. Keep (B), but check the remaining answers just in case. Choice (C) becomes $.60(400) = 240$, so eliminate it. Choice (D) becomes $55 + .25(400) = 55 + 100 = 155$, so eliminate it. Thus, the correct answer is (B).

11. **A** Use POE to solve this problem. The question states that the urban population is decreasing by 50,000 per year. Therefore, the correct answer should include a $-50,000$. For this reason, eliminate (C) and (D) because both of these answers add 50,000. 50% greater than the current suburban population means $1.5S$, so eliminate (B). Therefore, the correct answer is (A).

12. **B** Start with a Bite-Sized Piece, and label an element in the equation. If the weight of a rat is represented by w, then w is always the weight; label w wherever it appears in the equation. Now use POE. Choice (A) doesn't work here, because w will be multiplied by 0.017, so if the weight is greater than 1 gram, the equation will be greater than 0.017; eliminate (A). Choice (B) seems consistent so far, so keep it, as does (C). Choice (D) does not work because the metabolic rate changes based on the weight, so eliminate it. Because (C) gives you a value for w, this is a good time to Plug In. If you make $w = 100$ in the equation, you get $E = 1.7t + (d - 20)(4.7)t$. This may or may not equal 17, depending on the values of t and d, so (C) isn't necessarily true; eliminate (C) and select (B).

13. **C** Use POE. According to the question, M is directly proportional to the square of the number of hours of sleep or h^2. Therefore, h would be directly proportional to $\sqrt{M}$. The only answer that has h directly proportional to $\sqrt{M}$ is (C).

14. **2** Whenever the question includes two equations with the same two variables, think Simultaneous Equations. Rewrite the second equation to read $-3x + y = 6$. Multiply the entire equation by -1 to get $3x - y = -6$.

Stack the two equations on top of each other:

$$2x + y = 16$$
$$\underline{+\ (3x - y = -6)}$$
$$5x\qquad = 10$$

Solve for x to get $x = 2$. The correct answer is 2.

15. $\dfrac{16}{7}$ The equation described can be written as $\dfrac{1}{4}z = 2z - 4$. Multiply the entire equation by 4 to get $z = 8z - 16$. Combine like terms to get $-7z = -16$. Solve for z to get $z = \dfrac{16}{7}$. The correct answer is $\dfrac{16}{7}$.

16. **9** Because angle C is a right angle, the length of BC can be calculated using the Pythagorean theorem: $a^2 + 8^2 = 10^2$, $a + 64 = 100$, $a = 36$, and $a = 6$. Because the two triangles are similar triangles, $BC = \dfrac{2}{3}CE$. Therefore, $6 = \dfrac{2}{3}CE$. Solve for CE to get $18 = 2CE$ and $9 = CE$. The correct answer is 9.

17. $\dfrac{1}{3}$ Set the equation to 0 to get $6x^2 + 4x - 2 = 0$. Divide the entire equation by 2 to get $3x^2 + 2x - 1 = 0$. Factor to get $(3x - 1)(x + 1) = 0$. Because $x > 0$, $3x - 1 = 0$. Solve for x to get $3x = 1$ and $x = \dfrac{1}{3}$. The correct answer is $\dfrac{1}{3}$.

Section 4—Math (Calculator Allowed)

1. **A** Subtract 17 from both sides to get $2x = 22$. Divide both sides by 2 to get $x = 11$. The correct answer is (A).

2. **B** There are 12 inches in a foot. Therefore, the dimensions of the frame in feet are $36 \div 12 = 3$ feet by $24 \div 12 = 2$ feet. The perimeter of the frame in feet is therefore $2(3) + 2(2) = 6 + 4 = 10$ feet. The correct answer is (B).

3. **C** Use POE. The question does not provide any information about what happens after the end of the third week. Therefore, eliminate (A) and (D). It is clear from the question that the number of mice is increasing, not decreasing. Therefore, eliminate (B). Therefore, the correct answer is (C).

4. **C** The graph shows a positive correlation between the number of hours practiced and goals scored. In other words, as the number of hours of practice increased, the number of goals scored also increased. Only (C) expresses this relationship.

5. **B** Use FOIL to expand the equation to get $x^2 - 7x + 4x - 28 = 0$. Combine the two middle terms to get $x^2 - 3x - 28 = 0$. Therefore, the correct answer is (B).

6. **D** Use POE to solve this question. In (A), $0.10 \times 200{,}000 = 20{,}000$. However, we know from the information given that far more scientists believe the mass extinction to be caused by the Chicxulub Asteroid. Therefore, eliminate (A). In (B), $0.25 \times 200{,}000 = 50{,}000$. Again, far more scientists

believe the mass extinction to be caused by the Chicxulub Asteroid. Eliminate (B). In (C), $0.50 \times 200,000 = 100,000$. Again, the number of scientists who believe the mass extinction to be caused by the Chicxulub Asteroid is much higher. Therefore, the answer must be (D).

7. **D** There are 3 yards to a foot. The football field is $3 \times 100 = 300$ feet long. Adam has already run 240 feet. Therefore, he has $300 - 240 = 60$ feet left to run. The correct answer is (D).

8. **C** Use POE to eliminate (A) and (B) because both of these equations are the equation for a straight line. Remember the rules of graph transformation. Because the picture is a parabola that has been moved up 4, the equation should include $a + 4$. On this basis eliminate (D). The correct answer is (C).

9. **B** According to the chart, $0.44 \times 50 = 22$ participate in an after-school sport. Therefore, $50 - 22 = 28$ do not participate in an after-school sport. The ratio $22 : 28$ can be reduced to $11 : 14$. The correct answer is (B).

10. **B** According to the chart, 14% have an after-school job, and $0.14 \times 50 = 7$. Therefore, the correct answer is (B).

11. **B** Translate the English to an equation. The equation becomes $2x - 15 = 7x$. Solve for x to get $-15 = 5x$, and $-3 = x$. The correct answer is (B).

12. **A** Median means the middle number when the numbers are listed in numerical order. In order for list A to have a median of 7, x must be larger than 7. In order for list A to also have two distinct modes (mode = the number that appears most frequently), x must be equal to either 9 or 13. The correct answer is (A).

13. **D** If $a^3 - 7 = 20$, then $a^3 = 27$. Eliminate (A). To solve for a take the cube root of both sides of the equation: $a = \sqrt[3]{27} = 3$. Eliminate (C). Also eliminate (B) because $a^2 = 3^2 = 9$. Therefore, the correct answer is (D).

14. **C** Whenever there are variables, think Plugging In. If $x = 2$, then the number of casualties suffered would be $2 \times 259 = 518$. Plug 2 into the answer choices to see which answer equals 518. Choice (A) becomes $y = 2 + 259 = 261$, so eliminate it. Choice (B) becomes $y = 2 - 259 = -257$, so eliminate it. Choice (C) becomes $y = 259(2) = 518$. Keep (C), but check the remaining answer just in case. Choice (D) becomes $y = \frac{1}{259}(2) = \frac{2}{259}$, so eliminate it. The correct answer is (C).

15. **C** Start by figuring out how many portions of mac and cheese Chef Gordon could make with the milk he has available. He needs 4 cups of milk per serving: 4 cups = $4 \times 8 = 32$ ounces. 1 gallon of milk = 128 ounces. Therefore, the number of mac and cheese portions Chef Gordon can make is $128 \div 32 = 4$. In 4 portions, Chef Gordon uses $3 \times 4 = 12$ cups of water. Convert the 12 cups to ounces: $12 \times 8 = 96$ ounces of water. 1 gallon of water = 128 ounces. Therefore, he has $128 - 96 = 32$ ounces of water remaining. The correct answer is (C).

16. **B** The first step is to find the value of x by setting the function of $f(x)$ equal to 17 and solving for the value of x. The equation becomes $x^2 + 1 = 17$. The resulting value of x can then be plugged into the function $g(x)$. Only (B) correctly outlines this series of steps.

17. **B** The equation to find the slope of a line is $m = \dfrac{y_2 - y_1}{x_2 - x_1}$. The slope for the line shown can be calculated as $40 = \dfrac{277 - b}{5 - 0}$. Simplify the fraction to get $40 = \dfrac{277 - b}{5}$. Multiply both sides of the equation by 5 to get $200 = 277 - b$. Solve for b to get $-77 = -b$ and $77 = b$. The correct answer is (B).

18. **D** According to the question, the geology experts receive as many rare stones in the third month as they had received in the first two months combined. The resulting equation is $x + 2x + 18 = 4x - 30$. Simplify the equation to get $3x + 18 = 4x - 30$. Combine like terms to get $18 = x - 30$ and $x = 48$. The geologists received the following number of rare stones:

	Number of rare stones received
Month 1	48
Month 2	2(48) + 18 = 114
Month 3	4(48) – 30 = 162

The total number of rare stones received is $48 + 114 + 162 = 324$. Therefore the correct answer is (D).

19. **D** 2015 is 3 years after 2012. Therefore $y = 3$, and the function becomes $c(3) = 17(3) + 112 = 51 + 112 = 163$. Given that 20 additional cheetahs joined, the total population is $163 + 20 = 183$. The correct answer is (D).

20. **A** Start by drawing the two triangles. Recognize that triangle ABC is a 3-4-5 triangle and that $AC = 5$. Similar triangles have sides that are proportional to each other. Therefore, triangle DEF is a 6-8-10 triangle with $DF = 10$, so $2(DF - AC) = 2(10 - 5) = 2(5) = 10$. The correct answer is (A).

21. **C** Use POE. The equation $ax^2 + bx + c = 0$ is the equation of a parabola. If $a = 1$, the parabola opens up. On this basis, eliminate (B) and (D). The zeroes of a parabola are where the line crosses the x-axis which, according to the question, is at 3 and –4, so eliminate (A). The correct answer is (C).

22. **D** Start by determining the total As, Bs, and B+s for each teacher:

Final Grade	Ms. Fisher	Mr. Murphy	Mr. Cuda	Mrs. Flores	Ms. Rodgers
A	5	4	3	2	6
B	8	7	3	3	1
B+	3	4	7	3	2
Total	16	15	13	8	9

By Kristine's criteria, Ms. Fisher is the most effective teacher. The correct answer is (D).

23. **C**   Equations for $f(x)$, $g(x)$, and $h(x)$ must be derived. Therefore, Plugging In will not work here. Start with $f(x)$ and note that it passes points $(-3, 0)$ and $(0, 9)$. Then calculate the slope and determine that $f(x) = 3x + 9$. For $g(x)$, the line is reflected over the x-axis, so $g(x)$ passes through points $(-3, 0)$ and $(0, -9)$. After calculating the slope, you arrive at $g(x) = -3x - 9$. For $h(x)$, $g(x)$ is reflected over the y-axis. So $h(x)$ passes through points $(3, 0)$ and $(0, -9)$. Calculate the slope and get that $h(x) = 3x - 9$. $h(x) - g(x) = 3x - 9 - (-3x - 9) = 6x$. Thus, (C)'s $f(x) + h(x) = 3x + 9 + 3x - 9 = 6x$ is correct.

24. **D**   The equation $y = 32x - 32$ represents a linear equation. However, according to the question, as Andy spends more time reading his book, he starts to comprehend the content more quickly and will read pages at a faster rate. However, a linear function would mean he would always read at a constant rate and not speed up. For that reason, eliminate (A) and (B). A slope of $32x$ would not imply a slower rate over time, so eliminate (C). The correct answer is (D).

25. **A**   The question is asking for the solution to the following equation: $\frac{3}{2}x - 6 = 3^x - 81$. When there are variables in the question and numbers in the answers, think Plugging In the Answers. Start with (B). If $x = 3$, the equation becomes $\frac{3}{2}(3) - 6 = 3^3 - 81$. Solve both sides of the equation to get $\frac{9}{2} - 6 = 27 - 81$ and $-1.5 = -54$. Eliminate (B). It may not be clear which direction to go from here so pick a direction. In (A), $x = 4$, so the equation becomes $\frac{3}{2}(4) - 6 = 3^4 - 81$. Solve both sides of the equation to get $6 - 6 = 81 - 81 = 0$ and $0 = 0$. The correct answer is (A).

26. **C**   Let s = sofa and l = loveseat. According to the question, two sofas and one loveseat cost $1,200, which can be translated as $2s + l = 1,200$, and one sofa and three loveseats cost $1,350, which can be translated as $s + 3l = 1,350$. Whenever there are two equations and two variables, think Simultaneous Equations. Multiply the second equation by 2 to get $2s + 6l = 2,700$. Stack the two equations on top of each other and subtract them:

$$2s + 6l = 2,700$$
$$\underline{- (2s + l = 1,200)}$$
$$5l = 1,500$$

Solve for l, to get $l = 300$. Plug this value into the equation: $s + 3l = 1,350$ to get $s + 3(300) = 1,350$. Solve for s to get $s + 900 = 1,350$ and $s = 450$. The regular price of three sofas and five loveseats is $3(450) + 5(300) = 1,350 + 1,500 = 2,850$. The discount during the special sale can be calculated as $0.10 \times 2,850 = 285$ and $2,850 - 285 = 2,565$. Therefore, the correct answer is (C).

27. **B**   Begin by drawing all the information from the problem onto the figure. After drawing diameter BC, draw radii OA and OB, and label the radii as 6. After drawing the segment AB and labeling that 6 as well, the equilateral triangle OAB is created, making $\angle AOB$ a $60°$ angle. Taking

the $\frac{part}{whole}$ concept of circles, a proportion can be set up now that the value of the central angle is known. The relationship between the value of the central angle to the whole circle's 360° is equal to the relationship between the sector's area to the area of the whole circle, giving $\frac{60}{360} = \frac{x}{36\pi}$, in which x represents the sector's area. Solve for x to get 6π. Now read the full question. The question asks for the area of sector AOC, so because that makes up the remaining part of the upper semi-circle, (B)'s value of 12π is correct.

28. **153** Whenever there are two equations and two variables, think Simultaneous Equations. Start by multiplying the first equation by 2 to get $3x + 10y = 144$. Next, stack the two equations on top of each other and subtract them.

$$
\begin{array}{r}
3x + 10y = 144 \\
-(2x + 10y = 90) \\
\hline
x \qquad\quad = 54
\end{array}
$$

Plug 54 in for x into the equation $2x + 10y = 90$ to get $2(54) + 10y = 90$. Solve for y to get $108 + 10y = 90$, $10y = -18$, and $y = -1.8$. Therefore, $3x + 5y = 3(54) + 5(-1.8) = 162 - 9 = 153$. The correct answer is 153.

29. **2,288** The smallest two-digit prime number less than the square root of 144 is 11. The smallest odd number with 4 distinct prime factors is $3 \times 5 \times 7 \times 11 = 1,155$. Subtracting 11 from 210 gets 1,144, and $2 \times 1,144 = 2,288$. Therefore, the correct answer is 2,288.

30. **38.7** According to the question, any individual who responded "interested" for *Escape from Marley's Manor* also responded "interested" for both *Fire and Ice* and *Sands of Devastation*. Therefore, 53 people responded "interested" for *Fire and Ice*, which means 53 people are "not interested" in *Escape*. $\frac{53}{137} \approx 38.7$. Thus, the correct answer is 38.7.

31. **95** According to the table, 168 people surveyed are interested in *Sands of Devastation*. $0.875 \times 168 = 147$ people who are interested in *Winds of Change*, and $168 - 147 = 21$ people who are uninterested in *Winds of Change*. According to the table, 116 people are uninterested in *Escape from Marley's Manor*. $116 - 21 = 95$. Therefore, the correct answer is 95.

1.

YOUR NAME: _____
(Print)　　　Last　　　　　First　　　　　M.I.

SIGNATURE: _____　　DATE: __ / __ / __

HOME ADDRESS: _____
(Print)　　　Number and Street

_____
City　　　　State　　　　Zip Code

PHONE NO.: _____
(Print)

IMPORTANT: Please fill in these boxes exactly as shown on the back cover of your test book.

2. TEST FORM

3. TEST CODE

4. REGISTRATION NUMBER

5. YOUR NAME

First 4 letters of last name				FIRST INIT	MID INIT

6. DATE OF BIRTH

Month	Day		Year	
JAN				
FEB	0	0	0	0
MAR	1	1	1	1
APR	2	2	2	2
MAY	3	3	3	3
JUN		4	4	4
JUL		5	5	5
AUG		6	6	6
SEP		7	7	7
OCT		8	8	8
NOV		9	9	9
DEC				

7. SEX

MALE
FEMALE

The Princeton Review®

Test ①　Start with number 1 for each new section.
If a section has fewer questions than answer spaces, leave the extra answer spaces blank.

Section 1—Reading

1. A B C D
2. A B C D
3. A B C D
4. A B C D
5. A B C D
6. A B C D
7. A B C D
8. A B C D
9. A B C D
10. A B C D
11. A B C D
12. A B C D
13. A B C D
14. A B C D
15. A B C D
16. A B C D
17. A B C D
18. A B C D
19. A B C D
20. A B C D
21. A B C D
22. A B C D
23. A B C D
24. A B C D
25. A B C D
26. A B C D
27. A B C D
28. A B C D
29. A B C D
30. A B C D
31. A B C D
32. A B C D
33. A B C D
34. A B C D
35. A B C D
36. A B C D
37. A B C D
38. A B C D
39. A B C D
40. A B C D
41. A B C D
42. A B C D
43. A B C D
44. A B C D
45. A B C D
46. A B C D
47. A B C D

Section 2—Writing and Language Skills

1. A B C D
2. A B C D
3. A B C D
4. A B C D
5. A B C D
6. A B C D
7. A B C D
8. A B C D
9. A B C D
10. A B C D
11. A B C D
12. A B C D
13. A B C D
14. A B C D
15. A B C D
16. A B C D
17. A B C D
18. A B C D
19. A B C D
20. A B C D
21. A B C D
22. A B C D
23. A B C D
24. A B C D
25. A B C D
26. A B C D
27. A B C D
28. A B C D
29. A B C D
30. A B C D
31. A B C D
32. A B C D
33. A B C D
34. A B C D
35. A B C D
36. A B C D
37. A B C D
38. A B C D
39. A B C D
40. A B C D
41. A B C D
42. A B C D
43. A B C D
44. A B C D

Test ❶

Start with number 1 for each new section.
If a section has fewer questions than answer spaces, leave the extra answer spaces blank.

Section 3—Mathematics: No Calculator

1. Ⓐ Ⓑ Ⓒ Ⓓ
2. Ⓐ Ⓑ Ⓒ Ⓓ
3. Ⓐ Ⓑ Ⓒ Ⓓ
4. Ⓐ Ⓑ Ⓒ Ⓓ
5. Ⓐ Ⓑ Ⓒ Ⓓ
6. Ⓐ Ⓑ Ⓒ Ⓓ
7. Ⓐ Ⓑ Ⓒ Ⓓ
8. Ⓐ Ⓑ Ⓒ Ⓓ
9. Ⓐ Ⓑ Ⓒ Ⓓ
10. Ⓐ Ⓑ Ⓒ Ⓓ
11. Ⓐ Ⓑ Ⓒ Ⓓ
12. Ⓐ Ⓑ Ⓒ Ⓓ
13. Ⓐ Ⓑ Ⓒ Ⓓ

14. [grid-in answer space]
15. [grid-in answer space]
16. [grid-in answer space]
17. [grid-in answer space]

Section 4—Mathematics: Calculator

1. Ⓐ Ⓑ Ⓒ Ⓓ
2. Ⓐ Ⓑ Ⓒ Ⓓ
3. Ⓐ Ⓑ Ⓒ Ⓓ
4. Ⓐ Ⓑ Ⓒ Ⓓ
5. Ⓐ Ⓑ Ⓒ Ⓓ
6. Ⓐ Ⓑ Ⓒ Ⓓ
7. Ⓐ Ⓑ Ⓒ Ⓓ
8. Ⓐ Ⓑ Ⓒ Ⓓ
9. Ⓐ Ⓑ Ⓒ Ⓓ
10. Ⓐ Ⓑ Ⓒ Ⓓ
11. Ⓐ Ⓑ Ⓒ Ⓓ
12. Ⓐ Ⓑ Ⓒ Ⓓ
13. Ⓐ Ⓑ Ⓒ Ⓓ
14. Ⓐ Ⓑ Ⓒ Ⓓ
15. Ⓐ Ⓑ Ⓒ Ⓓ
16. Ⓐ Ⓑ Ⓒ Ⓓ
17. Ⓐ Ⓑ Ⓒ Ⓓ
18. Ⓐ Ⓑ Ⓒ Ⓓ
19. Ⓐ Ⓑ Ⓒ Ⓓ
20. Ⓐ Ⓑ Ⓒ Ⓓ
21. Ⓐ Ⓑ Ⓒ Ⓓ
22. Ⓐ Ⓑ Ⓒ Ⓓ
23. Ⓐ Ⓑ Ⓒ Ⓓ
24. Ⓐ Ⓑ Ⓒ Ⓓ
25. Ⓐ Ⓑ Ⓒ Ⓓ
26. Ⓐ Ⓑ Ⓒ Ⓓ
27. Ⓐ Ⓑ Ⓒ Ⓓ

28. [grid-in answer space]
29. [grid-in answer space]
30. [grid-in answer space]
31. [grid-in answer space]

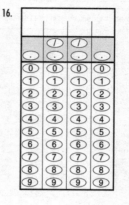

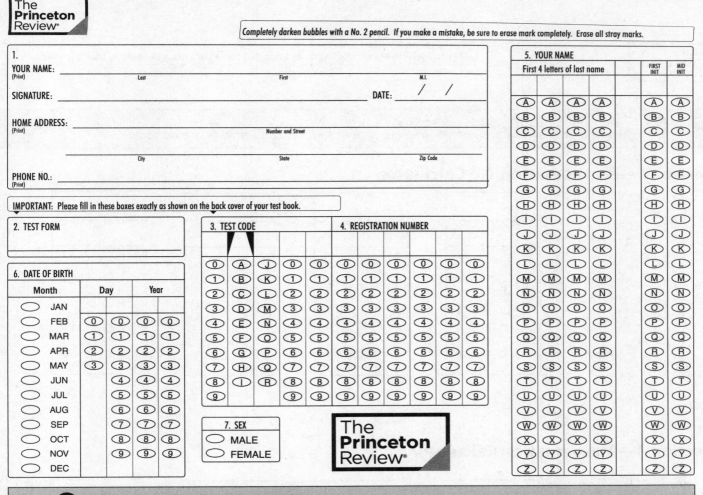

The Princeton Review

1.

YOUR NAME: _____
(Print)
             Last   First   M.I.

SIGNATURE: _____   DATE: __/__/__

HOME ADDRESS: _____
(Print)
        Number and Street

    City   State   Zip Code

PHONE NO.: _____
(Print)

IMPORTANT: Please fill in these boxes exactly as shown on the back cover of your test book.

2. TEST FORM

3. TEST CODE

4. REGISTRATION NUMBER

5. YOUR NAME

First 4 letters of last name   FIRST INIT   MID INIT

6. DATE OF BIRTH

Month	Day	Year
◯ JAN		
◯ FEB	0 0	0 0
◯ MAR	1 1	1 1
◯ APR	2 2	2 2
◯ MAY	3 3	3 3
◯ JUN	4	4 4
◯ JUL	5	5 5
◯ AUG	6	6 6
◯ SEP	7	7 7
◯ OCT	8	8 8
◯ NOV	9	9 9
◯ DEC		

7. SEX
◯ MALE
◯ FEMALE

The Princeton Review

Test ②

Start with number 1 for each new section.
If a section has fewer questions than answer spaces, leave the extra answer spaces blank.

Section 1—Reading

1. A B C D
2. A B C D
3. A B C D
4. A B C D
5. A B C D
6. A B C D
7. A B C D
8. A B C D
9. A B C D
10. A B C D
11. A B C D
12. A B C D
13. A B C D
14. A B C D
15. A B C D
16. A B C D
17. A B C D
18. A B C D
19. A B C D
20. A B C D
21. A B C D
22. A B C D
23. A B C D
24. A B C D

25. A B C D
26. A B C D
27. A B C D
28. A B C D
29. A B C D
30. A B C D
31. A B C D
32. A B C D
33. A B C D
34. A B C D
35. A B C D
36. A B C D
37. A B C D
38. A B C D
41. A B C D
39. A B C D
40. A B C D
41. A B C D
42. A B C D
43. A B C D
44. A B C D
45. A B C D
46. A B C D
47. A B C D

Section 2—Writing and Language Skills

1. A B C D
2. A B C D
3. A B C D
4. A B C D
5. A B C D
6. A B C D
7. A B C D
8. A B C D
9. A B C D
10. A B C D
11. A B C D
12. A B C D
13. A B C D
14. A B C D
15. A B C D
16. A B C D
17. A B C D
18. A B C D
19. A B C D
20. A B C D
21. A B C D
22. A B C D

23. A B C D
24. A B C D
25. A B C D
26. A B C D
27. A B C D
28. A B C D
29. A B C D
30. A B C D
31. A B C D
32. A B C D
33. A B C D
34. A B C D
35. A B C D
36. A B C D
37. A B C D
38. A B C D
39. A B C D
40. A B C D
41. A B C D
42. A B C D
43. A B C D
44. A B C D

Completely darken bubbles with a No. 2 pencil. If you make a mistake, be sure to erase mark completely. Erase all stray marks.

Test ❷ Start with number 1 for each new section.
If a section has fewer questions than answer spaces, leave the extra answer spaces blank.

Section 3—Mathematics: No Calculator

1. Ⓐ Ⓑ Ⓒ Ⓓ
2. Ⓐ Ⓑ Ⓒ Ⓓ
3. Ⓐ Ⓑ Ⓒ Ⓓ
4. Ⓐ Ⓑ Ⓒ Ⓓ
5. Ⓐ Ⓑ Ⓒ Ⓓ
6. Ⓐ Ⓑ Ⓒ Ⓓ
7. Ⓐ Ⓑ Ⓒ Ⓓ
8. Ⓐ Ⓑ Ⓒ Ⓓ
9. Ⓐ Ⓑ Ⓒ Ⓓ
10. Ⓐ Ⓑ Ⓒ Ⓓ
11. Ⓐ Ⓑ Ⓒ Ⓓ
12. Ⓐ Ⓑ Ⓒ Ⓓ
13. Ⓐ Ⓑ Ⓒ Ⓓ

14. 15. 16. 17.

Section 4—Mathematics: Calculator

1. Ⓐ Ⓑ Ⓒ Ⓓ
2. Ⓐ Ⓑ Ⓒ Ⓓ
3. Ⓐ Ⓑ Ⓒ Ⓓ
4. Ⓐ Ⓑ Ⓒ Ⓓ
5. Ⓐ Ⓑ Ⓒ Ⓓ
6. Ⓐ Ⓑ Ⓒ Ⓓ
7. Ⓐ Ⓑ Ⓒ Ⓓ
8. Ⓐ Ⓑ Ⓒ Ⓓ
9. Ⓐ Ⓑ Ⓒ Ⓓ
10. Ⓐ Ⓑ Ⓒ Ⓓ
11. Ⓐ Ⓑ Ⓒ Ⓓ
12. Ⓐ Ⓑ Ⓒ Ⓓ
13. Ⓐ Ⓑ Ⓒ Ⓓ
14. Ⓐ Ⓑ Ⓒ Ⓓ
15. Ⓐ Ⓑ Ⓒ Ⓓ
16. Ⓐ Ⓑ Ⓒ Ⓓ
17. Ⓐ Ⓑ Ⓒ Ⓓ
18. Ⓐ Ⓑ Ⓒ Ⓓ
19. Ⓐ Ⓑ Ⓒ Ⓓ
20. Ⓐ Ⓑ Ⓒ Ⓓ
21. Ⓐ Ⓑ Ⓒ Ⓓ
22. Ⓐ Ⓑ Ⓒ Ⓓ
23. Ⓐ Ⓑ Ⓒ Ⓓ
24. Ⓐ Ⓑ Ⓒ Ⓓ
25. Ⓐ Ⓑ Ⓒ Ⓓ
26. Ⓐ Ⓑ Ⓒ Ⓓ
27. Ⓐ Ⓑ Ⓒ Ⓓ

28. 29. 30. 31.

NOTES

NOTES

NOTES

International Offices Listing

China (Beijing)
1501 Building A,
Disanji Creative Zone,
No.66 West Section of North 4th Ring Road Beijing
Tel: +86-10-62684481/2/3
Email: tprkor01@chol.com
Website: www.tprbeijing.com

China (Shanghai)
1010 Kaixuan Road
Building B, 5/F
Changning District, Shanghai, China 200052
Sara Beattie, Owner: Email: sbeattie@sarabeattie.com
Tel: +86-21-5108-2798
Fax: +86-21-6386-1039
Website: www.princetonreviewshanghai.com

Hong Kong
5th Floor, Yardley Commercial Building
1-6 Connaught Road West, Sheung Wan, Hong Kong
(MTR Exit C)
Sara Beattie, Owner: Email: sbeattie@sarabeattie.com
Tel: +852-2507-9380
Fax: +852-2827-4630
Website: www.princetonreviewhk.com

India (Mumbai)
Score Plus Academy
Office No.15, Fifth Floor
Manek Mahal 90
Veer Nariman Road
Next to Hotel Ambassador
Churchgate, Mumbai 400020
Maharashtra, India
Ritu Kalwani: Email: director@score-plus.com
Tel: + 91 22 22846801 / 39 / 41
Website: www.score-plus.com

India (New Delhi)
South Extension
K-16, Upper Ground Floor
South Extension Part–1,
New Delhi-110049
Aradhana Mahna: aradhana@manyagroup.com
Monisha Banerjee: monisha@manyagroup.com
Ruchi Tomar: ruchi.tomar@manyagroup.com
Rishi Josan: Rishi.josan@manyagroup.com
Vishal Goswamy: vishal.goswamy@manyagroup.com
Tel: +91-11-64501603/ 4, +91-11-65028379
Website: www.manyagroup.com

Lebanon
463 Bliss Street
AlFarra Building - 2nd floor
Ras Beirut
Beirut, Lebanon
Hassan Coudsi: Email: hassan.coudsi@review.com
Tel: +961-1-367-688
Website: www.princetonreviewlebanon.com

Korea
945-25 Young Shin Building
25 Daechi-Dong, Kangnam-gu
Seoul, Korea 135-280
Yong-Hoon Lee: Email: TPRKor01@chollian.net
In-Woo Kim: Email: iwkim@tpr.co.kr
Tel: + 82-2-554-7762
Fax: +82-2-453-9466
Website: www.tpr.co.kr

Kuwait
ScorePlus Learning Center
Salmiyah Block 3, Street 2 Building 14
Post Box: 559, Zip 1306, Safat, Kuwait
Email: infokuwait@score-plus.com
Tel: +965-25-75-48-02 / 8
Fax: +965-25-75-46-02
Website: www.scorepluseducation.com

Malaysia
Sara Beattie MDC Sdn Bhd
Suites 18E & 18F
18th Floor
Gurney Tower, Persiaran Gurney
Penang, Malaysia
Email: tprkl.my@sarabeattie.com
Sara Beattie, Owner: Email: sbeattie@sarabeattie.com
Tel: +604-2104 333
Fax: +604-2104 330
Website: www.princetonreviewKL.com

Mexico
TPR México
Guanajuato No. 242 Piso 1 Interior 1
Col. Roma Norte
México D.F., C.P.06700
registro@princetonreviewmexico.com
Tel: +52-55-5255-4495
+52-55-5255-4440
+52-55-5255-4442
Website: www.princetonreviewmexico.com

Qatar
Score Plus
Office No: 1A, Al Kuwari (Damas)
Building near Merweb Hotel, Al Saad
Post Box: 2408, Doha, Qatar
Email: infoqatar@score-plus.com
Tel: +974 44 36 8580, +974 526 5032
Fax: +974 44 13 1995
Website: www.scorepluseducation.com

Taiwan
The Princeton Review Taiwan
2F, 169 Zhong Xiao East Road, Section 4
Taipei, Taiwan 10690
Lisa Bartle (Owner): lbartle@princetonreview.com.tw
Tel: +886-2-2751-1293
Fax: +886-2-2776-3201
Website: www.PrincetonReview.com.tw

Thailand
The Princeton Review Thailand
Sathorn Nakorn Tower, 28th floor
100 North Sathorn Road
Bangkok, Thailand 10500
Thavida Bijayendrayodhin (Chairman)
Email: thavida@princetonreviewthailand.com
Mitsara Bijayendrayodhin (Managing Director)
Email: mitsara@princetonreviewthailand.com
Tel: +662-636-6770
Fax: +662-636-6776
Website: www.princetonreviewthailand.com

Turkey
Yeni Sülün Sokak No. 28
Levent, Istanbul, 34330, Turkey
Nuri Ozgur: nuri@tprturkey.com
Rona Ozgur: rona@tprturkey.com
Iren Ozgur: iren@tprturkey.com
Tel: +90-212-324-4747
Fax: +90-212-324-3347
Website: www.tprturkey.com

UAE
Emirates Score Plus
Office No: 506, Fifth Floor
Sultan Business Center
Near Lamcy Plaza, 21 Oud Metha Road
Post Box: 44098, Dubai
United Arab Emirates
Hukumat Kalwani: skoreplus@gmail.com
Ritu Kalwani: director@score-plus.com
Email: info@score-plus.com
Tel: +971-4-334-0004
Fax: +971-4-334-0222
Website: www.princetonreviewuae.com

Our International Partners

The Princeton Review also runs courses with a variety of
partners in Africa, Asia, Europe, and South America.

Georgia
LEAF American-Georgian Education Center
www.leaf.ge

Mongolia
English Academy of Mongolia
www.nyescm.org

Nigeria
The Know Place
www.knowplace.com.ng

Panama
Academia Interamericana de Panama
http://aip.edu.pa/

Switzerland
Institut Le Rosey
http://www.rosey.ch/

All other inquiries, please email us at
internationalsupport@review.com